Number Four:
The W. L. Moody, Jr., Natural History Series

WILD FLOWERS
OF THE
BIG THICKET
East Texas, and
Western Louisiana

By GEYATA AJILVSGI

TEXAS A&M UNIVERSITY PRESS
College Station and London

Library of Congress Cataloging in Publication Data

Ajilvsgi, Geyata, 1933–
    Wild flowers of the Big Thicket, east Texas, and
western Louisiana.

        Bibliography: p.
        Includes index.
        1. Wild flowers—Texas—Big Thicket—Identification.
2. Wild flowers—Louisiana—Identification. 3. Big
Thicket, Tex. I. Title.
QK188.A37   582′.13′097642   78-21781
ISBN 0-89096-064-X
ISBN 0-89096-065-8 pbk.

Manufactured in the United States of America
FIRST EDITION

There still exist vast strips of virgin forest protecting a ground cover of some of the most beautiful and interesting low trees and shrubs in the world, which in turn protect many forms of vegetable life which are worth many a day's travel just to look upon.

H. B. Parks, V. L. Cory, et al.
BIOLOGICAL SURVEY OF THE EAST TEXAS
BIG THICKET AREA (1936)

Contents

Acknowledgments

MANY individuals have been helpful in the compiling of this book and to them I am most grateful. Foremost has been Dr. D. S. Correll, whose early encouragement, plant identification, and helpful suggestions have kept me at my work. I am especially grateful to Jerry Flook, formerly of Southern Methodist University, and Dr. Paul A. Fryxell at Texas A&M University for their phonetic pronounciations which appear in the descriptions. Appreciation is extended Dr. A. Y. (Pete) Gunter and Jenkins Publishing Company for permission to use the map on page 5. Illustrations for the glossary are from the talented pen of Martha Bell. To Dr. Paul Harcombe for ecological consultation, Dr. Jerry Grubb for bibliography corrections and advice, and Dr. John J. Sperry for plant description review, I am indebted. I have frequently relied upon the cooperation and advice of many capable professional botanists; outstanding among them have been Dr. Marshall C. Johnston and the late Dr. Eula Whitehouse.

To Dr. William F. Mahler and Barney Lipscomb at the Southern Methodist University Herbarium for final corrections of plant descriptions and many hours of helpful advice and instruction, I offer a most profound thanks.

The generosity of Francis Wier in making her cabin "The Barn" available during the many photographic trips to the Thicket is most deeply appreciated. To me it was *Ahwenvsv Adohi*—"my home in the woods." I miss it.

My deepest appreciation and thanks go to my friend Geraldine Watson, with whom I traveled the back roads of the Thicket and shared the joy of discovering its wild flowers. Through her eyes and words the Big Thicket was interpreted with a rare and special sensitivity.

It has long been my wish to share some of the beauty of our native wild flowers with more people, and I am most grateful for the opportunity to bring this small representation of the Big Thicket to the reader.

Portions of this book are based on works by Geraldine E. Watson.

Wild Flowers of the Big Thicket

Introduction

THE Big Thicket is an area fascinating in its diversity, complexity, and biological richness. Frequently referred to as the "biological crossroads of North America," it sprawls across Southeast Texas as a paradoxical semitropical wilderness of junglelike swamps, densely wooded uplands, and arid-appearing sandylands.

Once a vast region of over three million acres, today the Big Thicket has been greatly reduced by farming, lumbering, oil production, and other land uses. Thousands of acres of the formerly magnificent woodlands have been planted with evenly spaced rows of pine, which form large tracts ecologists have termed "biological deserts."

Fortunately, the growth rate of the vegetation is phenomenal, and cut or cleared lands quickly become thick with young trees and shrubs if not planted to pine. In such open spots wild flowers usually appear in large numbers until the canopy of maturing trees closes and shades them out.

Remnants of virgin forest remain, mostly in remote, nearly inaccessible swamps. The most easily seen representation of virgin forest today is on the Alabama-Coushatta Indian Reservation near Livingston.

The establishment of a portion of the Big Thicket as a national preserve seems a certainty at this writing. It has not come too soon. Some of the wild flowers shown in this book were the first findings for the state; many times the photographs were taken within sound of chainsaw and bulldozer. The plants photographed in those particular locations exist no longer.

PURPOSE

ONE of the objectives of this book is to provide a ready means for discovering and identifying the wild flowers of the Big Thicket and adjacent areas. Colored photographs are used along with relatively nontechnical descriptions. The photographs have been separated into natural plant associations so the book can be more easily used by amateurs, students, or professionals.

This guide is designed specifically to cover those wild flowers which occur in the Big Thicket of Southeast Texas. However, most of the wild flowers which occur in East Texas as a whole and in the western portion of Louisiana also occur in the Thicket. The book will be useful in those areas, also.

A second objective of this book is to make more people aware of plant associations and the fragility of most of the associations in the Big Thicket. Many of the plants found in the Thicket have evolved to live and survive in a particular habitat. A successful transplanting of these plants is virtually impossible, and any attempt to do so only hastens their extinction. However, some less sensitive plants may be propagated by seeds; descriptions of the fruits are given within the text for this purpose. The only way to insure preservation of all the plant species in the Big Thicket is to set aside the land where they grow naturally. It is hoped that this guide will encourage more people to work toward this end before the rarer species have entirely disappeared. It is also hoped that this work will stimulate further study of the area by specialists in many fields of science so that eventually the Big Thicket will be better understood as an ecological entity.

HISTORICAL SETTING AND BOUNDARIES

The geographical region known as the Big Thicket has never known a definite boundary. To the Indians it was a vague land called the "Big Woods," and they seldom traveled through the dim, forbidding forest. Occasionally canoes were used for following game through the numerous sloughs and streams, but mostly the watery swamps were shunned.

The first Spanish explorers and missionaries avoided the area and skirted it with their primitive roads. To the American pioneers the Thicket was an area extending southward from the Old San Antonio Road (El Camino Real) to the coastal prairies, bordered on the east by the Sabine River and on the west by the Brazos River, and to them it was a place to be traveled around, not through.

Later, hunters knew the Thicket as the wooded swamps and junglelike palmetto flats around Pine Island and Little Pine Island bayous. This area is known today as the Traditional Thicket.

The 1936 biological survey by Parks and Cory contains a map whose boundaries are similar to those recognized by the early pioneers except that the western boundary has been moved eastward from the Brazos about halfway to the Trinity River and the northern boundary has been slightly retracted. The Thicket, as described in that survey, encompassed all or part of fifteen counties, comprising 3,350,000 acres or approximately 5,234 square miles.

A more recent survey by Professor Claude A. McLeod (1972), using certain groups of plant species as indicators, has retracted the northern boundary still further to about thirty miles south of the Old San Antonio Road but has extended the southern boundary southward to include the northeastern tip of Harris County. A sizable area north of Orange County has been deleted.

Even the carefully studied boundaries outlined by McLeod have been the

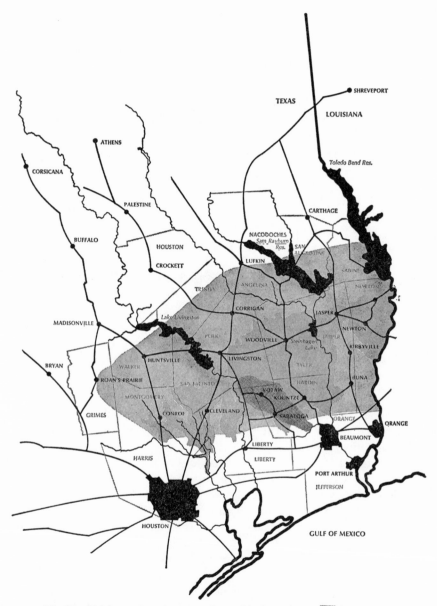

The Big Thicket—three interpretations of its boundaries. ▨ Biological Survey (Parks et al., 1936), ▨ Ecological Analysis (McLeod, 1972), ▨ Traditional (Hunter's) Thicket (1890–1900).

subject of much controversy. There are numerous places outside these boundaries that are much like the Thicket, even though one of the "indicator" species is absent. Conservationists generally insist that the Big Thicket as an ecological entity includes more than is indicated by McLeod's boundaries.

TOPOGRAPHY AND GEOLOGY

THE Big Thicket lies somewhat like a wide, shallow, slightly tipped, rimmed basin. The northern portion is the highest, rising to about 250 feet above sea level, and is moderately rolling country with well-developed drainage patterns. The eastern and western rims are relatively flat and slope gradually to the southern rim except where they are broken by streams. The central portion has some higher areas, but generally elevation drops southward until it is near sea level on the flat, poorly drained area around Pine Island Bayou.

The geological formations underlying the Thicket consist of bands of alluvium and marine sediments. In earlier times sea level rose and fell depending upon the amount of ice frozen in the polar caps. During warming periods powerful rivers cut through the land. As the sea filled, sediments were deposited in the great bay that was later to become the Thicket. The different strata laid down during those times later tilted downward into the Gulf because of the weight of sediments in the Gulf and the loss of weight inland when the sea drained, so that now the oldest stratum is exposed farthest from the Gulf and the youngest is exposed nearest the Gulf.

SOILS

SOILS of the Thicket are influenced but not dominated by substrate type. Factors affecting soil development in the Thicket are climate, substrate, topography, vegetation, and time.

The high rainfall of the Thicket has leached much of the calcium from the soils, and surface soils vary from strongly acid to slightly acid, rarely neutral. Subsoils vary from strongly acid to neutral. Generally the Thicket soils have not been leached to such an extent that they are very low in fertility. In the southern portion, and near streams elsewhere, sediments are still being deposited and the soils are not well developed. Two of the most important factors influencing soil development, and thereby the plant community, are permeability and topography. Soils of the lower Thicket are clayey and mostly flat, features which in conjunction with climate cause waterlogged, swampy conditions and little herbaceous vegetation. Soils of the upper Thicket and parts of the central Thicket are sandier and hence more permeable, and the drainage system is well developed. Considerable herbaceous vegetation grows on these well-aerated, favorably moist soils. Around the Trinity River there are some soils with a fairly high calcium content. These are of more western and more recent origin and support some interesting floral differences.

This brief outline is vastly oversimplified. Because of the method of formation of the Thicket, with soils having been shifted about for eons, and still being shifted about, soils are locally quite complex. According to Dr. C. L. Lundell of the University of Texas, "No area of comparable size in the United States contains as varied soil conditions as the Big Thicket." According to the Soil Conservation Service, more than fifty soil types can be found in Hardin County alone.

CLIMATE

THE climate of the Big Thicket is one of the major factors contributing to its floral richness. Generally warm and temperate, the Thicket is moderated in winter by warm air masses from the Gulf of Mexico. The temperature falls below freezing only about 20 days per year and exceeds ninety degrees approximately 110 days yearly. Monthly temperature averages vary from a mild fifty-six degrees in January to eighty-three degrees in August. Relative humidity averages nearly 75 percent. Annual rainfall is abundant, ranging from about fifty inches in the upper Thicket to almost sixty inches in the lower portion.

Although the climate of the Big Thicket is almost tropical, the seasonal changes are still prominent. Spring, summer, and fall have their own special wild flowers. In winter the conifers, hollies, and magnolias splash the bare woodlands with green and provide an appropriate setting for those wild flowers which continue to bloom through this Gulf-moderated season.

NATURE OF VEGETATION

THE vegetation of the Big Thicket is extremely abundant and diverse, in part due to the environmental forces which shape all of the Southern Mixed Forest, to which the Big Thicket belongs. The Southern Mixed Forest extends across the southern states, with the Big Thicket area forming its westernmost border. This mesophytic pine-hardwood forest is exceedingly varied in overstory, understory, and ground-cover vegetation, an inherent richness which is amplified in the Thicket by the effect of the Thicket's geographical location as an ecotone.

Invaded on its western fringe by species from the Blackland Prairie and the drier Post Oak Savannahs and on its southern border by coastal and tropical species, the Thicket is a maze of plant associations that can overwhelm even the experienced ecologist. Adding still further to this diversity are the Thicket's many relict plant species, once widespread but because of climatic changes now found only in tolerant areas like the Thicket.

Besides conditions favorable to these many plant species, a method of introduction was also required to achieve the diversity of species characteristic of the Thicket. This method is based on geological formation. According to Parks (1938), seeds were left behind by early rivers from the west. Flooding of the Mississippi River brought seeds from the north and east, some of Appalachian origin. Southern Gulf waters deposited tropical plants where they have survived in isolated patches.

A great many plants reach the limit of their distribution in the Thicket and are partly cut off from their main gene pool. As these plants adapt to the favorable but different conditions, some begin to show extreme variation. Dr. D. S. Correll states: "The variations are often so great that the plant has to be separated as a distinct species." Even when the variations are not so pronounced, they are often sufficient to justify subspecies classification, and these subspecies, plus the different morphological forms of many of the Thicket plants, often make for taxonomic difficulties.

Perhaps it would be appropriate here to define *species* and associated terms: a species is a group of biological organisms that breed preferentially among themselves. Preferentially, of course, means on a statistical basis, but in populations separated from each other it is difficult indeed to determine preferential breeding, so taxonomists are forced to use morphological characters that they normally find to be consistent within a group, along with habitat requirements, to assign species status. Regardless of the difficulty man has in defining a species, the concept is a natural one. On the other hand, race, subspecies, and variety are arbitrary terms given to a spatially separated subset within a species, the members of which demonstrate certain constant distinct characters.

A group of species having similar characteristics is assigned to a genus, a number of genera which have characters in common make up a family, and so on through order, class, and phylum until the level of kingdom is reached. These are classifications devised by man to bring a degree of order to an astronomical amount of information.

The majority of plants are capable of considerable morphological change in response to their environment. In the Thicket, with so many different soil types and hydrologic situations in close proximity, almost every species exhibits a wide range of phenotypic expression. Sometimes plants even of the same subspecies are scarcely recognizable as being related.

PLANT ASSOCIATIONS

ANOTHER subject that demands a full discussion is the notion of plant associations and the concepts surrounding it. Given time, the vegetation of a region will proceed to a uniform association of a relatively small number of dominant species which, theoretically, remain thereafter in harmony with the natural environmental forces, if those forces are static. This permanent association of plants is referred to as the climax vegetation for the region. In proceeding to this climax, the vegetation passes through a number of transient stages known as subclimax communities. A climax influenced mainly by soil properties is said to be an edaphic climax. A climax influenced by physical features is said to be a physiographic climax, and, finally, a climax controlled by the climate is said to be a climatic climax. The last is the most fundamental of the three, since climate, over the aeons, will contribute heavily to the formation of physical features and to the soil type.

The Thicket region has not yet reached its climatic climax and hence has been the subject of considerable speculation. Some ecologists believe the longleaf pine–bluestem association to be the climax. This hypothesis depends mainly on whether or not fire is considered a climatic factor—an arbitrary decision. If fire is excluded, the oak-hickory association might be the climax.

The climatic climax of a region depends on well-developed soils and a mature drainage system. Because of the Thicket's nearness to the sea, it may never develop an efficient drainage pattern, in which case it will be held in an arrested physiographic climax, or rather, several of them. Professor McLeod believes that the American beech (*Fagus grandifolia*), southern magnolia (*Magnolia grandiflora*), white oak (*Quercus alba*), and loblolly pine (*Pinus taeda*) forest type is the climax of the Thicket, and this is the association he uses as the "indicator" in delineating the Thicket, except in the lower Thicket, where beech is absent and its place is taken by chestnut oak (*Q. prinus*) and laurel oak (*Q. laurifolia*). He considers this climax to arise from edaphic influences. *Edaphic* can be used in a way that applies to the drainage system as well as the intrinsic properties of the soil itself. Besides being dependent on soil properties, the beech–magnolia–loblolly pine association of the northern Thicket is tied to topographic relief. One can quickly see that edaphic and physiographic influences are not readily separable, and this difficulty often applies to climatic factors as well.

It is obvious that the Big Thicket resists separation into plant associations, which is to be expected, since interspersion and diversity are the most striking characteristics of the Thicket. Nevertheless, I feel that the concept of plant associations is basic to our understanding of living things and how they relate to their environment. The search for the understanding of plant associations is as fascinating as the search for wild flowers.

No matter what the true climax association is going to be, at this time the Thicket can be reasonably well divided into eight plant associations and has been so divided in this book. A ninth association, "Roadsides," while not technically an association, has been added in order to include those plants found in that artificial but prominent habitat.

Plant associations are properly named for the dominant and subdominant plants of the community, these being the plants that are the most conspicuous, that cover the most ground, or that have the greatest total biomass. Usually dominants will lead in all three characteristics. Most often the dominant is named because it is the most conspicuous plant, especially if it is an overstory tree.

Plants form associations for two reasons. The first is that they are found together because of similar general requirements of nutrients and water. The amount of water is controlled by several factors in addition to rainfall. Some of these factors are topsoil type, subsoil type, concentration of salts, local slope, and the overall drainage pattern. Soil porosity is a major factor in this regard.

The other reason is that plants interact with each other, both by physical action, such as providing shade and windbreak, and by the chemical action of releasing substances into the soil and taking substances from the soil. The organisms of decay are an important part of this interaction. Often plants are found together not because one directly benefits from the other, but because one has become resistant to a toxin produced by the other or has evolved the ability to do without certain nutrients which the other robs from the soil, thereby gaining a competitive edge over close rivals.

The propensity of plants to form associations can be used as a taxonomic tool. In trying to distinguish or "key out" a plant from a number of similar species, the knowledge of the dominants with which the likely prospects associate is as important as knowing their geographic ranges and often as important as the morphological characters of the plants themselves. Therein lies the reason for the format of this book. Each wild-flower photograph has been placed with the association in which it is most often found. In other words, the wild flowers found in a particular association have been grouped together.

In the descriptions of the plant associations which follow, environmental concepts and factors are discussed under the association in which they are most applicable and are not usually explained again elsewhere. For example, the effect of sand as a soil ingredient can be seen in the Longleaf-Bluestem Uplands, but it is more dramatic in the Oak-Farkleberry Sandylands and so is discussed under the sandylands.

Mixed-Grass Prairies (MGP)

One of the factors contributing toward the "biological crossroads" concept of the Big Thicket is the existence there of Mixed-Grass Prairies—areas of nearly level, slowly drained plains mostly of grassland but with a scattering of shrubs and trees throughout, especially on slight elevations or along drainages.

With the changes of climate and drainage patterns during the geological past, the division line for the prairies changed many times. Today, the prairies lie mostly along the western edge of the Big Thicket, mainly on the uplands between Pine Island Bayou and the Trinity River. They are probably disjunct extensions of the Blackland Prairies further to the west and the Coastal Prairies to the south, as many of the plant species are the same.

Soils of the Mixed-Grass Prairies are mostly of uniformly dark-colored, tight clays with some gray, sandy loam. These soils have developed under a grass vegetation. With the natural tall-grass cover, the top soil layer has a friable, granular structure and is only slightly sticky and hard. Under cultivation or overgrazing it rapidly loses organic matter and becomes puddled when wet and hard and crumbly when dry. The tight, impervious subsoils resist root penetration and prevent the downward percolation of water as well as the upward movement of capillary water and are partly responsible for the almost treeless condition of the prairies.

Fire was perhaps another factor in maintaining the Mixed-Grass Prairies in a grass-vegetation climax. Fired by natural causes and by early Indians to flush game, the burning of these openings was continued by the settlers. These already cleared sites were natural selections for homesteading and grazing. Today, much of the burning is controlled, and non-prairie plants such as wax-myrtle (*Myrica cerifera*), sea-myrtle (*Baccharis halimifolia*), and various hawthorns (*Crataegus* spp.) are rapidly encroaching, changing the vegetation to an as yet undetermined type.

In addition to their distinctive vegetation, the prairies are characterized by an unusual microrelief topography. Conspicuous mounds, generally called "mima" mounds, are scattered about this otherwise relatively flat land. The mounds are composed of fine, sandy loam and are one to four feet high and ten to fifty feet in diameter. The higher and better-drained soils of these mounds support a different plant community than the tighter clay soils of the intermound areas.

Small saline places mostly formed by saltwater overflow from oil wells, seawater incursion, or natural salt outcroppings occur in the western and southwestern portions of the Thicket. Plants found here are typical of the Coastal Prairies and include salt marsh-mallow (*Kosteletzkya virginica*), sea-side heliotrope (*Heliotropium curassavicum*), and powdery-thalia (*Thalia dealbata*).

Prairies can be found in the eastern portion of the Thicket but are not prominent and often grade into savannahs which are also locally called "prairies." Plants of the Blackland Prairies are uncommon in the eastern Thicket, and such wild flowers as bluebells (*Eustoma grandiflorum*) and herbertia (*Alophia drummondii*) occur only in the western portion.

While grasses are the dominant plants of the Mixed-Grass Prairies, species composition varies with numerous factors such as exact location, combination of soils, amount of mowing and grazing, and season. Some of the typical and more conspicuous grasses which will be encountered on almost all of the Thicket prairies are Indian grass (*Sorghastrum avenaceum*), eastern gamagrass (*Tripsacum dactyloides*), and tall dropseed (*Sporobolus asper*).

One of the best examples of a virgin Mixed-Grass Prairie in the Big Thicket is Marysee Prairie near Batson. Many typical prairie wild flowers and more than forty grasses can be found there.

Palmetto-Oak Flats (POF)

The Palmetto-Oak Flats lie within the Traditional Big Thicket and for the most part remain wild, nearly inaccessible junglelike areas. Situated on the lowest, flattest terrain of the Thicket, the Palmetto-Oak Flats are typically composed of broad swamplands and tortuous bayous formed by the sluggish, uncertain drainage characteristic of the coastal region. Seen today as extensive, shallow, alluvium-filled depressions, these areas are the old floodplains and levees of past rivers.

Many low ridges and swales occur in the Palmetto-Oak Flats. The ridges, from one to ten acres in size, are composed of silty sands and are slightly better drained than the surrounding areas.

The Palmetto-Oak Flats appear at first glance to be either alluvial floodplains or baygalls. A closer look uncovers enough differences to separate these areas as distinct plant associations. Frequently inundated much the same as the stream floodplains are, and with large areas of standing water similar to those of baygalls, the Palmetto-Oak Flats do not contain the exact vegetation of either of the other associations. Lacking are the richness and diversity of the floodplains and the lush sphagnum moss (*Sphagnum* spp.), orchids, and ferns of the baygalls. Water stands for much longer periods here than in the floodplains because of the tight, impermeable soils and the low, slow drainage, preventing the establishment of many typical floodplain species. During the summer months much of the water evaporates, leaving the clay soils hard and cracked and unable to support the aquatic or bog species.

One of the most extensive Palmetto-Oak Flats is located along Pine Island Bayou and Little Pine Island Bayou. These two low-banked streams twist and turn beneath a dense canopy of bald cypress (*Taxodium distichum*), gum, and oak. The bayou water is dark brown, murky, and heavily stained with tannic acid from fallen leaves and rotting debris. Stretching for miles on either side of the streams are dense stands of water-tolerant trees and vines draped with Spanish moss (*Tillandsia usneoides*). Overcup oak (*Quercus lyrata*) and laurel oak are dominant components of this forest, mingling with other hardwoods. Hawthorns are scattered throughout the understory, often growing to the size of small trees. Dwarf palmetto (*Sabal minor*) is the most distinctive plant of this habitat and covers the forest flats in open formation with little vegetation in between. Often this plant does not exceed four feet in height, but occasionally plants are found with large trunks seven to ten feet tall. These stands of larger plants may cover many acres with a dense, heavy growth. In some botanical works this larger form has been separated and is known as Louisiana palm (*S. louisiana*).

Shade, frequent inundations, and hard, cracking soils all combine to make the Palmetto-Oak Flats the poorest of all the Big Thicket plant associations in understory and ground-cover plants. Creeping spot-flower (*Spilanthes americana*), Missouri ironweed (*Vernonia missurica*), lance-leaved water-willow (*Justicia lanceolata*), and stinking-fleabane (*Pluchea foetida*) are some of the common species growing between the palmettos on level terrain. On the low ridges Hooker eryngo (*Eryngium hookeri*), Virginia buttonweed (*Diodia virginiana*), and sharp-sepal penstemon (*Penstemon tenuis*) can be found. Loblolly pine often occurs on these slightly drier areas.

Sweet Gum–Oak Floodplains (SOF)

The Sweet Gum–Oak Floodplains, locally known as "bottoms," are broad, nearly flat expanses adjacent to the rivers and larger creeks of the Thicket. The flora is dominated by deciduous trees which in the natural state are truly massive. Although the various floodplains are similar, each has its own characteristics. Because several different habitats are contained within this major association, the floodplains support a wide variety of wildlife and wild flowers, making them among the most interesting places to visit in the Thicket.

Sweet gum (*Liquidambar styraciflua*) and various oaks are the prominent trees of the floodplains. Chestnut oak, colloquially called "basket oak" or "cow oak," and willow oak (*Quercus phellos*) are found throughout. Water oak (*Q. nigra*) and southern red oak or cherry bark oak (*Q. falcata*) are frequent on the terraces and raised areas, while overcup oak is the dominant oak in and around standing water. Other important trees are water hickory (*Carya aquatica*) and black gum (*Nyssa sylvatica*). The Trinity River basin, with its western aspect, also contains species such as blueberry hawthorn (*Crataegus brachyacantha*), bois d'arc (*Maclura pomifera*), cedar elm (*Ulmus crassifolia*), and Texas sugarberry (*Celtis laevigata*).

The floodplains were formed by the deposition of suspended matter carried downstream by floodwaters and deposited when the water slowed as it stacked up and fanned out over the land. The alluvial soils are rich, are generally composed of silty, sometimes sandy loams, and are slowly permeable. Water stands for long periods after flooding, but during some summers the surface becomes very dry. The soils of the Trinity River basin are notably different in that they have a higher calcium content, which partly accounts for the floristic differences of this basin.

Physiographic features of the Sweet Gum–Oak Floodplains consist of a levee near the main stream, timbered flatlands broken irregularly by ridges and swales, and one or more terraces at the outer reaches. Besides the main stream, the floodplains are laced with backwater sloughs, oxbow lakes, potholes, and wide, watery, tree-filled depressions.

The levee, when it exists, is from a few inches to a few feet higher than most of the floodplain and is usually immediate to the river or a few yards back, but it can be quite a distance back. It is formed by the deposition of the larger suspended particles and coarse materials as soon as they pass out of the swift main channel during flooding. The finer silts and organic debris are carried out over the floodplain. On the levee's coarser, better-drained soils are small trees and shrubs such as common elder-berry (*Sambucus canadensis*), scarlet maple (*Acer rubrum*), Carolina ash (*Fraxinus caroliniana*), alder (*Alnus serrulata*), pines, and oaks. Below the levee and on low banks are found pioneer plants such as sycamore (*Platanus occidentalis*), river birch (*Betula nigra*), and black willow (*Salix nigra*). Where the bank is sandy, characteristic semishrubs are bastard indigo (*Amorpha fruticosa*), showy sesbania (*Sesbania punicea*), and rattlebush (*Sesbania drummondii*). Many wild flowers grow in these more open areas, among them the beautiful halberd-leaved rose-mallow (*Hibiscus militaris*) and the cardinal flower (*Lobelia cardinalis*).

Like the levees, the ridges scattered through the Sweet Gum–Oak Floodplains are well-drained but shaded instead of open. Occasionally beech and southern magnolia are found here, and stands of American holly (*Ilex opaca*) are frequent. Along the outer fringes of the lower floodplain may be the terraces of higher, older floodplains with vegetation much like that of the ridges, or the floodplain may grade gradually into drier associations.

The still, backwater environs of the floodplains are the home of tupelo (*Nyssa aquatica*) and the gigantic bald cypress. Some of the understory plants of these quiet, watery places are water elm (*Planera aquatica*), common buttonbush (*Cephalanthus occidentalis*), and mock-orange (*Styrax americana*). Among the showier wild flowers found here are shore milkweed (*Asclepias perennis*) and spotted touch-me-not (*Impatiens capensis*).

Outside of the banks and ridges the shrub understory and ground cover of the floodplains are sparse. Subdominants here are the small trees American hornbeam (*Carpinus caroliniana*) and eastern hop-hornbeam (*Ostrya virginiana*) and the vines muscadine (*Vitis rotundifolia*) and rattan-vine (*Berchemia scandens*), which loop and twist about the smaller trees in their search for the sun. Particularly spectacular flowers of the bottoms are rattlesnake root (*Prenanthes barbata*) and Indian-pink (*Spigelia marilandica*). In autumn, ladies' tresses orchids (*Spiranthes cernua*) form large colonies of fragrant blossoms.

Access into the Sweet Gum–Oak Floodplains is limited mostly to the major highways which cross the rivers. But due to this ready access, the areas near the highways have been frequently logged and in most places are not in a mature, natural state. One of the best means for the adventuresome spirit to enjoy the floodplains is by canoeing the slow-moving rivers and winding creeks. Some of my fondest memories are of back-paddling up some quiet, remote slough and slipping slowly among huge, moss-hung trees, searching the banks for new and special wild flowers.

Bay–Gallberry Holly Bogs (BGB)

Among the various plant associations within the Big Thicket the Bay–Gallberry Holly Bogs are one of the most complex, diverse, and unique. In these wet and often dense confines, some of the rarest and most beautiful wild flowers can be found.

The association defined as bogs in this field guide is composed of two communities locally known as "acid bogs" and "baygalls." These communities are slightly dissimilar in origin and appearance, but they contain many of the same species, so for convenience they are combined. The bogs are composed of sandy-loam soils underlain by an impermeable clay stratum. Drainage is very slow, especially in the baygall; consequently the bogs are perpetually moist, boggy, or marshy.

The phenomenon responsible for the strong acidity (pH 4.5) of the bogs is imperfectly understood, but it involves much more than a simple leaching of bases, which is the common cause for the slight acidity of many soils in a region of high precipitation. A short, blocked drainage system and a precipitation rate that exceeds evaporation rate are important in the development of an acid bog. Most bogs occur in the north, and low temperature is thought to be a factor, but low temperature is obviously not essential, since bogs occur in the Thicket. Sphagnum moss is an influential ingredient of most acid bogs. It is not found in all acid bogs, but it is found in all acid bogs of the Thicket. Sphagnum and peat (dead, compressed sphagnum) have the ability to absorb bases from dissolved salts and thus free acids (Smith, 1966).

Oxygen is low in acid bogs due to reduced water circulation. Low oxygen and strong acidity effectively "pickle" dead organic debris so that decomposition is nearly at a standstill. Deep, soft mats of partially decayed vegetation called a "false bottom" build up, and nutrients become tied up in the dead matter. Hydrogen sulfide gas often bubbles from bogs as a result of the activity of the anaerobic sulfur bacteria. Acid bogs are particularly low in nitrogen, potassium, phosphorus, and calcium, so life in an acid bog must be adapted to low concentrations of these important nutrients, and many strange plants occur there.

Communities locally referred to as acid bogs are most often formed where underground water follows a clay stratum to the surface. Such places may cover several acres. Wet spots from surface drainage sometime occur in low, sandy depressions in the higher wooded uplands, forming a small acid-bog community. Small seeps on a slope or hillside are known as "hanging bogs" and are usually not as marshy because of the more rapid drainage. Sometimes a topographically higher acid bog will form the beginning of a small stream or grade into the similar but larger baygall.

Acid bogs may or may not contain sweet bay (*Magnolia virginiana*) or gallberry holly (*Ilex coriacea*), but the more extensive ones usually do. Sphagnum moss is present in varying degrees, depending on the amount and constancy of the water. Small patches of the rare little rose-flowered bogmoss (*Mayaca aubletii*) are sometimes found, and while never common, several species of orchids occur here, most notably the water-spider orchid (*Habenaria repens*), the green rein-orchid (*Habenaria clavellata*), and the rose pogonia (*Pogonia ophioglossoides*). Pitcher-plants (*Sarracenia alata*) and annual sundew (*Drosea annuus*) are two of the most frequently encountered insectivorous plants. Various species of ferns, such as cinnamon fern (*Osmunda cinnamomea*), royal fern (*Osmunda regalis*), and sensitive fern (*Onoclea sensibilis*) may be found in the acid bog, often with several species together.

Baygalls are larger and generally deeper in standing water than the acid bogs and contain larger and more exuberant vegetation. Some baygalls are quite extensive, being more than a mile across, while others are only small pools. Sweet bay and gallberry holly are the two dominant plants of this community, and the colloquial name "baygall" is derived from these two species.

Many of the older baygalls are in various rather complex transitional stages to a drier forest type of vegetation. As the bodies of water gradually fill with organic debris, more and different species of plants become established. These encroaching species form well-defined concentric rings, depending on their water tolerance. The center of a baygall may be open water or contain some floating aquatics such as fragrant water-lily (*Nymphaea odorata*). Sedges, rushes, and shrubs like water-willow (*Decodon verticillatus*) and wax-myrtle grow along the shallow edges. Water-tolerant trees, usually with an understory of black titi (*Cyrilla racemiflora*), Virginia sweet-spire (*Itea virginica*), red bay (*Persea borbonia*), and gallberry holly densely line the drier outer edges.

In the younger, less developed and more remote baygalls the vegetation grows to exceptional size and lushness. The clear, dark-tinted water, often covered with thick mats of sphagnum moss, spreads out through the trees and surrounding shrub thickets. Black gum and bald cypress are commonly found growing tall and straight in the larger baygalls, the branches of the trees heavily festooned with long strands of Spanish moss. Cypresses in this watery habitat develop wide, flaring bases surrounded by numerous tall "knees."

Small debris-formed knolls covered with mosses and liverworts provide footholds for various shrubs and small trees. Orchids and rare saprophytic plants such as burmannia (*Burmannia biflora*) and nodding-nixie (*Apteria aphylla*) cling to decaying logs and stumps. Ferns are often shoulder high in these baygalls, and vines of laurel green-brier (*Smilax laurifolia*) rise from the bases of broad-buttressed trees, hanging in long, graceful loops from the lower branches. Interlacing boughs form a closed canopy overhead, with little sunlight penetrating the depths of the baygalls. It is these dense, swampy bogs more than any other association which give the Big Thicket its dim, mysterious atmosphere.

Longleaf–Black Gum Savannahs (LBS)

The Longleaf–Black Gum Savannahs are broad, grassy flatlands with a widely spaced overstory of longleaf pine (*Pinus palustris*) and small, stunted black gum, while loblolly pine and sweet gum are recent invaders. The groundcover is predominantly indigenous grasses, sedges, and rushes. Mixed with these is an array of wild flowers of which more than a few are strange and rare; there are four species of carnivorous plants here, and at least five orchids.

A fluctuating water table and fire are usually important factors in maintaining a savannah vegetation, and they are probably important in maintaining the Big Thicket savannahs also. The soils are of fine, hard-packed, slow-draining sand and shallowly underlaid by hardpan, a stratum of cemented material. This impermeable layer causes a persistent high water table during periods of frequent rain, but during periods of drought the soils become very dry because moisture cannot rise by capillary action from below the hardpan. As a rule, shrubs do not do well under these conditions, but fire-resistant annual plants and some trees with sufficient root systems can thrive here.

Decomposition is slow in the acid to strongly acid soils of the savannahs, and large amounts of the nutrients are tied up in organic debris and not usable. Therefore, these soils support mainly carbonaceous plants, lending credence to the idea that fire could be a factor controlling the savannah nature of this association. This soil condition also contributes to the evolution and perpetuation of carnivorous plants, there being a greater need to trap certain nutrients.

The Longleaf–Black Gum Savannah area is more sensitive to local elevation than any other area of the Thicket. A very slight change, sometimes of only a few inches, will produce a completely different plant association.

Small mounds are scattered throughout the longleaf pine–black gum association, possibly suggesting a former coastal dune history. These mounds are drier than the surrounding areas and are usually dominated by longleaf pine. Numerous depressions are likewise found in the savannahs, and most often these are wet and boggy, due to the hardpan bottom, and strongly acidic in reaction. Although surrounded by Longleaf–Black Gum Savannahs, these mounds and acid bogs belong to, and are discussed in, the Longleaf-Bluestem Uplands and the Bay–Gallberry Holly Bogs, respectively.

Transition zones often contain the rarest and most delicate plants, and the borders of the savannahs are no exception. Just where they begin to grade into the higher, drier Longleaf-Bluestem Uplands grow some of the most sensitive plants of this association. Species that are quite moisture specific, such as Arkansas blueberry (*Vaccinium arkansanum*), stagger bush (*Lyonia mariana*), and the little carnivorous butterwort (*Pinguicula pumila*) grow in this zone, where their exacting requirements can be met.

Where the savannahs grade into the slightly lower and wetter acid bogs, plants such as yellow fringed orchid (*Habenaria ciliaris*), grass-pink (*Calopogon pulchellus*), and annual sundew become more common.

The savannahs bloom long and beautifully. One of the showiest and most characteristic species is the well-known carnivorous pitcher-plant, which sometimes covers large areas with bright greenish yellow trumpet-shaped leaves and large, drooping, pale yellow flowers. Such rare specialties as spring bartonia (*Bartonia verna*), and bottle-gentian (*Gentiana saponaria*) are found only in the savannahs. Other beauties which grow in the Longleaf–Black Gum Savannahs and may occur frequently here are snowy orchid (*Habenaria nivea*), yellow sunny-bell (*Schoenolirion croceum*), yellow meadow beauty (*Rhexia lutea*), Barbara's-buttons (*Marshallia tenuifolia*), and colic-root (*Aletris aurea*).

Longleaf-Bluestem Uplands (LBU)

The Longleaf-Bluestem Uplands are scattered throughout the Thicket area—on the hills and slopes in the northern portion, on the ridge tops between the Trinity and Sabine rivers, and even on the low mounds in the Longleaf–Black Gum Savannahs. It is in the hillier, northern region that the uplands are best represented. Where they are not disturbed, and where the forest remains unbroken, the uplands have an open, spacious, parklike appearance. There the longleaf pine still reigns supreme, the tall, stately trees overtopping an understory of small trees, shrubs, grasses, and wild flowers.

Soils in the uplands are composed of medium- to coarse-grained sands varying in depth but usually several feet deep and underlaid by a clay stratum. The topographic relief and moderately permeable soils provide rapid drainage, and the uplands are generally dry. Because of the clay substratum, however, local depressions often contain water. These shallow ponds are typically filled with grasses and sedges and are ringed by buttonbush, wax-myrtle, black titi, and various viburnums. Water moving horizontally along the clay substratum sometimes surfaces on the sides of hills and gullies; there an acid bog or the beginning of a small stream may be found. In places in the north-eastern part of the Thicket the upland soils show a red clay, and on this soil longleaf pine shares dominance with shortleaf pine (*Pinus echinata*) and various hardwoods.

The plant association of the uplands is considered to be subclimax in nature and is held in this arrested state primarily by fire, which was once frequent in the uplands. The high fiber content of the plants in the uplands and the thick ground cover of resinous pine needles allow fire to occur easily, preventing the establishment of tree seedlings and most woody plants. Long-leaf pine and many grasses are tolerant of fire, and with fire, a grassland dominated by the bluestems (*Andropogon* spp.) and overstoried by longleaf pine is maintained. Some ecologists believe that with total fire suppression, successional development would ultimately lead to an oak-hickory forest.

The Longleaf-Bluestem Uplands are not now as the earlier settlers found them. Changes have occurred through fire suppression, timber management, and sporadic attempts at agriculture. Today wildfires are largely controlled, and many species normally repressed by fire have invaded the longleaf habi-tat. Where once the longleaf pine stood in almost pure stands with a thinly scattered understory of beautifully shaped shrubs such as flowering dogwood (*Cornus florida*) and American holly, now in many areas nonrepresentative trees and shrubs are encroaching.

Logging has left scattered openings with tangles of tree limbs and de-bris. In this situation semishade species are stimulated into phenomenal growth and quickly replace the original shade-tolerant understory. Some plants which respond in this manner include hawthorns, blueberries (*Vac-cinium* spp.), and American beautyberry (*Callicarpa americana*). In larger abandoned clearings grasses are the early invaders along with more sun-tolerant plants such as southern dewberry (*Rubus trivialis*), wax-myrtle, su-mac (*Rhus* spp.), sea-myrtle, grape (*Vitis* spp.), and tree seedlings. These seedlings often include loblolly and shortleaf pine, sweet gums, oaks, and others from contiguous forest types which compete with the original longleaf association.

Although the impact of man has often disturbed the spacious continuity of the uplands, large areas of this association still remain. Wild flowers in these semishaded confines are many and include such lovely species as bird-foot violet (*Viola pedata*), wine-cup (*Callirhoë papaver*), purple pleat-leaf (*Eustylis purpurea*), and rose vervain (*Verbena canadensis*). In more shaded areas of this upland forest, Texas Dutchman's-pipe (*Aristolochia reticulata*), false foxglove (*Aureolaria grandiflora*), and the yellow-blossomed vine Carolina-jessamine (*Gelsemium sempervirens*) can be found. Flowering shrubs such as red buckeye (*Aesculus pavia*) and New Jersey tea (*Ceanothus americanus*) grow along the stream banks, mingling with various ferns, mosses, and liverworts. Large colonies of the fern southern bracken (*Pteridium aquilinum*) are frequent in the uplands and are a conspicuous feature of this association.

Beech-Magnolia-Loblolly Slopes (BMLS)

A magnificent mingling of deciduous, broad-leaved evergreen, and coniferous trees forms the forest of the Beech-Magnolia-Loblolly Slopes association. Among the age-old trees the diffused light and deep stillness convey a cathedrallike quality to these mystical woodlands. Beneath the high, interwoven crowns of this forest is sheltered a fascinating mixture of shrubs, vines, and many rare and interesting herbs.

It is the presence of American beech, southern magnolia, and loblolly pine which defines this association. The stately white oak is also common in this forest, and sugar maple (*Acer saccharum*) is a frequent subdominant.

The most extensive beech-magnolia-loblolly forests have developed on the elevated terrain in the northern portion of the Thicket and for the most part occur on the slopes between the drier uplands and wetter lowlands. There on the moist transition zone of the slopes they have been partly protected from the once frequently occurring wildfires of the uplands. The soils of these slopes are well developed, relatively fertile, and composed mostly of fine, sandy loams usually underlaid by well-aerated, friable subsoils.

The Beech-Magnolia-Loblolly Slopes are dissected by numerous small, spring-fed creeks with cool, clear water. Along the banks of these streams certain plants reach their largest growth and loveliest flowering. Among them are small trees and shrubs such as redbud (*Cercis canadensis*), fringe-tree (*Chionanthus virginica*), silver-bell (*Halesia dipteria*), hoary azalea (*Rhododendron canescens*), and the winter-flowering Virginia witch-hazel (*Hamamelis virginiana*). One of the rarest plants of the Thicket, silky camellia (*Stewartia malacodendron*), is found in this moist, shaded habitat.

Beech is often the most abundant tree along these streams and accompanies magnolia and loblolly pine along the stream courses into the lower lands of the Thicket to the south and east. Both magnolia and loblolly pine continue along the streams southward, but beech is largely replaced in the lowest portion of the Thicket by chestnut oak and laurel oak. Rarely does beech occur in the forest community of the more level, slow-draining southern flatlands.

Along the steeper slopes where the beech-magnolia-loblolly association overlaps the uplands, a narrow borderline plant community sometimes occurs. Many of the plants in this unstable community are uncommon or rare. One of the showiest wild flowers which is found only in this fragile niche is the Carolina-lily (*Lilium michauxii*).

The herb layer of the Beech-Magnolia-Loblolly Slopes is most conspicuous in the spring before the deciduous trees are fully leaved and cast their shadows on the forest floor. It is then that may-apples (*Podophyllum peltatum*), and wake-robin (*Trillium gracile*) form large colonies, interrupted by occasional patches of the lower-growing partridge-berry (*Mitchella repens*) or dark purple-blossomed Walter's violet (*Viola walteri*). Orchids which are usually found in close proximity to beech trees are whorled pogonia (*Isotria verticillata*) and crippled crane-fly (*Tipularia discolor*). Beech-drops (*Epifagus virginiana*), which are parasitic on the roots of beech trees, are found only where this tree grows.

Some of the wild flowers found in this association are typical of the eastern Appalachian Mountain region; they include bloodroot (*Sanguinaria canadensis*), yellow dog's-tooth-violet, (*Erythronium rostratum*), five-leaved Jack-in-the-pulpit (*Arisaema quinatum*), and the lovely yellow lady's-slipper orchid (*Cypripedium calceolus*).

The Beech-Magnolia-Loblolly Slopes are perhaps best remembered for the magnolia trees whose large, creamy white blossoms fill the summer forest with a sweet, heady fragrance.

Oak-Farkleberry Sandylands (OFS)

The Oak-Farkleberry Sandylands are the least expected plant association found in the Big Thicket. Composed of deep deposits of whitish sands, these areas appear harsh and dry, but they nevertheless support a rich variety of herbaceous plants. Many of the species growing there are typical of a more arid environment.

The sands of the sandylands were laid down by early rivers and streams and by the longshore currents of ancient seas. They are composed of quartz grains of various sizes, contain little clay, and are low in fertility. The porous nature of sand as a soil type is primarily responsible for the sandylands' xeric qualities. Humidity is nearly as high as in other parts of the Thicket, and rainfall is about the same, but water moves rapidly downward through the sand, leaving the upper soil layers relatively dry. The overstory is sparse, and the intense glare and reflected heat from the sand contribute heavily to the xeric effect.

These extreme conditions make it difficult for the young plants common to most of the Thicket to get started. However, the sandylands do offer certain advantages to those plants which are adapted to the environment. Light is abundant, of course, but more important, the sandy soil becomes neither hard, cracked, and extremely dry during a drought nor waterlogged for long periods after flooding. The soil is friable at all times, and the soil moisture content, although low, is more consistent than that of clay soils.

Adaptations exhibited by the plants of this community include such things as hairs, waxy coatings, small leaf surfaces, and recessed leaf pores to prevent wind drying and radiation damage. Plants may have deep root systems, tubers, succulent stems, or leaves of spongy tissue for absorbing and storing water.

A few plants generally associated with wet or swampy habitats are found in the Oak-Farkleberry Sandylands and seem out of place. Spanish moss is one of these. This plant flourishes in the sandylands because it is dependent not on soil moisture but on high humidity.

Plants typical of the sandylands may be found in scattered locations throughout the Thicket where there are spots of deep sand or gravel. In places where they receive an abundant supply of water, as they do near the artesian springs of the gravel deposits along the Trinity River, they grow tall and rank, reaching atypical size and making identification difficult.

Sand jack or blue jack (*Quercus incana*) and longleaf pine are the dominant trees of the sandylands in the lower portion of the Thicket. In the northern portion, blackjack (*Q. marilandica*), post oak (*Q. stellata*), and black hickory (*Carya texana*) are also common. Farkleberry (*Vaccinium arboreum*) is the dominant understory shrub throughout. The largest and most typical sandylands occur on the higher areas of the Village Creek watershed.

Despite the apparently inhospitable conditions of the Oak-Farkleberry Sandylands, numerous species of wild flowers, some of them uncommon or endemic, thrive there. Among the more common species are Louisiana yucca (*Yucca louisianensis*), eastern prickly pear (*Opuntia compressa*), and weak-stem sunflower (*Helianthus debilis*). Some uncommon and endemic species include Carolina vervain (*Stylodon carneus*), Oklahoma prairie clover (*Petalostemum griseum*), trailing phlox (*Phlox nivalis*), green-thread (*Thelesperma flavodiscum*), and Hooker palafoxia (*Palafoxia hookeriana*).

Roadsides (R)

Roadsides in the Big Thicket are a mosaic of diverse habitats usually supporting plant species representative of the immediately adjacent association but also containing a strange assortment of species from other regions. They provide a unique sampling of the various plant associations and a hint of the richness and diversity of the Big Thicket vegetation. This diversity, plus the accessibility, makes the roadsides especially enjoyable.

There are many factors which influence the roadside plants, often causing quite atypical responses. Sunlight and the abundant moisture draining from the road surface are the most obvious environmental properties. Due to the extra sunlight and moisture available, many species are able to extend their normal range into other, nearby habitats. Frequently a plant will be found growing in a sunny but moist situation along the roadside and doing quite well when ordinarily it would be found in dry, shaded woodlands. At other times full sun, exposed conditions, and fast drainage will make it possible for xerophytic types to survive where moisture is more abundant than usual. Where water stands permanently for long periods, as in the "borrow ditches," aquatic and semiaquatic plants become established.

Less obvious are three other important factors which contribute to the composition of wild flowers along the Roadsides: the corridor effect, Texas Highway Department practices, and the exposure of different soil types by the road cut.

The Roadsides offer a ready pathway for the establishment of new species into an area. Seeds and roots brought in by vehicles, tourists, and road crews often find the environmental conditions of the Thicket ideal for survival and propagation. This situation adds to the diversity and confusion of the Thicket's plant associations.

The various roadside associations are in a more or less unstable condition, mostly due to disturbance by the Texas Highway Department. Mowing, construction, and spraying with herbicides all influence the plants of any given habitat. Mowing of the herbaceous growth probably has the most influential effect. This constant disturbance can be both beneficial and detrimental to the roadside flora. It is particularly favorable for the more "weedy" or hardy plants such as ironweed (*Vernonia* spp.) and goldenrod (*Solidago* spp.). These plants are beautiful, but by invading a disturbed area first, they prevent the establishment of more fragile species. Yet at different times mowing provides the openings necessary for rare or unusual plants.

Along the Roadsides, as in other plant associations, plants are indicators of the type of soil present. During road construction, surface soils are often removed, exposing different subsoils. In these places an entirely different plant community may become established. An example of such a situation can be found in the northeastern portion of the Thicket, where low hills or ridges have been cut through and reworked, exposing the underlying calcareous soils. In these small, scattered locations many of the plants are different from those of the surrounding habitat and are representative of species of distant origin, not being found in the Thicket except on such exposed soils.

Some species of roadside wild flowers are found blooming throughout the year in the Thicket. The greatest variety occurs in the spring, when showy primrose (*Oenothera speciosa*), Philadelphia fleabane (*Erigeron philadelphicus*), and self-heal (*Prunella vulgaris*) make great splashes of pink, white, and purple. Summer and fall are also well represented when bitterweed (*Helenium amarum*), late brown-eyed Susan (*Rudbeckia hirta*), and Indian blanket (*Gaillardia pulchella*) form long, continuous ribbons of bright colors. The cold-tolerant Dakota vervain (*Verbena bipinnatifida*) and several species of fall composites continue blooming in protected areas, mingling in late winter with the first spring flowers.

How to Use This Guide

To best identify wild flowers in the Big Thicket and adjacent areas with this guide, use the following procedure:

When a flower has been selected for identification, turn first to the photographs of the plant associations at the beginning of the color plates section and choose the one which most closely resembles the selected flower's surroundings. Read the description of the chosen association, given in the Introduction, to be sure it is the best selection, then turn to the wild-flower photographs for that particular association and match the flower in question. If the flower cannot be found in the chosen association, then select the association which next best resembles the flower's surroundings. Repeat this process until a photograph is found which most closely matches the flower to be identified.

Beneath each flower photograph is given the page number of the written description of the plant. Turn to that page and check identification of the plant by comparing its parts with the description. A small hand lens of about 10× power will often prove helpful in examining flower parts. Then, for verification, compare the plant with the descriptions and photographs of other plants in the same genus. Plants in the same genus will be adjacent to one another in the descriptions, and their photographs may be quickly found from the page number given opposite the flower's name along the right-hand margin of each description.

The ecological approach of using plant associations for identification may not always be the fastest, but it yields the most positive identification and is definitely the most educational and rewarding. Of course a certain amount of botanical maturity is required, but this will come rapidly to the eager beginner.

The most obvious problem is not knowing the dominant plants or being able to recognize the major associations. Also, a keen awareness of one's surroundings is necessary to notice a subtle or quick change of plant associations. For example, a deep sandbar along a river should be considered part of the Oak-Farkleberry Sandylands, not the Sweet Gum–Oak Floodplains. Many plants exhibit different growth patterns in different situations. The "feel" for what these changes will be in a new set of circumstances can only be acquired through experience.

The written descriptions of the plants give each species by common and scientific name. Opposite the common name is the number of the page on which that species is illustrated. Following the names, a brief, general description of the entire plant is followed in consistent form by a description of the leaf, the inflorescence (flower cluster), and the individual flower of the plant. The fruit is also described, for often it aids in identification, is the best means of propagation, or has other interest. Information is frequently given in a note at the end of the description to comment on rarity, uses of the plant, or other interesting features.

The plant associations in which a species occurs are given by abbreviation on the last line of that plant's description, with the most likely association listed first. Because most wild flowers have some tolerance for associations other than the one in which they are most common, alternate associations that a wild flower might also be found in are listed in parentheses following the preferred one. For example, the letters POF (MGP) at the end of a plant description would indicate that the plant is usually found in the Palmetto-Oak Flats, and is illustrated in that section, but may also be found in the Mixed-Grass Prairies. However, R for Roadsides is not listed as an alternate association for any wild flower. It is understood that any wild flower can occasionally be found on the side of the road near its preferred habitat.

Representative letters for the plant associations are MGP for Mixed-Grass Prairies, POF for Palmetto-Oak Flats, SOF for Sweet Gum–Oak Floodplains, BGB for Bay–Gallberry Holly Bogs, LBS for Longleaf–Black Gum Savannahs, LBU for Longleaf-Bluestem Uplands, BMLS for Beech-Magnolia-Loblolly Slopes, OFS for Oak-Farkleberry Sandylands, and R for Roadsides.

The peak flowering period for each species is also given on the last line of the plant's description. For example, March–May means that flowering usually begins in March and continues through April and part or all of May. These bloom dates cannot be absolute or inclusive in the Thicket area, for because of the mildness of the winter months and the abundant moisture available, many species continue to bloom sporadically throughout the year.

NAMES AND TERMS IN THE TEXT

AN effort has been made to keep the text straightforward and simple. Technical terms are held to a minimum in order not to confuse the botanically untrained; those technical terms used are the more common ones and are explained in the glossary.

Scientific terms, scientific and common names, and the botanical order of plants in the plant descriptions closely follow Correll and Johnston's *Manual of the Vascular Plants of Texas* (1970). When no common name was given for a plant in the *Manual*, Gould's "Texas Plants—a Checklist and Ecological Summary" (1962) was used. If no name was found there, other references were sought. Sometimes more than one common name is listed when an alternate name is widely used. At least one common name is given for each plant even though it may not be dependable, for frequently it provides the only means of communication for those unfamiliar with scientific names.

The scientific name of each plant species consists of two Latin or latinized words: a generic name, or genus, which is capitalized, and a specific name, or species, which is not capitalized. If a subspecies or variety name is used, it follows the species name and is not capitalized. The personal name or abbreviation following the scientific name stands for the author who first described the plant. If the scientific name has been changed, the original author is given in parentheses and the current author is given last.

The scientific names of plants are sometimes difficult for the uninitiated to pronounce, so directly beneath each scientific name in the plant descriptions is given a phonetic spelling of that name. These are the pronunciations in common usage and may not always coincide with classical Latin. I suggest that learning to pronounce a few scientific names will quickly facilitate the pronunciation of others.

MEASUREMENTS

MEASUREMENTS in this book are given in inches and feet due to the unfamiliarity of most nonprofessionals with the metric system. However, a metric scale is given below, on the back of the paperback, and on the hardbound book jacket flap for those interested in learning the metric system. The following are approximate metric equivalents:

1 inch = 2.54 centimeters (cm) or 25.4 millimeters (mm)

3 feet, 3.4 inches = 1 meter (m)

Color Plates

Plant Associations

Mixed-Grass Prairies (MGP; p. 10)

Palmetto-Oak Flats (POF; p. 12)

Sweet Gum–Oak Floodplains (SOF; p. 13)

Bay–Gallberry Holly Bogs (BGB; p. 15)

Longleaf–Black Gum Savannahs (LBS; p. 17)

Longleaf-Bluestem Uplands (LBU; p. 18)

Beech-Magnolia-Loblolly Slopes (BMLS; p. 20)

Oak-Farkleberry Sandylands (OFS; p. 21)

Roadsides (R; p. 22)

Mixed-Grass Prairies (MGP)

Wild onion (p. 113)

Evening-star rain-lily
(p. 118)

Dotted blue-eyed grass
(p. 119)

Herbertia (p. 121)

Powdery-thalia (p. 122)

Spring ladies' tresses
(p. 128)

Swamp smartweed (p. 133)

White prickly poppy (p. 146)

Macartney rose (p. 156)

Carolina rose (p. 156)

Powderpuff (p. 158)

Bush-pea (p. 161)

Yellow-puff (p. 159)

Texas bluebonnet (p. 162)

Plains wild indigo (p. 160)

Purple prairie clover
(p. 166)

Plains prairie clover (p. 166)

Snow-on-the-prairie
(p. 184)

Least snoutbean (p. 177)

Salt marsh-mallow
(p. 191)

Scarlet hibiscus (p. 193)

Lance-leaf loosestrife
(p. 206)

White gaura (p. 209)

Uruguay water-primrose (p. 211)

Dog-sunshade (p. 213)

Simple-leaf eryngo (p. 216)

Centaury (p. 227)

Bluebell gentian (p. 227)

Bluebells (p. 228)

Antelope-horn (p. 231)

Whorled milkweed (p. 234)   Purple stylisma (p. 236)

Salt-marsh morning glory (p. 239)   Prairie phlox (p. 241)

Drummond phlox (p. 242)   Prairie phacelia (p. 242)

Seaside heliotrope (p. 243)

Brazilian vervain (p. 246)

Texas vervain (p. 246)

Florida bluehearts (p. 266)

Violet ruellia (p. 273)

Downy lobelia (p. 283)

Western ironweed (p. 284)

Slender-headed euthamia (p. 292)

Tall goldenrod (p. 294)   Texas aster (p. 295)   Annual aster (p. 296)

Slender silphium (p. 302)   Marsh cone-flower (p. 306)   Shiny cone-flower (p. 307)

Mexican-hat (p. 308)   White marshallia (p. 313)   Lance-leaf Indian plaintain (p. 320)

Palmetto-Oak Flats (POF)

Dwarf palmetto (p. 104)

Bristly smartweed (p. 134)

Rough-seed buttercup (p. 141)

Carolina buttercup (p. 141)

Blueberry hawthorn (p. 153)

Common balloon-vine (p. 189)

Bladder pod (p. 168)

Shrubby water-primrose
(p. 211)

Hooker eryngo (p. 215)

Dodder (p. 240)

Blue waterleaf (p. 243)

One-flowered waterleaf
(p. 243)

Disc water-hyssop (p. 260)

Sharp-sepal penstemon
(p. 262)

Green-flowered yeatesia
(p. 274)

Lance-leavéd water-willow
(p. 275)

Common buttonbush
(p. 276)

Virginia buttonweed
(p. 278)

Missouri ironweed (p. 284)

Stinking-fleabane (p. 301)

Southern arrow-wood (p. 278)

Creeping spot-flower (p. 304)

Burhead (p. 101)

Delta arrowhead (p. 102)

Wapato (p. 102)

Arrow-arum (p. 106)

Spanish moss (p. 108)

Ohio spiderwort (p. 110)

Water-hyacinth (p. 110)

Pickerel-weed (p. 111)

Yellow iris (p. 120)

Spider-lily (p. 117)

Southern swamp lily (p. 118)

Southern iris (p. 120)

Short-stem iris (p. 121)

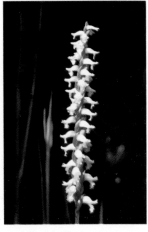

Nodding ladies' tresses (p. 129)

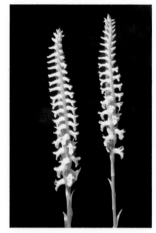

Fragrant ladies' tresses
(p. 129)

Lizard's-tail (p. 131)

Water smartweed (p. 134)

Alligator-weed (p. 135)

Spatterdock (p. 138)

Yellow lotus (p. 139)

Yellowroot (p. 139)

Purple meadow-rue
(p. 140)

White clematis (p. 142)

Blue jasmine (p. 143)

Spider flower (p. 149)

Ditch-stonecrop (p. 151)

Indian strawberry (p. 154)

Wild strawberry (p. 154)

Big-tree plum (p. 157)

Bastard indigo (p. 165)

Rattlebush (p. 168)

Kentucky wisteria (p. 167)

Showy sesbania (p. 169)

Amberique bean (p. 178)

Joint vetch (p. 170)

Drummond wax-mallow
(p. 191)

Spotted touch-me-not
(p. 190)

Halberd-leaved rose-mallow
(p. 192)

Bayou violet (p. 203)

Small-flowered St. John's–
wort (p. 198)

Axocatzin (p. 195)

Passion-flower (p. 205)

Spiked loosestrife (p. 207)

Tooth-cup (p. 207)

Golden Alexanders (p. 212)

Creeping eryngo (p. 216)

Spadeleaf (p. 217)

Red-osier dogwood (p. 218)

Trailing loosestrife (p. 221)

Indian-pink (p. 223)

Hornpod (p. 224)

Blue-star (p. 229)

Climbing dogbane (p. 230)

Shore milkweed (p. 235)

Milkvine (p. 236)

Pitted morning glory (p. 239)

Four-spike heliotrope
(p. 244)

Turnsole (p. 244)

American germander
(p. 249)

Slender-leaf betony
(p. 253)

Hedge-nettle (p. 254)

Lion's-ears (p. 255)

Cut-leaf ground-cherry (p. 258)

Monkey-flower (p. 261)

Cross-vine (p. 268)

Trumpet-creeper (p. 268)

Dicliptera (p. 274)

Common elder-berry (p. 279)

Japanese honeysuckle (p. 279)

Chicken spike (p. 281)

Cardinal flower (p. 283)

Texas ironweed (p. 285)

Mist-flower (p. 290)

Climbing hemp-weed (p. 288)

Calico aster (p. 296)

Wrinkle-leaved goldenrod
(p. 294)

Camphor-weed (p. 301)

Cut-leaf cone-flower
(p. 306)

Frostweed (p. 310)

Butterweed (p. 319)

Rattlesnake root (p. 324)

Bay–Gallberry Holly Bogs (BGB)

Water-weed (p. 103)

Bogmoss (p. 106)

Bunchflower (p. 112)

Texas trillium (p. 115)

Burmannia (p. 122)

Nodding-nixie (p. 123)

Water-spider orchid
(p. 124)

Green rein-orchid (p. 125)

Rose pogonia (p. 127)

Fragrant water-lily (p. 138)

Green adder's mouth
(p. 130)

Sweet bay (p. 145)

Virginia sweet-spire (p. 151)

Black titi (p. 187)

Gallberry holly (p. 187)

Water-willow (p. 206)

Sweet pepper-bush (p. 218)

White azalea (p. 219)

Mock-orange (p. 222)

Floating heart (p. 229)

Red milkweed (p. 234)   Water-horehound (p. 258)   Carolina water-hyssop
(p. 260)

Zigzag bladderwort   Purple bladderwort   Floating bladderwort
(p. 270)   (p. 271)   (p. 271)

Cone-spur bladderwort   Joe-Pye-weed (p. 289)
(p. 272)

Longleaf–Black Gum Savannahs (LBS)

Grassy arrowhead (p. 101)

White-topped umbrella grass (p. 103)

Yellow-eyed grass (p. 107)

Ten-angle pipewort (p. 107)

Sticky tofieldia (p. 111)

Yellow sunny-bell (p. 112)

Colic-root (p. 116)

Yellow fringed orchid (p. 124)

Snowy orchid (p. 125)

Bearded grass-pink (p. 128)

Grass-pink (p. 128)

Pitcher-plant (p. 150)

Annual sundew (p. 150)

Red chokeberry (p. 153)

Single-stem scurfpea
(p. 164)

Multi-bloom tephrosia
(p. 167)

Maryland milkwort
(p. 181)

Pink milkwort (p. 181)

Bachelor's button (p. 182)

Yellow savannah milkwort
(p. 183)

White rose-mallow (p. 192)

Rough rose-mallow
(p. 193)

St. Peter's–wort (p. 197)

Sand-weed (p. 198)

Primrose-leaved violet
(p. 200)

Lance-leaved violet (p. 200)

Meadow beauty (p. 208)

Yellow meadow beauty
(p. 208)

Common meadow beauty
(p. 209)

Spindle-root (p. 212)

Thread-leaf mock
bishop's-weed (p. 213)

Ribbed mock bishop's-weed
(p. 213)

Leafless cowbane (p. 215)

Wand hornpod (p. 224)

Pine-woods rose-gentian
(p. 225)

Rose-pink (p. 225)

Meadow-pink (p. 226)

Bottle-gentian (p. 228)

Prairie rose-gentian
(p. 226)

Spring bartonia (p. 228)

Long-leaf milkweed (p. 235)

Rough skullcap (p. 250)

Desert-lavender (p. 251)

Green gerardia (p. 264)

False dragon-head (p. 253)

American bluehearts
(p. 266)

Rush bladderwort (p. 270)

Small butterwort (p. 272)

Soft-leaved lobelia (p. 282)

Sharp gay-feather (p. 286)

Kansas gay-feather
(p. 287)

Hyssop-leaf eupatorium
(p. 288)

Justice-weed (p. 289)

Slender bigelowia (p. 292)   Low aster (p. 297)   Flat-top aster (p. 297)

Clasping cone-flower
(p. 307)

Ashy helianthus (p. 309)

Flax-leaved coreopsis
(p. 311)

Barbara's-buttons (p. 313)

Purple-head sneezeweed
(p. 315)

Fringed sneezeweed
(p. 316)

Sunbonnets (p. 321)

Longleaf-Bluestem Uplands (LBU)

Erect day-flower (p. 108)

Hairy-flowered spiderwort (p. 109)

Yellow star-grass (p. 117)

Yellow blue-eyed grass (p. 118)

Blue-eyed grass (p. 119)

Purple pleat-leaf (p. 121)

Texas Dutchman's-pipe
(p. 132)

Long-leaf wild buckwheat
(p. 132)

Heart-sepal wild buckwheat
(p. 133)

Agrimony (p. 155)

Partridge pea (p. 159)

White false indigo (p. 161)

Scarlet pea (p. 164)

Pencil-flower (p. 171)

Bare-stem tick-trefoil
(p. 172)

Panicled desmodium
(p. 172)

Pigeon-wings (p. 175)

Butterfly pea (p. 175)

Groundnut (p. 175)

Perennial wild bean
(p. 178)

Stiff-stem flax (p. 180)

Red buckeye (p. 188)

New Jersey tea (p. 190)

Wine-cup (p. 194)

St. Andrew's cross (p. 197)

Field pansy (p. 199)

Bird-foot violet (p. 201)

Thicket violet (p. 204)

Lovell violet (p. 201)

Yellow passion-flower (p. 204)

Button snake-root (p. 215)

Flowering dogwood (p. 217)

Stagger bush (p. 220)

Carolina-jessamine (p. 223)

Indian hemp (p. 230)

Savannah milkweed
(p. 232)

Green milkweed (p. 233)

White-flowered milkweed
(p. 233)

White stylisma (p. 237)

Puccoon (p. 245)

Rose vervain (p. 247)

Forked blue curls (p. 249)   Egg-leaf skullcap (p. 251)   Blunt false dragon-head
(p. 252)

Blue sage (p. 256)   Tropical sage (p. 256)   Loose-flowered penstemon
(p. 262)

Mountain-mint (p. 258)   Old-field toad-flax (p. 263)

False foxglove (p. 264)

Scale-leaved gerardia (p. 265)

Purple gerardia (p. 265)

Low ruellia (p. 273)

Fine-leaf bluets (p. 275)

Southern bluets (p. 276)

Small bluets (p. 276)

Wahlenbergia (p. 281)

Slender gay-feather
(p. 286)

Silk-grass (p. 291)

Maryland golden aster
(p. 291)

Boott goldenrod (p. 293)

Downy goldenrod (p. 295)

Meadow aster (p. 296)

Savory-leaf aster (p. 298)

Small-head boltonia
(p. 299)

Everlasting (p. 300)

Purple cone-flower (p. 304)

Brown-eyed Susan (p. 305)

Rough cone-flower (p. 305)

Stiff-haired sunflower
(p. 308)

Swamp sunflower (p. 309)

Tickseed (p. 312)

Woolly-white (p. 318)   Woolly groundsel (p. 319)   Cat's-ear (p. 323)

Beech-Magnolia-Loblolly Slopes (BMLS)

Green dragon (p. 104)   Jack-in-the-pulpit (p. 105)   Featherbells (p. 111)

Five-leaved Jack-in-the-pulpit (p. 105)

Carolina-lily (p. 114)

Yellow dog's-tooth-violet
(p. 114)

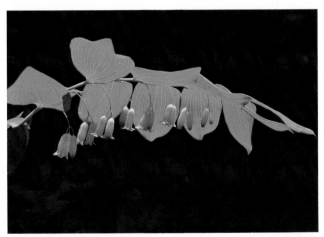

Great Solomon's seal (p. 115)

Wake-robin (p. 116)

Yellow lady's-slipper
(p. 123)

Southern twayblade
(p. 126)

Three birds orchid (p. 126)

Whorled pogonia (p. 127)

Crippled crane-fly (p. 130)

Spring coral-root (p. 131)

Southern magnolia (p. 144)

May-apple (p. 144)

Bloodroot (p. 145)

Spring-cress (p. 147)

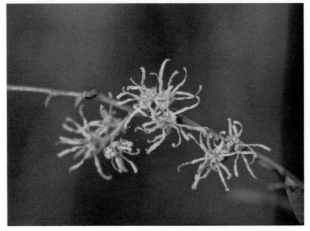

Virginia witch-hazel (p. 152)

American-ipecac (p. 152)

Redbud (p. 159)

Wood vetch (p. 174)

Violet wood-sorrel (p. 179)

Strawberry-bush (p. 188)

Silky camellia (p. 196)

Walter's violet (p. 200)

Trilobe violet (p. 202)

Woolly blue violet (p. 202)

Carolina violet (p. 203)

Hoary azalea (p. 219)

Indian-pipe (p. 220)

Silver-bell (p. 221)

Fringe-tree (p. 222)

Wood-betony (p. 267)

Beech-drops (p. 269)

Partridge-berry (p. 277)

Elephant's-foot (p. 285)

Oak-Farkleberry Sandylands (OFS)

Shaggy portulaca (p. 136)

Drummond's whitlow-wort (p. 137)

Small-flowered dayflower (p. 109)

Louisiana yucca (p. 115)

Snake-cotton (p. 135)

Catchfly (p. 137)

Leather flower (p. 143)

Blue larkspur (p. 140)

Twist-flower (p. 147)

Clammy-weed (p. 149)

Little-leaf sensitive brier (p. 158)

Viperina (p. 171)

Oklahoma prairie clover
(p. 165)

Devil's shoestring (p. 166)

Coral bean (p. 176)

MaCree's milkpea (p. 176)

Broad-leaf snoutbean (p. 177)

Yellow wood-sorrel (p. 180)

Bitter milkwort (p. 182)

Queen's delight (p. 183)

Bull nettle (p. 184)

Flowering spurge (p. 185)

Heart-leaf euphorbia (p. 186)

Showy sida (p. 195)

Carolina rockrose (p. 199)

Eastern prickly pear (p. 205)

Common evening primrose (p. 210)

Rattlesnake-weed (p. 214)

Blunt-leaf milkweed (p. 231)

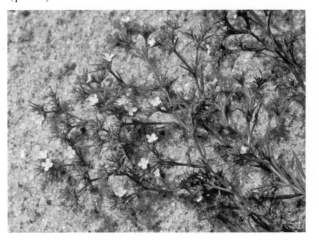

Juniper-leaf (p. 225)

Butterfly-weed (p. 232)

Bracted stylisma (p. 237)

Standing cypress (p. 240)

Trailing phlox (p. 241)

Carolina vervain (p. 247)

Wild bergamot (p. 257)

Spotted beebalm (p. 257)

Carolina horse-nettle
(p. 259)

Cup-leaf penstemon
(p. 262)

Texas toad-flax (p. 263)

Common devil's claw
(p. 269)

Tropical Mexican-clover (p. 277)

Venus' looking-glass
(p. 281)

Pink-scale gay-feather
(p. 287)

Scratch-daisy (p. 290)

Golden-aster (p. 290)

Arkansas lazy daisy
(p. 299)

Fragrant cudweed (p. 300)

Green-eyes (p. 302)

Weak-stem sunflower
(p. 309)

Plains coreopsis (p. 311)

Winkler gaillardia (p. 314)

Reverchon palafoxia
(p. 317)

Hooker palafoxia (p. 317)

Green-thread (p. 312)

Bristle-leaf dyssodia (p. 316)

Roadsides (R)

False garlic (p. 113)

Spring beauty (p. 136)

Forked catchfly (p. 137)

Carolina anemone (p. 142)

Southern corydalis (p. 146)

Charlock (p. 148)

Peppergrass (p. 148)

Southern dewberry (p. 155)

Bristly sensitive brier (p. 157)

Coffee senna (p. 160)

Bluebonnet (p. 162)

Low hop clover (p. 163)

White clover (p. 163)

Bristly locust (p. 169)

Bent-pod milk-vetch (p. 170)

Slender bush clover
(p. 173)

Sericea (p. 173)

Japanese bush clover
(p. 174)

Carolina geranium (p. 179)

Wild poinsettia (p. 185)

Carolina modiola (p. 194)

Broom-wood (p. 196)

Showy primrose (p. 210)

Cut-leaved evening primrose (p. 210)

Wild carrot (p. 214)

Scarlet pimpernel (p. 221)

Hairy cluster-vine (p. 237)

Cypress vine (p. 238)

Wild potato (p. 238)

Tuber vervain (p. 245)

Dakota vervain (p. 247)

Texas frog-fruit (p. 248)

West Indian lantana (p. 248)

Self-heal (p. 251)

Intermediate false
dragon-head (p. 252)

Henbit (p. 254)

Lyre-leaf sage (p. 255)

Silver-leaf nightshade
(p. 259)

Yellow-flowered
mecardonia (p. 261)

Sticky parentucellia
(p. 266)

Texas paintbrush (p. 267)

Trumpet honeysuckle (p. 280)

Corn salad (p. 280)

Eared lobelia (p. 282)

Thin-leaf goldenrod
(p. 293)

Philadelphia fleabane
(p. 298)

False ragweed (p. 303)

Ox-eye (p. 303)

Late brown-eyed Susan (p. 304)

Lance-leaved coreopsis
(p. 310)

Indian blanket (p. 314)

Bitterweed (p. 315)

Common yarrow (p. 318)

Bull thistle (p. 320)

Soft thistle (p. 320)

Potato-dandelion (p. 321)

Dwarf dandelion (p. 322)

Carolina false dandelion (p. 322)

Sow thistle (p. 323)   Red-seeded dandelion (p. 324)

Plant Descriptions

ALISMATACEAE
(Water Plantain Family)

Burhead [p. 44]
Echinodorus cordifolius (L.) Griseb.
(Eh-kih-noh′-doh-rus kor-dih-foh′-lee-us)

Erect to sprawling, coarse annual or short-lived perennial to 4 ft. tall, often lower, from thickened roots, growing in either mud or shallow water.

LEAVES: basal, erect, long-petioled; petiole to 8 in. long; blade broadly lanceolate, to 8 in. long and as wide, deeply notched at base, rounded at tip.

INFLORESCENCE: flowers numerous, short-pedicelled, in remote whorls at nodes around long slender scape; scape arching or lying on ground; leaves occasionally appearing with flowers. *Flower*: white, perfect; sepals 3, persistent, with ridges which bear minute round projections; petals 3, to ½ in. long, falling early.

FRUIT: achene, ribbed, beaked; achenes numerous, in rounded compact burlike head.
SOF (POF)   April–June

Grassy arrowhead [p. 59]
Sagittaria graminea Michx.
(Saj-it-tair′-ee-ah gra-min′-ee-ah)

Erect, slender, mostly aquatic perennial to 24 in. tall, often lower, from stolons, usually forming colonies; plants containing milky juice.

LEAVES: basal, erect, often surpassing flowering scape, to 8 in. long, 1 in. wide; leaves may occur either below or above water and vary from only thin broadly linear bladeless petioles to slender petioles with tapering narrowly lanceolate blades.

INFLORESCENCE: flowers few to numerous, pedicelled, in whorls of 3 at nodes in terminal portion of erect scape; whorls 2–12, subtended by bracts, usually showy; lower flowers usually pistillate with erect or recurved pedicels; upper flowers staminate with threadlike erect pedicels. *Flower*: white; sepals 3, persistent; petals 3, approximately ¼ in. long, falling early; stamens numerous in staminate flowers.

FRUIT: achene, small, flattened, thinly winged; achenes numerous, spirally arranged in crowded globelike head.
LBS (SOF)   March–December

Delta arrowhead   [p. 44]
Sagittaria platyphylla Engelm.
(Saj-it-tair'-ee-ah plat-ih-fil'-lah)

Erect perennial 2–3 ft. tall from small tubers formed at tips of rhizomes, usually forming colonies in mud or shallow water; plants containing milky juice.

LEAVES: basal, erect, long-petioled, usually taller than bloom scape; base of petiole sheathing stem; blade unlobed at base, prominently veined, elliptic to broadly lanceolate, to 7½ in. long, 3½ in. wide, frequently smaller.

INFLORESCENCE: flowers few to numerous, small, pedicelled, in whorls of 3 at nodes in terminal portion of weak leafless scape; whorls 3–7, subtended by soft pliable bracts; lower whorls of pistillate flowers with thick, soon recurving pedicels; upper whorls of staminate flowers with erect or spreading pedicels. *Flower*: white; sepals 3, persistent; petals 3, longer than sepals, falling early.

FRUIT: achene, small, flattened; achenes numerous, in crowded head; heads to ⅔ in. across.
SOF (POF)   April–October

Wapato (duck-potato)   [p. 44]
Sagittaria latifolia Willd.
(Saj-it-tair'-ee-ah lat-ih-foh'-lee-ah)

Erect to spreading, rather coarse aquatic perennial to 4 ft. tall, usually lower, from tuber-bearing rhizome; plants containing milky juice.

LEAVES: basal, erect, conspicuously large, long-petioled, growing either above or below water; petiole to 40 in. long; blade rounded or sharp-pointed at tip, sharply lobed at base; portion above lobes to 10 in. long and 10 in. wide, basal lobes one-half as long to longer than upper portion.

INFLORESCENCE: flowers few to numerous, pedicelled, in whorls of 3; whorls 2–10, subtended by bracts, at nodes in terminal portion of scape; scape slender, angled, occasionally branching from lower whorls; lower flowers usually all pistillate with pedicels shorter than the pedicels of upper staminate flowers. *Flower*: white; sepals 3, reflexed, persistent; petals 3, soon falling.

FRUIT: achene, flattened, with broad marginal wings, beaked at tip; achenes numerous, spirally arranged in crowded globelike head.
SOF (POF)   May–August

HYDROCHARITACEAE
(Frog's-bit Family)

Water-weed [p. 55]
Egeria densa Planch.
(Ee-jer'-ee-ah den'-sah)

Submerged aquatic perennial; stem slender, to 1/16 in. thick, rooted in mud, growing to top of water, sometimes sparingly branched in upper portion.

LEAVES: opposite or whorled, sessile, somewhat transparent; lower leaves opposite or in whorls of 3; middle and upper leaves thickly crowded, in whorls of 4–8, linear, approximately 1½ in. long, less than ¼ in. wide, rounded or sharp-pointed at tip, finely and inconspicuously toothed.

INFLORESCENCE: pistillate and staminate flowers on separate plants; staminate flowers 2–4, raised to surface of water on long, threadlike floral tubes from axillary spathe; spathes sessile, borne in axils of upper leaves; pistillate plants not seen. *Flower*: white; sepals 3, less than ¼ in. long; petals 3, thin, pliable, approximately ½ in. long and wide; stamens 9.

FRUIT: no fruit seen.

NOTE: native of South America, escaping cultivation; commonly used in aquariums.

BGB   April–June

CYPERACEAE
(Sedge Family)

White-topped umbrella grass [p. 59]
Dichromena latifolia Ell.
(Dye-kroh'-meh-nah lat-ih-foh'-lee-ah)

Stiffly erect, tufted perennial 16–32 in. tall, from slender rhizomes.

LEAVES: basal, crowded, erect, shorter than flowering culm, glabrous, linear, about ¼ in. wide at base; margins rolled toward upper surface near tip.

INFLORESCENCE: flowers few to numerous, minute, inconspicuous, in very small spikelets arranged in globelike head; heads terminal on stiffly erect culm, subtended by bracts; bracts 6–10, unequal, basally erect then spreading or reflexed, white in basal half, green in tip half, linear to narrowly lanceolate, to 6 in. long, ¼ in. wide in basal portion; head and bracts showy in the aggregate. *Flower*: whitish; sepals and petals absent; stamens 3, style 2-cleft.

FRUIT: achene, very small, wrinkled, crowned with persistent base of style; achenes numerous, in globelike head.

NOTE: uncommon in the Big Thicket.

LBS   (MGP)   April–August

PALMAE
(Palm Family)

Dwarf palmetto   [p. 41]

Sabal minor (Jacq.) Pers.

(Say'-bal mye'-nor)

Somewhat clumped, shrublike, coarse, glabrous perennial; base usually not rising above surface of ground.

LEAVES: from base, petioled, persistent; petiole long, extending on undersurface of blade as midrib; blade fan-shaped, stiff, bluish, not glaucous, spreading to 60 in. wide, divided to two-thirds its length into few to numerous segments.

INFLORESCENCE: flowers in small clusters along short branches, the branches crowded along a slender scapelike structure and the whole forming a terminal panicle; "scape" elongate, leafless, often arching, to 6 ft. long, arising from base of plant. *Flower*: whitish, very small, perfect; calyx 3-parted; petals 3; stamens 6; pistils 3, united into 1; stigma usually not divided.

FRUIT: drupe, black, outer portion somewhat fleshy when young, dry and hard at maturity, globelike to larger in tip portion, less than 1/2 in. across; seed often only 1 per drupe, white, shiny, commonly flattened, very hard.

POF (SOF)   May–July

ARACEAE
(Arum Family)

Green dragon   [p. 77]

Arisaema dracontium (L.) Schott

(Air-ih-see'-mah dra-kon'-chee-um)

Erect, succulent perennial to 3 ft. tall from rounded corm; corm containing acrid juice.

LEAVES: from corm, solitary, petioled, compound; petiole to 20 in. long, sheathing flowering scape at base; blade divided into 5–15 unequal leaflets; leaflets sometimes connected together in basal portions, the central leaflet to 8 in. long, the outer leaflets successively smaller.

INFLORESCENCE: flowers numerous, minute, crowded on spadix; enclosed by spathe; spadix and spathe terminal on flower scape; spadix conspicuous, to 6 in. or more long, exserted, often bent, with long tapering tip, enclosed basally by short, inrolled, leaflike spathe; spathe thin, pale green, about 2 1/2 in. long; spadix with pistillate flowers at base, staminate flowers in middle portion, no flowers in tip portion. *Flower*: whitish; no sepals or petals present.

FRUIT: berry, scarlet, glistening, globelike, less than 1/2 in. across; berries

numerous, tightly clustered in showy globelike or elongated head; seeds 1–3 per berry.
BMLS   (SOF)   May–June

Jack-in-the-pulpit (Indian-turnip)   [p. 77]
Arisaema triphyllum (L.) Schott
(Air-ih-see'-mah   try-fil'-lum)

Erect, succulent perennial to 2 ft. tall, occasionally taller, from corm; corm containing acrid juice.

LEAVES: from corm, usually 2, petioled, compound; petiole to 16 in. long, sheathing flowering scape at base; blade divided into 3 leaflets; leaflets sessile, green on both sides, with lengthwise veins, broadly lanceolate, 3–8 in. long, 1½–3½ in. wide; lateral leaflets sometimes lobed.

INFLORESCENCE: flowers numerous, minute, inconspicuous, crowded on spadix and surrounded and hidden by large leaflike spathe; spadix and spathe terminal on flower scape; spathe ¾–1¼ in. wide, striped with purple, curved or folded downward, abruptly sharp-pointed at tip, forming hood over spadix; spadix straight, with pistillate flowers at base, staminate flowers in middle portion, no flowers in tip portion. *Flower*: whitish; sepals and petals absent.

FRUIT: berry, scarlet, shining, globelike, to ¼ in. across; berries few to several, tightly clustered into showy globelike or somewhat elongated head.

NOTE: corms containing crystals of calcium oxalate.
BMLS   (SOF, BGB)   April–June

Five-leaved Jack-in-the-pulpit   [p. 78]
Arisaema quinatum (Nutt.) Schott
(Air-ih-see'-mah   kwih-nay'-tum)

Erect, slender, soft-stemmed perennial 12–20 in. tall from corm; corm containing acrid juice.

LEAVES: from corm, usually 1, sometimes 2, petioled, compound; petiole to 12 in. long; blade divided into 5 leaflets; leaflets glaucous on lower surface, elliptic to broadly lanceolate, to 6½ in. long, 4 in. wide, irregular at base; lower 2 leaflets conspicuously smaller.

INFLORESCENCE: flowers numerous, minute, inconspicuous, crowded on short spadix, enclosed and hidden by large hooded spathe; spadix and spathe terminal on flower scape; spathe green or yellowish green, not striped with purple, 1¼–2½ in. wide, sharp-pointed at tip, folded over spadix and forming hood; spadix curved, noticeably wider at base, tapering into tip; spadix with pistillate flowers at base, staminate flowers in middle portion, no flowers in tip portion. *Flower*: whitish; sepals and petals absent.

FRUIT: berry, scarlet, globelike, to ¼ in. across; berries few to several, tightly clustered in showy somewhat elongated head.

NOTE: uncommon in the Big Thicket.

BMLS   April–May

Arrow-arum (white-arum)   [p. 44]
Peltandra virginica (L.) Kunth
(Pel-tan′-drah   vir-jin′-ih-kah)

Erect, clumped, dark green perennial 14–20 in. tall from tuft of thick fibrous roots.

LEAVES: basal, petioled; petiole to 16 in. long; blade with 3 main veins from base and numerous side veins, glaucous on lower surface, oblong to broadly triangular, to 8 in. long, 6 in. wide, deeply lobed at base, the lobes to 3 in. across.

INFLORESCENCE: flowers numerous, minute, inconspicuous, crowded on spadix, enclosed by spathe; spadix and spathe terminal on scape; spathe green, tightly inrolled in basal portion, usually somewhat open in upper portion; margins of spathe leathery, wavy, white or creamy yellow; spadix slender, tapering, with pistillate flowers in basal portion, staminate flowers in upper portion, no sterile portion present or only at tip; scape erect during flowering, curving downward and usually beneath water during fruiting. *Flower*: whitish; sepals and petals absent.

FRUIT: berry, dark green; berries several, in ovoid fleshy head.

NOTE: uncommon in East Texas and western Louisiana.

SOF   (BGB)   April–May

MAYACACEAE
(Bogmoss Family)

Bogmoss   [p. 55]
Mayaca aubletii Michx.
(Mah-yah′-kah   oh-blet′-ee-eye)

Small, mosslike perennial spreading or creeping in wet soil or forming mats and floating in shallow water; stems to 8 in. long, usually shorter, branched.

LEAVES: alternate, sessile, numerous, crowded on stem; blade 1-veined, narrowly lanceolate, less than ¼ in. long, notched at tip.

INFLORESCENCE: flowers solitary, small, on slender pedicels from leaf axils; pedicels longer than leaves. *Flower*: maroon to pink, sometimes whitish; sepals 3, persistent; petals 3, spreading, wider in tip portion, less than ¼ in. long; stamens 3, opposite sepals.

FRUIT: capsule, globelike, about 3/16 in. across.

NOTE: unccmmon to rare in East Texas and western Louisiana.

BGB   May–July

XYRIDACEAE
(Yellow-eyed Grass Family)

Yellow-eyed grass   [p. 59]
Xyris ambigua Kunth
(Zye′-ris   am-big′-yoo-ah)

Slender, grasslike perennial; plants solitary or several in tuft, from hard deep fibrous base.

LEAVES: basal, smooth or slightly roughened, spreading, broadly linear, 4–16 in. long, to 3/4 in. wide, narrowing gradually and becoming inrolled toward upper surface at tip, brownish or reddish at base, dark shiny green in upper two-thirds; margins rough to the touch; new leaves usually mixed with stubble of dead leaf bases.

INFLORESCENCE: flowers numerous, 1–3 opening together, from axils of close-packed scales, in terminal spike; spike short, cylindrical, on slender scape; scape leafless, 28–40 in. tall, twisted, many-grooved in lower portion, becoming flat and 2-edged in upper portion. *Flower*: yellow; petals 3, approximately 1/4 in. long, opening in morning, lasting only a few hours.

FRUIT: capsule; seeds minute, shiny.

NOTE: Several similar species of *Xyris* occur in the Big Thicket.

LBS   (BGB)   May–July

ERIOCAULACEAE
(Pipewort Family)

Ten-angle pipewort   [p. 59]
Eriocaulon decangulare L.
(Eh-ree-oh-kaw′-lon   dek-ang-yoo-lair′-ee)

Erect, tufted, grasslike perennial from fibrous roots.

LEAVES: basal, forming rosette, sessile and clasping at base, mostly rigid, 10-ribbed, linear, to 14 in. long, less than 1/2 in. wide near middle; margins often rolled toward lower surface.

INFLORESCENCE: flowers pistillate and staminate, numerous, minute, inconspicuous, intermixed with minute bracts and clustered in small terminal peduncled head; bracts longer than flowers; head round, tough, hard, approximately 1/2 in. across, remaining on peduncle after drying; peduncles 1–2 ft. tall, slender, many-ribbed, rigid, leafless, 1–3 per plant. *Flower*: whitish;

staminate flowers usually with 2 sepals and 2 or 3 petals, the petals forming tube which is lobed at rim; pistillate flowers usually with 2 sepals and 2 petals.

FRUIT: capsule, thin-walled; seeds 2 or 3 smooth, minute.

LBS   (BGB)   May–October

BROMELIACEAE
(Pineapple Family)

Spanish moss   [p. 44]
Tillandsia usneoides (L.) L.
(Til-land'-zee-ah   us-nee-oh'-ih-deez)

Epiphyte, hanging from high supports and forming slender branching strands to several feet long; stem curled and wiry; entire plant essentially gray-colored or slightly greenish.

LEAVES: rosettelike, clustered, or scattered along stem, threadlike, 1–3 in. long, covered with small silvery scales.

INFLORESCENCE: flowers solitary, sessile, inconspicuous, from leaf axils. *Fower*: green, fragrant; sepals 3, green, about 1/4 in. long; petals, 3, green, about 1/2 in. long; stamens 6.

FRUIT: capsule, slender, cylindrical, to 1 1/4 in. long; seeds numerous, erect, with feathery appendages at base.

NOTE: fruit shown; plants harmless to trees unless becoming so thick they smother the tree.

SOF   (POF, BGB, BMLS, OFS)   February–June

COMMELINACEAE
(Spiderwort Family)

Erect day-flower   [p. 67]
Commelina erecta L. var. *deamiana* Fern.
(Kom-meh-lye'-nah   ee-rek'-tah   dee-mee-ay'-nah)

Erect to sprawling, thin, succulent perennial 2–3 ft. tall, overwintering by tuberous roots, sprouting in spring from buds along roots; stem slender, branched, erect or arching at base when young, later becoming lax with tips erect.

LEAVES: alternate, forming sheath at base; sheath to 1 in. long, with white pubescence on margins and in throat; blade flat or somewhat channeled, parallel-veined, pubescent above and rough to the touch, glabrous below, linear to lanceolate, to 6 in. long, 1 in. wide, more than 5 times as long as wide, entire.

INFLORESCENCE: flowers 1–several, pedicelled, in terminal or axillary cyme; pedicels elongating and emerging from spathe with flowers opening one at a time; spathes glabrous or densely pubescent, to 1¼ in. long, usually about 1⅛ in. long, open and tapering to point in upper portion, closed in basal portion. *Flower*: blue, closing early in day; sepals 3, unequal in size; petals 3; upper 2 petals blue; lower petal whitish, much reduced and inconspicuous; stamens 3; filaments conspicuously bearded with fine hairs.

FRUIT: capsule, 1–3 per spathe; seeds 1–3 per capsule.

LBU   (MGP, SOF)   May–October

Small-flowered dayflower   [p. 83]

Commelina erecta L. var. *angustifolia* (Michx.) Fern.

(Kom-meh-lye′-nah   ee-rek′-tah   an-gus-tih-foh′-lee-ah)

Erect to sprawling, pubescent perennial 2–3 ft. tall, usually much lower, from tuberous roots.

LEAVES: alternate, forming sheath at base; sheath to 1 in. long, with white pubescence on margins and in throat; blade parallel-veined, pubescent on upper surface, glabrous on lower surface, linear to lanceolate, to 6 in. long, 1 in. wide, entire.

INFLORESCENCE: flowers 3–5, pedicelled, in terminal or axillary cyme; pedicels elongating and exserted beyond boat-shaped spathe with flowers opening one at a time; spathes glabrous or pubescent, ½–⅞ in. long, usually ⅝–¾ in. long, closed in basal portion. *Flower*: blue, lasting only until midday; sepals 3; petals 3, with 1 noticeably much reduced; stamens 3; filaments conspicuously bearded with fine hairs.

FRUIT: capsule, 1–3 per spathe; seeds 1–3 per capsule.

OFS   (POF, SOF)   May–October

Hairy-flowered spiderwort   [p. 67]

Tradescantia hirsutiflora Bush

(Tra-des-kan′-chee-ah   hir-soo-ti-floh′-rah)

Erect to nearly erect, succulent perennial to 20 in. tall from long and somewhat fleshy root; stem with short, coarse pubescence or occasionally glabrous; nodes along stem 2–5, to 8½ in. between nodes.

LEAVES: alternate, sessile, sheathing stem at base; blade dark green to glaucous, thin but firm in texture, glabrous to pubescent, linear, 5½–13 in. long, ¾ in. wide, entire.

INFLORESCENCE: flowers few to many, pedicelled, in terminal usually solitary flat-topped cymes; cyme subtended by 2 leaflike bracts. *Flower*: blue, lavender, or rarely pink, lasting a day or less; sepals 3, pubescent, dull green, frequently tinged or edged with rose; petals 3, separate, all alike, to ¾ in. long; stamens 6; filaments with numerous hairs.

FRUIT: capsule, obovoid, about ¼ in. long, splitting into 3 parts; seeds 6–12, very small.

LBU   (MGP, SOF, OFS)   March–June

Ohio spiderwort   [p. 44]
Tradescantia ohioensis Raf.

(Tra-des-kan'-chee-ah   oh-hye-oh-en'-sis)

Erect or nearly erect, clumped, glabrous perennial, conspicuously glaucous almost throughout, 2½–3 ft. tall, often lower, from slender root; stem with 3–8 nodes spaced to 7 in. apart, containing gluey sap.

LEAVES: alternate, sessile; blade firm, linear, to 18 in. long, 1¾ in. wide, folded and clasping at base, long-pointed in tip portion, entire.

INFLORESCENCE: flowers few to many, pedicelled, showy, in axillary or terminal cymes; cyme subtended by 2 leaflike bracts; bracts short, usually sharply reflexed. *Flower*: deep blue, lavender, or pinkish, rarely white; sepals 3, glabrous or with tuft of hair at tip; petals 3, about ¾ in. long, falling early; stamens 6; filaments covered with conspicuous hair.

FRUIT: capsule, longer than wide, to ¼ in. long; seeds 6–12, very small.

SOF   February–May

PONTEDERIACEAE
(Pickerel-weed Family)

Water-hyacinth   [p. 45]
Eichhornia crassipes (Mart.) Solms

(Ike-horn'-ee-ah   kras'-sih-peez)

Low, aquatic perennial, free-floating or occasionally rooted in mud; floating roots long, feathery; plants reproducing primarily from stolons.

LEAVES: alternate, mostly in basal rosette, petioled; petiole spongy, conspicuously inflated at base, to 10 in. long; blade leathery, almost round, 1¼–4¼ in. long, usually broader than long; submerged leaves, if present, long and narrow.

INFLORESCENCE: flowers many, sessile, in large showy peduncled spike exserted from spathe; spike 6–16 in. long; spathe subtended by sheath; sheath with small, leaflike blade at tip. *Flower*: light blue to bluish purple, 1½–2½ in. long and broad, lasting a day or less; tepals united below into tube, deeply 6-lobed at rim; lobes petallike; upper 3 lobes prominently streaked with purple, the middle lobe with conspicuous yellow spot; lower 3 lobes with lighter purple markings.

FRUIT: capsule, ellipsoid, less than ½ in. long; seeds many, ribbed.

NOTE: beautiful, but plants sometimes clogging waterways; native of Brazil.

SOF   April–July

Pickerel-weed   [p. 45]
Pontederia cordata L.
(Pon-teh-der'-ee-ah   kor-day'-tah)

Erect, stout perennial to 36 in. tall, usually growing in water, from short thick creeping rhizomes rooting in mud.

LEAVES: alternate, mostly basal, erect, glabrous, long-petioled; blade to 8 in. long, lanceolate to broadly lanceolate, deeply notched or abruptly squared off at base; solitary leaf occurring on flower scape.

INFLORESCENCE: flowers several, sessile, in showy peduncled spike; spike erect, pubescent, to 6 in. long, from a sheathing spathe. *Flower*: violet blue, lasting 1 day or less; tepals 6, united below into tube, 6-lobed at rim; lobes petallike; stamens 6, the lower 3 exserted; anthers blue.

FRUIT: achenelike, somewhat ellipsoid, about ¼ in. long; seed 1, red, gluey.
SOF   (POF)   June–September

LILIACEAE
(Lily Family)

Sticky tofieldia (false asphodel)   [p. 59]
Tofieldia racemosa (Walt.) Small
(Toh-feel'-dee-ah   ray-see-moh'-sah)

Erect, tufted, slender perennial to 2 ft. tall from short or creeping rhizomes.

LEAVES: alternate, mostly basal, erect, grasslike, all about equal in length; blade linear, to 16 in. long, less than ¼ in. wide; 1 small, bractlike leaf occuring along flower scape.

INFLORESCENCE: flowers numerous, small, pedicelled, 2 or 3 at each node of a terminal raceme; raceme to 6 in. long; flowers opening from tip of raceme downward; flower scape 1–2 ft. tall, minutely pubescent, especially in flowering portion; each flower subtended by very small 3-lobed bract. *Flower*: creamy white; tepals 6, in 2 circles of 3, petallike, separate, spreading, less than ¼ in. long; stamens 6, exserted; styles 3.

FRUIT: capsule, firm, narrow, obovoid, subtended by persistent tepals, tipped by enlarged styles; seeds reddish brown, minute.
LBS   June–July

Featherbells   [p. 77]
Stenanthium gramineum (Ker.) Morong
(Sten-an'-thee-um   gra-min'-ee-um)

Erect, slender, glabrous perennial 1–5 ft. tall from bulbous base; fibrous remains of old leaves persistent.

LEAVES: alternate, numerous, mostly crowded toward base, usually erect, grasslike; blade linear, keeled, to 8 in. long, 1¼ in. wide; leaves in upper portion of stem much reduced.

INFLORESCENCE: flowers numerous, in showy elongated wandlike terminal panicle of racemes; panicle to 32 in. long, the lower portion much-branched and usually bearing staminate flowers; branches occasionally slanting downward; terminal portion unbranched and bearing perfect flowers. *Flower*: white, greenish, or purplish; tepals 6, petallike, narrow, less than ½ in. long; stamens 6.

FRUIT: capsule, small, erect or drooping, shortly cylindrical, 3-beaked at tip; seeds purple brown, not winged.

BMLS   (BGB)   June–August

Yellow sunny-bell   [p. 59]

Schoenolirion croceum (Michx.) Wood

(Skee-noh-lir′-ee-on   kroh′-see-um)

Erect, slender, glabrous perennial to 18 in. tall, frequently lower, from bulbous base and fibrous roots.

LEAVES: alternate, basal, tufted, grasslike, rather rigid; blade prominently ribbed, flat, elongated, linear, 1–16 in. long, to 3/16 in. wide.

INFLORESCENCE: flowers numerous, pedicelled, subtended by bracts, in showy raceme; raceme unbranched, to 6 in. long, 1½ in. across; flowers opening from base of raceme upward. *Flower*: yellow, often tinged with red; tepals 6, petallike, distinctively 3- to 5-veined, about ¼ in. long, exceeding stamens.

FRUIT: capsule, deeply 3-lobed, persisting on pedicels after maturity; seeds black, shiny, flattened on one side, with 1 or 2 in each section.

LBS   March–May

Bunchflower   [p. 55]

Melanthium virginicum L.

(Meh-lan′-the-um   vir-jin′-ih-kum)

Erect perennial 2–5 ft. tall from thick rhizome; stem covered with very small scales, pubescent throughout or glabrous in lower portion.

LEAVES: alternate, mostly basal; blade firm, flat, broadly linear, 8–36 in. long, to 1¼ in. wide; leaves becoming gradually reduced toward upper portion of plant.

INFLORESCENCE: flowers numerous, pedicelled, subtended by bracts, in slender branched racemes forming a large loose showy terminal panicle; lower flowers perfect; upper flowers staminate. *Flower*: creamy, becoming green or purple in aging; tepals 6, petallike, flat, narrowly clawed, with 2 dark-colored conspicuous glands at base; claw slender, one-half or less length of blade; stamens 6, on claw.

FRUIT: capsule, erect, 3-lobed, 3-beaked at tip, with tepals persistent; seeds whitish or yellowish, flat, broadly winged, about 10 in each section.

NOTE: uncommon in East Texas and western Louisiana.

BGB   May–July

Wild onion   [p. 33]
Allium canadense L. var. *mobilense* (Regel) M. Ownbey
(Al'-lee-um   kan-ah-den'-see   moh-bih-len'-see)

Erect, clumped, slender, glabrous perennial 8–24 in. tall from small rounded bulb; bulb with fine grayish or brownish meshlike outer covering.

LEAVES: from bulb, 2 or more, shorter than bloom scape, sheathing at base; blade soft, shiny, flat, with central lengthwise groove, narrowly linear, less than 1/8 in. wide, entire.

INFLORESCENCE: flowers many, pedicelled, in large solitary erect showy umbels at ends of slender scapes; pedicels of unequal lengths, threadlike, becoming elongated and rigid when in fruit; umbel subtended by spathe; spathe brownish, leaflike, persistent, splitting into 3 separate or partially united bracts before time of flowering; no small bulblets present. *Flower*: pale to dark pink, cupped; tepals 6, petallike, thin, broadly lanceolate, about 1/4 in. long.

FRUIT: capsule, small, 3-lobed; seeds black, shiny.

NOTE: plant with odor and taste of onion; edible.

MGP   (POF, SOF, LBU)   April–May

False garlic   [p. 90]
Nothoscordum bivalve (L.) Britt.
(Noh-tho-skor'-dum   bye-val'-veh)

Erect, glabrous perennial 6–22 in. tall from small membrane-coated bulb.

LEAVES: basal, several, sheathing at base; blade soft, flat or with lengthwise central groove on upper surface, narrowly linear, 4–16 in. long, less than 1/8 in. wide, no longer than flower scape.

INFLORESCENCE: flowers 6–12, small, long-pedicelled, in erect terminal umbel on leafless scape; umbel surrounded by 2 thin, papery bracts. *Flower*: whitish to creamy with narrow but prominent stripes of green, red, or purple on outer surface; tepals 6, petallike, narrowly oblong, about 1/2 in. long, persisting after withering.

FRUIT: capsule, obovoid, somewhat 3-angled, less than 1/4 in. long; seeds black, pebbled, angled or flattened.

NOTE: resembles the wild onion but without onion odor or taste.

R   (MGP, POF, SOF, LBU, OFS)   Throughout year

Carolina-lily   [p. 78]

Lilium michauxii Poir.

(Lil'-ee-um   mee-shoh'-zee-eye)

Erect, unbranched, glabrous perennial 1–4 ft. tall from scaly rhizomelike bulb.

LEAVES: usually in whorls of 3–7, occasionally some opposite or alternate, sessile; blade rather fleshy or leathery, glaucous when young, linear to lanceolate, to 4¾ in. long, 1 in. wide.

INFLORESCENCE: flowers 1–3 per plant, large, showy, peduncled, in terminal portion of stem; buds erect; flowers nodding when fully open. *Flower*: orange red, becoming yellow in throat, purple-spotted on inner surface; tepals 6, petallike, sharply recurved from about the middle, to 4 in. long, ½ in. wide; stamens 6, conspicuous.

FRUIT: capsule, erect, somewhat cylindrical to ovoid, to 2 in. long, 1 in. across, opening into 3 sections; seeds numerous, flat, densely packed in 2 rows in each section of capsule.

NOTE: only native lily known from the Big Thicket.

BMLS   (LBU)   July–August

Yellow dog's-tooth-violet (trout lily)   [p. 78]

Erythronium rostratum Wolf

(Eh-rith-roh'-nee-um   rost-ray'-tum)

Erect, glabrous perennial 4–8 in. tall from bulb; bulb deep, small, scaly, with long slender underground shoots; new plants produced at tips of shoots, forming colonies.

LEAVES: from corm, 2 in flowering plants, 1 in immature plants, petioled; petiole sheathing stem below ground; blade flat, smooth, shiny, usually conspicuously mottled with purplish brown, borne near middle of stem and appearing as a basal leaf.

INFLORESCENCE: flower solitary, lilylike, showy, nodding, terminal on slender scape. *Flower*: yellow; tepals 6, petallike, wide-spreading or sharply recurved, mostly ¾–1½ in. long; outer 3 segments sometimes with purplish brown spots on inner surface near base; stamens 6; anthers yellow.

FRUIT: capsule, obovoid to ellipsoid, beaked at tip, erect at maturity, opening into 3 sections; seeds numerous.

NOTE: rare in the Big Thicket, more common eastward.

BMLS   (SOF)   February–April

Louisiana yucca   [p. 83]
Yucca louisianensis Trel.
(Yuk'-kah   loo-iz-ee-an-in'-sis)

Erect perennial 6–8 ft. tall from short underground stem.

LEAVES: mostly from base, many, forming clump; blade linear, stiff but not rigid, straight or somewhat recurved, to 2 ft. long, commonly 3/4–1 1/2 in. wide, sharp-pointed at tip; margins white-bordered and with few hairlike fibers; leaves along scape few, much reduced, scalelike.

INFLORESCENCE: flowers numerous, in large showy panicle; panicle 2–3 ft. long, usually pubescent, terminal on long slender scape. *Flower*: creamy white, perfect; tepals 6, thick, waxy, 1–1 1/4 in. long; inner 3 tepals broader than outer 3; stamens 6, shorter than inner tepals; style often dark green; stigmas 3.

FRUIT: capsule, erect, dry, stout, short, angular before maturity, opening into 3 segments; seeds numerous in each segment, flattened, about 3/8 in. wide, blackish.

NOTE: Development of the fruit of the yuccas depends on pollination by the yucca moth, *Pronuba yuccasella*.

OFS   April–June

Great Solomon's seal   [p. 78]
Polygonatum biflorum (Walt.) Ell.
(Pol-ih-gon-ay'-tum   bye-floh'-rum)

Erect or usually arching, slender to stout, glabrous perennial to 3 ft. tall from thick white knotty rhizome; old stem scars on rhizome conspicuous.

LEAVES: alternate, sessile, often clasping basally; blade prominently several-veined, somewhat glaucous on lower surface, broadly elliptic to broadly lanceolate, to 6 in. long, 2 3/4 in. wide, rounded at tip.

INFLORESCENCE: flowers 1–few, short-pedicelled, in peduncled umbel; peduncles threadlike, drooping, in leaf axils along middle portion of stem. *Flower*: greenish white; tepals 6, united basally into long cylindrical tube; tube to 2/3 in. long, 6-lobed; lobes much shorter than tube, not spreading.

FRUIT: berry, dark blue or black, globelike, pulpy; seeds several, yellowish tan to olive, about 1/8 in. long.

BMLS   (SOF)   March–April

Texas trillium   [p. 55]
Trillium texanum Buckl.
(Tril'-lee-um   tex-ay'-num)

Erect, slender, delicate perennial 4–12 in. tall from creeping tuberlike rhizome.

LEAVES: absent; bracts 3, in whorl at top of flower scape, sessile, leaf-like, somewhat mealy or granular to the touch on upper surface, narrowly lanceolate to broadly lanceolate, most commonly 1½–2½ in. long, ½–¾ in. wide, rounded at tip.

INFLORESCENCE: flower solitary, pedicelled, subtended by bracts, terminal on slender scape; pedicel slender, erect. *Flower*: white, becoming pink or reddish with age; sepals 3, green, separate, spreading, lanceolate, usually larger than petals; petals 3, spreading, lanceolate, commonly ¾–1 in. long, to ⅜ in. wide.

FRUIT: berry, 3-sided, larger near base, nonopening; seeds 8–15.

NOTE: rare in the Big Thicket.

BGB   March–May

Wake-robin   [p. 78]
Trillium gracile J. D. Freeman
(Tril'-lee-um   gras'-ih-lee)

Erect, glabrous perennial 8–12 in. tall from creeping tuberlike rhizome.

LEAVES: absent; bracts 3, in whorl at top of flower scape, sessile, leaflike, dark green, usually distinctively mottled with darker green, elliptic to lanceolate, commonly 2¾–4 in. long, 1¼–2½ in wide, broadly triangular at base, rounded or sharp-pointed at tip.

INFLORESCENCE: flower solitary, sessile, small, subtended by bracts, terminal on slender scape. *Flower*: dark purple, rarely yellowish; sepals 3, usually dark purple on upper surface, widely spreading, sometimes reflexed near tip; petals 3, erect, commonly ¾–1½ in. long, about ¼ in. wide; stamens 6, about half as long as petals.

FRUIT: berry, ovoid, smooth; seeds usually many.

BMLS   (SOF)   April–May

Colic-root   [p. 60]
Aletris aurea Walt.
(Al-ee'-tris   aw'-ree-ah)

Erect, glabrous perennial 1–3 ft. tall from short thickened rhizome; plants containing very bitter juice.

LEAVES: mostly basal, forming rosettes; blade yellow green, flat, thin, soft, pliable, lanceolate, to 4¾ in. long; stem leaves much reduced.

INFLORESCENCE: flowers several, small, in slender spikelike raceme; raceme terminal on slender scape. *Flower*: orange yellow, about ¼ in. long; tepals 6, united basally into tube; tube short, broad, 6-lobed at tip with the lobes incurved; outer surface of tube wrinkled and roughened with small projections and mealy to the touch.

FRUIT: capsule, small, ovoid, long-beaked, enclosed by the persistent withered tepals; seeds numerous, minute.

LBS   May–July

AMARYLLIDACEAE
(Amaryllis Family)

Spider-lily [p. 45]
Hymenocallis liriosme (Raf.) Shinners
(Hye-men-oh-kal'-lis   lir-ee-oz'-mee)

Erect, fleshy, glabrous perennial to 40 in. tall, growing in watery or very wet places, from bulb; bulb large, onionlike, with black outer covering, white inner covering.

LEAVES: from bulb, pale green, shiny, elongated, linear or straplike, to 30 in. long, commonly much shorter, to 1½ in. wide but often less than 1 in. wide.

INFLORESCENCE: flowers 4–6, sessile, in showy umbel at top of scape; scapes from bulb, 1–2 ft. tall, spongy, sharply 2-edged, the sides rounded; umbel subtended by bracts; bracts 2, dry, thin, papery. *Flower:* snowy white tinged with yellow in center, very fragrant; tepals 6, petallike, linear to narrowly lanceolate, spreading; stamens 6; filaments connected in basal portion by thin, membranous tissue to form large spreading cup, then extending from rim of cup as slender elongated segments; anthers conspicuous.

FRUIT: capsule, opening into 3 sections; seeds few.

SOF   (POF)   March–May

Yellow star-grass [p. 67]
Hypoxis hirsuta (L.) Cov.
(Hye-pok'-sis   hir-soo'-tah)

Low, pubescent perennial from small cormlike rhizome; rhizome covered with brownish sheaths which do not become fibrous.

LEAVES: basal, rather firm, grasslike, narrowly linear, 5- to 9-veined, 4–14 in. long, to ¼ in. wide.

INFLORESCENCE: flowers 2–7, pedicelled, in loose cluster at top of peduncle; cluster subtended by 2–several linear bracts; peduncles threadlike, stiff, leafless, 1½–14 in. tall, shorter than leaves. *Flower:* yellow; tepals 6, petallike, ¼–⅝ in. long, greenish and pubescent on outer surface.

FRUIT: capsule, to ¼ in. long, densely pubescent; seeds black, shiny, minute, closely covered with rough sharp projections.

LBU   (MGP, POF, BMLS)   March–May

Evening-star rain-lily   [p. 33]
Cooperia drummondii Herb.
(Koo-per'-ee-ah   drum-mun'-dee-eye)

Erect to spreading, variable perennial to about 12 in. tall from bulb; bulb globelike, to 1¼ in. across, long-necked, with black outer covering.

LEAVES: from bulb, erect or somewhat lax, smooth, slender, grasslike, gray green, usually glaucous, elongating after flowering, to 12 in. long.

INFLORESCENCE: flower solitary, subtended by spathe, at top of long erect hollow scape; spathe rather dry, greenish, often fading to red, slit or looped at tip, persistent. *Flower*: white, sometimes pink-tinted on outer surface, fragrant, opening in evening, lasting to 4 days before withering; tepals 6, united into trumpet shape; tube slender, 3¼–7¼ in. long; rim shallowly lobed, opening flat; anthers creamy yellow, erect.

FRUIT: capsule, globelike; seeds numerous, black, flat, shaped like a D.

NOTE: usually blooming after fall rains but occasionally appearing in spring or summer; plants easily grown from seed.
MGP   (POF)   May–September

Southern swamp lily   [p. 45]
Crinum americanum L.
(Kry'-num   a-mer-ih-kay'-num)

Erect, clumped, stout, succulent, aquatic perennial to 3 ft. tall from large stolon-producing bulb; bulb with large, short neck.

LEAVES: from bulb, often persistent, 2–4 ft. long, to 2 in. wide, thick and curved near base, thinner and flatter toward tip; margins sparingly small-toothed.

INFLORESCENCE: flowers 2–6, in showy umbel at top of scape; umbel subtended by spathe; spathe to 3½ in. long, split into 2 parts; scape from bulb, slender, fleshy, solid. *Flower*: white, sometimes marked with pink, fragrant; tepals 6, united into deeply lobed tube; tube slender, greenish, to 4¾ in. long; lobes petallike, slender, wide-spreading, recurved; stamens 6, red, spreading, conspicuous.

FRUIT: capsule, globelike, prominently beaked, less than 1¼ in. across; seeds large, green.

NOTE: uncommon in the Big Thicket.
SOF   (POF)   May–November

IRIDACEAE
(Iris Family)

Yellow blue-eyed grass   [p. 67]
Sisyrinchium exile Bickn.
(Sis-ih-rin'-kee-um   ek-zye'-lee)

Erect to nearly erect, delicate, glabrous annual 2–7½ in. tall from fibrous roots; stem slender, 2-winged.

LEAVES: basal, arranged in 2 vertical rows, grasslike, clasping basally, threadlike to narrowly linear, to about ⅛ in. wide.

INFLORESCENCE: flowers 1–few in cluster, pedicelled; cluster at top of scape, emerging from linear leaflike spathe; scape slender, flat, similar to the leaves. *Flower*: yellow with red brown eye ring; tepals 6, petallike, ¼–½ in. long, sometimes alternating wide and narrow, usually spreading; stamens 3.

FRUIT: capsule, reddish brown, globelike, about ⅛ in. across; seeds black, minute.

NOTE: uncommon; native of South America.

LBU   April–June

Blue-eyed grass [p. 67]

Sisyrinchium sagittiferum Bickn.

(Sis-ih-rin′-kee-um saj-it-tif′-er-um)

Erect, clumped, delicate, glabrous perennial 4–12 in. tall, with small matted fibers at base; stem slender, 2-winged.

LEAVES: basal, erect, grasslike, 2–9 in. long, arranged in 2 vertical rows.

INFLORESCENCE: flowers few to several, pedicelled, in terminal cluster from spathe; spathe dry, brown, violet-tinged. *Flower*: blue purple; tepals 6, alternating; outer 3 tepals usually longer and pointed; inner 3 tepals occasionally slightly shorter; stamens 3.

FRUIT: capsule, globelike, less than ¼ in. long; seeds black, minute.

NOTE: Many species of *Sisyrinchium* occur in the Thicket area, and *S. sagittiferum* hybridizes with several of them, producing plants with various features which make identification difficult.

LBU (MGP, LBS)   March–April

Dotted blue-eyed grass [p. 33]

Sisyrinchium pruinosum Bickn.

(Sis-ih-rin′-kee-um proo-ih-noh′-sum)

Erect to sprawling, clumped, delicate, glabrous perennial 3½–12 in. tall from fibrous roots; stems slender, usually numerous, not broadly winged.

LEAVES: basal, grasslike, arranged in 2 vertical rows, to 9 in. long, ⅛ in. wide; leaflike bracts along stem.

INFLORESCENCE: flowers 1–few in cluster, pedicelled; cluster terminal, emerging from spathe; pedicels usually about ¼ in. longer than spathe; spathe short-peduncled, green or sometimes purple at the nodes, arising from the leafy bract. *Flower*: violet purple to purple blue, rarely white; tepals 6, petallike, often alternating wide and narrow, wide-spreading; stamens 3.

FRUIT: capsule, glabrous, somewhat globelike, to ¼ in. tall, on drooping or spreading pedicels; seeds black, minute.

NOTE: Dotted blue-eyed grass readily hybridizes with several other species where their ranges overlap.

MGP   (LBU)   April–May

Yellow iris (yellow-flag)   [p. 45]
Iris pseudacorus L.
(Eye′-ris   soo-dak′-oh-rus)

Erect, glabrous perennial to about 3 ft. tall from stout creeping rhizome; plants sometimes forming extensive colonies, usually standing in water.

LEAVES: alternate, mostly basal, forming clumps, bright green, erect to somewhat arching at tip, linear, to 3 ft. long, about $\frac{3}{4}$ in. wide, sheathing at base.

INFLORESCENCE: flowers 1 or 2, showy, emerging from spathelike bract, terminal or from axil of upper leaf. *Flower*: yellow; tepals 6; outer 3 tepals drooping, to 3 in. long, 1–2 in. wide; inner 3 tepals much smaller, erect or spreading, $\frac{3}{4}$–1$\frac{1}{4}$ in. wide; style parted into 3 segments; style segments petallike, arched over and covering anthers, 2-cleft and curling upward at tip.

FRUIT: capsule, bright green, somewhat cylindrical, 3-angled, 2–3 in. long; seeds numerous, flattened, usually somewhat angular, corky.

NOTE: introduced from Eurasia and Africa; known only from Hardin County in the Big Thicket, but more common eastward.

SOF   April–May

Southern iris (southern blue-flag)   [p. 45]
Iris virginica L.
(Eye′-ris   vir-jin′-ih-kah)

Erect to sprawling, aquatic perennial to about 3 ft. tall from stout creeping rhizome; stems unbranched or branched in upper portion; plants forming extensive colonies.

LEAVES: alternate, mostly basal, sheathing at base, soon arching or lying on ground, linear, to 30 in. long, 1$\frac{1}{4}$ in. wide; basal leaves pale brown or buffy at base.

INFLORESCENCE: flowers 1–few, showy, emerging from green spathelike terminal bract; flower stalk weak, soon arching downward and ripening seeds on ground or in water. *Flower*: pale to light blue with darker streakings; tepals 6; outer 3 tepals about 1$\frac{1}{2}$ in. wide, reflexed, the midrib yellow and expanding into yellow pubescent patch on upper surface; inner 3 tepals erect or spreading; style parted into 3 segments; style segments petallike, spreading, covering anthers, recurved at tips.

FRUIT: capsule, obscurely 3-angled, ovoid to somewhat cylindrical, 1$\frac{1}{4}$–4$\frac{1}{4}$ in. long, disintegrating early; seeds numerous, flattened, rounded or irregularly shaped; outer covering deeply pitted, brittle, and corky.

SOF   April–June

Short-stem iris [p. 45]

Iris brevicaulis Raf.

(Eye′-ris brev-ih-caw′-lis)

Erect to loosely sprawling, glabrous perennial from slender rhizome.

LEAVES: alternate, mostly basal, sheathing at base, linear, 12–24 in. long, 1/2–1 3/8 in. wide.

INFLORESCENCE: flowers 1–few, showy, emerging from spathe; spathes terminal and essentially sessile or short-peduncled from upper leaf axils, subtended by broad prolonged leaflike bracts; flower stem prominently zigzag, 6–20 in. tall, lower than leaves. *Flower*: deep blue or blue purple, 3–4 in. wide; tepals 6; outer 3 tepals drooping downward, 2 3/4–3 1/2 in. long, 1–1 1/2 in. wide; inner 3 tepals erect or spreading, greenish yellow near base with darker lines; style greenish, 3-branched; style branches wide-spreading, covering anthers.

FRUIT: capsule, prominently 6-angled, ovoid to ellipsoid, 1 1/4–2 in. long, tardily opening; seeds numerous, with thick outer covering.

SOF   April–June

Herbertia [p. 34]

Alophia drummondii (Grah.) Foster

(A-loh′-fee-ah drum-mun′-dee-eye)

Erect, delicate, slender perennial to 12 in. tall from deep globelike brown-coated bulb; plants usually forming large colonies.

LEAVES: alternate, mostly basal, in 2 rows, sheathing flower scape at base, folded along rest of length, narrowly linear, to 12 in. long.

INFLORESCENCE: flowers 1 or 2, subtended by spathe, terminal on slender erect scape; spathe thin, dryish, bractlike. *Flower*: pale to dark lavender, white near base, about 2 in. across; tepals 6; outer 3 tepals wide-spreading, heavily spotted with violet outlined in purple on basal portion, broadly sharp-pointed at tip; inner 3 tepals much smaller, blackish violet on basal portion, violet near tip; style 3-branched, each branch tipped with 2 sharp-pointed stigmas.

FRUIT: capsule, erect, thin-walled, usually cylindrical, to 1 in. long, pale yellowish brown at maturity.

NOTE: rare in East Texas and western Louisiana.

MGP   (POF)   March–May

Purple pleat-leaf (pinewoods-lily) [p. 67]

Eustylis purpurea (Herb.) Engelm. & Gray

(Yoo′-stih-lis pur-poo′-ree-ah)

Erect, rather delicate, glabrous perennial to 30 in. tall from shallow-rooted bulb; bulb covered with chocolate brown scales; plants scattered in thin colonies.

LEAVES: alternate, mostly basal, conspicuously veined, clasping at base and folded for rest of length, narrowly lanceolate, 18–24 in. long, to ¾ in. wide.

INFLORESCENCE: flowers few to several, showy, opening for several days in succession from terminal spathe; flower stalk slender, wiry, often zigzag, more or less branched, usually taller than leaves. *Flower*: velvety purplish in outer portion, yellowish and spotted with reddish brown toward center, withering early in day; tepals 6; outer 3 tepals broadly rounded in tip portion, to about 1 in. long; inner 3 tepals much smaller, cupped, crimped near tip; style forming tube, then dividing near tip into 3 slender curved sections.

FRUIT: capsule, ellipsoid, about ¾ in. long; seeds numerous, brown, wrinkled.

LBU   (OFS)   May–October

MARANTACEAE
(Arrowroot Family)

Powdery-thalia   [p. 34]
Thalia dealbata Roscoe
(Thay'-lee-ah   dee-al-bay'-tah)

Erect, robust, rather coarse, glabrous aquatic perennial to 7 ft. tall from thick rhizome; plant densely covered with a white powdery coating mostly throughout.

LEAVES: basal, 3, sheathing basally, long-petioled, with a joint at top of petiole; blade smooth, elliptic to broadly lanceolate, 8–16 in. long, 3–5 in. wide.

INFLORESCENCE: flowers several, subtended by leathery bracts, in spikes forming panicle; panicle terminal on leafless scape. *Flower*: purple, sepals 3, minute, usually much shorter than petals; petals 3, united at base, about ¼ in. long, with 1 much narrower than other 2; stamens united, petallike; 1 stamen much larger, sterile, dark purple, forming a deflexed lip about ½ in. long; 2 of inner stamens much shorter, fertile.

FRUIT: capsule, ovoid, about ⅜ in. across; seed 1 per capsule, erect.

MGP   (POF)   October–November

BURMANNIACEAE
(Burmannia Family)

Burmannia   [p. 55]
Burmannia biflora L.
(Bur-man'-nee-ah   bye-floh'-rah)

Erect, delicate, saprophytic annual to 18 in. tall, usually much lower, from fibrous roots; stem threadlike, occasionally branched in upper portion; plants usually in colonies.

LEAVES: alternate, minute, scalelike.

INFLORESCENCE: flowers small, inconspicuous, strictly erect; 1 flower terminal; other flowers, when present, in lateral spikes or racemes. *Flower*: bluish; floral tube broadly and conspicuously 3-winged in lower portion, 6-lobed at rim; outer 3 lobes well developed, very small; inner 3 lobes minute or lacking; stamens 3, sessile, attached in throat of floral tube below lobes.

FRUIT: capsule, winged, less than ¼ in. long; seeds minute, yellowish, translucent.

NOTE: uncommon or perhaps overlooked.

BGB (BMLS) August–November

Nodding-nixie [p. 56]

Apteria aphylla (Nutt.) Barnh.

(Ap-ter′-ee-ah ay-fil′-lah)

Erect, delicate, saprophytic annual to 8 in. tall, frequently much lower; stem threadlike, wiry, blackish, unbranched or branched in upper portion; plants usually in colonies.

LEAVES: alternate, reduced to minute scales, to ⅛ in. long, not green.

INFLORESCENCE: flower solitary, nodding, on long pedicel at or near top of stem. *Flower*: whitish to purple, appearing not fully open, about ½ in. long; floral tube 6-lobed at rim; outer 3 lobes much larger than inner 3; stamens 3, sessile, attached deep in throat of tube.

FRUIT: capsule, minute; seeds numerous.

NOTE: uncommon or perhaps overlooked.

BGB (BMLS) August–November

ORCHIDACEAE
(Orchid Family)

Yellow lady's-slipper [p. 78]

Cypripedium calceolus L. var. *pubescens* (Willd.) Correll

(Sip-rih-pee′-dee-um kal-see′-oh-lus pyoo-bes′-senz)

Erect, rather stout, coarse, terrestrial perennial to 28 in. tall from short or elongated rhizome with fibrous roots; plants essentially glandular pubescent throughout.

LEAVES: alternate, several, sheathing basally, somewhat folded for rest of length, prominently ribbed, elliptic to broadly lanceolate, to 8 in. long, 4 in. wide.

INFLORESCENCE: flowers 1 or 2, showy, terminal; each flower subtended by large leaflike bract. *Flower*: cream-colored to golden yellow and brownish to purplish; sepals 3, greenish yellow to brownish purple; upper sepal larger, usually erect, 1¼–3½ in. long; lower 2 sepals united and appearing as one beneath lip, 2-toothed at tip; petals 3; 2 lateral petals very long and narrow, 2–2½ in. long, greenish yellow to purplish brown, spirally twisted, spreading; lip creamy or yellow, usually veined with purple, 2–2½ in. long, inflated or cupped to form moccasin shape; stamens, style, and stigma united to form column.

FRUIT: capsule, obovoid to ellipsoid; seeds numerous, minute.

NOTE: rare; the largest and most showy orchid in East Texas and western Louisiana.

BMLS   (BGB)   April–June

Water-spider orchid   [p. 56]
Habenaria repens Nutt.
(Hab-en-air′-ee-ah   ree′-penz)

Erect to somewhat sprawling, leafy-stemmed, glabrous, aquatic perennial 8–36 in. tall.

LEAVES: alternate, sheathing basally; blade pale green, 3-ribbed and prominently veined, linear to narrowly lanceolate, 2–9½ in. long, to 1 in. wide; upper leaves smaller.

INFLORESCENCE: flowers many, short-pedicelled, in usually dense solitary showy elongated raceme; flowers intermixed with small, greenish, leaflike bracts. *Flower*: greenish white or creamy; sepals 3, petallike; middle sepal erect and forming hood; lateral sepals spreading; petals 3, less than ⅓ in. long; each lateral petal deeply cleft and appearing as 2 threadlike segments; lip in lowermost position, reflexed, deeply divided into 3 threadlike segments; middle segment slightly broader, shorter, long-spurred; stamens, style, and stigma united to form column.

FRUIT: capsule, narrowly cylindrical to ellipsoid; seeds numerous, minute.

NOTE: can be found in moist bogs, but usually grows on floating mats of sphagnum moss or other vegetation in shallow or slow-moving acidic water.

BGB   May–November

Yellow fringed orchid   [p. 60]
Habenaria ciliaris (L.) R. Br.
(Hab-en-air′-ee-ah   sil-ee-air′-is)

Erect, slender to stout, glabrous perennial to 36 in. tall, usually much lower; from tuberous roots.

LEAVES: alternate, sheathing basally, often prominently keeled; lower leaves solitary or few, to 12 in. long, 1¼ in. wide, sharp-pointed at tip, reduced upward and becoming bracts.

INFLORESCENCE: flowers many, pedicelled, in dense showy solitary terminal raceme; raceme 2–6 in. long, to 3 in. wide. *Flower*: dark orange to yellow orange, to 1½ in. long; sepals 3, petallike, erect, almost round; petals 3; lateral petals about 2/5 in. long, toothed at tip, often hidden by lateral sepals; lip in lowermost position, about ½ in. long, spurred at base, with margin deeply cut into fringe of numerous threadlike segments; spur slender, to 1¼ in. long; stamens, style, and stigma united to form column.

FRUIT: capsule, narrowly cylindrical to ellipsoid; seeds numerous, minute.

NOTE: uncommon in the Big Thicket.

LBS   (BGB)   June–October

Green rein-orchid   [p. 56]
Habenaria clavellata (Michx.) Spreng.
(Hab-en-air'-ee-ah   kla-vel-lay'-tah)

Erect, glabrous aquatic or terrestrial perennial to 18 in. tall from cluster of thick roots; stem somewhat angled and narrowly winged.

LEAVES: along stem, sheathing basally; larger leaves 1 or 2, near middle of stem; blade narrowly spatulate, to 7¼ in. long, usually shorter, pointed at tip; upper leaves reduced to bracts.

INFLORESCENCE: flowers few to several, pedicelled, in solitary terminal raceme; raceme ¾–2½ in. long. *Flower*: greenish or yellowish white; sepals 3, petallike, erect; petals 3; lip in lowermost position, oblong, about ½ in. long, blunt or squarish at tip and minutely 3-lobed, extending into spur at base; spur slender, club-shaped, extending sideways and appearing distorted; stamens, style, and stigma united to form column.

FRUIT: capsule, narrowly cylindrical; seeds numerous, minute.

NOTE: infrequent to rare in the Big Thicket.

BGB   (BMLS)   June–August

Snowy orchid   [p. 60]
Habenaria nivea (Nutt.) Spreng.
(Hab-en-air'-ee-ah   niv'-ee-ah)

Rigidly erect, slender, glabrous, terrestrial perennial to 3 ft. tall, usually lower, from small ellipsoid fleshy tubers.

LEAVES: alternate, mostly basal, usually 2 or 3; blade firm, sometimes folded lengthwise, with midrib prominent on lower surface, linear to narrowly lanceolate, 4–12 in. long, ¼–½ in. wide; upper leaves reduced to bracts.

INFLORESCENCE: flowers numerous, pedicelled, in showy solitary terminal raceme; raceme dense, compact, 1½–6 in. long. *Flower*: white; sepals 3 and petals 3, mostly similar, ⅛–¼ in. long; lip in uppermost position, to ⅜ in. long, spurred; spur slender, conspicuous, approximately ¾ in. long, extending toward side with tip curving upward; stamens, style, and stigma united to form column.

FRUIT: capsule, cylindrical, prominently ribbed, covered with minute, rounded projections; seeds numerous, minute.

NOTE: uncommon in the Big Thicket, becoming rare due to destruction of habitat.

LBS   May–August

Southern twayblade [p. 78]

Listera australis Lindl.

(Lis'-ter-ah   aw-stray'-lis)

Erect, slender, delicate, inconspicuous terrestrial perennial rarely more than 6 in. tall from matted fibrous roots; stem unbranched, purplish.

LEAVES: opposite, 2, above middle of stem, sheathing basally; blade typically elliptic to broadly lanceolate, to 1½ in. long, commonly smaller.

INFLORESCENCE: flowers few–several, pedicelled, small, inconspicuous, in open solitary terminal raceme; raceme to 4 in. long; pedicels threadlike, to ¼ in. long. *Flower*: reddish purple or greenish; sepals 3 and petals 3, mostly similar, almost equal, only about 1/16 in. long; lip sessile, in lowermost position, ¼–½ in. long, deeply cleft into 2 segments; segments narrow, slightly spreading, with minute appendages on each side near base.

FRUIT: capsule, very small, slender, pedicelled; seeds numerous, minute.

NOTE: uncommon in East Texas and western Louisiana.

BMLS   (BGB)   February–May

Three birds orchid (nodding pogonia) [p. 79]

Triphora trianthophora (Sw.) Rydb.

(Try-foh'-rah   try-an-tho-foh'-rah)

Low, slender, delicate, inconspicuous, succulent terrestrial perennial usually about 6 in. tall from fleshy tubers which produce stolons and form large colonies of plants; stem fragile, thin, reddish to deep maroon, often hidden among fallen leaves.

LEAVES: alternate, usually 2, clasping basally; blade usually tinged and veined with maroon, broadly lanceolate, about ¾ in. long.

INFLORESCENCE: flowers 1–3, peduncled, borne from the axils of the uppermost leaves, nodding in bud, erect when open, lasting about a day. *Flower*: white tinged with pink, about 1¼ in. long; sepals 3 and petals 3, mostly similar; lip larger, 3-lobed, with 3 lengthwise crests; middle lobe larger, broadly rounded; stamens, style, and stigma united to form column.

FRUIT: capsule, erect or drooping, somewhat ellipsoid, to ¾ in. long; seeds numerous, minute.

NOTE: rare in East Texas and western Louisiana; plants may not be found for several years in succession.

BMLS   August–October

Whorled pogonia [p. 79]
Isotria verticillata (Willd.) Raf.
(Eye-soh'-tree-ah   ver-tih-sil-lay'-tah)

Erect, terrestrial perennial to 16 in. tall from long slender pubescent roots; roots producing new plants at tips, forming large colonies; stem purplish or reddish brown.

LEAVES: whorled, 5 or 6, near top of stem; blade green on upper surface, glaucous beneath, small at time of flowering, later expanding, elliptic to broadly lanceolate, wider near tip, becoming to 4 in. long, 2 in. wide.

INFLORESCENCE: flower solitary, peduncled, erect or drooping, showy, terminal; peduncle 1–2 in. long, subtended by the leaves. *Flower*: brown purple and yellowish green; sepals 3, brown purple, very narrow, to $2\frac{1}{2}$ in. long, about $\frac{1}{8}$ in. wide, wide-spreading, conspicuous; lateral petals yellowish green, broadly lanceolate or broader in tip portion, about $\frac{3}{4}$ in. long; lip in lowermost position, to 1 in. long, $\frac{3}{8}$ in. wide, streaked with purple, crested with broad fleshy ridge, lobed at tip.

FRUIT: capsule, erect, cylindrical or ellipsoid, to $1\frac{1}{2}$ in. long, persistent into winter months.

NOTE: rare in East Texas and western Louisiana.

BMLS (BGB)   March–July

Rose pogonia (snake-mouth) [p. 56]
Pogonia ophioglossoides (L.) Ker.
(Poh-goh'-nee-ah   oh-fee-oh-glos-so'-ih-deez)

Rigidly erect, slender, glabrous terrestrial perennial to 2 ft. tall, usually about 16 in. tall, from fibrous roots; stem delicate, green or brownish green.

LEAVES: solitary, near middle of stem, sheathing basally; blade broadly lanceolate, to $4\frac{3}{4}$ in. long, usually shorter, to $1\frac{1}{4}$ in. wide.

INFLORESCENCE: flowers usually solitary, occasionally 2, subtended by small leaflike bract, short-peduncled, terminal on stem. *Flower*: rose or pink to white, fragrant, usually lasting for several days; sepals 3, petallike; petals 3; lip in lowermost position, coarsely toothed at tip, densely bearded near throat with short fleshy yellow white bristles.

FRUIT: capsule, erect, ellipsoid, to $1\frac{1}{8}$ in. long; seeds numerous, minute.

NOTE: uncommon in East Texas and western Louisiana.

BGB (LBS)   April–July

Bearded grass-pink   [p. 60]
Calopogon barbatus (Walt.) Ames
(Kal-oh-poh′-gon   bar-bay′-tus)

Erect, glabrous terrestrial perennial 6–18 in. tall from globelike corm.

LEAVES: basal, usually 1, sometimes 2, grasslike, sheathing basally; blade threadlike to linear, less than 8 in. long.

INFLORESCENCE: flowers 2–5, pedicelled, opening almost at same time, in short dense showy solitary terminal raceme; pedicels slender, to 3/8 in. long. *Flower*: deep lavender to magenta; sepals 3 and petals 3, mostly similar, spreading, to about 3/4 in. long; lip in uppermost position, about 1/2 in. long, heavily bearded with orange or rust red hairs; stamens, style, and stigma united to form column; column usually less than 1/2 in. long, extending downward then curving upward near tip, broadly winged on each side near tip.

FRUIT: capsule, erect, cylindrical or ellipsoid; seeds numerous, minute.

NOTE: rare in East Texas and western Louisiana.

LBS   (BGB)   March–May

Grass-pink   [p. 60]
Calopogon pulchellus (Salisb.) R. Br.
(Kal-oh-poh′-gon   pul-kel′-lus)

Stiffly erect, wandlike, terrestrial perennial usually about 20 in. tall from globelike corm.

LEAVES: basal, solitary, sheathing basally; blade linear to narrowly lanceolate, to 20 in. long, 2 in. wide.

INFLORESCENCE: flowers 8 or more, pedicelled, opening upward in slow succession in rather lax showy solitary terminal raceme. *Flower*: purplish to magenta; sepals 3 and petals 3, mostly similar, to about 1 in. long, spreading; lip in uppermost position, usually more than 1/2 in. long, conspicuously bearded with orange and crimson hairs; column prominently incurved, to 2/3 in. long, broadly winged on each side near tip.

FRUIT: capsule, erect, cylindrical or ellipsoid; seeds numerous, minute.

NOTE: uncommon in East Texas and western Louisiana.

LBS   (BGB)   April–June

Spring ladies' tresses   [p. 34]
Spiranthes vernalis Engelm. & Gray
(Spy-ran′-theez   ver-nay′-lis)

Strictly erect, slender to stout, pubescent perennial 6 in. to 3 ft. tall, commonly about 20 in. tall, from elongated tuberous roots.

LEAVES: basal or some along stem, erect, sheathing basally; blade firm, usually thick, often prominently keeled, linear to narrowly lanceolate, to 12 in. long, 1/2 in. wide, usually smaller.

INFLORESCENCE: flowers numerous, sessile, subtended by small leaflike bracts, in spiraled solitary terminal spike; flower stem and bracts with dense, reddish brown, sharp-pointed pubescence. *Flower*: white or yellowish, sometimes marked with green, fragrant, less than 1/2 in. long; middle sepal and 2 lateral petals connected at base and forming hood; lip larger, fleshy, curved downward, spreading, glistening, crisped at tip; ovaries densely pubescent; stamens, style, and stigmas united to form short column.

FRUIT: capsule, erect, somewhat ellipsoid; seeds numerous, minute.

NOTE: one of the more common species of orchids.

MGP   (POF, LBS)   April–July

Nodding ladies' tresses [p. 45]
Spiranthes cernua (L.) Rich. var. *cernua*
(Spy-ran'-theez sern'-oo-ah)

Erect, very slender perennial usually to about 16 in. tall, sometimes taller, glabrous in lower portion, becoming pubescent in upper parts; new plants produced from stolons, usually forming large colonies.

LEAVES: basal or on lower portion of stem, often withering early; blade linear to narrowly lanceolate, 8–10 in. long, about 1/2 in. wide, reduced upward to bracts.

INFLORESCENCE: flowers numerous, sessile, nodding, subtended by small leaflike bracts, in dense solitary terminal spike; spike to 6 in. long, spirally twisted; flowers in 2–4 rows; stem and bracts softly pubescent. *Flower*: white, fragrant, less than 1/2 in. long, densely pubescent on outer surface; middle sepal and lateral petals united, forming hood over column; lip larger, oblong, less than 3/8 in. long, widely flaring, crisped at tip; stamens, style, and stigma united to form column.

FRUIT: capsule, erect, somewhat ellipsoid; seeds numerous, minute.

NOTE: uncommon in East Texas and western Louisiana.

SOF   (POF)   July–December

Fragrant ladies' tresses [p. 46]
Spiranthes cernua (L.) Rich. var. *odorata* (Nutt.) Correll
(Spy-ran'-theez sern'-oo-ah   oh-doh-ray'-tah)

Erect, delicate perennial 4–24 in. tall, sometimes taller, glabrous in lower portion, with soft pubescence above, forming colonies from stolons.

LEAVES: basal or extending up stem, sheathing basally; blade dark green, linear to lanceolate, 8–16 in. long, 3/8–13/8 in. wide, not much reduced upward.

INFLORESCENCE: flowers numerous, sessile, in showy solitary terminal spike; spike dense, compact, spiraled, to 7 in. long; flowers in 2–4 rows, intermixed with small green bracts. *Flower*: white or cream-colored, sometimes marked with green, fragrant; middle sepal and lateral petals united, forming hood over column; lip much larger, about 1/2 in. long, thickish, broadly oval, wider near base, curved downward, crisped at tip; stamens, style, and stigma united to form short column.

FRUIT: capsule, erect, somewhat ellipsoid; seeds numerous, minute.

NOTE: rare in the Big Thicket; occurs sparingly throughout same area as *S. cernua* var. *cernua*, but usually in moister situations, often growing in shallow water.

SOF   (POF)   November–December

Green adder's mouth   [p. 56]
Malaxis unifolia Michx.

(Mal-ax'-is   yoo-nih-foh'-lee-ah)

Erect, low, delicate, bright green, glabrous, rather inconspicuous terrestrial perennial to 12 in. tall, frequently much lower, from swollen or cormlike base.

LEAVES: on stem, near the middle, solitary, sheathing basally; blade glossy, rounded to broadly lanceolate, to 3 1/2 in. long, 2 1/2 in. wide, frequently much smaller.

INFLORESCENCE: flowers few to many, very small, pedicelled, in dense solitary terminal raceme; pedicels threadlike, to 3/8 in. long; raceme 1/2–6 in. long, elongating as flowers open. *Flower*: green; sepals 3, narrow, spreading, to 1/8 in. long; petals 3; lateral petals threadlike, prominently recurved; lip in lowermost position, 3-lobed at tip, the middle lobe much smaller.

FRUIT: capsule, somewhat ovoid to ellipsoid, to 1/4 in. long, 1/8 in. across; seeds numerous, minute.

NOTE: uncommon in East Texas and western Louisiana.

BGB   (BMLS)   March–July

Crippled crane-fly (crane-fly orchid)   [p. 79]
Tipularia discolor (Pursh) Nutt.

(Tip-yoo-lair'-ee-ah   dis'-kuh-lor)

Erect, slender, glabrous, inconspicuous terrestrial perennial 6–24 in. tall from horizontal series of corms, forming colonies; plant leafless at flowering time.

LEAVES: from corm, solitary, slender-petioled; blade dull green above, purplish below, deeply and conspicuously veined, broadly lanceolate, to 4 in. long, 2 3/4 in. wide, notched at base; leaves produced in late autumn, living through the winter then withering away before the bloom scape appears.

INFLORESCENCE: flowers numerous, slender-pedicelled, nodding, in loose solitary raceme at top of scape; raceme 5–10 in. long; scape brownish green tinged with yellow brown or purple. *Flower*: greenish or yellowish, tinged with purple, about ½ in. across; sepals 3 and petals 3, alike, to ⅓ in. long, ⅛ in. or less wide; lip 3-lobed, spurred; spur long, slender, straight or curved, often twice as long as flower; stamens, style, and stigma united to form column.

FRUIT: capsule, ovoid, drooping, persistent for several months; seeds numerous, minute.

NOTE: uncommon in East Texas and western Louisiana; almost always found closely associated with beech trees.

BMLS   July–August

Spring coral-root   [p. 79]
Corallorhiza wisteriana Conrad
(Kor-ral-loh-rye'-zah wis-ter-ee-ay'-nah)

Erect, succulent, inconspicuous, glabrous, saprophytic perennial to 16 in. tall, frequently lower, from rhizome; rhizome pink, elongated, much-branched, toothed, appearing like pieces of sea coral; stem reddish brown, yellowish, or purplish; plant producing no chlorophyll and with no green coloring at any time.

LEAVES: alternate, along stem, reduced to several small thin sheathing scales.

INFLORESCENCE: flowers few to several, sometimes nodding, pedicelled, in loose solitary terminal raceme. *Flower*: greenish yellow tinged with purplish brown; sepals 3 and petals 3, almost equal, to ⅓ in. long, spreading; lip white, heavily spotted with magenta purple, sharply curved downward, toothed or wavy at tip; stamens, style, and stigma united to form column.

FRUIT: capsule, ovoid, nodding, less than ½ in. long, to ¼ in. across; seeds numerous, minute.

NOTE: uncommon in East Texas and western Louisiana.

BMLS   February–May

SAURURACEAE
(Lizard's-tail Family)

Lizard's-tail   [p. 46]
Saururus cernuus L.
(Saw-roo'-rus ser'-noo-us)

Erect, succulent, jointed-stemmed, usually branched perennial to 36 in. tall from pungently fragrant rhizome; rhizome producing extensively creeping stolons and forming large colonies of plants in shallow water or mud.

LEAVES: alternate, mostly in upper portion of plant, usually long-petioled; petiole sheathing stem at node; blade broadly lanceolate, 2–6 in. long, 3/4–3½ in. wide, deeply notched at base.

INFLORESCENCE: flowers numerous, minute, sessile, congested in elongated peduncled spike; spike opening from base upward, wandlike, to 12 in. long, conspicuously drooping at tip, terminal but often surpassed by axillary branches. *Flower*: white, perfect; sepals and petals absent; stamens 6–8, with long slender filaments; pistils 3 or 4, united at base only, each with an outwardly curved style.

FRUIT: capsule, fleshy, wrinkled, separating into 3 or 4 sections; seeds 1 per section.

SOF   (POF)   April–August

ARISTOLOCHIACEAE
(Birthwort Family)

Texas Dutchman's-pipe   [p. 68]
Aristolochia reticulata Nutt.
(A-ris-toh-loh'-kee-ah   reh-tik-oo-lay'-ta)

Erect to sprawling, rather delicate perennial to 20 in. tall from slender fibrous-rooted rhizome; plants with stiff, spreading pubescence; stems 1–several, angled, zigzag, unbranched or branched in lower portion.

LEAVES: alternate, few, almost sessile, clasping basally; blade firm, somewhat thickened, prominently net-veined on lower surface, somewhat pubescent along veins on both surfaces, oblong to broadly lanceolate, to 4¾ in. long, 2½ in. wide, usually smaller; margins often wavy.

INFLORESCENCE: flowers several, in raceme; racemes from lower nodes of stem, often lying on ground and hidden by fallen leaves or other woods-floor debris. *Flower*: dark brown or purplish, pubescent, about ½ in. long; calyx tubular, corollalike, curved into U or S shape, shallowly 3-lobed; no petals present.

FRUIT: capsule, reddish brown, prominently 6-angled, globelike, to ⅔ in. across, opening from top; seeds numerous, concave, with minute projections on rounded surface.

LBU   (BMLS)   May–July

POLYGONACEAE
(Knotweed Family)

Long-leaf wild buckwheat   [p. 68]
Eriogonum longifolium Nutt.
(Er-ee-og'-oh-num   lon-jih-foh'-lee-um)

Erect, rather coarse, sparsely pubescent to glabrous perennial 3–6 ft. tall; stem much-branched in upper portion.

LEAVES: alternate; basal leaves petioled; petiole 1½–4 in. long, winged at base; blade sparsely pubescent on lower surface, glabrous or almost so on upper surface, oblong to lanceolate, 4–8 in. long, to 1¼ in. wide; stem leaves sessile, similar to basal leaves but reduced in size.

INFLORESCENCE: flowers few, small, short-pedicelled, in small umbel; umbels numerous, forming peduncled flat-topped terminal cymes; umbels from pubescent, bell-shaped structure; peduncles subtended by small, leaflike bracts. *Flower*: white to silvery pubescent on outside, yellow and glabrous on inside; calyx segments 6, lanceolate, in 2 whorls of 3; corolla absent; stamens and style branches exserted.

FRUIT: achene, less than ¼ in. long, covered with dense, woolly white pubescence.
LBU   (OFS)   June–August

Heart-sepal wild buckwheat   [p. 68]
Eriogonum multiflorum Benth.
(Er-ee-og'-oh-num   mul-tih-floh'-rum)

Erect, usually thin annual or frequently biennial, 2–7½ ft. tall; plants with tufts of soft, woolly, whitish or brownish pubescence nearly throughout.

LEAVES: alternate, sessile or short-petioled, mostly in lower portion of plant; blade densely pubescent on both surfaces, elliptic to broadly lanceolate, to 1½ in. long, ⅝ in. wide; margins entire, wavy, or curled under.

INFLORESCENCE: flowers few, small, short-pedicelled, in umbel; umbels numerous, forming rather compact flat-topped terminal cymes; umbels from pubescent, bell-shaped structure; cymes short-peduncled or sessile. *Flower*: white, becoming tan with age, glabrous; calyx segments 6, in 2 whorls of 3; outer 3 segments larger than inner 3; corolla absent; stamens 9.

FRUIT: achene, brown, glabrous, to 1/16 in. long.
LBU   (OFS)   September–November

Swamp smartweed   [p. 34]
Persicaria coccinea (Muhl.) Green
(Per-sih-kair'-ee-ah   kok-sin'-ee-ah)

Stiffly erect to sprawling, greenish, aquatic or terrestrial perennial to 5 ft. tall, usually much lower, from creeping rhizome; aquatic forms have floating, often inflated stems.

LEAVES: alternate, stipuled, petioled; stipules sheathing nodes, much longer than wide, pubescent but not fringed with hairs on margin; petiole ¾–2¾ in. long; blade usually pubescent beneath, lanceolate, 2–10 in. long, ½–2½ in. wide, blunt or tapering to petiole at base.

INFLORESCENCE: flowers numerous, small, in terminal raceme; racemes slender, peduncled, 1½–6 in. long, about ½ in. wide; peduncle with gland-tipped pubescence. *Flower*: pink to reddish pink; calyx segments 6, less than ¼ in. long, prominently veined; corolla absent; stamens included or exserted, always of different length than styles; styles 2, included or exserted.

FRUIT: achene, small, black, shiny, 2-sided, convex on sides, seldom produced.

NOTE: This plant is quite variable in form in response to conditions.
MGP   (POF, SOF)   June–October

Water smartweed   [p. 46]
Persicaria punctata (Ell.) Small
(Per-sih-kair′-ee-ah   punk-tay′-tah)

Erect to loosely spreading, slender, glabrous or sparsely pubescent annual or perennial 4–40 in. tall; stem green, unbranched or much-branched.

LEAVES: alternate, stipuled, petioled; stipules sheathing nodes, 2–4 times longer than wide, fringed with bristles; bristles to ¼ in. long; petiole to ¾ in. long; blade dotted or pitted on lower surface with small glands, lanceolate, 1¼–6 in. long, ¼–¾ in. wide.

INFLORESCENCE: flowers numerous, small, in terminal raceme; racemes numerous, slender, peduncled, erect or arching; peduncles usually glabrous, gland-dotted. *Flower*: white or greenish; calyx segments 6, conspicuously dotted with yellowish glands; corolla absent; stamens included; styles 3.

FRUIT: achene, small, shiny, dark brown or black, 3-sided.
SOF   (MGP, POF, LBU)   February–December

Bristly smartweed   [p. 41]
Persicaria setacea (Baldw.) Small
(Per-sih-kair′-ee-ah   see-tay′-see-ah)

Erect to sprawling, stout, rough perennial 2–4 ft. tall; stem green and usually much-branched in upper portion, to ½ in. across at base, often lying on ground and rooting at nodes.

LEAVES: alternate, stipuled, short-petioled; stipules sheathing nodes, pubescent, ¼–¾ in. long, fringed with bristles; bristles ¼–¾ in. long; blade with rough, stiff pubescence, lanceolate, 2¾–9½ in. long, ½–2½ in. wide.

INFLORESCENCE: flowers numerous, small, pedicelled, in terminal raceme; racemes erect or slightly drooping, tapering at tip, mostly 1⅛–3¼ in. long. *Flower*: white to pinkish white; calyx segments 6, less than ⅛ in. long, without glands; corolla absent; stamens included; styles 3.

FRUIT: achene, shiny, dark brown to black, 3-sided.
POF   (MGP, SOF)   June–October

AMARANTHACEAE
(Amaranth Family)

Alligator-weed [p. 46]

Alternanthera philoxeroides (Mart.) Griseb.

(Al-ter-nan'-ther-ah fih-lox-eh-roh'-ih-deez)

Erect or creeping and mat-forming, stout, mostly aquatic perennial 4–24 in. tall from stolons; stem unbranched or branched, often rooting at nodes, forming large colonies.

LEAVES: opposite, sessile; blade thick, somewhat succulent, glabrous, linear to narrowly lanceolate, 3/4–4 1/4 in. long, 1/4–3/4 in. wide, narrowed to base, shortly pointed at tip, entire.

INFLORESCENCE: flowers numerous, minute, subtended by minute bracts, compacted into small peduncled terminal or axillary headlike spikes; peduncles 3/4–2 3/4 in. long. *Flower*: silvery white, fragrant; tepals 4 or 5, glabrous, about 1/4 in. long, finely toothed near tip.

FRUIT: achenelike, bladdery, flattened, nonopening; seed flattened, lens-shaped, smooth.

NOTE: native of South America; becoming a problem in some waters of southern North America.

SOF (POF) March–August

Snake-cotton (cottonweed) [p. 83]

Froelichia floridana (Nutt.) Moq.

(Freh-lik'-ee-ah floh-rih-day'-nah)

Stiffly erect, wandlike, stout-stemmed annual 1 1/2–5 ft. tall, more commonly only 2–3 ft. tall, sparsely branching in upper portion; branches with short, often sticky whitish or brownish pubescence.

LEAVES: opposite, short-petioled; blade pubescent, lanceolate or broadly spatulate, 1 1/4–4 in. long, to 3/4 in. wide.

INFLORESCENCE: flowers several, sessile, small, intermixed with bracts, forming dense elongated spike; bracts minute, thin, dry; spikes peduncled, often branched, terminal or from leaf axils. *Flower*: whitish or pinkish, perfect; calyx tubular, 5-lobed, becoming flattened and enlarged in fruit, the sides with spinelike ridges; stamens 5; filaments united, forming tube.

FRUIT: achenelike, ovoid, nonopening, enclosed within filament tube; seed 1, minute, reddish brown, smooth, lens-shaped.

OFS May–November

PORTULACACEAE
(Purslane Family)

Shaggy portulaca   [p. 82]
Portulaca mundula I. M. Johnst.
(Por-choo-lak'-ah   mun'-doo-lah)

Sprawling and matlike or somewhat erect, much-branched, succulent, pubescent annual to 6 in. tall from thickened taproot.

LEAVES: alternate, numerous, erect or spreading; blade fleshy, threadlike to linear, to ⅝ in. long; hair in leaf axils white, woolly, conspicuously kinky, as long as shortest leaves or longer.

INFLORESCENCE: flowers 2–8, crowded in densely pubescent head at top of stem or branch; each head subtended by 6–10 small, linear, succulent leaves. *Flower*: deep rose to purplish; calyx 2-parted; petals usually 5, about ¼ in. long, less than ¼ in. wide; stamens usually 10–15, sometimes more.

FRUIT: capsule, small, somewhat globelike, opening around middle; upper portion shiny, covered with withered calyx and corolla; seeds numerous, black.

OFS   (MGP)   July–November

Spring beauty   [p. 90]
Claytonia virginica L.
(Klay-toh'-nee-ah   vir-jin'-ih-kah)

Erect or sprawling, tufted, succulent, glabrous perennial 4–12 in. tall from small globelike corm; stems 1–several, unbranched or sparsely branched in upper portion.

LEAVES: alternate, succulent, faintly 3-ribbed; basal leaves linear to narrowly lanceolate or wider near tip, slowly tapering into slender petiole, 8–10 in. long including petiole; stem leaves 2, opposite, short-petioled.

INFLORESCENCE: flowers 6–15, small, pedicelled, in terminal raceme; pedicels threadlike, to 1½ in. long, drooping in bud and in fruit, erect or nearly erect in flower; lowest pedicel often subtended by small, oval bract. *Flower*: white or rose-colored, conspicuously veined with rose or red; sepals 2, persistent; petals 5, about ½ in. long, oval, usually rounded at tip.

FRUIT: capsule, globelike, less than ¼ in. across; seeds 1–6, blackish brown, flat, rounded, shiny.

R   (POF, SOF, LBU, BMLS)   February–April

CARYOPHYLLACEAE
(Pink Family)

Forked catchfly [p. 90]
Silene gallica L.
(Sih-lee'-nee   gal'-lih-kah)

Erect or sprawling, much-branched slender annual or biennial to 18 in. tall from taproot; plant with dense, stiff, coarse pubescence throughout, the upper portion also with sticky, gland-tipped hair.

LEAVES: opposite; basal leaves petioled, spatulate, 2–3 in. long, basally tapering into pubescent petiole, sharp-pointed at tip; upper leaves sessile, lanceolate, usually about 1 in. long, ¼ in. wide.

INFLORESCENCE: flowers few to several, pedicelled, in 1-sided raceme; pedicels from axils of small, bractlike leaves; raceme to 6 in. long. *Flower*: white to pinkish; calyx conspicuous, tubular, 10-veined, with long, soft pubescence, less than ½ in. long, becoming inflated at maturity; margin deeply toothed; petals 5, very small, entire or barely toothed at tip, usually a little longer than calyx and slightly twisted.

FRUIT: capsule, ovoid, about ¼ in. long; seeds numerous, blackish.

NOTE: native of Europe.

R   April–May

Catchfly [p. 83]
Silene subciliata Robins.
(Sih-lee'-nee   sub-sil-ee-ay'-tah)

Erect, unbranched or branched, glabrous or sparsely pubescent perennial to 3½ ft. tall, usually much lower.

LEAVES: opposite, 2 at each node; blade rather fleshy, glabrous or with scattered hairs along margins, linear to narrowly spatulate, to 6½ in. long, ½ in. wide.

INFLORESCENCE: flowers 1–few, showy, scattered or terminal on stem or slender branches. *Flower*: scarlet, to 1 in. long; calyx tubular, glabrous, smooth, 10-veined, to 1 in. long; petals 5, long-clawed; blade ½–¾ in. long, entire to barely toothed at tip; filaments exserted, pubescent at base.

FRUIT: capsule; seeds numerous, dark brown, minute.

NOTE: plants worthy of cultivation.

OFS   July–October

Drummond's whitlow-wort [p. 82]
Paronychia drummondii T. & G.
(Pair-oh-nik'-ee-ah   drum-mun'-dee-eye)

Erect or sprawling, delicate, minutely pubescent annual or biennial 4–10 in. tall from woody base; stem densely branching above base, the branches spreading.

LEAVES: opposite, sessile, stipuled; stipules silvery, lanceolate, shorter than leaves; blade flat, rigid, pubescent on both surfaces, narrowly oblong to narrowly spatulate, to 1 in. long, 1/16 in. wide, abruptly sharp-pointed at tip; margins fringed with hairs.

INFLORESCENCE: flowers minute, in flat-topped terminal cymes. *Flower*: red brown at base with distinct white margin; calyx subtended by ring of hooked hairs, deeply 5-lobed; lobes wedge-shaped, about 1/16 in. long, flattened and broadened into a white hood; petals none.

FRUIT: achenelike, bladdery, minute; seed 1.

NOTE: endemic to southeastern Texas.

OFS   April–October

NYMPHAEACEAE
(Water-lily Family)

Fragrant water-lily   [p. 56]
Nymphaea odorata Ait.
(Nim-fee′-ah   oh-doh-ray′-tah)

Aquatic, glabrous perennial from stout elongated horizontal rhizome, rooted in mud.

LEAVES: from rhizome, long-petioled; blade bright green on upper surface, reddish or purplish on lower surface, almost round, narrowly and deeply cleft at base, to 10 in. wide, floating on surface of water or sometimes emergent.

INFLORESCENCE: flower solitary, showy, usually floating, terminal on elongated scapes from submersed leaf axils. *Flower*: white, very fragrant, 2–6 in. across, opening for 3 or 4 days in early morning, closing about noon; sepals 4, petallike, often purplish on back; petals usually more than 25, thickish, 3/4–4 in. long, sharp-pointed at tip; stamens usually more than 70; outer stamens petallike, gradually becoming smaller toward center.

FRUIT: berry, leathery, globelike, somewhat flattened, about 1 in. across, maturing under water; seeds many.

BGB   March–October

Spatterdock (yellow cow-lily)   [p. 46]
Nuphar luteum subsp. *macrophyllum* (Small) E. O. Beal
(Noo′-far   loo′-tee-um   mak-roh-fil′-lum)

Aquatic perennial from large branching rhizome, rooted in mud.

LEAVES: from rhizome, long-petioled, usually floating on water or emergent and erect; petiole cylindrical to somewhat flattened in upper portion, containing numerous minute air cavities; blade glabrous on upper surface, glabrous to more or less pubescent on lower surface, broadly oval or almost round, to 12 in. long or more, 10 in. wide, deeply cleft at base.

INFLORESCENCE: flower solitary, floating or emergent, terminal on long slender leafless scape. *Flower*: waxy yellow, to 1¾ in. across; sepals 6, rather thick, rounded, cupped; outer sepals green, inner ones yellow and petallike; petals small, numerous, thickish and stamenlike, mixed with the numerous stamens.

FRUIT: berry, large, leathery, globelike, maturing under water; seeds numerous.

SOF   March–October

Yellow lotus (water-chinquapin) [p. 46]
Nelumbo lutea (Willd.) Pers.
(Nee-lum'-boh loo'-tee-ah)

Aquatic, large, coarse, glabrous perennial from slender rhizome, rooted in mud.

LEAVES: from rhizome, long-petioled, floating or raised high above water; petiole stout, attached in center of blade; blade glaucous, almost round, uncleft, to 28 in. across, depressed or cupped in center.

INFLORESCENCE: flower solitary, large, showy, to 10 in. across, on stout scape; scapes usually raised above surface of water and flowers not floating. *Flower*: pale yellow; sepals and petals alike, numerous, spreading; stamens numerous, closely surrounding pistil; anthers to ¾ in. long, tipped with slender hooked appendages.

FRUIT: nutlike, dry, hard, unopening, resembling an acorn; each "nutlet" embedded in separate cavity in top of enlarged flat-topped receptacle; 15–20 nutlets per receptacle.

SOF   (POF)   May–July

RANUNCULACEAE
(Crowfoot Family)

Yellowroot [p. 46]
Xanthorhiza simplicissima Marsh.
(Zan-thoh-rye'-zah sim-pli-sis'-si-mah)

Erect or nearly erect, slender shrub 24–28 in. tall, usually forming colonies; inner bark and roots dark yellow and very bitter.

LEAVES: alternate, petioled, terminal, compound; blade divided into usually 5 leaflets; leaflets broadly lanceolate, 1–3 in. long; margins toothed, cleft, or divided.

INFLORESCENCE: flowers numerous, small, in slender raceme; racemes compound, drooping, pubescent; racemes and leaves forming crowded terminal clusters. *Flower*: purplish brown; sepals 5, spreading, lanceolate, to about ¼ in. long, soon falling; petals 5, glandlike; stamens 5–10; pistils 5–15.

FRUIT: follicle, yellowish, shiny, flattened, curved, elliptic, about ⅛ in. long; seed 1, reddish, ovoid, minute.

NOTE: rare in East Texas and western Louisiana.

SOF   March–May

Purple meadow-rue [p. 47]
Thalictrum dasycarpum Fisch. & All.
(Tha-lik'-trum   das-ih-kar'-pum)

Erect, stout perennial to 6 ft. tall, usually much lower; stem thick near base, often purplish, branching in upper portion.

LEAVES: alternate, compound; lower leaves long-petioled; upper leaves sessile; blade 2 or 3 times divided into numerous leaflets; leaflets firm, thick, entire to 3-lobed, to 2¼ in. long, 1½ in. wide; lower surface of leaflets prominently veined, glabrous or pubescent or sometimes glaucous.

INFLORESCENCE: flowers numerous, in loose delicate showy elongated terminal panicles; flowers either pistillate or staminate; panicles of staminate flowers more conspicuous. *Flower*: greenish or yellowish; sepals 4 or 5, lanceolate, usually slender-tipped; petals absent; filaments of staminate flowers threadlike, soon drooping and becoming entangled.

FRUIT: achene, ribbed lengthwise, in clusters of 4–15.

NOTE: uncommon in the Big Thicket.

SOF   March–July

Blue larkspur [p. 83]
Delphinium carolinianum Walt.
(Del-fin'-ee-um   kair-oh-lin-ee-ay'-num)

Erect, slender perennial to about 3 ft. tall from cluster of shallow tuber-like roots; stem straw-colored or bluish in upper portion, slightly pubescent throughout or with gland-tipped pubescence in upper portion and almost glabrous in lower portion.

LEAVES: alternate, pedicelled, equally spaced along stem and not much reduced in size upward; blade glabrous on upper surface, sparsely and minutely pubescent below, to 2¾ in. wide, cut and lobed into numerous linear ultimate segments; leaves occasionally forming winter rosettes; lower leaves often withering before flowers finish blooming.

INFLORESCENCE: flowers few to numerous, short-pedicelled, slowly opening in an erect narrow dense terminal raceme. *Flower*: rich dark blue, occasionally whitish blue; sepals 5, petallike, to about ½ in. long, ¼ in. wide;

upper sepal spurred; petals 4, much shorter than sepals; upper 2 petals with long, nectar-bearing spurs extending into sepal spur; lower 2 petals often paler or whitish and with sparse wide-spreading pubescence.

FRUIT: follicle, slender, beaked at tip; 3 united follicles per pedicel, splitting apart at maturity; seeds numerous, brownish, to 1/16 in. long, prominently scaly-winged.

OFS (MGP) April–July

Rough-seed buttercup [p. 41]
Ranunculus muricatus L.
(Ra-nun'-kyoo-lus moo-rih-kay'-tus)

Erect or sprawling, glabrous winter annual or sometimes perennial; stem hollow, not rooting at nodes, 8–20 in. long, freely branching.

LEAVES: alternate; basal leaves petioled; petiole 1½–6 in. long; blade ¾–2 in. long, ¾–2½ in. wide, deeply 3-cleft, each segment again shallowly lobed and rounded at tip; upper leaves short-petioled or sessile.

INFLORESCENCE: flowers solitary, pedicelled, from leaf axils; pedicel glabrous, slender, ¼–¾ in. long in flower, becoming ¾–2½ in. long in fruit. *Flower*: yellow, shiny, appearing waxy; sepals usually greenish, falling early; petals 5, about ¼ in. long, ⅛ in. wide, each petal with narrow, nectar-bearing scale at base; stamens few.

FRUIT: achene, outer surface covered with stout curved spines; margin prominent, without spines, keeled, forming stout curved beak at tip; achenes in cluster of 10–20, forming globelike head.

NOTE: native of Old World, now widespread.

POF (SOF) March–May

Carolina buttercup [p. 41]
Ranunculus carolinianus D.C. var. *villicaulis* Shinners
(Ray-nun'-kyoo-lus kair-oh-lin-ee-ay'-nus vil-li-kaw'-lis)

Erect or usually weak and sprawling, pubescent perennial from thick fibrous roots; stem noticeably pubescent, creeping, rooting at nodes, developing long trailing branches after flowering.

LEAVES: alternate; early basal leaves small, broadly lanceolate, entire or 3-lobed; later leaves larger, long-petioled, the blade divided into 3 leaflets; leaflet deeply 3-cleft or lobed, sharply toothed.

INFLORESCENCE: flowers 1–10 along stem; stems slender, lax, pubescent, elongating and finally becoming trailing branches to 20 in. long. *Flower*: yellow, shiny, appearing waxy; sepals usually 5, reflexed; petals 5, broader near tip, ¼–½ in. long, to ¼ in. broad.

FRUIT: achene, smooth, flattened, beaked at tip; margin wide and corky, forming straight erect beak at tip; achenes in cluster of 10–20, forming globe-like head.

POF   (SOF)   February–April

Carolina anemone   [p. 90]
Anemone caroliniana Walt.

(A-nem′-oh-nee   kair-oh-lin-ee-ay′-nah)

Erect, slender, essentially glabrous perennial to 12 in. tall from small globelike tuber and slender rhizomes or stolons.

LEAVES: basal leaves 1–3, long-petioled, compound; blade once or twice divided into narrow segments; stem leaves few, sessile, in whorl at top of stem, subtending peduncle; blade 3-parted, with the segments narrow and again 3-parted.

INFLORESCENCE: flower solitary, showy, at top of slender peduncle. *Flower*: white to rose, purple or dark blue on back side of outer sepals, or all sepals solid dark lavender blue to dark violet; sepals 10–20, petallike, narrowly oblong, to 1 in. long; petals absent; stamens and pistils numerous.

FRUIT: achene, flattened, beaked, densely pubescent; achenes numerous and forming dense woolly globe-like or elongated head.

R   (LBU)   February–April

White clematis   [p. 47]
Clematis dioscoreifolia Lévl. & Van.

(Klem′-ah-tis   dye-os-koh-ree-ih-foh′-lee-ah)

Sprawling to high-climbing, essentially glabrous perennial vine 10 ft. or more long, supported by twining of leaflet petioles.

LEAVES: opposite, petioled, compound; blade divided into 5 leaflets; leaflets petioled, mostly entire, leathery in texture, triangular to broadly lanceolate, to 3 in. long, rounded to notched at base, rounded to sharp-pointed at tip; terminal leaflet conspicuously long petioled.

INFLORESCENCE: flowers numerous, in showy panicle; panicle peduncled, flattened, terminal or axillary; peduncles opposite. *Flower*: white, about 1 in. across; sepals 4, petallike, wide-spreading, conspicuous, 1/2–2/3 in. long, glabrous on inner surface; margins with dense short white pubescence; petals absent; stamens numerous; pistils numerous; styles elongating in maturity, persistent on fruit as tail.

FRUIT: achene, brown, flattened, terminated by feathery tail; achenes numerous in conspicuous feathery ball.

NOTE: native of Japan; cultivated and escaped, well established in Hardin County.

SOF   July–September

Blue jasmine [p. 47]
Clematis crispa L.
(Klem'-ah-tis   kris'-pah)

Sprawling, trailing or climbing, essentially glabrous perennial vine to several feet long, often blooming when quite small; stems many-angled; plant climbing by twining of leaflet petioles.

LEAVES: opposite, petioled, compound; blade divided into 3–11 leaflets; leaflets petioled, thin, soft, obscurely net-veined, linear to broadly lanceolate or rarely 3-cleft, wedge-shaped or notched at base.

INFLORESCENCE: flower solitary, nodding, terminal, on long peduncle from leaf axils. *Flower*: rose-colored to violet; sepals 4, petallike, 1–2 in. long, united at base, recurved or spreading from near middle; sepal margins thin, crisped or wavy; petals absent; stamens numerous; pistils numerous; styles elongating in maturity, persistent on fruit as tail.

FRUIT: achene, small, flattened, terminated by tail; tail 3/4–1 1/4 in. long, essentially glabrous or finely pubescent; achenes numerous in conspicuous ball.
SOF   March–October

Leather flower [p. 83]
Clematis pitcheri T. & G.
(Klem'-ah-tis   pitch'-er-eye)

Twining or climbing, thin, delicate, essentially glabrous perennial vine; stem reddish brown, 6-angled, occasionally branched, supported by tendrils at tip of leaves.

LEAVES: opposite, petioled, compound; blade divided into 3–5 pairs of leaflets; leaflets petioled, entire or 2- to 5-lobed, stiff, almost glabrous to densely pubescent below and obscurely to prominently net-veined; lowest leaflets 1 1/2–4 in. long; ultimate leaflets varying greatly in size and shape; terminal portion of leaf often ending in tendril.

INFLORESCENCE: flowers usually solitary, nodding, on long slender peduncles from leaf axils. *Flower*: dull purple to brick red on outside, dark purple, red, or greenish white on inside; sepals 4, petallike, thick, ribbed, united at base, recurved or only slightly spreading near tip; petals absent; stamens numerous; pistils numerous; styles elongating in maturity, persistent on fruit as tail.

FRUIT: achene, flattened, terminated by tail; tail glabrous to pubescent but not feathery; achenes numerous in conspicuous ball.
OFS   (MGP, POF, SOF)   April–September

BERBERIDACEAE
(Barberry Family)

May-apple (mandrake)   [p. 79]
Podophyllum peltatum L.
(Poh-dof'-il-lum   pel-tay'-tum)

Erect, succulent, solitary-stemmed glabrous perennial to 20 in. tall, forming large colonies from creeping rhizome and thick fibrous roots.

LEAVES: from rhizome, solitary or 2 in flowering plants, on long petioles from top of flower stem; petiole attached toward center of blade; blade flat, shiny, almost round in general outline, to 12 in. across, 3- to 9-parted around margin.

INFLORESCENCE: flower solitary, nodding, short-peduncled, at junction of leaf petioles. *Flower*: waxy white, sweetly fragrant; sepals 6, falling early; petals 6–9, cupped, to 1½ in. long; stamens twice as many as petals; stigma ruffled.

FRUIT: berry, yellow to purplish at maturity, lemon-shaped, to 2 in. long; edible only when ripe; seeds many, poisonous.

NOTE: All parts of this plant except the pulp of the ripe fruit are reported to be poisonous.
BMLS   (LBU)   March–April

MAGNOLIACEAE
(Magnolia Family)

Southern magnolia   [p. 79]
Magnolia grandiflora L.
(Mag-noh'-lee-ah   gran-dih-floh'-rah)

Large tree to 90 ft. tall; bark smooth, tight, rarely flaky.

LEAVES: alternate, petioled, evergreen; petiole stout, with rusty red pubescence, to ¾ in. long; blade thick, leathery, dark green and shiny on upper surface, with conspicuous rusty red pubescence on lower surface, elliptic, to 8 in. long, 3½ in. wide, somewhat wedge-shaped at base, rounded or shortly-pointed at tip, entire.

INFLORESCENCE: flowers solitary, pedicelled, terminal; pedicels stout, pubescent. *Flower*: white or creamy white, conspicuously fragrant, cupped, to 8 in. across; sepals 3, petallike; petals usually 6, thick, somewhat spatulate, to 4 in. long; stamens numerous, spiraled; filaments purple; pistils numerous, spirally arranged and inserted on elongated receptacle.

FRUIT: a woody conelike aggregate of follicles formed from numerous carpels; cone pubescent, ovoid, to 4 in. long, 2½ in. across; carpels opening

on the back, from which the seeds hang by an extendable silky thread; seeds red, obovoid, somewhat flattened, to $\frac{1}{2}$ in. long.
BMLS   June–August

Sweet bay [p. 56]
Magnolia virginiana L.
(Mag-noh'-lee-ah   vir-jin-ee-ay'-nah)

Tall shrub or more often slender tree to 60 ft. tall; bark bitter, aromatic when crushed; young branches slender, bright green, densely pubescent, soon glabrous.

LEAVES: alternate, petioled, usually persistent; petiole slender, silky pubescent to glabrous, to $\frac{3}{4}$ in. long; blade thick, leathery, glabrous on upper surface, conspicuously white on lower surface, silky pubescent on lower surface when young, elliptic to broadly lanceolate, 4–6 in. long, to $2\frac{1}{2}$ in. wide, tapering or rounded at base, rounded or pointed at tip, entire.

INFLORESCENCE: flowers solitary, showy, peduncled, terminal. *Flower*: white, cupped, pleasantly fragrant, to $2\frac{3}{4}$ in. across; sepals 3, similar to but shorter than petals, spreading; petals 9–12, somewhat spatulate, cupped or concave, to $2\frac{1}{2}$ in. long; stamens numerous, spirally arranged; pistils numerous, spirally arranged and inserted on an elongated receptacle.

FRUIT: a woody conelike aggregate of follicles formed from numerous carpels; mature carpels opening on the back from which the seeds hang by an extendable silky thread; seeds red, obovoid, flattened, to $\frac{1}{4}$ in. long.
BGB   April–June

PAPAVERACEAE
(Poppy Family)

Bloodroot [p. 79]
Sanguinaria canadensis L. var. *rotundifolia* (Greene) Fern.
(San-gwih-nair'-ee-ah   kan-ah-den'-sis   roh-tun-di-foh'-lee-ah)

Erect, succulent, glabrous perennial $3\frac{1}{4}$–12 in. tall from rhizome; rhizome elongated, thick, sometimes forked, containing abundant and very bitter red orange juice.

LEAVES: from rhizome, solitary, long-petioled, encircling bloom scape when young, later overtopping fruit; blade pale green, thin, soft, pliable, prominently veined, often glaucous on lower surface, rounded in outline, to 8 in. long and wide, usually smaller; margin deeply lobed or toothed.

INFLORESCENCE: flower solitary, showy, at top of leafless scape; bud erect. *Flower*: white; petals 8 or more, to $1\frac{1}{4}$ in. long, oblong or elliptic, usually 4 larger and 4 smaller; stamens 24.

FRUIT: capsule, ellipsoid, to 2 in. long; seeds black or russet, conspicuously crested.

NOTE: uncommon to rare in the Big Thicket.

BMLS   February–March

White prickly poppy [p. 34]

Argemone albiflora Hornem. subsp. *texana* G. Ownbey
(Ar-jem'-oh-nee   al-bih-floh'-rah   tex-ay'-nah)

Erect, glaucous annual or biennial to 5 ft. tall, usually lower, with recurved prickles sparsely throughout, containing yellow acrid sap; stem usually solitary, branched in upper portion.

LEAVES: alternate, sessile or clasping; basal and lower leaves often lobed to near midrib; upper and middle leaves smaller, widely spaced along stem, more shallowly lobed, smooth or with few prickles.

INFLORESCENCE: flowers 1–several, usually subtended by 1 or 2 leaflike bracts, short-peduncled, showy, in cyme; cymes axillary or terminal; flower buds erect. *Flower*: white; sepals 2 or 3, with small horn near tip, prickly, falling early; petals 4–6, large, cupped, crinkly, stamens numerous, yellow, conspicuous.

FRUIT: capsule, prickly, to about 1½ in. long, opening into 3–5 segments; seeds blackish brown, crested.

MGP   (POF)   March–June

FUMARIACEAE
(Fumitory Family)

Southern corydalis [p. 90]

Corydalis micrantha (Engelm.) Gray var. *australis* (Chap.) Shinners
(Koh-rid'-ah-lis   mye-kran'-thah   aw-stray'-lis)

Erect to sprawling, glaucous winter annual to 24 in. tall, often less than 12 in. tall; stems 1–several, rather weak, containing bitter watery juice.

LEAVES: alternate, short-petioled or sessile, compound; blade divided into 5–7 primary segments which are divided twice more; ultimate segments linear to elliptic.

INFLORESCENCE: flowers few to numerous, short-pedicelled, intermixed with short bracts in an elongated raceme; racemes often exceeding leaves; short racemes of cleistogamous flowers often present, inconspicuous. *Flower*: pale yellow; petals 4; outer 2 petals enclosing inner 2; 1 outer petal with saclike spur at base; spur short, straight, not globelike at tip.

FRUIT: capsule, erect, slender; seeds numerous, black, minute, nearly smooth.

R   (LBU, OFS)   February–April

CRUCIFERAE
(Mustard Family)

Twist-flower [p. 83]

Streptanthus hyacinthoides Hook.

(Strep-tan'-thus   hye-ah-sin-thoh'-ih-deez)

Stiffly erect, slender, glabrous annual 12–40 in. tall; stems 1–few, unbranched or branched in upper portion.

LEAVES: alternate; basal leaves absent; stem leaves sessile or short-petioled; blade narrowly lanceolate, to 6 in. long, entire.

INFLORESCENCE: flowers few to numerous, short-pedicelled, in terminal racemes; flowers erect in bud, then turning at right angles to stem and finally conspicuously curved downward when fully open. *Flower*: dark lavender to purple or magenta; calyx urn-shaped, purplish; petals 4, longer than calyx; stamens 6; outer stamens 2, not paired; inner stamens 4, in pairs; upper stamen pair exserted, with filaments free or united; lower stamen pair not exserted and with filaments united.

FRUIT: silique, essentially sessile, very narrow, to 4 in. long, 1/16 in. across, opening from base; seeds many, flattened, winged, arranged in one row.

OFS   May–June

Spring-cress [p. 79]

Cardamine bulbosa (Schreb). B.S.P.

(Kar-dam'-ih-nee   bul-boh'-sah)

Erect perennial 8–24 in. tall from short tuber; stems solitary or several and clumplike, unbranched or branched in upper portion of plant, usually finely pubescent in lower portion.

LEAVES: alternate; basal leaves long-petioled; blade almost round, notched at base; margins shallowly toothed; lower stem leaves short-petioled; upper leaves sessile, narrowly lanceolate, reduced in size.

INFLORESCENCE: flowers several, pedicelled, in loose showy terminal raceme; racemes elongating after flowering; fruit usually forming in lower portion of raceme while flowers still opening in upper portion. *Flower*: white; sepals 4, greenish with white margins; petals 4, to ⅝ in. long.

FRUIT: silique, long-pedicelled, narrow, ¾–1¼ in. long, opening from base into 2 parts; seeds numerous, flattened, usually longer than broad, smooth.

BMLS (SOF, LBU)   February–May

Charlock [p. 90]
Brassica kaber (DC.) Wheeler
(Bras'-sih-kah kay'-ber)

Erect, rough, branched annual 12–32 in. tall; plant with coarse spreading pubescence.

LEAVES: alternate; basal leaves petioled; blade 1–6 in. long, ½–3⅛ in. wide, cleft into several lobes; terminal lobe toothed, rounded, and larger than side lobes; middle and upper leaves sessile or almost so, oblong to lanceolate; margins entire to sharply toothed.

INFLORESCENCE: flowers numerous, in elongating showy raceme; fruit present in lower portion of racemes while terminal buds still unopened. *Flower*: bright yellow; sepals 4, spreading during flowering; petals 4, about ½ in. long, long-clawed, spreading wide to form cross shape.

FRUIT: silique, erect, glabrous, rather cylindrical, to 1½ in. long, opening from base, beaked at tip; beak flattened, forming about ⅓ the entire length of silique and containing 1 or 2 seeds; seeds red or black.

NOTE: native of Eurasia, now a naturalized escape.

R   April–June

Peppergrass [p. 91]
Lepidium virginicum L.
(Leh-pid'-ee-um vir-jin'-ih-kum)

Erect or essentially so, usually pubescent annual or biennial to 28 in. tall; stem usually single from base, much-branched from upper leaf axils.

LEAVES: alternate, in basal rosette and along stem; basal leaves usually absent at flowering time; blade of basal leaves somewhat spatulate in outline, deeply lobed or cleft to sharply double-toothed, to 6 in. long, 1 in. wide; blade of lower stem leaves similar to basal leaves but less divided; leaves in upper portion of plant becoming smaller, less lobed or toothed.

INFLORESCENCE: flowers several in slender raceme, pedicelled; pedicels to ⅜ in. long, slender, spreading, often nearly horizontal; racemes numerous, solitary on slender scapes, to 4 in. long. *Flower*: white; sepals 4, very small, white-margined, usually falling early; petals 4, usually 2–3 times longer than sepals; stamens usually 2.

FRUIT: silicle, glabrous, flattened, somewhat rounded, to 3/16 in. long, ⅛ in. wide, broadly winged in tip portion, the wings forming notch; style included in notch; seeds reddish brown, narrowly winged, minutely pitted.

R   (MGP, LBU, OFS)   February–July

CAPPARIDACEAE
(Caper Family)

Clammy-weed [p. 83]

Polanisia erosa (Nutt.) Iltis

(Poh-lah-nee'-zee-ah ee-roh'-sah)

Erect to sprawling, slender-branched annual to 24 in. tall, glabrous or with sparse gland-tipped pubescence almost throughout; plant with strong, unpleasant oder when touched.

LEAVES: alternate, petioled, compound; petiole to 3/4 in. long; blade divided into 3 leaflets; leaflets threadlike to linear or spatulate, to about 1 1/2 in. long, less than 1/4 in. wide, often folded lengthwise.

INFLORESCENCE: flowers 10–17, long-pedicelled, subtended by 3-lobed bracts, in raceme; racemes open, to 1 in. long. *Flower*: white to pale yellow or pinkish; petals 4, in dissimilar pairs, long-clawed, the claw darker in color; larger petals to 1/2 in. long, broadly rounded at tip, 3- to 9-lobed; smaller petals to about 1/4 in. long and deeply cut into threadlike segments; stamens 6–15, pink, 1/4–1/2 in. long, conspicuous; nectar-bearing gland between corolla and stamens yellow, tubular, prominent.

FRUIT: capsule, erect, short-stalked, glandular, narrow, somewhat cylindrical, 3/4–2 1/4 in long; seeds 6–36, dark reddish brown.

OFS   April–October

Spider flower [p. 47]

Cleome hassleriana Chod.

(Klee-oh'-mee has-sler-ee-ay'-nah)

Erect, robust, shrubby, much-branched annual 3–6 ft. tall, prominently armed with stout prickles; plant with gland-tipped pubescence throughout, strongly and unpleasantly scented when touched.

LEAVES: alternate, petioled, compound; petiole with pair of prickles at base; blade divided into 5–7 leaflets; leaflets glandular, narrowly elliptic, long-pointed at both ends, to 4 3/4 in. long, 1 1/4 in. wide, finely and sharply toothed.

INFLORESCENCE: flowers numerous, intermixed with small leaflike bracts, in dense showy terminal raceme; racemes elongating to 3 ft. *Flower*: pink to purple, rarely white; sepals 4, falling early; petals 4, long-clawed, all ultimately in row on upward side, 3/4–1 1/2 in. long; stamens 6; filaments longer than petals, conspicuous and drooping downward opposite the petals.

FRUIT: capsule, long-pedicelled, glabrous, narrowly cylindrical, 1 1/2–4 in. long, usually recurved at maturity.

NOTE: native of Latin America, occasionally escaping cultivation.

SOF   April–October

SARRACENIACEAE
(Pitcher-plant Family)

Pitcher-plant   [p. 60]
Sarracenia alata Wood
(Sar-rah-see′-nee-ah   a-lay′-tah)

Stiffly erect, cluster-forming, carnivorous perennial to 28 in. tall from rhizome.

LEAVES: basal, erect, yellow green, hollow, tubular or trumpet-shaped, terminated by rounded, expanded hood; hood inconspicuously veined with red, arching over opening; leaves usually partially filled with liquid and decaying insects or other small invertebrates.

INFLORESCENCE: flower solitary, nodding, surrounded by bracts, showy, terminal on long leafless scape; bracts 3, small, appressed, persistent. *Flower*: greenish yellow; sepals 5, curved downward, 1½–2 in. long, 1½ in. wide; petals 5, rounded near tip, drooping, soon falling, 2–2½ in. long, 1½ in. wide; style 5-lobed, large, expanded into upside-down umbrella shape, remaining after petals fall and becoming somewhat reddish and conspicuous during summer months; stigmas 5, attached at tips of recurved style lobes.

FRUIT: capsule, large, globelike, the outer covering rough with short firm sharp projections; seeds numerous, warty, winged on one side.

NOTE: becoming rare in the Big Thicket. Many pitcher-plant bogs in the Big Thicket have been ditched for drainage.
LBS   (BGB)   March–April

DROSERACEAE
(Sundew Family)

Annual sundew   [p. 60]
Drosera annua E. L. Reed
(Dros′-er-ah   an′-yoo-ah)

Flattened, very small carnivorous annual, sometimes perennial or biennial, with gland-tipped pubescence mostly throughout.

LEAVES: basal, in rosette or tuft, greenish to bright reddish, coiled when young, petioled; petiole glandular; blade almost round to broadly wedge-shaped, to about ⅜ in. long and wide, about ⅓ as long as petiole, densely covered on upper surface with gland-tipped hairs exuding clear sticky liquid which attracts and traps insects or other small invertebrates.

INFLORESCENCE: flowers 1–6 in 1-sided raceme at tip of threadlike scape; raceme covered with gland-tipped hairs, nodding at tip in immaturity, becoming erect and elongating to 4¾ in. tall as flowers open. *Flower*: pink to rose-colored; sepals 5, united at base; petals 5, to ⅜ in. long, opening only in sunlight, soon withering but persisting.

FRUIT: capsule, obovoid, about ⅛ in. long, opening into 3–5 segments; seeds numerous, black, deeply pitted in 10–12 rows.

LBS   (BGB)   February–July

SAXIFRAGACEAE
(Saxifrage Family)

Ditch-stonecrop   [p. 47]
Penthorum sedoides L.
(Pen'-thoh-rum   seh-doh'-ih-deez)

Erect or sprawling, essentially glabrous perennial to 32 in. tall, usually much lower, from stolons; stem reddish, often branched in upper portion.

LEAVES: alternate, essentially sessile, scattered along stem; blade elliptic to broadly lanceolate, to 6 in. long, 1½ in. wide, narrowly wedge-shaped at base, sharp-pointed at tip, sharply toothed.

INFLORESCENCE: flowers few to several, rather inconspicuous, sessile, loosely arranged along upper side of terminal coiled cyme; cymes usually 3-branched, the branches uncoiling as flowers open. *Flower*: yellowish green; calyx lobes 5 or 7, green, erect; petals usually absent; stamens 10; pistils 5 or 7, united in lower portion.

FRUIT: capsule, 5-angled, 5-horned, 5-celled; seeds numerous, pink, ellipsoid, prickly.

SOF   (POF)   June–July

Virginia sweet-spire (Virginia willow)   [p. 57]
Itea virginica L.
(Eye'-tee-ah   vir-jin'-ih-kah)

Slender-branched, essentially glabrous shrub to 6 ft. tall, usually lower.

LEAVES: alternate, short-petioled, deciduous; blade broadly elliptic to oblong or broadly spatulate, to 3¼ in. long, rounded or narrowed at base, abruptly sharp-pointed at tip, minutely and sharply toothed.

INFLORESCENCE: flowers numerous, short-pedicelled, in terminal raceme; racemes slender, loose, open, more or less drooping, to 8 in. long. *Flower*: white, less than ¼ in. long; calyx united to base of ovary, deeply 5-cleft at rim; petals 5, spreading, longer than calyx and stamens.

FRUIT: capsule, with 2 united styles persistent at tip, 2-grooved, pubescent, rather cylindrical, becoming 2-parted when mature; seeds several, dark brown, smooth, shiny; empty capsules remaining on plant for a year or more.

BGB   (BMLS)   April–June

HAMAMELIDACEAE
(Witch-hazel Family)

Virginia witch-hazel   [p. 80]
Hamamelis virginiana L.
(Ham-ah-mee′-lis   vir-jin-ee-ay′-nah)

Coarse, sparsely branched large shrub or small tree to 6 ft. tall, occasionally sprouting from base; branches and twigs glabrous or with scattered pubescence.

LEAVES: alternate, short-petioled, deciduous; blade prominently veined, glabrous or pubescent on lower surface, broadly spatulate to oval or almost round, to 6 in. long and 3 in. wide at maturity, rounded or wedge-shaped at base, rounded to abruptly sharp-pointed at tip, wavy-toothed.

INFLORESCENCE: flowers 1–3 in cluster on short peduncle; peduncles 1 or more at each leaf axil. *Flower*: yellow; calyx united to base of ovary, 4-lobed at rim; petals 4, to 1 in. long, linear, spirally twisted in bud, usually curled or crinkled when fully open.

FRUIT: capsule, densely pubescent, woody, obovoid, to $5/8$ in. long, opening from top and ejecting seeds; seeds 2, black, shiny.

BMLS (BGB)   September–January

ROSACEAE
(Rose Family)

American-ipecac (Indian-physic)   [p. 80]
Gillenia stipulata (Muhl.) Baill.
(Gil-len′-ee-ah   stip-oo-lay′-tah)

Erect to somewhat lax, woody-based perennial to 3 ft. tall from horizontal rhizome, more or less pubescent throughout; stems 1–several, branched in upper portion.

LEAVES: alternate, essentially sessile, stipuled, compound; stipules leaf-like, to $3/4$ in. long, double-toothed or cleft, persistent; blade divided into 3 leaflets; leaflets thin, sparsely pubescent, narrowly lanceolate, 2–3 in. long; lower leaflets deeply cleft into narrow segments or lobes; upper leaflets deeply and sharply double-toothed.

INFLORESCENCE: flowers few, long-pedicelled, in terminal panicle; panicles loose, open, leafy. *Flower*: usually white, sometimes pinkish; floral tube to $1/4$ in. long; calyx 5-lobed; petals 5, narrow, clawed, rather disorderly, about $1/2$ in. long; stamens 20, included within floral tube.

FRUIT: follicle, less than $1/4$ in. long; 5 united follicles per pedicel, splitting apart at maturity, persistent; seeds 2–4 in each follicle, large, flattened.

BMLS   April–June

Red chokeberry [p. 60]
Pyrus arbutifolia (L.) L. f.
(Pye'-rus ar-byoo-tih-foh'-lee-ah)

Shrub or small slender tree to 21 ft. tall, usually only about 6 ft. tall; plants forming thin colonies from underground offsets; branches erect to spreading, slender, with whitish pubescence when young.

LEAVES: alternate, petioled; blade dark green and glabrous on upper surface except for gland-tipped hairs along midrib, pubescent and pale on lower surface, broadly spatulate to elliptic, to about 3½ in. long, 1½ in. wide, tapering to base, sharp-pointed at tip, sharply toothed.

INFLORESCENCE: flowers as many as 25 in cluster, pedicelled; clusters terminal on stem and short axillary branches, sometimes overtopped by young sterile shoots. *Flower*: white or pink-tinged, about ⅜ in. across; floral tube pubescent; sepals 5, with numerous glands; petals 5; stamens numerous.

FRUIT: pome, bright or dull red, fleshy, obovoid to globelike, about ¼ in. across, ripening in late autumn; seeds several.

LBS   March–May

Blueberry hawthorn [p. 41]
Crataegus brachyacantha Sarg. & Engelm.
(Kra-tee'-gus bra-kee-uh-kan'-thah)

Large shrub or small round-topped tree to 40 ft. tall; bark on old trunks becoming furrowed or divided into flattened ridges, loosening with age into thin scales and exposing reddish brown inner bark; branches pale green and somewhat pubescent when young, becoming ashy gray and glabrous in age, armed with numerous short stout usually somewhat curved spines.

LEAVES: alternate, petioled, deciduous; petiole ½–¾ in. long, slender, sometimes winged; blade of mature leaves leathery, glabrous, dark green and shiny on upper surface, paler beneath, narrowly lanceolate to somewhat ovate, to 2 in. long, 1 in. wide, tapering to petiole, abruptly sharp-pointed to rounded at tip; margins sharply toothed or occasionally lobed; leaves on young growth usually much larger and variously lobed or deeply toothed, appearing quite distinct from those on older growth.

INFLORESCENCE: flowers numerous in cluster, pedicelled; clusters glabrous, usually somewhat crowded along branches. *Flower*: white, becoming orange with age, about ⅓ in. across; sepals 5, short, triangular, narrowed at tip and with gland; petals 5, rounded, wide-spreading, soon-falling; stamens 15–20; anthers yellow, oblong.

FRUIT: pome, bright blue, glaucous, somewhat globelike, to ½ in. across; nutlets 3–5, pale brown, about ¼ in. long, hard; seeds 1 per nutlet; few to several pomes in cluster, on erect pedicels, ripening in August–September.

NOTE: A French name for this tree is *pomette bleu*, in reference to the blue fruit, which is uncommon for a hawthorn; a rare white-fruited form occurs in western Louisiana.

POF   (SOF)   March–May

Wild strawberry   [p. 47]

Fragaria virginiana Duchn.

(Fra-gair′-ee-ah   vir-jin-ee-ay′-nah)

Erect to matlike pubescent perennial to 6 in. tall from rhizome; rhizome short, thick, producing stolons and forming large colonies of new plants.

LEAVES: basal, stipuled, usually long-petioled, compound; stipules united to base of petiole; blade divided into 3 leaflets; leaflets very short-petioled or sessile, wedge-shaped at base, sharply toothed; terminal leaflet larger in tip portion; lateral leaflets somewhat more rounded; old leaves firm or leathery, often reddish to wine-colored; new leaves thinner, conspicuously wrinkled, bright green.

INFLORESCENCE: flowers few to many in loose cyme on long scape; scapes leafless, pubescent, often lower than leaves; pistillate, staminate, and perfect flowers occasionally occurring on same plant. *Flower*: white, to 1 in. across; pistillate flowers much smaller than staminate flowers; calyx flat, deeply 5-lobed with a bract between each lobe, the whole appearing as 10 bracts; petals 5, to $\frac{1}{2}$ in. long, usually rounded.

FRUIT: achene, small, dry, numerous and lightly embedded in surface of globelike receptacle commonly called "berry"; berry red, juicy, pulpy, to $\frac{3}{4}$ in. across, edible when ripe.

SOF   (LBU)   March–April

Indian strawberry   [p. 47]

Duchesnea indica (Andrz.) Focke

(Doo-ches′-nee-ah   in′-dih-kah)

Low perennial from short rhizome; plant producing above-ground stolons which root at tips and form large colonies.

LEAVES: from rhizome and along stolons, long-petioled, compound; blade divided into 3 leaflets; leaflets broadly lanceolate to elliptic, $\frac{3}{4}$–$1\frac{1}{2}$ in. long, sparsely pubescent on lower surface, sharply toothed.

INFLORESCENCE: flower solitary on long peduncle from nodes; peduncles often lower than leaves. *Flower*: yellow; calyx deeply 5-lobed, the lobes alternating with much larger bracts; bracts spreading, 3-toothed at tip; petals 5, rounded; stamens 20.

FRUIT: achene, small, numerous and imbedded in globelike receptacle commonly called "berry"; berry spongy but rather dry, bright red, pulpy, edible but tasteless.

NOTE: resembles the wild strawberry, *Fragaria virginiana*, except for yellow flowers and insipid fruit. According to most authors, this plant is a native of Asia.

SOF   (MGP, POF, LBS, LBU)   March–August

Southern dewberry   [p. 91]
Rubus trivialis Michx.
(Roo'-bus   triv-ee-ay'-lus)

Trailing or arching perennial rooting at tips of canes and forming colonies; canes slender, tough, bristly with gland-tipped pubescence and hard curved prickles.

LEAVES: alternate, stipuled, compound; stipules persistent, united to base of petiole; leaves on first-year nonflowering canes long-petioled, tough, semi-evergreen, divided into usually 5 leaflets; leaflets smooth, oblong to lanceolate, to 4 in. long, $1\frac{1}{4}$ in. wide, coarsely toothed; leaflets of second-year flowering canes similar but smaller.

INFLORESCENCE: flowers solitary or few in cyme, pedicelled; cymes rather loose, flattened, showy, terminal or axillary; pedicels bristly. *Flower*: white to pinkish, about 1 in. across; sepals 5, spreading or reflexed; petals 5, erect or spreading, less than $\frac{1}{2}$ in. wide; stamens and pistils numerous.

FRUIT: drupelet, pulpy, numerous and in the aggregate forming globe-like or elongated head commonly called "berry"; berry black and edible when ripe.

R   (MGP, SOF, LBU, OFS)   March–April

Agrimony   [p. 68]
Agrimonia microcarpa Wallr.
(Ag-rih-moh'-nee-ah   mye-kroh-kar'-pah)

Erect or nearly erect, slender perennial seldom more than 3 ft. tall from tuberous thickened roots; stem with long, soft pubescence in lower portion.

LEAVES: mostly toward base, stipuled, petioled, compound; stipules small, leaflike; petioles of principal leaves pubescent; blade divided into 3–7 leaflets interspersed with much smaller leaflets; leaflets pubescent, without glands on lower surface, thin, narrowly spatulate to elliptic, rounded at tip, coarsely toothed; lowest pair of leaflets much reduced.

INFLORESCENCE: flowers few to many, scattered, essentially sessile, in terminal spikelike raceme; raceme long, slender, pubescent. *Flower*: yellow, $\frac{1}{4}$ in. across or less; floral tube somewhat bell-shaped, the throat with hooked bristles which become hardened in fruit; sepals 5, folding inward after flowering; petals 5; stamens 5–15.

FRUIT: achene, small, enclosed at maturity by floral tube and hardened bristles; 2 achenes per floral tube.
LBU   (BMLS)   July–October

Macartney rose   [p. 34]
Rosa bracteata Wendl.
(Roh'-zah   brak-tee-ay'-tah)

Erect, trailing or arching, robust, woody, prickly, evergreen perennial, with dense soft glandular pubescence especially on younger parts; plants usually forming tangled masses.

LEAVES: alternate, stipuled, petioled, compound; stipules leaflike, partially united to petiole, about 1/4 in. long, cleft into slender segments, conspicuously toothed, subtended at base by prominent pair of curved broad-based prickles; blade divided into 5–9 leaflets; leaflets dark green, tough and leathery in texture, shiny on upper surface, broadly spatulate, 1/2–1 1/4 in. long, rounded or sharp-pointed at tip, finely toothed.

INFLORESCENCE: flowers solitary or few in cluster, short-pedicelled, subtended by bracts, showy, from leaf axils; bracts large, leaflike, pubescent, cleft into segments. *Flower*: white, 2–2 3/4 in. across; floral tube cup-shaped, contracted at mouth, pubescent; sepals 5, narrowly sharp-pointed at tip, reflexed at maturity; petals 5, abruptly pointed at tip, 1–1 3/8 in long, wide-spreading; stamens numerous.

FRUIT: achene, numerous and enclosed by the pulpy floral tube forming "hip"; hip orange red, woolly, globelike, to 1 in. across.

NOTE: native of China; planted as a living fence and readily escaping.
MGP   April–December

Carolina rose   [p. 34]
Rosa carolina L.
(Roh'-zah   kair-oh-lye'-nah)

Erect or trailing, slender perennial to 40 in. tall, usually lower; canes usually borne singly from stolons, woody and with prickles at base; prickles few or none in upper portion of plant; plants forming small colonies.

LEAVES: alternate, stipuled, petioled, compound; stipules leaflike, partially united to petiole, deeply cleft, to 2/3 in. long, less than 1/8 in. wide, subtended at base by pair of firm straight needlelike prickles; blade divided into 5–9 leaflets; leaflets firm, leathery, dull or barely shiny on upper surface, elliptic to lanceolate or narrowly spatulate, blunt to sharp-pointed at tip; margins coarsely toothed in tip portion of blade, the teeth tipped with glands.

INFLORESCENCE: flowers mostly solitary, short-pedicelled, terminal or from leaf axils. *Flower*: pink, 1/4–2 1/4 in. across; floral tube cup-shaped, contracted at mouth, glabrous or with gland-tipped hairs; sepals 5, green, narrowly tapering in tip portion, glabrous or with gland-tipped hairs; petals 5, spreading flat.

FRUIT: achene, numerous and enclosed by pulpy floral tube forming "hip"; hip red, globelike, about ½ in. long.

MGP   (LBU)   May–July

Big-tree plum (Mexican plum) [p. 47]

Prunus mexicana Wats.

(Proo′-nus   mex-ih-kay′-nah)

Small, stout tree to 36 ft. tall, not growing in colonies; young branches and twigs slender, glabrous or pubescent.

LEAVES: alternate, stipuled, petioled; blade pubescent, thick at maturity, net-veined on lower surface, broadly spatulate, 2½–4¾ in. long, abruptly sharp-pointed at tip, sharp-toothed and often double-toothed.

INFLORESCENCE: flowers 2–4 in umbel, pedicelled; umbels showy, from leaf axils of previous season; flowers opening before or with first leaves. *Flower*: white, about ½–¾ in. across; floral tube cup-shaped; sepals 5, pubescent on inner surface; petals 5, clawed, spreading; stamens numerous.

FRUIT: drupe, purplish red, glaucous, usually globelike, ¾–1¼ in. long; "seed" 1, correctly a stone.

NOTE: fruit edible, often used for jellies and preserves, ripening July–September.

SOF   (POF, BMLS)   February–March

LEGUMINOSAE
(Legume Family)

Bristly sensitive brier [p. 91]

Schrankia hystricina (Britt. & Rose) Standl.

(Shrank′-ee-ah   his-trih-sye′-nah)

Trailing or wide-spreading, coarse, herbaceous perennial from somewhat globelike or irregularly shaped taproot; essentially glabrous throughout with few prickles present; stems 8–12 ft. long.

LEAVES: alternate, stipuled, petioled, compound; blade divided into 4 or 5 pairs of opposite segments; segments divided into 10–15 pairs of small leaflets; leaflets firm, prominently net-veined on lower surface, narrow, to ¼ in. long, with small sharp point at tip; leaflets closing at dusk, during cloudy weather, or at slightest touch.

INFLORESCENCE: flowers numerous, minute, subtended by bracts, clustered in round head; heads peduncled, to ⅔ in. across, from leaf axils; peduncle slender, prickly; bracts minute, protruding from flower head before flowers open. *Flower*: pink, sessile; sepals 5, united, minute; corolla small, tubular, 5-lobed; stamens 8–12, overtopping corolla.

FRUIT: legume, very densely prickly, narrow, almost cylindrical, ½–1½ in. long; seeds several to numerous.

NOTE: endemic to southeastern Texas and adjacent Louisiana.

R   (LBU)   February–May

Little-leaf sensitive brier   [p. 84]
Schrankia microphylla (Sm.) Macbr.
(Shrank´-ee-ah   mye-kroh-fil´-lah)

Weakly arching, sprawling, or trailing perennial to 3 ft. long from thick woody root; lower portion of stem round, not distinctly 4- or 5-sided as in some species; stem and fruit smooth, otherwise plant armed with prickles mostly throughout.

LEAVES: alternate, stipuled, petioled, compound; blade divided into 8 pairs of segments with 10–17 pairs of tiny leaflets per segment; leaflets smooth beneath or with only midrib prominent, usually with short sharp point at tip; leaflets closing at dusk, during cloudy weather, or at slighest touch.

INFLORESCENCE: flowers numerous, minute, clustered in terminal globe-like head on slender prickly peduncle; heads about ½ in. across. *Flower*: pale pink, sessile; calyx very small; petals united to form 5-lobed tube; stamens 10, conspicuously exserted.

FRUIT: legume, beaked at tip, narrow, 4-angled, not conspicuously flat-tened, 2¼–4¾ in. long; beak almost ½ in. long; seeds several to numerous.

NOTE: uncommon in the Big Thicket.

OFS   July–September

Powderpuff   [p. 35]
Mimosa strigillosa T. & G.
(Mih-moh´-sah   strih-jil-loh´-sah)

Sprawling or trailing, much-branched perennial with annual stems 3–6 ft. long; plant usually densely covered with stiff, spreading, bristlelike spines but not noxious to the touch.

LEAVES: alternate, stipuled, long-petioled, compound; blade divided into 4–8 pairs of small segments; segments divided into usually 10–15 pairs of small leaflets; leaflets threadlike to linear, about ¼ in. long.

INFLORESCENCE: flowers numerous, minute, in small globelike head; heads peduncled, terminal, from leaf axils. *Flower*: pink to purplish; sepals 5, minute, united most of length; petals 5, united; stamens 10 or fewer, con-spicuously exserted.

FRUIT: legume, minutely bristly, flattened, oblong, to ¾ in. long, ½ in. wide, separating into 1–few sections at maturity; seeds 1 in each section.
MGP   May–October

Yellow-puff [p. 35]
Neptunia lutea (Leavenw.) Benth.
(Nep-too′-nee-ah loo′-tee-ah)

Sprawling or trailing, prickly, few-stemmed herbaceous perennial from orange-colored roots.

LEAVES: alternate, stipuled, petioled, prickly, compound; blade divided into 2–11 pairs of opposite segments; segments divided into 8–18 pairs of tiny leaflets; leaflets conspicuously veined on lower surface.

INFLORESCENCE: flowers 30–60, minute, densely crowded into slightly elongated peduncled head; peduncles long, slender, axillary. *Flower*: yellow; sepals 5; petals 5; stamens 10, alike, anther-bearing.

FRUIT: legume, softly pubescent, thin, flat, often curved, to 2 in. long, promptly opening at maturity; seeds few to several.

NOTE: As in the *Schrankia*, the leaflets close at dusk, during cloudy weather, or when touched.
MGP   (POF)   April–October

Redbud [p. 80]
Cercis canadensis L.
(Ser′-sis kan-ah-den′-sis)

Erect, usually wide-spreading, smooth-barked small tree to 35 ft. tall, commonly much lower; trunk frequently curved or forked.

LEAVES: alternate, petioled; blade thin, pale or dull green on both surfaces, pubescent beneath when young, almost as broad as long, 3–6 in. across, notched at base, short-pointed at tip.

INFLORESCENCE: flowers few to several in cluster, small, pedicelled; clusters showy, on last year's wood, usually appearing before leaves expand. *Flower*: pink purplish to dark rose; calyx reddish, persistent; petals 5; banner smaller than wing petals; keel petals not united.

FRUIT: legume, dark-brown, flattened, thin-walled, conspicuously veined, 1½–4 in. long, ¼–¾ in. wide; seeds several.
BMLS   (SOF, LBU)   February–March

Partridge pea [p. 68]
Cassia fasciculata Michx.
(Kas′-see-ah fas-sik-yoo-lay′-tah)

Erect, glabrous annual 1–5 ft. tall, commonly slender and few-branched, occasionally several-branched; plants often forming dense stands.

LEAVES: alternate, stipuled, petioled, compound; stipules linear, to ⅜ in. long; petiole bearing minute, sessile, saucer-shaped gland near middle; blade divided into 8–15 opposite pairs of leaflets; leaflets distinctly veined, narrowly oblong, to ¾ in. long, to ⅛ in. wide, abruptly sharp-pointed at tip.

INFLORESCENCE: flowers 2–7, short-pedicelled, in shortened raceme from just above leaf axils; one flower opening at a time. *Flower*: bright yellow; sepals 5, sharp-pointed at tip; petals 5, broadly spatulate, to ¾ in. long, unequal in size; upper petals red-spotted at base; lower petal larger, cupped; stamens 10, essentially equal in length; anthers yellow or dark-colored, stiff; style conspicuously protruding to side opposite stamens.

FRUIT: legume, glabrous, flattened, linear, to 2¾ in. long, ¼ in. wide, opening explosively and the 2 halves twisting; seeds 10–20, dark brown, flattened, hard and shiny.

LBU (MGP, OFS) June–October

Coffee senna [p. 91]
Cassia occidentalis L.
(Kas'-see-ah ok-sih-den-tay'-lis)

Erect, glabrous, unpleasant-scented annual 3½–6 ft. tall; stem grooved lengthwise, usually with few to several erect branches.

LEAVES: alternate, petioled, compound; petiole with small, globelike, sessile gland at base; blade divided into 4–6 pairs of leaflets, with terminal pair the largest; leaflets glaucous on lower surface, lanceolate to broadly lanceolate, 1⅛–2⅜ in. long, 1 in. wide.

INFLORESCENCE: flowers 2–5, intermixed with bracts in short raceme; racemes from leaf axils. *Flower*: yellow or yellow orange, wilting by midday; sepals to ⅜ in. long; petals 5, spreading, usually unequal, to ¾ in. long; stamens 10, the lower 3 with elongated filaments.

FRUIT: legume, erect, slender, 3–4¾ in. long, to ⅜ in. wide, flat when young, becoming inflated at maturity; seeds many, dull brown, ovoid, somewhat flattened, to 3/16 in. long.

NOTE: seeds still used in some regions as a coffee substitute and in medicinal remedies; extracts show antibiotic activity.

R (SOF) August–November

Plains wild indigo [p. 35]
Baptisia leucophaea Nutt.
(Bap-tee'-zee-ah loo-koh-fee'-ah)

Erect, moundlike, stout, solitary-stemmed, bushy-branched perennial 12–30 in. tall from deeply buried rhizome.

LEAVES: alternate, stipuled, short-petioled, compound; stipules large, persistent, to 1½ in. long; blade divided into 3 leaflets; leaflets 1¼–4 in. long, entire.

INFLORESCENCE: flowers numerous, pedicelled, subtended by persistent bracts, in showy raceme; racemes from near base of plant, horizontal or down-curved, sometimes lying on ground, 4–10 in. long. *Flower*: creamy to dark yellow; calyx bell-shaped, persistent, 5-lobed, to ⅜ in. long; petals 5; banner wide-spreading, notched at tip, about ¾ in. long.

FRUIT: legume, short-stalked, tough, inflated, somewhat cylindrical, 1⅛–2 in. long, ½–1 in. across, with slender beak at tip; seeds few to many, small.

NOTE: In late summer the entire above-ground portion of the plant be-comes dry, turns dark gray, and breaks off at ground level.

MGP (LBU, OFS) March–April

White false indigo [p. 68]
Baptisia leucantha T. & G.
(Bap-tee'-zee-ah loo-kan'-thah)

Erect, stout, glabrous, glaucous, rather bushy perennial 3–6 ft. tall from large deeply buried rhizome; stem solitary, much-branched in upper portion.

LEAVES: alternate, stipuled, petioled or upper leaves sessile, compound; petioles of mature leaves slender, to ½ in. long; blade divided into 3 leaflets; leaflets firm, oblong to spatulate, 1–2½ in. long, ½–1¼ in. wide, rounded or pointed at tip, entire.

INFLORESCENCE: flowers few to many, short-pedicelled, in long, showy terminal or axillary raceme; racemes 8–24 in. long. *Flower*: white; calyx bell-shaped, to ⅜ in. long, deeply lobed; petals 5; banner about ½ in. long, with purple blotches; wing petals almost 1 in. long, usually solid white.

FRUIT: legume, long-stalked, drooping, black, tough, inflated, somewhat ellipsoid, 1–1½ in. long, short-beaked at tip, slow to open; seeds few to many, small.

NOTE: uncommon in East Texas and western Louisiana.

LBU April–June

Bush-pea [p. 35]
Baptisia sphaerocarpa Nutt.
(Bap-tee'-zee-ah sfer-oh-kar'-pah)

Erect, stout perennial to about 3 ft. tall, frequently lower; stems 1–several, glabrous or occasionally pubescent, bushy-branched in upper portion; entire plant turning dark gray or black in late summer.

LEAVES: alternate, petioled, mostly compound; petiole to ⅜ in. long; blade divided into 3 leaflets in lower portion of plant, reduced to 2 leaflets or 1 leaflet in upper portion; leaflets spatulate or broadly elliptic, 1–3¼ in. long, entire.

INFLORESCENCE: flowers numerous, pedicelled, in showy terminal raceme; upper racemes 8–12 in. long, lower racemes 6–10 in. long. *Flower*:
dark yellow; calyx bell-shaped, to ⅜ in. long; petals 5; banner ⅜–¾ in. long.

FRUIT: legume, woody, beaked at tip, globelike, about ¾ in. long; beak
about ½ in. long; seeds few to many, small.

MGP   (POF, LBU)   April–May

Texas bluebonnet   [p. 35]
Lupinus subcarnosus Hook.
(Loo-pye'-nus   sub-kar-noh'-sus)

Erect or sprawling, usually much-branched winter annual 6–16 in. tall,
with conspicuous soft silky pubescence throughout; branches from base, lax or
lying on ground; plants forming rosettes of leaves in fall or early winter and
blooming the following spring.

LEAVES: alternate, stipuled, petioled, compound; blade divided into usually 5 leaflets; leaflets essentially glabrous on upper surface, silky pubescent on
lower surface, spatulate, to 1 in. long, ½ in. wide, mostly rounded at tip;
margins silky pubescent.

INFLORESCENCE: flowers several, pubescent, pedicelled, in showy terminal peduncled raceme; racemes 2½–4¾ in. long, rounded at tip, not conspicuous from a distance as is *L. texensis*. *Flower*: bright blue, patched with
white, ½ in. or more long; calyx 2-lipped; petals 5; banner with white center
which usually turns purplish in age; wing petals inflated when young; keel
petals slenderly pointed, turning upward.

FRUIT: legume, silky, stout, flattened, broadly linear, 1–1⅜ in. long, less
than ½ in. wide, somewhat constricted between seeds; seeds 4 or 5, gray or
tannish, unmarked.

NOTE: endemic; adopted as the state flower of Texas in 1901. In 1971
all *Lupinus* taxa which occur in Texas were made the state flower.

MGP   March–April

Bluebonnet   [p. 91]
Lupinus texensis Hook.
(Loo-pye'-nus   tex-en'-sis)

Erect or sprawling, much-branched winter annual 6–16 in. tall, mostly
pubescent throughout; plants usually forming rosettes of leaves in the fall and
blooming the following spring.

LEAVES: alternate, stipuled, petioled, compound; basal leaves long-
petioled; blade divided into usually 5 leaflets; leaflets glabrous above, silky
pubescent on lower surface, spatulate, to 1 in. long, ½ in. wide, pointed at
tip; margins silky pubescent.

INFLORESCENCE: flowers many, in dense showy terminal raceme; tips of racemes pointed and conspicuous with silvery white pubescence of unopened buds. *Flower*: dark blue; calyx 2-lipped; petals 5; banner with white center which usually turns wine red or purplish in aging; wing petals on young flowers not inflated.

FRUIT: legume, stout, silky, flattened, broadly linear; seeds few.

NOTE: endemic to Texas; widely planted by the Texas Highway Department.

R (MGP, OFS) April–May

Low hop clover [p. 91]
Trifolium campestre Sturm
(Try-foh′-lee-um kam-pes′-tree)

Erect or sometimes sprawling, much-branched, weak-stemmed annual or biennial less than 2 ft. tall, mostly densely pubescent especially on younger parts.

LEAVES: alternate, stipuled, petioled, compound; stipules conspicuous, partially united to base of petiole, persistent; blade divided into 3 leaflets; leaflets very variable, usually about twice as long as broad, oblong to broadly spatulate, mostly about ⅜ in. long, pointed at tip.

INFLORESCENCE: flowers 20–40, in small globelike or elongated head; heads peduncled, terminal or axillary. *Flower*: yellow, turning brownish when dry, to ¼ in. long; calyx glabrous, 5-veined, unequally lobed; petals 5; banner conspicuously lined, folded forward instead of in usual erect position, noticeably longer than wing and keel petals.

FRUIT: legume, short-stalked, somewhat cylindrical, less than ⅛ in. long, exserted from calyx tube; seed 1.

NOTE: a native of Europe, now widely introduced.

R (LBU, OFS) May–September

White clover [p. 91]
Trifolium repens L.
(Try-foh′-lee-um ree′-penz)

Mat-forming, low, essentially glabrous perennial from creeping stems rooting at the nodes.

LEAVES: alternate, stipuled, long-petioled, compound; stipules conspicuous, partially united to base of petiole, persistent; blade divided into 3 leaflets; leaflets sessile or nearly so, usually with lighter-colored band near base, broadly elliptic to spatulate, less than 3 times as long as broad, mostly to ¾ in. long, rounded, pointed or notched at tip, finely and sharply toothed.

INFLORESCENCE: flowers many, pedicelled, in compact globelike terminal raceme; racemes about as thick as long, on long slender peduncles from leaf axils; flowers erect when young, becoming brown and turning downward with age. *Flower*: white, sometimes pinkish, less than ½ in. long; calyx tubular, 10-veined, lobed at rim; petals 5; banner folded forward, conspicuously longer than wing petals.

FRUIT: legume, about ¼ in. long, exceeding calyx tube; seeds 3 or 4.

NOTE: native of Europe; commonly cultivated and now a widespread escape.

R   April–September

Scarlet pea   [p. 68]
Indigofera miniata Ort. var. *leptosepala* (Nutt.) B. L. Turner
(In-dih-gof'-er-ah   min-ee-ay'-tah   lep-toh-see'-pal-ah)

Sprawling or trailing, somewhat shrubby pubescent perennial from tough woody taproot; stems 1–several, usually freely branched, to 20 in. long; pubescence hairs attached at the middle with both ends free.

LEAVES: alternate, stipuled, short-petioled, compound; blade divided into 5–9 leaflets; leaflets sessile or short-petioled, alternate with one leaflet terminal.

INFLORESCENCE: flowers numerous, in showy spikelike terminal raceme; racemes from leaf axils, much surpassing the subtending leaf. *Flower*: brick red or dark rosy red; calyx deeply 5-lobed, persistent; petals 5; banner rounded, abruptly bent backward from base, short-clawed; wing petals linear to oblong, short-clawed, the blades forming an earlike projection at base; keel petals united at tip, separate at base.

FRUIT: legume, sessile, usually straight, narrowly cylindrical, to 1½ in. long; seeds few to several.

LBU   (BGP, OFS)   April–September

Single-stem scurfpea   [p. 61]
Psoralea simplex T. & G.
(Soh-ray'-lee-ah   sim'-plex)

Erect, delicate, solitary-stemmed perennial 12–32 in. tall from thickened tuberous roots; plants with sharp, stiff pubescence mostly throughout.

LEAVES: alternate, stipuled, compound; stipules well developed, about ⅜ in. long, persistent; lower leaves long-petioled, the upper leaves almost sessile; blade divided into 3 leaflets; leaflets gland-dotted on upper surface, with sharp stiff pubescence beneath, narrowly lanceolate, ¾–2¾ in. long, to ⅝ in. wide, sharp-pointed at tip.

INFLORESCENCE: flowers numerous, in showy spikelike raceme; racemes erect, dense, elongated, to 2 in. long, on long peduncles from leaf axils; peduncles to 4 in. long. *Flower*: dark purple, to ⅜ in. long; calyx purple, tubular, 5-lobed; petals 5; banner extending forward, tapering into short claw at base; wing petals short-clawed; keel petals rounded, united at tip.

FRUIT: legume, thin, papery, wrinkled, shortly beaked, flat, somewhat rounded; seed 1, brown.

NOTE: infrequent in the Big Thicket.

LBS April–June

Bastard indigo (lead-plant) [p. 48]
Amorpha fruticosa L.
(A-mor'-fah froo-tih-koh'-sah)

Erect, often clumped, quite variable, thinly branched shrub 3–12 ft. tall, more or less pubescent throughout.

LEAVES: alternate, deciduous, rather long-petioled, compound; blade divided into 11–27 leaflets; leaflets dark green and obscurely net-veined on upper surface, paler and sparsely gland-dotted and somewhat pubescent along veins on lower surface, oblong or elliptic, to 1¼ in. long, ⅝ in. wide, rounded or narrowed at base, rounded or sometimes abruptly pointed at tip.

INFLORESCENCE: flowers numerous, small, short-pedicelled, in dense slender peduncled racemes at ends of stem and branches. *Flower*: dark blue or purplish; calyx essentially pubescent, tubular, 5-lobed, persistent; only banner petal present; other petals absent; stamens 10, exserted; anthers bright orange, conspicuous.

FRUIT: legume, slightly curved, glabrous, conspicuously gland-dotted, about ¼ in. long; seeds 1 or 2.

SOF (POF) April–July

Oklahoma prairie clover [p. 84]
Petalostemum griseum T. & G.
(Pet-ah-loh-stee'-mum gris'-ee-um)

Erect, sparsely pubescent perennial to 28 in. tall; stems 1–few, often clustered, usually reddish and marked with fine lengthwise grooves, branching in upper portion.

LEAVES: alternate, stipuled, numerous, spreading, compound; stipules sharp-pointed at tip, persistent; blades divided into 9–17 leaflets; leaflets with fine, long, silky pubescence, conspicuously gland-dotted on lower surface, oblong to spatulate, less than ½ in. long, abruptly sharp-pointed at tip.

INFLORESCENCE: flowers numerous, very small, in terminal short-peduncled spike; spikes dense, cylindrical, elongating as flowers open; each bud subtended by a minute, soon-falling bract. *Flower*: pink or pink purple; calyx 5-lobed, ribbed lengthwise, densely pubescent; corolla of 5 separate and similar petals, all with threadlike claws.

FRUIT: legume, pubescent, curved, somewhat obovoid, less than ¼ in. long, nonopening; seeds 1 or 2.

NOTE: endemic to East and Southeast Texas.

OFS May–July

Purple prairie clover   [p. 35]
Petalostemum purpureum (Vent.) Rudb.
(Pet-ah-loh-stee'-mum   pur-poo'-ree-um)

Erect, woody-based perennial 1–3 ft. tall; stems 1–several, grooved lengthwise, glabrous or pubescent, branching in upper portion.

LEAVES: alternate, numerous, stipuled, frequently with smaller leaves in axils, compound; blade divided into usually 5 leaflets; leaflets glabrous or with stiff pubescence, gland-dotted on lower surface, linear, to ¾ in. long, to ⅛ in. wide; margins rolled inward on upper surface.

INFLORESCENCE: flowers numerous, very small, subtended by minute bracts, in short-peduncled terminal spike; spikes dense, compact, elongating as flowers open. *Flower*: rose purple; calyx lobed, densely pubescent; petals 5; wing and keel petals shorter-clawed than banner.

FRUIT: legume, pubescent, to ⅛ in. long, nonopening; seeds 1 or 2.

NOTE: uncommon in the Big Thicket.

MGP   (LBU)   June–July

Plains prairie clover   [p. 36]
Petalostemum decumbens Nutt.
(Pet-ah-loh-stee'-mum   dee-kum'-benz)

Weakly erect or sprawling perennial, glabrous or with sparse short pubescence; stems 1–several, grooved lengthwise.

LEAVES: alternate, numerous, erect, stipuled, compound; blade divided into 5–7 leaflets; leaflets sparsely pubescent, gland-dotted on lower surface, linear or narrowly oblong, abruptly sharp-pointed at tip; margins slightly rolled inward on upper surface.

INFLORESCENCE: flowers numerous, small, subtended by bracts, in short terminal spike; spikes elongating as flowers open; bracts narrowly lanceolate, much longer than buds. *Flower*: pink or rose purple; calyx 5-lobed, with short silky pubescence; petals 5, separate, all about same length.

FRUIT: legume, pubescent; seeds 1 or 2.

NOTE: uncommon in the Big Thicket.

MGP   April–June

Devil's shoestring (goat's-rue)   [p. 84]
Tephrosia virginiana (L.) Pers.
(Tef-roh'-zee-ah   vir-jin-ee-ay'-nah)

Strictly erect perennial 12–28 in. tall, with silvery silky pubescence mostly throughout; roots and stem base woody; stems 1–several, usually not branching.

LEAVES: alternate, petioled, compound; blade divided into commonly 15–

25 leaflets; leaflets elliptic to narrowly oblong, $\frac{1}{2}$–$1\frac{1}{4}$ in. long, less than $\frac{1}{4}$ in. wide, sharply pointed at tip.

INFLORESCENCE: flowers numerous, short-pedicelled, with 2–10 at each node of a terminal or axillary raceme; racemes erect, short-peduncled, $1\frac{1}{4}$–4 in. long. *Flower*: white, yellow, and rose, $\frac{1}{2}$–$\frac{3}{4}$ in. long; calyx 5-lobed; petals 5; banner broad, clawed, lemon yellow to cream-colored on outer surface and silky-pubescent, cream to white on inner surface; wing petals rose or rarely white, broadly oblong, united near tip, the clawed blades with earlike appendages near base on upper surface; keel petals rose-colored.

FRUIT: legume, flattened, linear, straight or curved, $1\frac{3}{8}$–$2\frac{1}{8}$ in. long, about $\frac{1}{4}$ in. wide; seeds 6–11.

OFS (LBU) April–June

Multi-bloom tephrosia [p. 61]
Tephrosia onobrychoides Nutt.
(Tef-roh'-zee-ah oh-noh-brih-ko'-ih-deez)

Usually sprawling, stout, pubescent perennial from woody base; stems 1–several, 24–28 in. long.

LEAVES: alternate, petioled, compound; blade once divided into usually 13–25 leaflets; leaflets variable, mostly narrowly spatulate, narrowly elliptic or narrowly oblong, $\frac{3}{4}$–$2\frac{1}{8}$ in. long, $\frac{1}{4}$–$\frac{5}{8}$ in. wide, rounded or blunt at tip.

INFLORESCENCE: flowers several, pedicelled, loosely spaced in elongated showy raceme; racemes long-peduncled, narrow, slender, terminal or from leaf axils, 4–16 in. long. *Flower*: white, becoming pink to dark rosy red in age, pink or purple in drying, to $\frac{3}{4}$ in. long; calyx 5-lobed; petals 5; banner clawed, wide-spreading, erect, with silky pubescence on outer surface; wing petals broadly oblong, clawed, with earlike appendages near base of blade.

FRUIT: legume, pubescent, straight or curved in tip portion, $1\frac{1}{4}$–$3\frac{1}{4}$ in. long, to $\frac{1}{4}$ in. wide; seeds 3–10.

LBS (LBU) April–September

Kentucky wisteria [p. 48]
Wisteria frutescens (L.) Poir. var. *macrostachya* T. & G.
(Wis-tee'-ree-ah froo-tes'-senz mak-roh-stay'-kee-ah)

Trailing, sprawling, or high-climbing, robust, essentially glabrous woody vine.

LEAVES: alternate, stipuled, petioled, compound; blade once divided into usually 9 leaflets; leaflets opposite, with terminal leaflet, short-petioled, thin, broadly lanceolate, $1\frac{1}{4}$–$3\frac{3}{4}$ in. long, rounded or notched at base.

INFLORESCENCE: flowers numerous, pedicelled, in large showy raceme, racemes terminal and axillary, drooping, 8–12 in. long. *Flower*: purple, lilac, or bluish purple, about ¾ in. long, sweetly fragrant; calyx 2-lipped; petals 5; banner broad, erect; wing petals shorter than banner, with prominent earlike appendages at base of blade; keel petals united at tip.

FRUIT: legume, glabrous, linear, flattened, 2¾–8 in. long; seeds few to numerous.

NOTE: A native species, this plant is often placed under the name *W. macrostachya* T. & G. but has never been adequately transferred to the species level according to the *International Code of Botanical Nomenclature*.

SOF   (POF)   April–August

Bladder pod   [p. 42]
Sesbania vesicaria (Jacq.) Ell.
(Sez-bay'-nee-ah   veh-sih-kay'-ree-ah)

Erect, robust, glabrous or sparsely pubescent shrubby annual to 10 ft. tall, commonly lower, branching in upper portion; stems and branches bright green.

LEAVES: alternate, short-petioled, not crowded, compound; blade divided into 20–40 opposite leaflets; leaflets linear or narrowly oblong, to 1½ in. long, ¼ in. wide.

INFLORESCENCE: flowers few, short-pedicelled, in peduncled raceme; racemes showy, axillary, shorter than leaves; peduncle 2–4¾ in. long. *Flower*: yellowish, tinged with pink or red, to ⅜ in. long; calyx bell-shaped, usually wider than long, 5-lobed; petals 5; banner erect, longer than other petals; wing petals long-clawed; keel petals long-clawed, strongly arched.

FRUIT: legume, dry, elongated, inflated, beaked at tip, somewhat cylindrical to ellipsoid, 1–3⅛ in. long, ½–¾ in. thick, constricted between seeds, separating at maturity into 2 layers; seeds 2.

NOTE: probably native of West Indies; seeds reportedly poisonous to cattle.

POF   (SOF)   August–October

Rattlebush   [p. 48]
Sesbania drummondii (Rydb.) Cory
(Sez-bay'-nee-ah   drum-mun'-dee-eye)

Erect, conspicuously green, glabrous or sparsely pubescent herbaceous perennial 2–10 ft. tall; stem from woody base, usually much-branched in upper portion, occasionally dying back in winter.

LEAVES: alternate, short-petioled, 4–8 in. long, compound; blade once divided into 20–50 leaflets; leaflets linear or narrowly oblong, mostly ½–1¼ in. long, about ¼ in. wide.

INFLORESCENCE: flowers few to several, long-pedicelled, in raceme; racemes showy, peduncled, axillary, shorter than leaves; peduncles to 2 in. long.

Flower: yellow, often lined with red, about ½ in. long; petals 5; banner erect, longer than other petals; wing petals long-clawed; keel petals prominently arched.

FRUIT: legume, dry, short-beaked, elongated, 2–2⅜ in. long, about ⅜ in. wide, conspicuously 4-winged for total length; seeds several.

NOTE: native species; seeds reportedly poisonous to cattle; mature seeds are loose in pod and rattle when moved.

SOF (POF) June–September

Showy sesbania [p. 48]
Sesbania punicea (Cav.) Bent.
(Sez-bay'-nee-ah poo-nis'-ee-ah)

Erect, weak, deciduous shrub 3–6 ft. tall; stem branching in upper portion.

LEAVES: alternate, short-petioled, not crowded, compound; blade divided into 12–40 leaflets; leaflets linear or narrowly oblong, to 1¼ in. long, about ¼ in. wide.

INFLORESCENCE: flowers 10–30, pedicelled, in showy peduncled raceme; racemes axillary, often drooping, usually shorter than foliage; peduncles to 1¼ in. long. *Flower*: rose red to red orange, ½–¾ in. long; petals 5; banner erect, longer than other petals; wing petals long-clawed; keel petals prominently arched.

FRUIT: legume, dry, slender, conspicuously 4-winged, 2–3⅛ in. long, about ½ in. thick; seeds several.

NOTE: infrequent to rare in East Texas and western Louisiana; native of South America.

SOF (POF) May–July

Bristly locust [p. 92]
Robinia hispida L.
(Roh-bin'-ee-ah his'-pih-dah)

Erect, much-branched shrub or small tree to 8 ft. tall, forming colonies from rhizomes or root sprouts; stems and branches pubescent; pubescence dense, stiff, coarse, bristly to the touch.

LEAVES: alternate, short-petioled, stipuled, deciduous, densely pubescent, compound; stipules spinelike; blade once divided into 7–19 leaflets; leaflets alternate, broadly spatulate or oblong, ½–2 in. long, 1¾ in. wide, rounded at base, with short sharp point at tip.

INFLORESCENCE: flowers few to many, pedicelled, in raceme from leaf axil of current season's growth; racemes peduncled, drooping, open to dense, usually shorter than leaves. *Flower*: dark pink to rose; calyx bristly, 2-lipped, with upper 2 lobes shorter than lower 3; petals 5; banner erect, wide-spreading; wing petals with basal earlike appendages; keel petals incurved, united near tip.

FRUIT: legume, densely covered with gland-tipped pubescence, flattened, broadly linear; seeds few to several.

NOTE: uncommon in the Big Thicket, probably introduced from eastern mountainous states.

R   May–June

Bent-pod milk-vetch   [p. 92]

Astragalus distortus T. & G. var. *engelmannii* (Sheld.) M. E. Jones

(As-trag′-ah-lus   dis-tor′-tus   en-gel-man′-nee-eye)

Low, sprawling, short-lived perennial from knotty woody base; plant much-branched and wide-spreading in flattened, circular fashion, with sparse rather stiff pubescence.

LEAVES: alternate, stipuled, petioled, compound; blade divided into 13–25 leaflets; leaflets oval to almost round, less than ½ in. long, blunt or shallowly notched at tip; leaves in basal portion of plant often smaller.

INFLORESCENCE: flowers many, pedicelled, in rather dense erect axillary raceme; racemes usually many, opening almost together and forming a conspicuous circle. *Flower*: generally pink purple to pale lilac; calyx 5-lobed; petals 5; banner erect, pale in center, ⅜–½ in. long; wing petals pale on tip, shorter than banner; keel petals about ¼ in. long, united at tip.

FRUIT: legume, exserted from calyx, half-moon-shaped, to 1 in. long, ¼ in. across, becoming almost black at maturity, opening only after falling and weathering on ground; seeds 15–28.

R   (LBU)   April–June

Joint vetch   [p. 48]

Aeschynomene indica L.

(Es-kih-nom′-ih-nee   in′-dih-kah)

Erect, much-branched perennial 20 in. to 8 ft. tall, dying back to underground stem each year, glabrous to rough with bristly pubescence.

LEAVES: alternate, stipuled, short-petioled, compound; stipules with small appendages below point of attachment; blade once divided into 19–63 alternate leaflets; leaflets usually becoming smaller in tip portion of leaf; terminal leaflet present.

INFLORESCENCE: flowers 1–3, pedicelled, in raceme; racemes terminal or axillary; pedicels subtended by minutely toothed bracts. *Flower*: creamy to yellowish or pale salmon-colored; calyx 2-lipped, glabrous, persistent; petals 5; banner erect, to ⅜ in. long; wing and keel petals much smaller.

FRUIT: legume, long-stalked, with 5–14 joints, slender, flat, to 2 in. long,

$\frac{1}{8}$ in. wide, constricted between joints and falling apart when mature into 1-seeded sections.

NOTE: local in habitat; rare in East Texas and western Louisiana.

SOF (POF) August–September

Pencil-flower [p. 68]
Stylosanthes biflora (L.) B.S.P.
(Sty-loh-san′-theez bye-floh′-rah)

Erect to sprawling, herbaceous perennial 8 in. to 2 ft. tall, glabrous to densely pubescent; stems few to many, usually somewhat woody at base, often branching from base, becoming wiry and bushy-branched in upper portion.

LEAVES: alternate, stipuled, short-petioled, compound; stipules slightly shorter than petiole and united with petiole almost to full stipule length, bristly pubescent; petiole to $\frac{3}{4}$ in. long; blade divided into 3 leaflets; leaflets with bristly pubescence, conspicuously veined, commonly $\frac{1}{2}$–$\frac{3}{4}$ in. long, bristle-pointed at tip.

INFLORESCENCE: flowers 2–6, short-pedicelled, in short terminal raceme; racemes less than $\frac{1}{2}$ in. long, closely subtended by reduced leaves. *Flower*: orange yellow, to $\frac{3}{8}$ in. long; calyx glabrous, tubular in lower portion and pedicellike, 5-lobed; petals 5; banner broad, erect, less than $\frac{3}{8}$ in. long; wing petals oblong, folded forward; keel petals incurved.

FRUIT: legume, sessile, 2-jointed, flat, less than $\frac{1}{4}$ in. wide; joints separating at maturity with only the upper joint containing fertile seed.

LBU April–November

Viperina [p. 84]
Zornia bracteata J. F. Gmel.
(Zor′-nee-ah brak-tee-ay′-tah)

Low, herbaceous perennial from long tough woody root; stems several to numerous, wiry, much-branched, spreading or trailing and forming small to extensive mats on ground.

LEAVES: alternate, stipuled, petioled, compound; stipules free from petiole, broadly spatulate, with small flaplike lobe at base below point of attachment; petiole as long as leaflets; blade divided into 4 leaflets, the leaflets to $1\frac{1}{4}$ in. long.

INFLORESCENCE: flowers 3–10, opening 1 at a time, in slender erect spike; spikes becoming elongated in fruit; each flower subtended by 2 leaflike bracts; bracts grooved, erect, closely appressed, fringed with hairs. *Flower*: bright yellow, to $\frac{1}{2}$ in. long; calyx 2-lipped; petals 5; banner almost round, less than $\frac{1}{2}$ in. long, clawed, much larger than other petals; wing petals short-clawed; keel petals incurved, boat-shaped.

FRUIT: legume, flattened, elongated, divided into 2–7 bristly nonopening joints; seeds 1 per joint.

OFS   June–September

Bare-stem tick-trefoil   [p. 68]
Desmodium nudiflorum (L.) DC.
(Dez-moh'-dee-um   noo-dih-floh'-rum)

Erect to almost erect, slender, 2-stemmed perennial; one stem unbranched, sterile, bearing a whorl of leaves near top; flowering stem leafless, as tall as or exceeding leaves.

LEAVES: usually all whorled, 4–7, petioled, compound; petiole to 5 in. long, pubescent; blade divided into 3 leaflets; leaflets sparsely pubescent on upper surface, glaucous and somewhat pubescent on lower surface; terminal leaflet broadly elliptic to broadly lanceolate or broadly spatulate, 1¾–4¾ in. long, 1⅜–3⅛ in. wide, rather wedge-shaped at base, abruptly sharp-pointed at tip; lateral leaflets smaller, unequal on sides near base.

INFLORESCENCE: flowers few to many, small, pedicelled, in long narrow erect raceme; racemes usually several, forming terminal panicle. *Flower*: dark pink to purplish, rarely whitish, ¼–⅜ in. long; calyx 2-lipped, pubescent; petals 5; banner oblong to almost round, narrowed or clawed at base; wing petals oblong; keel petals nearly straight.

FRUIT: legume, exceeding calyx, with dense hooked pubescence, flat, separating into 1–4 joints at maturity; upper margin straight; lower margin deeply indented, the indentations broadly U-shaped; seeds 1 per joint.

NOTE: uncommon in East Texas and western Louisiana.

LBU   (BMLS)   July–September

Panicled desmodium   [p. 69]
Desmodium paniculatum (L.) DC.
(Dez-moh'-dee-um   pa-nik-yoo-lay'-tum)

Erect perennial to 3 ft. tall from elongated branching root; stems usually several, glabrous to sparsely pubescent, slender, angled, marked with lengthwise lines, often branched in upper portion of plant.

LEAVES: alternate, stipuled, long-petioled, compound; blade divided into 3 leaflets; leaflets usually somewhat pubescent on both surfaces, narrowly lanceolate to narrowly elliptic; terminal leaflet 1½–4 in. long, to 1 in. wide; lateral leaflets similar, slightly smaller, fringed with hairs.

INFLORESCENCE: flowers few to several, pedicelled, in loosely branched panicles. *Flower*: dark pink or magenta; calyx with stiff pubescence, 2-lobed; upper lobe deeply 2-toothed; petals 5; banner sharply curved backward, narrowed at base; wing petals oblong, somewhat folded together with keel petals between; keel petals united at tip.

FRUIT: legume, densely pubescent with hooked hairs, flat, straight on upper margin, abruptly angled on lower margin, separating at maturity into 1–5 triangular joints; seeds 1 per joint.

NOTE: one of the largest and showiest of the *Desmodiums* in East Texas and western Louisiana.

LBU   May–September

Slender bush clover [p. 92]

Lespedeza virginica (L.) Britt.

(Les-peh-dee′-zah   vir-jin′-ih-kah)

Strictly erect, slender, pubescent perennial 1–5 ft. tall; stems solitary or few from base and clumped, very leafy, occasionally branched in upper portion.

LEAVES: alternate, numerous, crowded along stem, stipuled, petioled, compound; blade divided into 3 leaflets; leaflets sparsely pubescent on upper surface, linear to narrowly oblong, $\frac{1}{2}$–$1\frac{1}{2}$ in. long, 3–10 times as long as broad.

INFLORESCENCE: flowers 4–8, borne in pairs, small, short-pedicelled, in very short axillary raceme; racemes numerous, crowded along stem, usually exceeded by subtending leaves; both chasmogamous and cleistogamous flowers present. *Flower*: purplish; calyx 5-lobed, pubescent, persistent; petals 5; banner erect, oblong or almost round; wing petals usually longer than banner and keel petals.

FRUIT: legume, pubescent, conspicuously net-veined, short, 1-jointed, flat, somewhat rounded, $\frac{1}{8}$–$\frac{1}{4}$ in. long, nonopening; seed 1.

R   (LBU)   August–October

Sericea (Chinese bush clover) [p. 92]

Lespedeza cuneata (Dumont) G. Don.

(Les-peh-dee′-zah   kyoo-nee-ay′-tah)

Erect, slender, somewhat shrubby, short-lived perennial 16–60 in. tall; stems solitary or clumped, wandlike, with sharp stiff pubescence, usually branched.

LEAVES: alternate, crowded on stem, stipuled, short-petioled, compound; blade divided into 3 leaflets; leaflets with short appressed pubescence, appearing silvery green, narrowly triangular, to $\frac{3}{4}$ in. long, blunt at tip.

INFLORESCENCE: flowers 2–4, borne in pairs, short-pedicelled, in very short axillary raceme; racemes numerous, mostly shorter than subtending leaves; both chasmogamous and cleistogamous flowers present. *Flower*: white or cream-colored with violet purple veins and purple throat, about $\frac{3}{8}$ in. long; calyx 5-lobed, persistent; petals 5; banner erect, oblong to almost round, clawed at base; wing and keel petals about equal in length.

FRUIT: legume, pubescent, 1-jointed, flattened, somewhat rounded, about ⅛ in. long, nonopening; seed 1.

NOTE: scattered and uncommon in East Texas and western Louisiana; native to eastern Asia and Australia.

R　　　August–October

Japanese bush clover [p. 92]
Lespedeza striata (Thunb.) H. & A.
(Les-peh-dee′-zah　stry-ay′-tah)

Erect or sprawling, pubescent annual mostly less than 16 in. tall from taproot; stem unbranched or much-branched.

LEAVES: alternate, stipuled, almost sessile, compound; blade divided into 3 leaflets; leaflets essentially glabrous, prominently and conspicuously veined, broadly spatulate to narrowly oblong, to ¾ in. long, ⅓–½ as wide.

INFLORESCENCE: flowers very small, short-pedicelled, solitary or 2–5 in short leafy axillary raceme; racemes many; only a few flowers opening at one time on plant. *Flower*: pale to dark pink; calyx 5-lobed, with bristly hairs along veins and margins; upper 2 lobes partly united; petals 5; banner erect, clawed, free or partially attached to the incurved keel.

FRUIT: legume, 1-jointed, very small, rather inconspicuously net-veined, almost covered by calyx, nonopening; seed 1, black, mottled.

NOTE: native of eastern Asia, becoming naturalized.

R　(LBU)　　June–September

Wood vetch [p. 80]
Vicia caroliniana Walt.
(Vis′-ee-ah　kair-oh-lin-ee-ay′-nah)

Trailing or climbing, slender, delicate, glabrous perennial to 3 ft. long, usually shorter.

LEAVES: alternate, stipuled, compound; blade divided into 10–24 leaflets, with terminal tendril; leaflets usually with 5–7 veins on each side, elliptic to broadly lanceolate, rounded at tip with sharp point.

INFLORESCENCE: flowers 7–20, pedicelled, in loose peduncled raceme; racemes 2¼–4 in. long, equal to or longer than subtending leaves. *Flower*: white, ¼–½ in. long; calyx densely pubescent; petals 5; wing petals united with keel; keel often blue-tipped.

FRUIT: legume, long-beaked, somewhat flattened, narrowly oblong, ½–1¼ in long; seeds 5–8.

NOTE: uncommon in the Big Thicket.

BMLS　　April–June

Pigeon-wings   [p. 69]
Clitoria mariana L.
(Kly-toh'-ree-ah   mair-ee-ay'-nah)

Erect to almost trailing but never twining, glabrous perennial 8–40 in. tall; stem slender, occasionally branched in upper portion.

LEAVES: alternate, stipuled, long-petioled, compound; stipules stiff, persistent; blade divided into 3 leaflets; leaflets much paler on lower surface, lanceolate, $3/4$–$3\frac{1}{8}$ in. long, entire.

INFLORESCENCE: flowers 1–3, pedicelled, showy, in peduncled axillary raceme; peduncles usually shorter than subtending petiole. *Flower*: bluish or lavender with darker markings, usually in upside-down position with banner at bottom; calyx somewhat tubular, 5-lobed, glabrous or pubescent; petals 5; banner to $2\frac{1}{2}$ in. long, $1\frac{1}{2}$ in. wide, not spurred at base, notched at tip; wing petals much smaller and attached to the prominently incurved keel.

FRUIT: legume, beaked, flattened, broadly linear, to $3\frac{1}{8}$ in. long, opening upon ripening; seeds 4–10, gluey.

NOTE: differs mainly from *Centrosema virginianum* in having more slender flowers and not twining.
LBU   (BMLS)   May–September

Butterfly pea   [p. 69]
Centrosema virginianum (L.) Benth.
(Sen-troh-see'-mah   vir-jin-ee-ay'-num)

Sprawling, trailing, usually vigorously twining, herbaceous perennial vine to 6 ft. long, more or less minutely pubescent throughout.

LEAVES: alternate, conspicuously net-veined, stipuled, long-petioled, compound; blade divided into 3 leaflets; leaflets quite variable in shape, from linear to broadly lanceolate or oblong, commonly $3/4$–$2\frac{1}{2}$ in. long, entire.

INFLORESCENCE: flowers 1–3, short-pedicelled, subtended by small leaf-like bracts, showy, in short axillary peduncled raceme; peduncles usually shorter than subtending leaves. *Flower*: purplish to pale lavender, often occuring in upside-down position with banner at bottom; calyx deeply 5-lobed, partly hidden by bracts; petals 5; banner $3/4$–$1\frac{1}{2}$ in. long, usually broader than long, wide-spreading, with small prominent spur at base, notched at tip; wing petals narrow; keel petals prominently curved.

FRUIT: legume, long-beaked, linear, flattened, $1\frac{1}{2}$–$4\frac{3}{4}$ in. long, the halves spirally twisted upon opening; seeds 4–10.
LBU   (OFS)   July–August

Groundnut   [p. 69]
Apios americana Medic. in Vorles
(Ay'-pee-us   a-mer-ih-kay'-nah)

Trailing or high-climbing, twining, herbaceous perennial vine 4–10 ft. long from rhizome; rhizome thickened at intervals to form series of small, potatolike tubers.

LEAVES: alternate, petioled, compound; petiole to 2¾ in. long; blade divided into 5–7 leaflets; leaflets usually pubescent, narrowly to broadly lanceolate, commonly ¾–2¾ in. long.

INFLORESCENCE: flowers numerous, pedicelled, in showy raceme; raceme short, dense, axillary, peduncled, usually shorter than foliage. *Flower*: brownish red to purplish brown, fragrant, about ⅜ in. long; calyx with short pubescence; petals 5; banner whitish on outer surface, brown red or purplish on inner surface; wing petals curved downward; keel petals very slender, prominently incurved.

FRUIT: legume, linear, somewhat flattened, 2–4 in. long, about ¼ in. wide, spirally twisted after opening; seeds 2–many.

NOTE: tubers edible; uncommon in East Texas and western Louisiana.
LBU   (SOF)   May–September

Coral bean (mamou)   [p. 84]
Erythrina herbacea L.
(Eh-rith-rye′-nah   her-bay′-see-ah)

Strictly erect, thorny perennial shrub to 6 ft. tall; stems usually several, often dying back in winter.

LEAVES: alternate, scattered along stem, stipuled, petioled, compound; petioles often prickly; blade divided into 3 leaflets; leaflets essentially glabrous, sometimes prickly beneath, broadly triangular in shape and basally shallowly lobed with the lobes wide-spreading, 3–5 in. long, ¾–4¼ in. wide.

INFLORESCENCE: flowers numerous, pedicelled, in showy peduncled terminal raceme; peduncles erect, leafless, 8–30 in. tall, from base of plant. *Flower*: red, 1¼–2⅛ in. long, appearing tubular; calyx somewhat tubular, glabrous, spurred basally; petals 5; banner long and narrow, to 2⅜ in. long, curved downward around style and filaments; wing and keel petals much smaller, mostly enclosed by folded banner.

FRUIT: legume, blackish, constricted between seeds, to 8¾ in. long; seeds several, large, scarlet, remaining in opened capsule, poisonous.
OFS   (SOF, LBU)   April–June

MaCree's milkpea   [p. 84]
Galactia macreei M. A. Curtis
(Ga-lak′-tee-ah   mak-ree′-eye)

Trailing or high-climbing, twining, minutely pubescent perennial vine; stems 20–60 in. long, branched, the branches alternate.

LEAVES: alternate, stipuled, compound; blade once divided into 3 leaflets;

leaflets thin, pliable, not conspicuously veined underneath as in some species, broadly linear to broadly lanceolate or oblong, usually 3/4–1 1/2 in. long, 1/4–3/4 in. wide, broadly rounded to shallowly notched at base, entire.

INFLORESCENCE: flowers solitary or in twos or threes, short-pedicelled, in axillary peduncled raceme; only 1 or 2 racemes at any node; peduncle long, slender, 1 1/2–2 3/4 in. long; raceme and peduncle together usually 4–12 in. long, sometimes longer. *Flower*: purple or pink with purple center, about 1/2 in. long; calyx 5-lobed, appearing 4-lobed; petals 5; banner erect; wing petals extending forward, shorter than keel; keel petals about 3/8 in. long.

FRUIT: legume, pubescent, straight, slender, 1 1/8–2 3/4 in. long, always above ground; seeds several.

NOTE: infrequent in the Big Thicket.

OFS   (LBU)   July–September

Least snoutbean   [p. 36]
Rhynchosia minima (L.) DC.
(Rin-koh'-zee-ah   min'-ih-mah)

Sprawling, trailing, or twining pubescent perennial vine; stems 1–several.

LEAVES: alternate, stipuled, long-petioled, compound; petiole as long as terminal leaflet to several times longer; blade divided into 3 leaflets; leaflets sparsely pubescent, resin-dotted, somewhat diamond-shaped to almost round, to 1 1/2 in. long.

INFLORESCENCE: flowers few to several, small, drooping, pedicelled, in axillary raceme; racemes 2–6 1/2 in. long, as long as subtending leaf petiole or longer. *Flower*: yellow, occasionally tinged with brown, about 1/4 in. long; calyx 5-lobed, the lobes narrowly lanceolate; petals 5, exceeding calyx; banner erect; wing petals shorter than keel.

FRUIT: legume, flattened, curved, 1/2–3/4 in. long; seeds 1 or 2.

MGP   (LBU, OFS)   April–December

Broad-leaf snoutbean   [p. 84]
Rhynchosia latifolia Nutt. in T. & G.
(Rin-koh'-zee-ah   lat-ih-foh'-lee-ah)

Erect, trailing or low-climbing, twining perennial vine, with dense soft pubescence at least on younger portions; stems 1–several, angled, branched.

LEAVES: alternate, stipuled, petioled, compound; petiole 1–3 in. long; blade divided into 3 leaflets; leaflets petioled, with soft downy pubescence on both surfaces, resin-dotted, broadly lanceolate to broadly diamond-shaped, 1 1/8–2 3/4 in. long; terminal leaflet largest and with longer petiole.

INFLORESCENCE: flowers few to several, pedicelled, in long raceme; raceme erect, axillary, peduncled, to 12 in. long, exceeding subtending leaves. *Flower*: yellow, to 1/2 in. long; calyx 2-lipped, to 2/3 in. long, deeply divided into 5 lanceolate lobes; petals 5, slightly shorter than calyx; banner extending forward to strictly erect; wing petals narrow; keel petals incurved.

FRUIT: legume, pubescent, flat, oblong; seeds 1 or 2.

OFS   (LBU)   May–August

Amberique bean [p. 48]
Strophostyles helvola (L.) Ell.

(Stroh-foh-sty′-leez   hel′-voh-lah)

Erect, later trailing or climbing annual vine; stems 1–several, sparsely pubescent, 1–8 ft. long.

LEAVES: alternate, stipuled, long-petioled, compound; stipules small, spreading, prominently veined, persistent; blade divided into 3 leaflets; leaflets broadly lanceolate or diamond-shaped to broadly elliptic, commonly 3-lobed and fiddle-shaped, broadly lobed to broadly triangular at base, if not lobed at base then 1–3 times as long as wide.

INFLORESCENCE: flowers few, short-pedicelled, subtended by bracts, in short raceme; raceme compact, axillary, peduncled; bracts at base of individual flowers sharp-pointed at tip, as long as calyx tube or longer; peduncles erect, 6–12 in. long. *Flower*: dark pink to purplish, fading greenish, to ⅝ in. long; calyx with short tube, more or less 2-lipped; petals 5; banner broad, recurved; keel petals united, very narrow, with darker-colored tip prominently incurved.

FRUIT: legume, sessile, pubescent, short-beaked, slender, somewhat cylindrical, 2–4 in. long, promptly opening at maturity; seeds several, woolly.

SOF   (POF, LBU)   June–September

Perennial wild bean [p. 69]
Strophostyles umbellata (Willd.) Britt.

(Stroh-foh-sty′-leez   um-bel-lay′-tah)

Trailing or climbing, twining pubescent vine from perennial root; stem slender, mostly branching horizontally from base, 2–6½ ft. long.

LEAVES: alternate, stipuled, petioled, compound; blade divided into 3 leaflets; leaflets variable, more or less lanceolate, never lobed, 2–8 times as long as broad, ¾–2 in. long, mostly broadly rounded at base and broadly rounded to sharp-pointed at tip.

INFLORESCENCE: flowers few, small, short-pedicelled, subtended by bracts, closley clustered in short axillary peduncled raceme; bracts at base of individual flowers blunt at tip, shorter than calyx; peduncles to 12 in. long. *Flower*: pink to purplish, fading greenish, about ½ in. long; calyx 2-lipped, twice as long as bracts or longer, fringed with hairs; petals 5; banner recurved or wide-spreading; keel petals very narrow, united, with darker-colored tip prominently incurved.

FRUIT: legume, sessile, pubescent, short-beaked, slender, somewhat cylindrical, 1⅛–2½ in. long; seeds several, woolly.
LBU   June–September

GERANIACEAE
(Geranium Family)

Carolina geranium   [p. 92]
Geranium carolinianum L.
(Jeh-ray'-nee-um   kair-oh-lin-ee-ay'-num)

Erect to sprawling, pubescent annual or biennial; stem unbranched or branching from base and in upper portion; branches occasionally lax and turning upward at tips, to 24 in. long.

LEAVES: alternate at base and along stem, usually opposite in flowering portion of plant, stipuled, petioled; blade to 2¾ in. long, almost round in outline, variously parted into 5–9 deeply toothed or lobed segments; ultimate segments narrowly oblong.

INFLORESCENCE: flowers paired, pedicelled, in cyme; cymes leafy, terminal on axillary peduncles or branches; pedicels subtended by narrow, pubescent bracts. *Flower*: pale pink to whitish; sepals 5, overlapping in bud, pubescent, with spinelike tips, persistent; petals 5, about ¼ in. long, about as long as sepals, broader near tip, alternating at base with 5 glands; pistil of 5 carpels, the carpels united and forming long beak.

FRUIT: capsulelike, composed of the 5 carpels; at maturity carpels split at base and coil toward tip; seeds 1 per carpel, prominently net-veined.
R   (LBU, OFS)   January–May

OXALIDACEAE
(Wood-sorrel Family)

Violet wood-sorrel   [p. 80]
Oxalis violacea L.
(Ox'-ah-lis   vye-oh-lay'-see-ah)

Erect, delicate, glabrous perennial 4–16 in. tall from scaly-coated bulb and slender stolons; plant containing acrid juice.

LEAVES: from base, long-petioled, compound; blade divided into 3 leaflets; leaflets fleshy, bright green on upper surface, sometimes reddish or purplish on lower surface, broadly spatulate, to 1 in. long, notched at tip, downwardly folded together at night or during cloudy weather.

INFLORESCENCE: flowers 4–19, pedicelled, in terminal peduncled cyme; peduncles slender, usually surpassing leaves; flowers closing at night and in cloudy weather, nodding in bud and after flowering. *Flower*: lavender to pinkish purple; sepals 5, glabrous, persistent; petals 5, wide-spreading, $1/2$–$3/4$ in. long; stamens 10; filaments united at base.

FRUIT: capsule, somewhat globelike, about $1/4$ in. long; seeds few to many, red, prominently net-veined.

NOTE: Plant blooms again August–October without leaves being present. BMLS   (LBU, OFS)   March–May

Yellow wood-sorrel [p. 85]
Oxalis priceae Small
(Ox'-ah-lis   pry'-see-ee)

Erect or sprawling, clumped, often moundlike, pubescent perennial to 16 in. tall, usually much lower, from slender elongate horizontal rhizome; stems usually leafy, much-branched.

LEAVES: alternate, long-petioled, compound; blade divided into 3 leaflets; leaflets mostly thin, bright green, sparsely pubescent, broadly spatulate, about $1/2$ in. wide, notched at tip, downwardly folded together at night or during cloudy weather.

INFLORESCENCE: flowers 1–7, pedicelled, in showy terminal peduncled umbel; peduncles much overtopping the stems or branches; flowers closing at night or during inclement weather, nodding before and after blooming. *Flower*: golden yellow; sepals 5, persistent; petals 5, $1/2$–$3/4$ in. long; stamens 10; filaments united at base.

FRUIT: capsule, about $1/2$ in. long; seeds few to many, red, prominently net-veined.

NOTE: plants with sour sap containing oxalic acid. OFS   (MGP, LBU)   April–May

LINACEAE
(Flax Family)

Stiff-stem flax [p. 69]
Linum rigidum Pursh var. *berlandieri* (Hook.) T. & G.
(Lye'-num   rig'-ih-dum   ber-lan-dee-er'-eye)

Stiffly erect, thin, glabrous annual 8–20 in. tall; stem unbranched in lower portion, few-branched in upper portion; branches slender, prominently angled.

LEAVES: alternate, sessile; blades erect, rigid, linear, $3/8$–$1\,1/4$ in. long, about $1/8$ in. wide; glands usually present at base of leaf.

INFLORESCENCE: flowers few, short-pedicelled, in open panicle. *Flower*: yellow, red at base of each petal; sepals 5, green, overlapping, about $1/2$ in. long; margins toothed, the teeth tipped with glands; petals 5, swirled in bud,

⅜–¾ in. long, falling early; stamens 5; pistil 1; styles 5, united almost entire length.

FRUIT: capsule, small, thick-walled, broadly ovoid, abruptly tapering to flattened base, composed of 5 carpels which open into 5 sections at maturity; seeds few to many, brown, flat, oily.

LBU   (OFS)   May–September

POLYGALACEAE
(Milkwort Family)

Maryland milkwort   [p. 61]
Polygala mariana Mill.
(Poh-lig'-ah-lah   mair-ee-ay'-nah)

Erect, slender annual 6–16 in. tall; stem unbranched or more frequently much-branched in upper portion of plant, sparsely pubescent.

LEAVES: alternate, sessile, usually erect; blade linear or the lower leaves spatulate, ¼–1 in. long, less than ⅛ in. wide, sharp-pointed at tip.

INFLORESCENCE: flowers numerous, essentially sessile, in terminal or axillary peduncled raceme; racemes at first compact and globelike, elongating as flowers open upward. *Flower*: pink or purplish; sepals 5; inner 2 sepals large, petallike, extending to sides as wings; petals 3, partly joined together into 3-lobed tube; lateral petal lobes longer than middle lobe; middle petal lobe thicker and fringed along margin; stamens usually 8, partly united with corolla tube.

FRUIT: capsule, very small, flattened, notched at tip, promptly falling; seeds 2, densely pubescent.

LBS   (LBU)   April–September

Pink milkwort   [p. 61]
Polygala incarnata L.
(Poh-lig'-ah-lah   in-kar-nay'-tah)

Erect, delicate, slender, glabrous, glaucous annual 6–24 in. tall; stem with lengthwise grooves, few-leaved, unbranched or sparsely branched.

LEAVES: opposite or whorled near base, alternate and scattered along stem, essentially sessile, soon falling; blade threadlike to linear, to about ¼ in. long, with sharp rigid point at tip.

INFLORESCENCE: flowers numerous, small, almost sessile, in terminal peduncled raceme; racemes dense, 2–3 times as long as thick, elongating as flowers open upward. *Flower*: rose purplish; sepals 5; inner 2 sepals large, petallike, extending to sides as wings; petals 3, forming long tube; tube prominently fringed at rim, about ¼ in. long, extending beyond wings; stamens usually 8, partially united with corolla tube.

FRUIT: capsule, small; seeds 2, pubescent; some or all of the fruit persistent below opened flowers.

LBS   (LBU)   May–September

Bitter milkwort (racemed milkwort) [p. 85]
Polygala polygama L.
(Poh-lig′-ah-lah   poh-lig′-ah-mah)

Erect to nearly erect, glabrous biennial or perennial 6–12 in. tall; stems 1–many, unbranched or sparsely branched.

LEAVES: alternate or lower leaves occasionally opposite, essentially sessile; blade fleshy, broadly linear to broadly spatulate, ½–1¼ in. long, to about ¼ in. wide, rounded or blunt at tip but with small sharp point.

INFLORESCENCE: flowers usually numerous, pedicelled, in very loose peduncled racemes from base of plant or late in season from axils of leaves; racemes elongating to 6 in. long; horizontal racemes of cleistogamous flowers borne at base of plant either below or just above soil surface. *Flower*: pink to pink purple, rarely whitish; sepals 5; outer 3 sepals green, with pink or white margins; inner 2 sepals large, petallike, extending to sides as wings, mostly pink; petals 3, forming tube, shorter than wings, with conspicuous tufted crest; stamens 8, partially united with corolla tube.

FRUIT: capsule, small, plump, to ⅛ in. long; seeds 2, black, densely pubescent, ellipsoid, short-pointed at base.

OFS   (LBU)   April–June

Bachelor's button [p. 61]
Polygala nana (Michx.) DC.
(Poh-lig′-ah-lah   nay′-nah)

Clumped, several-stemmed annual or biennial to 7 in. tall, usually much lower.

LEAVES: basal leaves clumped or rosettelike, usually numerous; blade succulent, 3- to 5-veined, spatulate, ½–1¾ in. long, to ⅝ in. wide; stem leaves alternate, few; blade linear or narrowly spatulate to broadly spatulate, ½–1½ in. long.

INFLORESCENCE: flowers numerous, essentially sessile, intermixed with mostly deciduous bracts, in short dense terminal peduncled raceme; racemes usually exceeding leaves. *Flower*: lemon yellow, turning green on drying; sepals 5; inner 2 sepals large, petallike, extending to sides as wings; petals 3, forming tube, the lower petal 3-lobed; stamens 6.

FRUIT: capsule, less than 1/16 in. across; seeds 2, woolly.

LBS   May–June

Yellow savannah milkwort [p. 61]

Polygala ramosa Ell.

(Poh-lig'-ah-lah ray-moh'-sah)

Erect, glabrous annual 6–16 in. tall from fibrous roots; stems 1–several, unbranched to few-branched.

LEAVES: basal leaves in small tuft or rosette; blade narrowly elliptic to broadly spatulate, to $\frac{3}{4}$ in. long, $\frac{1}{4}$ in. wide, narrowing into petiolelike base, rounded at tip; stem leaves very narrow, to 1 in. long; branch leaves linear, much reduced.

INFLORESCENCE: flowers numerous, small, pedicelled, intermixed with numerous bracts in loose showy raceme; racemes terminal or axillary; central raceme essentially sessile, with lateral racemes peduncled and forming a flat-topped panicle to $5\frac{1}{2}$ in. wide. *Flower*: yellow, turning dark bluish green on drying; sepals 5; inner 2 sepals large and petallike, extending to sides as wings; petals 3, united into tube, shorter than wings; tube fringed at rim; stamens 6.

FRUIT: capsule, very small; seeds 2, chestnut brown, plump, densely pubescent.

LBS   May–September

EUPHORBIACEAE
(Spurge Family)

Queen's delight [p. 85]

Stillingia sylvatica L.

(Stil-lin'-gee-ah sil-vat'-ih-kah)

Erect to wide-spreading, glabrous, herbaceous perennial with milky sap, to 3 ft. tall, from deep root; stems few to several from woody base, erect, thick, commonly forming shrubby clump, branched; branches short and immediately below an inflorescence, each branch usually ending in a terminal inflorescence.

LEAVES: alternate, short-petioled or almost sessile, with 2 small glands at base; blade narrowly lanceolate or broadly spatulate, commonly $1\frac{3}{8}$–$2\frac{3}{4}$ in. long, 4–7 times as long as broad, narrowed at base and tip; margins sharply toothed and with small deciduous glands between teeth.

INFLORESCENCE: flowers few to numerous, in terminal spike; spikes composed of staminate and pistillate flowers, each flower in the axil of a minute bract; bract with 2 conspicuous saucer-shaped glands near base; staminate flowers in clusters at upper nodes of spike; pistillate flowers few and at lower nodes of spike. *Flower*: yellowish; petals none; calyx of staminate flowers cup-shaped, minute, obscurely 2-lobed; stamens 2; calyx of pistillate flowers shallowly to deeply 3-lobed; stigmas 3, red.

FRUIT: capsule, green, hard, tough, globelike, prominently 3-lobed, less than ⅜ in. long, leaving a 3-lobed disk upon falling from plant; seeds 3, grayish white.

OFS   (LBU)   May–June

Bull nettle   [p. 85]
Cnidoscolus texanus (Muell. Arg.) Small
(Nye-dos′-koh-lus   tex-ay′-nus)

Erect or sprawling perennial with milky sap, to 40 in. tall, usually lower, from deep roots; roots to 40 in. long, 8 in. thick; stems green, several, branching above or below ground; entire plant covered with long stiff translucent stinging hairs.

LEAVES: alternate, long-petioled; blade rounded in outline, 3–6 in. across, deeply 3- to 5-lobed; lobes usually coarsely and irregularly toothed or lobed again; veins especially densely covered with stinging hairs.

INFLORESCENCE: flowers few, in compound, many-branched peduncled terminal cyme; each small cluster in cyme with both staminate and pistillate flowers; staminate flowers in outer portion of cluster; pistillate flower 1, truly terminal, in center of cluster. *Flower*: white, fragrant, about 1 in. across; sepals 5, petallike; petals absent; sepals of staminate flowers united basally into long tube, deeply 4-lobed at rim, bearing some stinging hairs on outer surface; stamens 10, within tube; sepals of pistillate flowers separated essentially to base, falling soon after fertilization; styles 3.

FRUIT: capsule, covered with stinging hairs, somewhat cylindrical, to ¾ in. long, separating into 3 sections; seeds 3, brownish white, smooth, somewhat cylindrical, edible when ripe.

OFS   (LBU)   March–September

Snow-on-the-prairie   [p. 36]
Euphorbia bicolor Engelm. & Gray
(Yoo-for′-bee-ah   bye′-kuh-lor)

Erect, rather stout annual with milky sap, 1–3 ft. tall; stem solitary, short-branching in upper portion; plant with long, shaggy pubescence in younger portions, becoming glabrous with age.

LEAVES: alternate, mostly sessile, with upper leaves usually occurring in threes; blade rather thick, narrowly oval or lanceolate, 2–4 in. long, 1/5 to ⅓ as wide.

INFLORESCENCE: flowers numerous, inconspicuous, in terminal cluster; clusters several, forming larger clusters and surrounded by numerous leaflike bracts; bracts conspicuously white-margined, linear, commonly 1⅛–2⅜ in. long, about ⅛ in. wide; both staminate and pistillate flowers borne in each cluster. *Flower*: white; petals absent; each staminate flower represented by 1 stamen; pistillate flower solitary, represented by 1 pistil; stamens and pistil borne in cup-shaped structure; cup with 5 glands around rim, each gland with very small petallike appendage and the whole appearing as a 5-petaled flower; stamens about 35, around inside margin of cup; pistil 1, pedicelled, in center of cup; pedicel slender, elongated at maturity.

FRUIT: capsule, globelike, separating into 3 sections; seeds 3, blackish, globelike.

NOTE: Contact with plant may cause dermatitis in some persons.

MGP   (POF)   July–October

Flowering spurge [p. 85]
Euphorbia corollata L.
(Yoo-for'-bee-ah   kor-oh-lay'-tah)

Erect or nearly erect perennial with milky sap, 8–32 in. tall, glabrous or minutely pubescent; stem usually solitary, branched; branches few, alternate in lower portion of plant, opposite or whorled and forking in pairs in upper portion.

LEAVES: alternate in lower portion, opposite or whorled in flowering portion of plant, glabrous; leaves along midstem short-petioled; blade mostly oblong, sometimes linear, $\frac{3}{4}$–$1\frac{1}{2}$ in. long, tapering to base, rounded at tip; leaves in flowering portion essentially sessile, much reduced.

INFLORESCENCE: flowers numerous, inconspicuous, in solitary peduncled cluster in forks of upper branches; both staminate and pistillate flowers in each cluster; flower cluster appearing as 1 flower. *Flower*: white, petals absent; each staminate flower represented by one stamen; pistillate flower solitary and represented by 1 pistil; stamens and pistil borne in cup-shaped structure; cup with 5 glands around rim, each gland with small petallike appendage, the whole appearing as a 5-petaled flower; stamens 10–15, around inside margin of cup; pistil 1, pedicelled, in center of cup; pedicel slender, elongated at maturity.

FRUIT: capsule, globelike, less than $\frac{1}{4}$ in. long, separating into 3 sections; seeds 3, white, smooth, minute.

OFS   (LBU)   May–December

Wild poinsettia [p. 92]
Euphorbia cyathophora Murr.
(Yoo-for'-bee-ah   sye-ah-thof'-oh-rah)

Erect, glabrous annual with milky sap, 8–20 in. tall, from yellowish taproot; stem solitary, thick, greenish, sparsely branched to much-branched; branches opposite and at right angles near base of plant, alternate at midstem, whorled and forking in terminal portion.

LEAVES: opposite, occasionally alternate; blade glossy green, rather thin, minutely pubescent on lower surface, linear to lanceolate or spatulate, fiddle-shaped if broad, 2½–6 in. long, sharp-pointed at both ends, entire or prominently and largely toothed; upper leaves often with conspicuous red blotches near base.

INFLORESCENCE: flowers many, inconspicuous, in terminal cluster; clusters several, forming larger cluster and closely subtended by upper leaves; both staminate and pistillate flowers borne in each cluster. *Flower*: greenish; petals absent; each staminate flower represented by 1 stamen; pistillate flower solitary, represented by 1 pistil; stamens and pistil borne in cup-shaped structure; cup with only 1 gland at rim; gland sessile, green, deeply cupped, with narrow oblong opening, without petallike appendage; stamens many per cup; pistil 1 per cup, pedicelled, pedicel long-exserted and drooping at maturity.

FRUIT: capsule, green, smooth, ovoid or globelike, about ⅛ in. long, separating into 3 sections; seeds 3, dark brown, covered with pale brown warty projections.

NOTE: often cultivated.

R   (OFS)   May–September

Heart-leaf euphorbia   [p. 85]
Euphorbia cordifolia Ell.
(Yoo-for′-bee-ah   kor-dih-foh′-lee-ah)

Trailing or mat-forming, glabrous annual, with milky sap, from taproot; stems numerous, reddish, usually 6–24 in. long.

LEAVES: opposite at nodes, stipuled, essentially sessile; stipules pubescent when young, parted to base into few to several threadlike segments; blade from almost round to oblong, to ½ in. long, often notched at base, entire.

INFLORESCENCE: flowers numerous, inconspicuous, in solitary clusters at nodes and branch tips; clusters often congested at upper, shortened internodes; both staminate and pistillate flowers in each cluster. *Flower*: white, petals absent; each staminate flower represented by 1 stamen; pistillate flower solitary, represented by 1 pistil; stamens and pistil borne in cup-shaped structure; cup with 5 glands around rim, each gland with very small petallike appendage, the whole appearing as a 5-petaled flower; stamens 29–44, around inside margin of cup; pistil 1, near center of cup, long-exserted at maturity.

FRUIT: capsule, glabrous, prominently 3-angled, wider in lower portion, very small; seeds 3, broad and thick, obscurely wrinkled.

OFS   June–September

CYRILLACEAE
(Cyrilla Family)

Black titi   [p. 57]

Cyrilla racemiflora L.

(Sye-ril'-lah   ra-see-mee-floh'-rah)

Tall shrub or small tree to 30 ft. tall, often lower, usually forming large colonies.

LEAVES: alternate, petioled, semievergreen, usually at ends of branches; petiole to ¼ in. long; blade thick, leathery, glabrous, somewhat spatulate, to 4 in. long, 1½ in. wide, rounded or pointed at tip, entire.

INFLORESCENCE: flowers numerous, pedicelled, in raceme; pedicels to ⅛ in. long, with persistent, conspicuous bract at base and 2 persistent bracts at tip just below calyx; racemes several, slender, lateral, clustered, wide-spreading, arising from base of new twigs, to 7 in. long. *Flower*: white, fragrant; calyx 5-parted, small, white, persistent, subtended by bracts; petals 5, separate, to ⅛ in. long; stamens 5, shorter than petals; style solitary, persistent; stigma 2-lobed.

FRUIT: drupelike, brown or gray, nonopening, less than ⅛ in. long, with spongy inner portion; seeds 2.

NOTE: There are two distinct forms of this plant: one form with racemes less than 4 in. long and almost round fruits blunt at the tip, and a second form with racemes over 4 in. long and narrowly ovoid fruits pointed at tip. BGB   May–July

AQUIFOLIACEAE
(Holly Family)

Gallberry holly   [p. 57]

Ilex coriacea (Pursh.) Chapm.

(Eye'-lex   kor-ee-ay'-see-ah)

Large shrub to 15 ft. tall, usually forming rather dense colonies; twigs slender, minutely pubescent.

LEAVES: alternate, petioled, evergreen; petiole stout, minutely pubescent; blade often rigid, leathery, dark green and shiny on upper surface, paler and gland-dotted beneath, the midrib conspicuous on both surfaces, elliptic to somewhat spatulate, to 3½ in. long, 1⅜ in. wide, tapering to base; margins entire or with several small teeth in upper portion.

INFLORESCENCE: flowers solitary or in small clusters, pedicelled, usually axillary; staminate and pistillate flowers appearing on separate plants; pedicels of staminate flowers glabrous, to ¼ in. long; pedicels of pistillate flowers pubescent, to ⅝ in. long. *Flower*: white; calyx glabrous, minute, 4- to 9-lobed, persistent; petals 4–9, united at base, irregularly toothed, to about ⅛ in. long; stamens in staminate flowers as long as petals; ovary in pistillate flowers flattened, somewhat globelike.

FRUIT: drupe, black, shiny, somewhat globelike, to 5/16 in. wide, crowned with persistent stigma; stones 4–9, flattened, smooth; seeds 1 per stone.

BGB   March–April

CELASTRACEAE
(Staff-tree Family)

Strawberry-bush   [p. 80]
Euonymus americanus L.
(Yoo-on'-ih-mus   a-mer-ih-kay'-nus)

Erect or sprawling shrub to 6 ft. tall, commonly much lower; branches slender, straight, green-barked, 4-sided.

LEAVES: opposite, essentially sessile, evergreen; blade glabrous, bright green on upper surface, pale below, broadly lanceolate to elliptic, to 4 in. long, 1⅜ in. wide; margins finely toothed, the teeth rounded.

INFLORESCENCE: flowers solitary or in few-flowered cymes from leaf axils. *Flower*: greenish purple, about ½ in. across; sepals 5, united at base, spreading flat; petals 5, rounded, spreading, distinctly short-clawed; stamens 5, short, inserted on margin of flat fleshy 5-angled disk; stigma in center of disk.

FRUIT: capsule, conspicuous, rose red, globelike, somewhat flattened, roughly warty on outer surface, splitting into 3–5 lobes at maturity; seeds 1–4, enclosed within the shiny scarlet ovary membrane, with the group of seeds appearing as one seed; one "seed" attached at each lobe of opened capsule, hanging downward.

NOTE: plant sometimes colloquially called "hearts-abusting-with-love."

BMLS   (SOF, BGB)   May–June

HIPPOCASTANACEAE
(Buckeye Family)

Red buckeye   [p. 69]
Aesculus pavia L.
(Esk'-yoo-lus   pay'-vee-ah)

Large shrub or small tree, often clumped, to 30 ft. tall, commonly much lower; bark smooth, gray or brownish, with unpleasant odor.

LEAVES: opposite, petioled, compound, deciduous; petiole to 6 in. long; blade dark green, shiny, divided into usually 5 leaflets; leaflets essentially sessile, glabrous or occasionally pubescent on lower surface, lanceolate to elliptic or spatulate, to 7 in. long, 2¾ in. wide, tapering to base, abruptly sharp-pointed at tip, irregularly sharply toothed.

INFLORESCENCE: flowers numerous, pedicelled, in large loose showy terminal panicle of both staminate and perfect flowers. *Flower*: scarlet or scarlet and yellow, to 1¼ in. long; calyx red, long, tubular, irregularly 5-lobed; petals 4, closely appressed, with gland-tipped hairs on margins; upper pair of petals longer than lower pair, long-clawed, with small spatulate blade; lower pair of petals with wide, almost round blade; stamens 6–8, sometimes slightly longer than upper petals.

FRUIT: capsule, pale brown, smooth, leathery, somewhat globelike, to 2⅜ in. across; seeds usually 2 or 3, sometimes 1 by abortion, dark brown with prominent pale scar, smooth, globelike, ¾–1½ in. across.

NOTE: seeds bitter, narcotic. Both seeds and young foliage are considered dangerous poisons.

LBU   (SOF, BMLS)   March–May

SAPINDACEAE
(Soap-berry Family)

Common balloon-vine   [p. 41]
Cardiospermum halicacabum L.
(Car-dee-oh-sper′-mum   hal-ih-kay′-keh-bum)

Sprawling or low-climbing, essentially glabrous to sparsely pubescent annual vine to several feet long, supported by tendrils; stem wiry, several-ribbed, much-branched.

LEAVES: alternate, stipuled, petioled, compound; blade once divided into 3 segments, these again divided into 3 leaflets; leaflets petioled, narrowly lanceolate to broadly lanceolate or oblong, to about 3⅛ in. long, 1¼ in. wide; margins deeply and sharply lobed and toothed.

INFLORESCENCE: flowers few, small, inconspicuous, in peduncled cluster; peduncles slender, axillary, bearing 2 threadlike tendrils at tip. *Flower*: whitish or pale yellowish; sepals 4, with 2 large and 2 small; petals 4, to about ⅛ in. long, 2 large and 2 small, with winglike appendage near base; stamens 8.

FRUIT: capsule, thin, soft, inflated and bladderlike, obovoid to somewhat globelike, 1⅛–1¾ in. across; seeds 3, black, less than ¼ in. across.

POF   (MGP)   June–November

BALSAMINACEAE
(Touch-me-not Family)

Spotted touch-me-not (jewel-weed)   [p. 49]
Impatiens capensis Meerb.
(Im-pay'-shenz ka-pen'-sis)

Erect, glabrous annual to 5 ft. tall; stem hollow, succulent, with watery juice, usually much-branched in upper portion.

LEAVES: alternate, petioled; petiole to 4 in. long; blade pale green on upper surface, pale or glaucous below, broadly lanceolate, to 4¾ in. long, 3 in. wide, broadly rounded at base, bluntly pointed at tip, coarsely toothed.

INFLORESCENCE: flowers solitary or few in cluster, long-pedicelled, showy, from leaf axils; pedicel threadlike, drooping, to ¾ in. long, appearing to be attached near lip of flower; both chasmogamous and cleistogamous flowers produced. *Flower*: orange with crimson spots, ¾–1¼ in. long; sepals apparently 4; 1 sepal very large, petallike and saclike, attached to pedicel, notched at tip, prominently spurred at base; spur somewhat curled or abruptly bent forward toward lip; petals 3; upper petal often broader than long; each lateral petal deeply 2-lobed.

FRUIT: capsule, to ¾ in. long, separating into 5 parts at maturity, sharply coiling upward from base and exposively ejecting seeds when touched; seeds several, ridged.

NOTE: rare in the Big Thicket.
SOF   May–August

RHAMNACEAE
(Buckthorn Family)

New Jersey tea   [p. 70]
Ceanothus americanus L. var. *pitcheri* T. & G.
(See-ah-noh'-thus a-mer-ih-kay'-nus pitch'-er-eye)

Low, small-stemmed shrub to 3 ft. tall, usually lower; flowering branches erect, new each year; plant from deep, reddish, extremely large, tough, burl-like roots.

LEAVES: alternate, short-petioled; blade green, more or less pubescent on both surfaces, prominently 3-veined beneath, broadly lanceolate to broadly elliptic, 1¼–3⅛ in. long, to 1½ in. wide, sharply toothed.

INFLORESCENCE: flowers numerous, small, pedicelled, in showy dense umbellike cluster; clusters either terminal on leafy branches or terminal on long nearly leafless peduncles from leaf axils; pedicels often white like petals. *Flower*: white, sepals 5, white, attached at rim of floral cup, incurved; petals 5; blade hooded, tapering into narrow claw at base; stamens 5, exserted.

FRUIT: drupe, somewhat fleshy, separating into 3 sections at maturity, subtended by persistent floral cup; floral cup remaining on pedicel after falling of drupe; seeds 3, smooth.

NOTE: dried leaves used as substitute for tea during colonial times; large roots popularly called "grubs."

LBU   (OFS)   May–July

MALVACEAE
(Mallow Family)

Drummond wax-mallow (Texas mallow)   [p. 49]
Malvaviscus arboreus Cav. var. *drummondii* (T. & G.) Schery
(Mal-va-vis'-kus   ar-boh'-ree-us   drum-mun'-dee-eye)

Erect to sprawling shrub usually 3–4 ft. tall, with short soft matted woolly pubescence; stems usually several, woody, much-branched.

LEAVES: alternate, stipuled, petioled; blade almost round, often shallowly 3-lobed, 1½–3½ in. long, fully as wide as long, deeply notched at base, rounded or sharp-pointed at tip, coarsely toothed.

INFLORESCENCE: flowers peduncled, solitary from leaf axils or in terminal racemes; each flower subtended by several very narrow bracts. *Flower*: vermillion red, ¾–1⅜ in. long; calyx deeply 5-lobed; petals 5, erect, forming tubular corolla, prominently swirled in bud; stamen filaments united basally, forming long, tubular column; styles 5, exserted beyond filament column; anthers numerous, below tip of styles.

FRUIT: capsule, red, shiny, globelike, fleshy and edible either raw or cooked when young; seeds 5.

SOF   (POF)   Throughout year

Salt marsh-mallow   [p. 36]
Kosteletzkya virginica (L.) Gray var. *althaefolia* Chapm.
(Kos-teh-letz'-kee-ah   vir-jin'-ih-kah   al-thee-foh'-lee-ah)

Erect, shrublike herbaceous perennial to 6 ft. tall from tough roots; plants with coarse, shaggy pubescence throughout; stems usually several, often forming clump.

LEAVES: alternate, petioled; blade gray green, densely pubescent; lower leaves rounded to oval, notched at base, coarsely toothed; upper leaves mostly lanceolate, sometimes lobed at base.

INFLORESCENCE: flowers 1–few, pedicelled, showy, in terminal or axillary, often leafy racemes or panicles; each flower subtended by 8–10 very narrow bracts. *Flower*: pale pink to rose pink; calyx 5-lobed, pubescent; petals 5, swirled in bud, opening wide, to 1¾ in. long, 1¼ in. wide; stamen filaments united basally, forming long tubular column; styles 5, exserted beyond filament column; anthers numerous, in upper portion of column and below stigmas.

FRUIT: capsule, densely pubescent, flattened, separating into 5 sections at maturity; seeds 5, one in each section, dark brown, smooth.

MGP   June–October

Halberd-leaved rose-mallow [p. 49]
Hibiscus militaris Cav.

(Hih-bis′-kus   mil-ih-tair′-is)

Erect, shrubby, essentially glabrous perennial to 8 ft. tall, usually much lower; stems and branches often tinged with red.

LEAVES: alternate, petioled; petiole slender, to 4 in. long; blade broadly lanceolate, usually prominently lobed at base with the lobes wide-spreading, sharply toothed.

INFLORESCENCE: flower solitary, subtended by whorl of bracts, pedicelled, showy, peduncled, from upper leaf axils; bracts 9 or 10, threadlike, to 1¼ in. long; pedicels to ¾ in. long, elongating in fruit; peduncles to 1½ in. long. *Flower*: pale to dark pink with maroon or purple throat; sepals 5, triangular at tips, to ⅜ in. long, longer in fruit; petals 5, swirled in bud, spreading wide upon opening, 2½–3¼ in. long; filaments united basally, forming long tubular column; styles 5, exserted beyond filament column; stigmas knoblike; anthers numerous, along upper portion of column.

FRUIT: capsule, essentially glabrous, ¾–1⅜ in. long, separating into 5 sections; seeds several in each section, covered with dense short reddish brown pubescence.

SOF   (POF)   May–November

White rose-mallow [p. 61]
Hibiscus leucophyllus Shiller

(Hih-bis′-kus   loo-koh-fil′-lus)

Erect, densely pubescent shrubby perennial to 3 ft. tall from succulent roots; stems few to several from base, branching in upper portion.

LEAVES: alternate, numerous, petioled; petiole about 1½ in. long; blade densely pubescent on both surfaces, pale green on upper surface, conspicuously white pubescent on lower surface, lanceolate, to 5½ in. long, 2½ in. wide, 7-veined at the rounded or notched base, long-tapering to tip; margins coarsely and bluntly toothed except at tip and base.

INFLORESCENCE: flower solitary, pedicelled, subtended by bracts, showy, on peduncle from leaf axils; bracts numerous, densely pubescent, threadlike, shorter than calyx. *Flower*: white with purplish red blotch in throat; calyx to 1 in. long, densely pubescent; petals 5, about 3 in. long, swirled in bud; filaments united basally, forming long, tubular column; styles 5, exserted beyond filament column; stigmas knoblike; anthers numerous, in upper portion of column.

FRUIT: capsule, short-beaked, densely pubescent when young, essentially glabrous at maturity, about ¾ in. long, separating into 5 sections; seeds several in each section, glabrous.

LBS   May–June

Rough rose-mallow [p. 61]
Hibiscus aculeatus Walt.
(Hih-bis'-kus   a-kyoo-lee-ay'-tus)

Erect or sprawling, coarse perennial to 4 ft. tall, with bristly pubescence mostly throughout and rough to the touch; stem unbranched or often many-branched from base.

LEAVES: alternate, long-petioled; petiole ¾–10 in. long; blade deeply cleft into 3–5 lobes, 1¼–3½ in. long, mostly wider than long, coarsely and irregularly toothed.

INFLORESCENCE: flowers short-pedicelled, showy, solitary or in terminal or axillary racemes; each flower subtended by bracts; bracts 8–10, linear, to ¾ in. long, usually 2 or 3 times cleft at tip. *Flower*: creamy to deep yellow with crimson throat, fading to pink, 2–3 in. across; calyx 5-lobed, about ½ in long, elongating in fruit, covered with long stiff hairs rising from blisterlike projections; lobes distinctly keeled; margins thickened and resembling keel; petals 5; filaments united into tubular column; styles 5, separated at tip and exserted from column of united filaments; anthers numerous, around column.

FRUIT: capsule, bristly pubescent, slender, to ¾ in. long, gradually tapering to beak at tip, separating into 5 sections at maturity; seeds several in each section, brown, with few minute white projections.

NOTE: rare in the Big Thicket.

LBS   (LBU)   July–October

Scarlet hibiscus [p. 36]
Hibiscus coccineus Walt.
(Hih-bis'-kus   kok-sin'-ee-us)

Erect, glabrous, glaucous perennial to 10 ft. tall.

LEAVES: alternate, long-petioled; blade deeply divided into 5 lobes; lobes linear to lanceolate, 6–12 in. long, slowly tapering to tip, usually prominently red on midrib; margins irregularly toothed except near tip.

INFLORESCENCE: flower solitary, subtended by whorl of bracts, showy, peduncled, from leaf axils; bracts 9–12, threadlike; peduncles 3–4 in. long. *Flower*: bright scarlet, 6–8 in. across; sepals 5, sharp-pointed at tip; petals 5, swirled in bud, spreading wide upon opening, long-clawed, sparsely pubescent near base; filaments united, forming long tubular column; styles 5, emerging from filament column; anthers numerous, along upper portion of column.

FRUIT: capsule, glabrous, somewhat angled, opening into 5 sections; seeds several in each section, pubescent.

NOTE: rare in the Big Thicket; one of the most showy species of *Hibiscus*, often cultivated.

MGP   July–September

Wine-cup (poppy-mallow) [p. 70]
Callirhoë papaver (Cav.) Gray
(Kal-lir'-oh-ee   pa-pav'-er)

Erect to sprawling or trailing, usually pubescent perennial, from long narrow woody root; stems often several, 12–24 in. long.

LEAVES: alternate, stipuled, petioled; stipules broadly lanceolate or oblong, to ½ in. long, ¼ in. wide; petiole equal to or many times longer than blade; blade deeply cleft into 3 or 5 segments; segments linear to lanceolate, curved; margins entire, toothed, or lobed; upper leaves sometimes reduced to a single lobe.

INFLORESCENCE: flower solitary, subtended by bracts, peduncled, showy, mostly from axils of upper leaves; bracts 3, linear, about half as long as calyx; peduncle long, slender, often 2–3 times longer than subtending leaf. *Flower*: rosy red to dark wine, 2–2½ in. across; calyx 5-lobed, with stiff bristly pubescence; petals 5, swirled in bud, slightly and irregularly toothed at tip; filaments united, forming short column; anthers numerous, in tip portion of column.

FRUIT: schizocarp; carpels short-beaked, prominently net-veined on sides; about 20 carpels arranged in flattened ring; seeds 1 in each carpel.

LBU (MGP)   March–August

Carolina modiola [p. 92]
Modiola caroliniana (L.) G. Don
(Moh-dee-oh'-lah   kair-oh-lin-ee-ay'-nah)

Low, trailing or creeping, densely pubescent perennial, freely branching and rooting at nodes.

LEAVES: alternate, stipuled, petioled; stipules conspicuous, to ¼ in. long, persistent; petiole about 1¼ in. long; blade ¾–2¾ in. long, ½–1½ in. wide, deeply cleft into 3–5 lobes, the lobes with jagged or coarsely toothed margins.

INFLORESCENCE: flower solitary, small, rather inconspicuous, subtended by 3 leaflike bracts, peduncled, from leaf axils. *Flower*: pale to brilliant salmon or purplish red, opening only during sunlight; calyx pubescent, 5-lobed; petals 5, swirled in bud, to ¼ in. long, only slightly longer than calyx; stamens 10–20.

FRUIT: schizocarp; carpels pubescent on outer side, extending into 2 claws at tip; about 15–25 carpels tightly compressed in flattened ring; seeds 1 per carpel, brown, smooth.

R   (MGP, POF, SOF)   March–May

Showy sida [p. 85]

Sida lindheimeri Engelm. & Gray

(Sye'-dah   lind-hye'-mer-eye)

Erect to sprawling, pubescent herbaceous perennial to about 3 ft. tall from woody base.

LEAVES: alternate, stipuled, petioled; petiole to about ½ in. long; blade minutely pubescent on lower surface, linear to narrowly lanceolate, ½–1½ in. long, blunt or rounded at base, rounded or sharp-pointed at tip; margins sharply toothed, often purplish.

INFLORESCENCE: flower solitary, pedicelled, showy, from axils of upper leaves; pedicels slender, to 2 in. long, often exceeding subtending leaf. *Flower*: yellow to dark salmon; calyx 5-lobed, to ⅜ in. long; margins often purplish; petals 5, about ½ in. long, conspicuously swirled in bud, not symmetrical at base; filaments united, forming column, separated into 5 bundles near tip of column; styles 7–15.

FRUIT: schizocarp; carpels prominently wrinkled and net-veined on sides, with 2 short rigid teeth at tip; about 10 carpels arranged in flattened ring; seeds 1 per carpel.

OFS   April–October

Axocatzin [p. 49]

Sida rhombifolia L.

(Sye'-dah   rom-bih-foh'-lee-ah)

Erect to weakly sprawling, somewhat shrubby annual or perennial 2–4 ft. tall; stem and branches pubescent, commonly woody in lower portion.

LEAVES: alternate, short-petioled; blade dark green and essentially glabrous on upper surface, pale and with short fine gray-colored pubescence on lower surface, diamond-shaped to broadly spatulate, to about 3⅛ in. long, 1½ in. wide, wedge-shaped or rounded at base, rounded to abruptly sharp-pointed at tip, sharply toothed.

INFLORESCENCE: flowers solitary, pedicelled, from axils of upper leaves; pedicels commonly many times longer than subtending petiole. *Flower*: cream to orange yellow, sometimes purplish or reddish near base; calyx 5-lobed, prominently 5- to 10-veined, sparsely pubescent; petals 5, less than ½ in. long, swirled in bud, not symmetrical at base; filaments united, forming short column, separated into 5 bundles near tip of column; styles 7–15.

FRUIT: schizocarp; carpels essentially smooth, sharp-pointed at tip; about 10 carpels arranged in flattened ring; seeds 1 per carpel.

SOF   (POF)   Throughout year

STERCULIACEAE
(Cacao Family)

Broom-wood (chocolate-weed)   [p. 93]

Melochia corchorifolia L.

(Meh-loh'-kee-ah   kor-koh-rih-foh'-lee-ah)

Erect, glabrous or sparsely pubescent, branched perennial to 2 ft. tall; branches erect, straight, slender, wandlike.

LEAVES: alternate, stipuled, petioled; stipules linear, falling early; petiole pubescent, to 2 in. long; blade glabrous except along main veins, lanceolate to broadly lanceolate, often slightly 3-lobed, to 3 in. long, 2 in. wide, irregularly and sharply double-toothed.

INFLORESCENCE: flowers few to several, small, in cyme; cymes compact, headlike, axillary; flowers intermixed with numerous bracts resembling stipules. *Flower*: whitish to purple, yellowish in throat; sepals 5, united; petals 5, about ¼ in. long; stamens 5; filaments united; pistil 5-parted.

FRUIT: capsule, pubescent, somewhat globe-like, separating into 5 sections; seeds 5, with 1 in each section, brown with blackish markings, wrinkled on outer side.

NOTE: native of Old World tropics.

R   August–October

THEACEAE
(Camellia Family)

Silky camellia   [p. 81]

Stewartia malacodendron L.

(Stoo-war'-tee-ah   mal-ah-koh-den'-dron)

Large, open-branched shrub or small tree to 20 ft. tall, commonly lower, pubescent on younger portions.

LEAVES: alternate, short-petioled, deciduous; blade prominently veined, glabrous on upper surface, pale green and with silky pubescence on lower surface, broadly lanceolate to elliptic or somewhat spatulate, to 4 in. long, 2 in. wide; margins sharply toothed and fringed with hairs.

INFLORESCENCE: flower solitary, showy, short-peduncled in leaf axils along branches. *Flower*: white, 2–3 in. across, commonly cupped; sepals 5, united at base, with silky pubescence; petals 5, commonly cupped, united at base, wider in tip portion, pubescent on outer surface; margins wavy or somewhat crisped; stamens numerous; filaments united basally, dark purple, conspicuous; anthers blue; styles 5, united; stigma 5-lobed.

FRUIT: capsule, woody, pubescent, globelike, somewhat flattened, about ½ in. long, opening into 5 sections; seeds 1 or 2 in each section, shiny, flattened, lens-shaped; margins not crested.

NOTE: rare in the Big Thicket.

BMLS   April–June

HYPERICACEAE
(St. John's–wort Family)

St. Peter's–wort   [p. 62]
Ascyrum stans Michx.
(As'-sih-rum   stanz)

Erect to nearly erect, glabrous, pale green, leafy, essentially evergreen perennial 12–32 in. tall; stem woody, 2-winged when young, unbranched or few-branched; bark shredding when old.

LEAVES: opposite, erect, short-petioled; blade leathery, oblong to elliptic, to 1¼ in. long, ½ in. wide, rounded to sharp-pointed at tip; upper leaves rounded and notched at base, clasping stem.

INFLORESCENCE: flowers mostly solitary from leaf axils, pedicelled, subtended by 2 small leaflike bracts. *Flower*: pale yellow; sepals 4, conspicuously 6- or 7-veined, pale green; outer 2 sepals broadly lanceolate to almost round, erect, pressed together, to ⅝ in. long and about as wide; inner 2 sepals linear, to ⅝ in. long, ⅛ in. wide; petals 4, spreading, forming cross, usually longer than sepals, falling early; stamens numerous, conspicuous, persistent; styles 3 or 4.

FRUIT: capsule, enclosed by sepals, exserted at maturity, ovoid; seeds numerous, black, net-veined.

LBS   June–September

St. Andrew's cross   [p. 70]
Ascyrum hypericoides L.
(As'-sih-rum   hye-per-ih-koh'-ih-deez)

Erect to somewhat lax or sprawling, glabrous, pale green, usually evergreen shrub to 3 ft. tall, often much lower; stem reddish brown, unbranched or sparsely branched near base, often much-branched in upper portion, 2-winged when young, with bark shredding in older portion.

LEAVES: opposite, sessile, numerous; blade linear to spatulate, to 1¼ in. long, about ¼ in. wide, narrowed at base, rounded at tip; margins somewhat rolled toward lower surface.

INFLORESCENCE: flowers solitary or with few in cymelike clusters, pedicelled, terminal or axillary; each flower subtended by a pair of small leaflike bracts. *Flower*: pale yellow; sepals 4; outer 2 sepals large, to ½ in. long and about as wide; inner 2 sepals much smaller or essentially absent; petals 4, narrowly oblong, about equaling outer sepals, spreading flat, cross-shaped, falling early; stamens numerous, conspicuous, persistent; styles 2.

FRUIT: capsule, surrounded by persistent calyx, ovoid; seeds numerous, black, net-veined.

LBU   (MGP, LBS, BMLS)   May–November

Sand-weed   [p. 62]
Hypericum fasciculatum Lam.

(Hye-per'-ih-kum   fas-sik-yoo-lay'-tum)

Erect, commonly moundlike, woody, much-branching shrub to 40 in. tall, often lower; bark on stem dark brown, thick, spongy, peeling in very thin sheets.

LEAVES: whorled, sessile, numerous, crowded, with cluster of smaller leaves in axils of larger leaves; blade leathery, threadlike to narrowly linear, to ¾ in. long; margins often rolled toward lower surface.

INFLORESCENCE: flowers solitary or with few in cymelike clusters, terminal or axillary, numerous in upper portion of the plant, showy in the aggregate. *Flower*: bright yellow; sepals 5, similar to leaves, persistent; petals 5, about ¼ in. long; stamens numerous.

FRUIT: capsule, ovoid, about ¼ in. long, 3-lobed; seeds numerous, shiny.

LBS   June–August

Small-flowered St. John's–wort   [p. 49]
Hypericum mutilum L.

(Hye-per'-ih-kum   myoo'-tih-lum)

Weakly erect to lax annual or perennial 1–3 ft. tall, sometimes forming large colonies; stem slender, widely branching in upper portion.

LEAVES: opposite, sessile, partially clasping basally; blade 3- to 5-veined, broadly lanceolate to narrowly oblong, to 1⅜ in. long, to ⅝ in. wide, rounded to blunt at tip.

INFLORESCENCE: flowers many, small, solitary or with few in leafy-bracted cymelike cluster; clusters terminal or axillary. *Flower*: pale yellow, about ¼ in. across; sepals 5, long, narrow, persistent, equal to or slightly exceeding capsule; petals 5, swirled in bud; stamens 6–12, conspicuous; styles 3, separate.

FRUIT: capsule, globelike, with persistent styles at tip; seeds yellow, minute, numerous.

SOF   (POF, BGB, LBS)   May–October

CISTACEAE
(Rockrose Family)

Carolina rockrose [p. 86]
Helianthemum carolinianum (Walt.) Michx.
(Hee-lee-an'-the-mum   kair-oh-lin-ee-ay'-num)

Erect, slender, solitary-stemmed, densely pubescent perennial to 10 in. tall from thick tuberlike roots.

LEAVES: alternate, short-petioled; basal leaves mostly in rosette; blade densely pubescent, to 1½ in. long; stem leaves 2–5, smaller, scattered, with lower surface visible through pubescence.

INFLORESCENCE: flowers few, short-pedicelled, in terminal coiled cyme; cyme short, loose, uncoiling as flowers open. *Flower*: yellow, appearing large for plant, lasting for 1 day or less; sepals 5; outer 2 sepals much smaller than inner 3; petals 5, to ¾ in. long; stamens numerous.

FRUIT: capsule, globelike, to ⅜ in. long; seeds 80–135, reddish black, covered with minute projections.

OFS   (LBU)   March–May

VIOLACEAE
(Violet Family)

Field pansy [p. 70]
Viola rafinesquii Greene
(Vye-oh'-lah   raf-ih-nes'-kee-eye)

Erect or sprawling, delicate, glabrous annual ¾–8 in. tall; stem slender, leafy, unbranched or branching basally; plant withering away after flowering.

LEAVES: alternate, stipuled, petioled; stipules conspicuous, deeply cleft, to 1 in. long, fringed with hairs; petiole varying from much shorter to much longer than blade; blade of basal leaves round; stem leaves linear to broadly spatulate, entire.

INFLORESCENCE: flower solitary, peduncled, axillary; peduncles usually exceeding leaves; both chasmogamous and cleistogamous flowers produced. *Flower*: creamy white to pale lavender or dark violet with darker markings, yellow in throat; sepals 5, shorter than petals, with short basal appendages, fringed with hairs; petals 5; lateral petals bearded; lowermost petal spurred at base; stamens 5.

FRUIT: capsule, about ¼ in. long, opening into 3 sections; seeds numerous, pale brown, minute.

NOTE: crushed roots have fragrance of wintergreen.

LBU   (OFS)   February–April

Walter's violet   [p. 81]

Viola walteri House

(Vye-oh′-lah   wal′-ter-eye)

Low, trailing perennial from slender rhizome; stems much-branched, at first erect, later falling to ground, rooting at tips and eventually forming large colonies of plants.

LEAVES: alternate, stipuled, petioled; stipules deeply cleft; blade dark-veined on upper surface and with short stiff pubescence, often purple-tinged on lower surface, from almost round to wider than long, 1–2 in. long, deeply notched at base, finely toothed; basal leaves partially evergreen.

INFLORESCENCE: flower solitary, long-peduncled from basal leaves, later from leaf axils of the elongating branches. *Flower*: blue violet, to 1 in. across; sepals 5, glabrous, with short basal appendages; petals 5; lowermost petal bearded, spurred at base; stamens 5; cleistogamous flowers produced late in season from upper leaf axils.

FRUIT: capsule, purplish, globelike, to ¼ in. long, opening into 3 sections; seeds numerous, brown, minute.

BMLS   March–April

Primrose-leaved violet   [p. 62]

Viola primulifolia L.

(Vye-oh′-lah   prim-yoo-lih-foh′-lee-ah)

Low perennial from rhizome; rhizome narrow, white, cordlike; plants producing above-ground runners which root at the nodes and form new plants.

LEAVES: from rhizome, stipuled, petioled; stipules to ½ in. long, deeply cleft into threadlike segments; petiole pubescent, as long as or longer than blade; blade pubescent, lanceolate to broadly lanceolate, 1½–2 times as long as broad, tapering into petiole at base; margins with small, rounded teeth.

INFLORESCENCE: flower solitary, peduncled; peduncles slender, from rhizome, often exceeding leaves. *Flower*: white with pale blue veins, to ⅔ in. wide; sepals 5, glabrous, with basal appendages; petals 5; lower petal bearded, spurred at base; stamens 5; cleistogamous flowers nodding, produced on short erect peduncles late in season.

FRUIT: capsule, green, glabrous, narrowly ellipsoid, about ¼ in. long, opening into 3 sections; seeds numerous, reddish brown, minute.

LBS (BGB)   March–May

Lance-leaved violet   [p. 62]

Viola lanceolata L.

(Vye-oh′-lah   lan-see-oh-lay′-tah)

Erect perennial from cordlike rhizome; during growing season plant producing numerous above-ground runners which root at the nodes and form new plants.

LEAVES: from rhizome, stipuled, petioled; petiole long, slender, reddish; blade glabrous, lanceolate, 3–5 times as long as wide, tapering into petiole at base; margins with small widely spaced teeth.

INFLORESCENCE: flower solitary, peduncled, from rhizome; peduncles slender, reddish, usually exceeding leaves. *Flower*: white with bluish veins; sepals 5, lanceolate, with short basal appendages; petals 5, usually all beardless; lowermost petal spurred at base; stamens 5; cleistogamous flowers nodding, on erect peduncles usually shorter than leaves.

FRUIT: capsule, ellipsoid, opening into 3 sections at maturity; seeds numerous, dark brown, minute.

LBS (BGB) February–April

Bird-foot violet [p. 70]
Viola pedata L.
(Vye-oh'-lah peh-day'-tah)

Clumped, glabrous perennial from short thick vertical rhizome.

LEAVES: alternate, from rhizome, stipuled, petioled; stipules pinkish or brownish, fringed with hairs, to $3/4$ in. long; petiole 4–6 in. long; blade almost round in outline, $3/4$–2 in. long, deeply cleft into 3–5 major segments, these again narrowly cleft or lobed.

INFLORESCENCE: flower solitary, showy, peduncled; peduncles as long as or exceeding leaves. *Flower*: pale to dark purple, broad, flat, pansylike, to $1\frac{1}{2}$ in. across; sepals 5, less than $1/2$ in. long, fringed with hairs, the basal appendages short; petals 5; upper 2 petals smaller than lower 3; lowest petal spurred at base, not bearded; stamens 5; stamen appendages brilliant orange, conspicuous; cleistogamous flowers none.

FRUIT: capsule, green, glabrous; seeds numerous, coppery or reddish brown, minute.

NOTE: The less common form with upper petals a dark, velvety purple and lower petals lavender can sometimes be found in East Texas and western Louisiana. *Viola pedata* is the only violet in this area reproducing strictly from seed.

LBU March–April

Lovell violet [p. 71]
Viola lovelliana Brainerd
(Vye-oh'-lah luh-vel-lee-ay'-nah)

Low, erect, often clumped perennial producing new plants by breaking of the horizontal rhizome.

LEAVES: from rhizome, erect to spreading, stipuled, long-petioled, moderately to densely pubescent; blade width ½ to nearly equal length, broadly lobed in lower portion, elongated in tip portion.

INFLORESCENCE: flower solitary, peduncled; peduncles long, usually exceeding leaves. *Flower*: dark lavender or violet; sepals 5; basal appendages short, rounded, fringed with hairs; petals 5; lower 3 petals conspicuously bearded near throat; lowermost petal spurred at base; stamens 5; cleistogamous flowers numerous, peduncled, lying on ground.

FRUIT: capsule, purple-dotted, to ⅔ in. long; seeds numerous, buff to brown, minute.

LBU   March–April

Trilobe violet   [p. 81]
Viola triloba Schwein. var. *dilatata* (Ell.) Brainerd
(Vye-oh'-lah   try-lob'-ah   dye-lah-tay'-tah)

Low perennial often producing new plants from broken fragments of horizontal rhizome.

LEAVES: from rhizome, spreading, stipuled, petioled; blade pubescent on both surfaces or glabrous, broader than long; main leaves at flowering time deeply cleft into 5–7 narrow lobes; early leaves and leaves after flowering unlobed, rounded in general outline.

INFLORESCENCE: flower solitary, peduncled; peduncles slender, as long as leaves or longer. *Flower*: violet purple, large, showy; sepals 5; petals 5; lateral petals bearded in throat near base; lower petal spreading, spurred at base; stamens 5; cleistogamous flowers short-peduncled, lying on ground.

FRUIT: capsule, pale green or purplish, ovoid; seeds numerous, buff or brown, minute.

BMLS (SOF)   March–April

Woolly blue violet   [p. 81]
Viola sororia Willd.
(Vye-oh'-lah   soh-ror'-ee-ah)

Tufted to moundlike pubescent perennial often reproducing from fragmented horizontal rhizomes.

LEAVES: from rhizome, spreading, stipuled, long-petioled; blade dark green, thick, pubescent on both surfaces, broadly lanceolate to wider than long, to 4 in. wide, notched at base; margins with 21–52 prominent teeth.

INFLORESCENCE: flower solitary, peduncled; peduncles slender, usually exceeding leaves. *Flower*: pale lilac to dark violet purple; sepals 5; basal appendages short, broad, fringed with hairs; petals 5, occasionally white near base; lateral petals broad, white-bearded; lower petal spurred at base; stamens

5; cleistogamous flowers underground or buried in leaf litter when young, erect at maturity.

FRUIT: capsule, purple sometimes mottled with brown, ovoid; seeds numerous, dark brown, minute.

NOTE: one of the most variable of the violets.

BMLS (POF, SOF, LBU) March–April

Carolina violet [p. 81]
Viola villosa Walt.

(Vye-oh'-lah vil-loh'-sah)

Very small, low, pubescent perennial frequently spreading from rather woody elongated horizontal rhizomes.

LEAVES: from rhizome, often flattened on ground and forming small rosettes, evergreen, stipuled, short-petioled; blade small, thick, red-veined, densely covered on both surfaces with long interwoven pubescence, broadly lanceolate to almost round, commonly 1–2 in. long, deeply notched at base, shallowly toothed.

INFLORESCENCE: flower solitary, peduncled, often hidden by leaves; peduncles short, slender, pubescent. *Flower*: violet or blue violet, appearing only partially open; sepals 5, fringed with hairs; basal appendages short; petals 5; lower 3 petals bearded; lowermost petal forming large rounded spur at base; stamens 5; cleistogamous flowers usually erect.

FRUIT: capsule, green, lower than leaves, ⅜ in. long; seeds numerous, dark brown or blackish, minute.

BMLS February–April

Bayou violet [p. 49]
Viola langloisii Green

(Vye-oh'-lah lang-lwa'-zee-eye)

Clumped, glabrous perennial 2–8 in. tall; plants often reproducing from fragmented horizontal rhizomes, usually forming large colonies.

LEAVES: from rhizome, stipuled, long-petioled; blade glabrous, thin, soft, spreading, broadly lanceolate to somewhat rounded, 1½–3 in. long, rounded and broadly notched at base, somewhat pointed at tip, prominently toothed.

INFLORESCENCE: flower solitary, peduncled, usually exceeding leaves. *Flower*: blue violet, ½–¾ in. wide; sepals 5, narrow, tapering at tip; basal appendages slightly elongated; petals 5; lateral petals bearded; lowermost petal spurred at base; stamens 5; cleistogamous flowers present.

FRUIT: capsule, to ½ in. long, opening into 3 sections; seeds numerous, minute.

SOF March–May

Thicket violet   [p. 70]
Viola affinis LeConte forma. *albiflora* Henz.
(Vye-oh'-lah af'-fih-nis al-bih-floh'-rah)

Erect, usually thinly clumped perennial from stout horizontal rhizome.

LEAVES: from rhizome, stipuled, long-petioled; stipules linear, sparsely cleft; blade lobed in lower portion, broadly rounded and notched at base, tapering to broad point in tip portion, toothed; basal lobes with stiff, scattered, white pubescence on upper surface; summer leaves much larger than early leaves.

INFLORESCENCE: flower solitary, peduncled; peduncles slender, usually exceeding leaves. *Flower*: white with purplish throat and veins; sepals 5, with basal appendages; petals 5; lateral petals bearded; lower petal bearded, spurred at base; stamens 5; cleistogamous flowers loosely erect or somewhat lax.

FRUIT: capsule, purple-dotted or green, glabrous or minutely pubescent, 1/4–1/2 in. long; seeds numerous, dark or pale and purple-dotted, minute.
LBU   March–June

PASSIFLORACEAE
(Passion-flower Family)

Yellow passion-flower   [p. 71]
Passiflora lutea L.
(Pas-sih-floh'-rah   loo'-tee-ah)

Trailing or climbing, slender perennial vine supported by tendrils from leaf axils, glabrous or slightly pubescent on new growth; stem to 10 ft. long.

LEAVES: alternate, petioled; petiole to 2 in. long, without glands at base; blade pale green or bluish, often mottled with silvery gray, 3-veined, thin, pliable, usually much wider than long, 1 1/4–2 3/4 in. long, 1 1/2–4 in. wide, rounded or blunt at base, bluntly 3-lobed in tip portion, entire.

INFLORESCENCE: flowers solitary or in pairs, short-pedicelled, peduncled, axillary; peduncles very slender, to 1 1/2 in. long, with no bracts present. *Flower*: greenish yellow, 3/4–1 in. across; sepals 5, united at base, fleshy, pubescent on outer surface, less than 1/2 in. long, 1/8 in. wide; petals 5, threadlike, about 1/4 in. long; corona with fringe of filaments; filaments numerous, threadlike, to 1/2 in. long; stamens 5, united below to form erect tube around pistil; styles 3, wide-spreading.

FRUIT: berry, purple to black, fleshy, glabrous, globelike to ovoid, to 1/2 in. long at maturity; seeds numerous, dark brown, ribbed, ovoid.
LBU (SOF, BMLS)   May–September

Passion-flower   [p. 49]
Passiflora incarnata L.
(Pas-sih-floh'-rah   in-kar-nay'-tah)

Climbing, trailing, or nearly erect herbaceous perennial vine supported by tendrils from leaf axils, glabrous or with minute soft pubescence; stem angular when young, to 25 ft. long.

LEAVES: alternate, petioled; petiole to 3 in. long, bearing 2 sessile glands at base of blade; blade dark green above, whitened beneath, thin, pliable, 3-veined, 2¼–6 in. long and as wide, deeply cleft into 3 lanceolate lobes, sharply toothed.

INFLORESCENCE: flower solitary, short-pedicelled, conspicuously showy, peduncled, axillary; peduncles stout, terminated with whorl of 3 bracts. *Flower*: pale to dark lavender, to 3 in. across; sepals 5, petallike, to 1⅜ in. long, green on back, hooded, with soft hornlike appendage near tip; petals 5, to 1½ in. long, less than ½ in. wide; corona with fringe of filaments; filaments numerous, threadlike, irregularly curled or crimped near tip, to 1¼ in. long; stamens 5, united basally and forming long tube around pistil, parted and wide-spreading in upper portion; anthers large, conspicuous; styles 3, wide-spreading; stigmas knoblike at tips.

FRUIT: berry, orange yellow when ripe, ovoid to globelike, 2–3 in. long, with edible pulp; seeds numerous, net-veined.
SOF   (MGP, POF, LBU, OFS)   April–September

CACTACEAE
(Cactus Family)

Eastern prickly pear   [p. 86]
Opuntia compressa (Salisb.) Macbr.
(Oh-pun'-chee-ah   kom-pres'-sah)

Erect to sprawling, clumped or mat-forming succulent perennial 12–18 in. tall from nontuberous roots; stems consisting of flattened pads; pads dark green to yellowish green or reddish purple in winter, almost round to elliptic or spatulate, to 4 in. long, commonly 3–4 in. wide.

LEAVES: scattered on pads, minute, falling early, usually absent from adult plants; leaf axils bearing 1 slender spine and a tuft of numerous fine barbed bristles; bristles painful to touch, coming loose from plant easily.

INFLORESCENCE: flower solitary, sessile, showy, at tip of large green ovary; usually few to several flowers forming row along margins of younger pads. *Flower*: solid yellow or with beige or reddish orange blotches in throat, 2–3 in. across; sepals and petals similar, cupped; stamens numerous, conspicuous.

FRUIT: berry, fleshy, somewhat pear-shaped, to 1½ in. long, with tufts of bristles scattered on surface, reddish or wine-colored when ripe, edible when peeled; seeds flattened, smooth.

OFS   (LBU)   April–June

LYTHRACEAE
(Loosestrife Family)

Water-willow   [p. 57]

Decodon verticillatus (L.) Ell.

(Dek'-oh-don   ver-tih-sil-lay'-tus)

Glabrous or pubescent aquatic perennial often somewhat woody at base; stems usually several, slender, 4- to 6-sided, arching downward and rooting at tips, to 8 ft. long; bark of submerged parts thick, spongy; plants usually forming large colonies.

LEAVES: opposite or in whorls of 3 or 4, short-petioled; blade lanceolate, to 6 in. long, $1\frac{1}{2}$ in. wide.

INFLORESCENCE: flowers few to several, short-pedicelled, in cluster; clusters from axils of leaves in upper portion of branches. *Flower*: magenta; calyx 5- to 7-toothed at rim with spreading appendages between teeth; petals 5, wavy or crisped, narrowed at base, about $\frac{1}{2}$ in. long; stamens 10, of 2 lengths, the longer 5 exserted.

FRUIT: capsule, dark brown to black, globelike, to $\frac{1}{4}$ in. across; seeds reddish.

BGB   July–October

Lance-leaf loosestrife   [p. 36]

Lythrum lanceolatum Ell.

(Lith'-rum   lan-see-oh-lay'-tum)

Erect, glabrous perennial to 5 ft. tall, with numerous creeping basal off-shoots, eventually forming large clumps; stems somewhat woody, 4-angled, usually branching in upper portion.

LEAVES: alternate in lower portion of plant; blade lanceolate, to $2\frac{1}{4}$ in. long, about $\frac{1}{2}$ in. wide, tapering to petiolelike base; leaves opposite and much reduced in flowering portion of plant.

INFLORESCENCE: flowers usually solitary from axils of small leaves in upper portion of branches. *Flower*: purple, reddish, or lavender blue; calyx tubular, ribbed, 5- to 7-toothed at rim and with longer appendages between teeth; petals 4–6, to $\frac{1}{4}$ in. long, spreading; stamens 8–12; styles exserted.

FRUIT: capsule, cylindrical, included within calyx; seeds numerous.

MGP   (POF, LBU)   April–October

Spiked loosestrife   [p. 50]
Lythrum salicaria L.
(Lith'-rum   say-lih-kair'-ee-ah)

Erect, stout, glabrous or pubescent perennial 3–6 ft. tall; plants producing basal offshoots and usually forming large clumps; stems angled, much-branched in upper portion.

LEAVES: opposite or in whorls of 3, sessile; blade broadly lanceolate, clasping or with rounded lobes at base, 2–4 in. long, about ½ in. wide.

INFLORESCENCE: flowers in almost sessile cyme; cymes numerous, intermixed with small leaflike bracts, forming dense showy terminal spike. *Flower*: purple, to ¾ in. across; calyx tubular, greenish, coarsely pubescent, toothed at rim, with longer appendages between teeth; petals 4–6; flowers of 3 types, all with 10 stamens; one type with all stamens from base of calyx tube and with a low style; second type with all stamens from near rim of tube and with a short style; third type with low and high stamens and a style of medium length.

FRUIT: capsule, cylindrical, included within calyx.

NOTE: rare in the Big Thicket; introduced, native of Eurasia; worthy of cultivation.

SOF   June–September

Tooth-cup   [p. 50]
Ammannia coccinea Rottb.
(Am-man'-nee-ah   kok-sin'-ee-ah)

Erect to spreading, glabrous, succulent annual to 20 in. tall; stem 4-angled, branched in lower portion, thick and spongy at base when growing in water.

LEAVES: opposite, sessile; blade linear to narrowly lanceolate, to 4 in. long, ½ in. wide, usually much smaller, clasping stem at base with earlike projections on each side.

INFLORESCENCE: flowers 2–5, essentially sessile, small, inconspicuous, in cyme from leaf axils. *Flower*: pink to purple; calyx funnel-shaped, 4-angled, 4-toothed at rim; petals 4, about ⅛ in. long, withering and falling early; style persistent.

FRUIT: capsule, globelike, opening irregularly; seeds numerous, yellow, shiny.

SOF   (POF)   April–November

MELASTOMATACEAE
(Melastoma Family)

Meadow beauty   [p. 62]
Rhexia petiolata Walt.
(Rex'-ee-ah   pet-ee-oh-lay'-tah)

Erect, slender perennial to 24 in. tall; stem rather woody in lower portion, 4-sided, flat on sides, narrowly winged on edges, glabrous, unbranched or forked in upper portion.

LEAVES: opposite, erect, numerous, essentially sessile; blade 3-veined, glabrous or with sparse coarse pubescence on upper surface, glabrous or almost so beneath, broadly elliptic to broadly lanceolate, to 1 in. long, about $\frac{1}{2}$ in. wide, less than three times as long as wide, fringed with bristly hairs.

INFLORESCENCE: flowers solitary or in cymes, sessile, showy, among terminal leaves. *Flower*: rose-colored; floral tube glabrous, united at base, constricted near tip, conspicuously urn-shaped; calyx 4-lobed, the lobes with fringed margins; petals 4, about $\frac{3}{4}$ in. long, falling early; stamens 8; anthers yellow, large, straight.

FRUIT: capsule, developing within the "urn" of the floral tube, to $\frac{1}{4}$ in. across; seeds numerous.

LBS   July–September

Yellow meadow beauty   [p. 62]
Rhexia lutea Walt.
(Rex'-ee-ah   loo'-tee-ah)

Erect perennial to 20 in. tall, mostly covered with coarse gland-tipped pubescence; stem 4-sided, flat on sides, winged on edges, usually much-branched.

LEAVES: opposite, essentially sessile; blade sparsely pubescent, 3-veined, elliptic to spatulate, about 1 in. long, $\frac{1}{4}$ in. wide, more than 3 times as long as wide, pointed at tip, fringed with hairs.

INFLORESCENCE: flowers solitary or in cymes from leaf axils, mostly toward top of plant, showy. *Flower*: yellow; floral tube urn-shaped, glabrous or with few scattered gland-tipped hairs; calyx 4-lobed, the lobes fringed with gland-tipped hairs; petals 4, falling early, to $\frac{1}{2}$ in. long; stamens 8; anthers curved.

FRUIT: capsule, ribbed, globelike, about $\frac{1}{8}$ in. across, maturing within the "urn" of the floral tube; seeds numerous.

NOTE: only species of *Rhexia* in North America with yellow flowers.

LBS   May–June

Common meadow beauty [p. 62]
Rhexia virginica L.
(Rex'-ee-ah vir-jin'-ih-kah)

Erect perennial 8–40 in. tall from tuberous roots, with short rough pubescence throughout; stem 4-angled, with the sides either flat or rounded and conspicuously winged on edges.

LEAVES: opposite, sessile or very short-petioled; blade 3- to 5-veined, sparsely pubescent, elliptic to broadly lanceolate, to 3 in. long, 1½ in. wide, sharply toothed and fringed with hairs.

INFLORESCENCE: flowers solitary or few to numerous in cymes, short-pedicelled, showy, from upper leaf axils. *Flower*: dark rose to purple, about 1 in. across, lasting only a few hours; floral tube urn-shaped, with short coarse gland-tipped pubescence; calyx 4-lobed, the lobes tipped with bristles; petals 4, to 1 in. long, fringed with gland-tipped hairs; anthers linear, curved.

FRUIT: capsule, developing within the "urn" of the floral tube; seeds numerous.

LBS   (LBU)   June–October

ONAGRACEAE
(Evening Primrose Family)

White gaura [p. 36]
Gaura lindheimeri Engelm. & Gray
(Gaw'-rah lind-hye'-mer-eye)

Erect to sprawling, slender perennial 1½–5 ft. tall; most parts of plants with long, soft pubescence; stems 1–several from base, much-branched in upper portion.

LEAVES: alternate, essentially sessile, greatly reduced in size in upper portion of plant; blade narrowly elliptic to spatulate, ¼–3⅓ in. long, to ½ in. wide, pointed at tip, entire or with scattered teeth.

INFLORESCENCE: flowers few to several, in elongated showy pubescent terminal spikes and on axillary branches; pubescence usually dense, often gland-tipped. *Flower*: white, turning pink in aging, opening near sunrise; sepals pink or purplish, reflexed, with long erect pubescence; petals 4, clawed, all ultimately in row on upward side, ½–⅔ in. long; stamens 8, long, erect to drooping downward opposite petals.

FRUIT: capsule, 4-angled, woody, nutlike, somewhat cylindrical, tapered at each end, nonopening.

MGP   (POF, LBU)   April–November

Showy primrose   [p. 93]
Oenothera speciosa Nutt.
(Ee-noh-ther'-ah   spee-shee-oh'-sah)

Erect to sprawling, slender, usually branched perennial to 2 ft. tall from
rhizome; plants with minute, short pubescence.

LEAVES: alternate, sessile or petioled; petiole to 1⅛ in. long; blade variable, entire to cleft near base or merely lobed with wavy margins, from linear
to elliptic to broader in tip portion, ¾–3½ in. long, to 1 in. wide, sometimes
toothed.

INFLORESCENCE: flowers solitary, pedicelled, showy, in upper leaf axils;
buds sharply nodding, rising to erect position as they open. *Flower*: whitish
to dark rosy pink with reddish veins, yellow at base, cupped, opening in
morning or evening depending upon populations; floral tube slender, to 1 in.
long; sepals 4, narrow, to 1¼ in. long; petals 4, broad, overlapping, 1–1½
in. long.

FRUIT: capsule, sessile, pubescent, tough, narrow, prominently 8-ribbed,
to ⅜ in. long; seeds numerous.
R   (MGP, LBU, OFS)   April–July

Cut-leaved evening primrose   [p. 93]
Oenothera laciniata Hill
(Ee-noh-ther'-ah   lah-sin-ee-ay'-tah)

Erect to sprawling annual to 2 ft. tall, variable, usually pubescent
throughout; stem unbranched or much-branched.

LEAVES: alternate, sessile or short-petioled in lower portion of plant;
blade usually cleft into few to several lobes but occasionally entire or toothed,
1–2 in. long.

INFLORESCENCE: flowers solitary from upper leaf axils. *Flower*: pale yellow, turning pink in aging, opening in evening, withering next morning;
floral tube slender, to 1 in. long, with short coarse pubescence; calyx 4-lobed;
lobes narrow, reflexed, much shorter than floral tube; petals 4, to 1 in. long.

FRUIT: capsule, pubescent, narrowly cylindrical, to 1½ in. long; seeds
numerous, pale brown, conspicuously pitted.
R   (MGP, LBU, OFS)   March–November

Common evening primrose   [p. 86]
Oenothera biennis L. subsp. *centralis* Munz
(Ee-noh-ther'-ah   bye-en'-nis   cen-tray'-lis)

Erect, somewhat coarse, glabrous or sparsely pubescent biennial to 6 ft.
tall, often lower, from woody taproot; stem green or purple-tinged, unbranched or branched in upper portion.

LEAVES: alternate, pubescent, spreading or erect; basal leaves in rosette, long-petioled; blade varying from deeply cleft into opposite narrow lobes to only toothed, 3–12 in. long, ½–2½ in. wide, narrowed at base; stem leaves essentially sessile, becoming bracts in flowering portion of stem, narrowed at base, entire to finely toothed.

INFLORESCENCE: flowers few to numerous, in elongated terminal raceme; racemes a showy combination of fruits, flowers, and buds; flowers and buds subtended by small, leaflike bracts. *Flower*: bright yellow, opening near sunset and remaining open a short time next morning; floral tube slender, to 1¼ in. long; calyx 4-lobed; lobes to 1¼ in. long, reflexed; petals 4, to 1¼ in. long.

FRUIT: capsule, pubescent, thick, cylindrical, to 1½ in. long, usually curved near base, tapering at tip; seeds numerous.

OFS   (LBU)   August–November

Shrubby water-primrose [p. 42]
Ludwigia octovalvis (Jacq.) Raven
(Lud-wig'-ee-ah   ok-toh-val'-vis)

Usually erect herb to 3 ft. tall, glabrous or with sharp stiff pubescence; stem usually much-branched from base.

LEAVES: alternate, stipuled, petioled; petiole to ½ in. long; blade lanceolate to broadly lanceolate, 1¼–5¾ in. long, ⅛–1½ in. wide, entire to minutely toothed.

INFLORESCENCE: flowers solitary, pedicelled, from upper leaf axils. *Flower*: yellow; sepals 4, to ½ in. long, persistent; petals 4, to ⅔ in. long; stamens 8.

FRUIT: capsule, thin-walled, slender, cylindrical, ½–1¾ in. long, 3/16–⅓ in. across, readily opening; seeds numerous.

POF   (SOF)   July–October

Uruguay water-primrose [p. 37]
Ludwigia uruguayensis (Camb.) Hara
(Lud-wig'-ee-ah   oo-roo-gway-en'-sis)

Creeping or floating aquatic perennial rooting at nodes; stem erect in flowering portion, mostly with long spreading pubescence especially in upper portion of plant, unbranched or branching, to 3 ft. long.

LEAVES: alternate, petioled; petiole usually less than ½ in. long; blade pale green, pubescent, linear, elliptic to spatulate, 1–4 in. long, less than ½ in. wide, abruptly pointed at tip, entire to minutely toothed.

INFLORESCENCE: flowers solitary, pedicelled, showy, from axils of upper leaves. *Flower*: bright yellow; sepals 5, pubescent, ¼–⅝ in. long; petals 5, to 1 in. long, ¾ in. wide; stamens 10.

FRUIT: capsule, tough, woody, pubescent, somewhat cylindrical, ½–1 in.

long, $\frac{1}{8}$ in. across, not readily opening; seeds numerous, each firmly embedded in a woody structure fused to capsule wall.

MGP   (POF)   June–September

Spindle-root   [p. 62]
Ludwigia hirtella Raf.

(Lud-wig′-ee-ah hir-tel′-lah)

Erect, densely and coarsely pubescent perennial to 3 ft. tall from cluster of spindle-shaped roots; stem unbranched or branched, dying back to ground each year.

LEAVES: alternate, essentially sessile; blade pubescent, narrowly lanceolate to elliptic, $\frac{1}{2}$–$2\frac{1}{2}$ in. long, to $\frac{3}{4}$ in. wide.

INFLORESCENCE: flowers solitary, pedicelled, from upper leaf axils. *Flower*: pale to dark yellow; sepals 4, erect to spreading, less than $\frac{1}{2}$ in. long, less than $\frac{1}{4}$ in. wide, persistent; petals 4, exceeding sepals, about $\frac{1}{2}$ in. long, to $\frac{3}{8}$ in. wide; stamens 4.

FRUIT: capsule, with coarse pubescence, somewhat globelike, 4-angled in upper portion, winged on angles, about $\frac{1}{4}$ in. long.

NOTE: uncommon in the Big Thicket.

LBS   June–September

UMBELLIFERAE
(Parsley Family)

Golden Alexanders   [p. 50]
Zizia aurea (L.) Koch

(Ziz′-ee-ah aw′-ree-ah)

Erect, glabrous, usually branching perennial 16–32 in. tall from loose cluster of roots.

LEAVES: alternate, petioled, compound; basal leaves to 4 in. long, $4\frac{3}{4}$ in. wide, twice divided into leaflets; leaflets lanceolate, sharply and finely toothed; upper leaves similar to basal leaves but becoming reduced and less divided.

INFLORESCENCE: flowers few to several in showy umbel; umbel flat-topped, terminal or axillary, peduncled; peduncles to 6 in. long; rays 10–15; central flower in each small umbel fertile, sessile or nearly so. *Flower*: golden yellow, less than $\frac{1}{8}$ in. long; sepals 5; petals 5; stamens 5.

FRUIT: schizocarp; mericarps 2, glabrous, finely ribbed, ovoid, about $\frac{1}{8}$ in. long; seeds 1 per mericarp.

SOF   (LBU)   April–August

Thread-leaf mock bishop's-weed [p. 63]

Ptilimnium capillaceum (Michx.) Raf.

(Tih-lim'-nee-um ka-pil-lay'-see-um)

Erect, slender, loosely branched, glabrous annual 4–36 in. tall.

LEAVES: usually in whorls at the nodes, compound; blade broadly oblong in outline, to 5 in. long, 1½ in. wide, several times narrowly divided into numerous threadlike segments.

INFLORESCENCE: flowers numerous, very small, in showy compound umbel; umbels terminal and axillary, peduncled; peduncles 1–4 in. long, exceeding leaves; rays subtended by whorl of threadlike bracts about half as long as ray; pedicels subtended by whorl of short, threadlike bracts. *Flower*: white; sepals minute; petals 5; stamens 5.

FRUIT: schizocarp; mericarps 2, glabrous, prominently 5-ribbed, broadly ovoid, to ⅛ in. long; seeds 1 per mericarp.

LBS   May–August

Ribbed mock bishop's-weed [p. 63]

Ptilimnium costatum (Ells.) Raf.

(Tih-lim'-nee-um kos-tay'-tum)

Erect, robust, usually much-branched glabrous annual 2–5 ft. tall.

LEAVES: alternate, appearing whorled around stem, compound; blade to 5½ in. long, 2¾ in. wide, divided into numerous segments about ⅓ in. long; ultimate segments crowded, threadlike.

INFLORESCENCE: flowers numerous, very small, arranged in showy compound umbels; umbels terminal or axillary, peduncled; peduncles 2¾–5½ in. long, exceeding leaves; rays 18–25, spreading, subtended by conspicuous leaflike bracts; pedicels 15–20, spreading, subtended by short, linear or threadlike bracts. *Flower*: white; sepals 5, minute, persistent, conspicuous; petals 5.

FRUIT: schizocarp; mericarps 2, glabrous, oval, about ⅛ in. long, with prominent threadlike ribs; seeds 1 per mericarp.

LBS   June–October

Dog-sunshade [p. 37]

Limnosciadium pumilum (Engelm. & Gray) Math. & Const.

(Lim-noh-sye-ad'-ee-um pyoo'-mih-lum)

Low, usually sprawling, glabrous annual 2–16 in. tall; stem slender, widely branching.

LEAVES: alternate; basal leaves entire or divided, narrowly lanceolate to lanceolate, to 3¼ in. long, less than ½ in. wide, tapering at base; stem leaves entire or divided into 3–7 threadlike to lanceolate segments.

INFLORESCENCE: flowers numerous, very small, arranged in terminal or axillary compound umbels; umbels peduncled or sometimes sessile; peduncles to 3 in. long; rays 3–8, slender, to 2 in. long; bracts usually absent; pedicels several, less than ¼ in. long, subtended by several short linear bracts. *Flower*: white; petals 5; tips of petals not turned inward as is common in this family.

FRUIT: schizocarp; mericarps 2, glabrous, somewhat ovoid to globelike, rounded at base and tip, less than ¼ in. long, with broad corky wings; seeds 1 per mericarp.

NOTE: endemic in central, southern, and southeastern Texas; infrequent in the Big Thicket.

MGP   March–June

Rattlesnake-weed   [p. 86]
Daucus pusillus Michx.
(Daw′-kus   pyoo′-sil-lus)

Erect, slender, pubescent annual to 3 ft. tall; stem usually solitary, ribbed, with stiff downward-pointing pubescence, unbranched or branched in upper portion.

LEAVES: alternate, petioled, compound; blade to 4¼ in. long, 2¾ in. wide, divided into opposite segments; ultimate segments variously lobed, bristly pubescent, threadlike to linear, sharp-pointed at tip.

INFLORESCENCE: flowers numerous, small, in compound umbels; umbels terminal and axillary, peduncled; peduncles 4¼–15 in. long, bristly pubescent; rays few to numerous, unequal, ¼–1½ in. long, drawing inward in fruit, subtended by leaflike bracts which exceed umbel; pedicels unequal, to ⅜ in. long, subtended by linear bracts which about equal pedicel in length; central flower of center umbel white. *Flower*: white; petals 5; stamens 5.

FRUIT: schizocarp; mericarps 2, flattened on back, ribbed; primary ribs 5, bristly; secondary ribs 4, winged, each wing with row of 10 or fewer prominently barbed bristles; seeds 1 per mericarp.

NOTE: easily identified by the bracts which extend beyond flower umbels.

OFS   (LBU)   April–May

Wild carrot (Queen Anne's lace)   [p. 93]
Daucus carota L.
(Daw′-kus   ka-roh′-tah)

Erect, slender, sometimes coarse, glabrous or stiffly pubescent, branching biennial to 4 ft. tall from stout fleshy taproot.

LEAVES: alternate, petioled, compound; blade to 6 in. long, 2¾ in. wide, divided into opposite narrow segments; ultimate segments entire or few-cleft, glabrous or with bristly pubescence especially on veins and margins, linear to lanceolate, less than ¼ in. wide.

INFLORESCENCE: flowers numerous, small, in showy compound umbel; umbels terminal and axillary, subtended by divided threadlike bracts, rounded

when in flower but concave in fruit and forming a conspicuous "bird nest."
Flower: white, except center flower in umbel which is dark wine red or blackish purple; petals 5.

FRUIT: schizocarp; mericarps 2, broader near middle, ribbed; primary
ribs 5, bristly; secondary ribs 4, winged; each wing with row of 12 or more
weakly hooked bristles; seeds 1 per mericarp.

R   (MGP, LBU)   April–May

Leafless cowbane [p. 63]
Oxypolis filiformis (Walt.) Britt.
(Ox-ip'-oh-lis   fil-ih-for'-mis)

Erect, slender, glabrous, hollow-stemmed perennial to 5½ ft. tall from
tight cluster of tubers.

LEAVES: alternate, consisting only of elongated, hollow, jointed petioles
1–18 in. long, becoming bractlike in upper portion of plant.

INFLORESCENCE: flowers numerous, small, in showy compound terminal or axillary umbels; umbel 2–4 in. across, subtended by 5 or more small
linear to lanceolate bracts. *Flower*: white; sepals 5; petals 5.

FRUIT: schizocarp; mericarps 2, winged, 5-ribbed; seeds 1 per mericarp.

LBS   (MGP)   July–September

Button snake-root [p. 71]
Eryngium yuccifolium Michx.
(Eh-rin'-jee-um   yuk-ih-foh'-lee-um)

Stiffly erect, stout, glabrous perennial 1–4 ft. tall from cluster of woody
tuberous roots; stem solitary, slender, branching in upper portion.

LEAVES: alternate, rigid, sheathing stem at base; blade parallel-veined,
broadly linear, to 36 in. long, usually much shorter, to 1¼ in. wide, sharp-
pointed at tip; margins with occasional solitary bristles; stem leaves becoming smaller upward.

INFLORESCENCE: flowers numerous, minute, sessile, in long-peduncled
globelike head; heads to 1 in. across, subtended by bracts; bracts 6–10, short,
spreading, sharp-pointed; each flower in head subtended by minute, stiff,
sharp-pointed bract. *Flower*: white or greenish; petals 5; styles exserted.

FRUIT: schizocarp; mericarps 2, about ¼ in. long, covered with small
scales; ribs essentially absent; seeds 1 per mericarp.

LBU   May–August

Hooker eryngo [p. 42]
Eryngium hookeri Walp.
(Eh-rin'-jee-um   hook'-er-eye)

Erect, slender, glabrous annual 12–24 in. tall; stem solitary, branching in
upper portion.

LEAVES: alternate; basal leaves petioled; petiole slender, sheathing stem at base; blade lanceolate, oblong, or spatulate, to 3½ in. long, 1⅛ in. wide, sharp-pointed at tip; margins somewhat sharply toothed; lower stem leaves essentially sessile, lanceolate; margins with long, slender, spine-tipped teeth; leaf base with a pair of small, spiny-margined segments; upper stem leaves deeply cleft into 5–7 spiny-toothed lobes, the lobes ¾–1¼ in. long.

INFLORESCENCE: flowers numerous, very small, sessile, in peduncled head; heads oval, about ½ in. across, subtended by numerous bracts; bracts rigid, exceeding head, narrowly lanceolate, broadly winged at base, with spiny-toothed margins. *Flower*: whitish to purplish; sepals 5, extremely sharp-pointed, persistent; petals 5; styles shorter than sepals.

FRUIT: schizocarp; mericarps 2, about 1/16 in. long, densely covered with tawny scales; ribs essentially absent; seeds 1 per mericarp.

POF   (MGP)   June–September

Simple-leaf eryngo   [p. 37]
Eryngium integrifolium Walt.
(Eh-rin'-jee-um   in-teg-rih-foh'-lee-um)

Erect, slender, glabrous perennial 12–32 in. tall from fleshy roots; stem solitary, branching in upper portion.

LEAVES: alternate; basal leaves petioled; petiole sheathing stem at base; blade oblong to broadly lanceolate, ¾–2½ in. long, ¼–2 in. wide, broadly notched at base, entire to shallowly toothed; lower stem leaves similar but short-petioled or sessile; leaves in upper portion becoming much reduced, linear, and spiny-margined.

INFLORESCENCE: flowers numerous, sessile, in globelike head; heads to ½ in. across, subtended by conspicuous spiny bracts; bracts 6–10, rigid, linear, exceeding head, to ¾ in. long, entire or usually with 3–5 spiny teeth. *Flower*: whitish to bluish or purplish; sepals persistent; petals 5; stamens 5; styles slender, exceeding sepals.

FRUIT: schizocarp; mericarps 2, densely covered with rows of white scales on angles, minute; seeds 1 per mericarp.

MGP   (POF)   August–October

Creeping eryngo   [p. 50]
Eryngium prostratum DC.
(Eh-rin'-jee-um   pros-tray'-tum)

Low, creeping or weakly erect, glabrous perennial; stems slender, often numerous, spreading, rooting at nodes, 6–28 in. long, unbranched or branched in upper portion.

LEAVES: basal leaves alternate, slender-petioled; blade lanceolate, unlobed or lobed, to 4¼ in. long, 1 in. wide, entire or irregularly and occasionally toothed; stem leaves much reduced, becoming sessile in upper portion and clustered at nodes.

INFLORESCENCE: flowers few, minute, in small head; heads cylindrical, from leaf axils, peduncled, 1/4–3/8 in. long, subtended by 5–10 reflexed bracts. *Flower*: pale to dark blue; sepals 5; petals 5; styles exceeding sepals.

FRUIT: schizocarp; mericarps 2, minute; ribs essentially absent; seeds 1 per mericarp.

SOF   May–September

Spadeleaf [p. 50]
Centella asiatica (L.) Urban
(Sen-tel′-lah   ay-zee-at′-ih-kah)

Low, creeping, glabrous to pubescent perennial; stems 4–20 in. long, rooting at nodes.

LEAVES: clustered at nodes, erect, petioled; petiole to 6 in. long, glabrous or with yellowish pubescence, sheathing stem at base, usually with tuft of hair at base of blade; blade thick, oblong to round, 1/2–1 1/2 in. long, 1/2–1 1/4 in. wide, sometimes larger, broadly notched or prominently blunt across base, rounded at tip, entire or slightly wavy and toothed.

INFLORESCENCE: flowers few, nearly sessile, in small peduncled axillary umbels; peduncle pubescent, often shorter than leaves; rays 2–5, to about 1/8 in. long; umbel subtended by 2 small bracts. *Flower*: white or rose-tinged; petals 5, soon falling.

FRUIT: schizocarp; mericarps 2, prominently ribbed and net-veined, flattened, broader than long; seeds 1 per mericarp.

SOF   (LBS)   May–September

CORNACEAE
(Dogwood Family)

Flowering dogwood [p. 71]
Cornus florida L.
(Kor′-nus   floh′-rih-dah)

Large shrub or small tree to 38 ft. tall, usually lower; bark reddish brown to black, broken into small squares in lower portion of trunk in older trees; younger branches usually greenish.

LEAVES: opposite, petioled, appearing with or after flowers; blade pale green on upper surface, pale and glabrous or with silky pubescence on lower surface, conspicuously veined, elliptic to broadly elliptic, to 4 3/4 in. long, 3 1/4 in. wide, rounded at base, somewhat pointed at tip, entire.

INFLORESCENCE: flowers several, small, sessile, in compact head; head surrounded by 4 bracts; bracts large, conspicuous, petallike, white or pinkish, occasionally pointed or notched at tip, to 2 in. long, 1¼ in. wide. *Flower*: yellowish green to greenish white; calyx minutely 4-toothed; petals 4, spreading; stamens 4; ovary inferior.

FRUIT: drupe, scarlet red, shiny, ellipsoid, to ¾ in. long, ⅜ in. wide; seeds 2, within hard bony stone.

LBU   (BMLS)   March–April

Red-osier dogwood   [p. 50]
Cornus foemina Mill.
(Kor'-nus   fem'-ih-nah)

Erect, much-branched, essentially glabrous tree or shrub to 14 ft. tall, frequently much lower; younger branches smooth, reddish brown, the pith usually white.

LEAVES: opposite, deciduous, petioled; petiole to ⅜ in. long; blade dark green on upper surface, paler beneath, glabrous or nearly so, lanceolate to narrowly elliptic, to about 4 in. long, 1½ in. wide, tapering to narrow elongated tip.

INFLORESCENCE: flowers numerous, very small, in showy peduncled cyme; peduncles 1–2¾ in. long; cymes large, convex. *Flower*: creamy white; sepals 4, minute; petals 4, oblong, spreading; stamens 4; anthers bluish.

FRUIT: drupe, bluish, fleshy, globelike, less than ¼ in. across, containing stone; stone furrowed, longer than broad, usually 2-seeded.

SOF   (POF)   May–June

CLETHRACEAE
(White Alder Family)

Sweet pepper-bush   [p. 57]
Clethra alnifolia L.
(Kleth'-rah   al-nih-foh'-lee-ah)

Erect to straggling, glabrous or pubescent shrub 3–9 ft. tall.

LEAVES: alternate, deciduous, petioled; petiole to ¾ in. long; blade prominently straight-veined, glabrous on upper surface, elliptic to spatulate, 1½–3½ in. long, tapering to petiole, finely toothed in tip portion.

INFLORESCENCE: flowers numerous, pedicelled, in showy raceme; racemes terminal or axillary, pubescent. *Flower*: white, very fragrant; calyx 5-parted, pubescent, persistent; petals 5, about ¼ in. long; stamens 10; filaments long, glabrous.

FRUIT: capsule, erect, densely pubescent, globelike, about ⅛ in. long; seeds many, pinkish to whitish tan, net-veined, minute.

BGB   (BMLS)   July–September

ERICACEAE
(Heath Family)

White azalea   [p. 57]
Rhododendron oblongifolium (Small) Millais
(Roh-doh-den'-dron ob-lon-jih-foh'-lee-um)

Erect to spreading, branching shrub to 8 ft. tall, glabrous or with red-dish pubescence.

LEAVES: alternate, commonly in terminal clusters, deciduous, short-petioled; blade pubescent to almost glabrous on lower surface; elliptic to spatulate, to 4 in. long, narrowed or rounded at base, rounded or abruptly pointed at tip.

INFLORESCENCE: flowers few to several, pedicelled, in showy terminal clusters opening after leaves appear; pedicels to ½ in. long, with gland-tipped pubescence. *Flower*: white, conspicuously sticky to touch, 1¼–1½ in. long; corolla trumpet-shaped, with gland-tipped pubescence on outside, 5-lobed; stamens 5, exserted; pistil much longer than stamens.

FRUIT: capsule, black, sometimes shiny, profusely covered with gland-tipped pubescence, to ¾ in. long, persistent.

NOTE: the most widespread and latest-flowering azalea in East Texas and western Louisiana.

BGB   (LBS)   April–September

Hoary azalea   [p. 81]
Rhododendron canescens (Michx.) Sweet
(Rho-doh-den'-dron   ka-nes'-senz)

Erect or spreading, thinly branched shrub to 10 ft. tall, frequently much lower, pubescent in upper portion.

LEAVES: alternate, petioled, deciduous, commonly in terminal clusters; blade thick, firm, pubescent on upper surface, with soft white or grayish wool and scattered gland-tipped hairs on lower surface, oblong to spatulate, 1¼–4 in. long, ¾–1¼ in. wide, wedge-shaped at base, abruptly pointed at tip; margins toothed, the teeth small and gland-tipped.

INFLORESCENCE: flowers few to several, in showy circular terminal clus-ters; flowers opening before or with first leaves. *Flower*: pale pink to dark rose, fragrant, sticky to the touch; corolla trumpet-shaped, slender-tubed, 1–2 in. long, to 1 in. across, 5-lobed at rim, densely pubescent on outer surface and with some scattered gland-tipped hairs; stamens and pistil much exserted beyond corolla, conspicuous.

FRUIT: capsule, dark brown, pubescent, wider in tip portion, to about ½ in. long.

NOTE: one of the most beautiful of our native shrubs.

BMLS   March–May

Stagger bush   [p. 71]
Lyonia mariana (L.) D. Don
(Lye-oh'-nee-ah   mair-ee-ay'-nah)

Erect shrub to 6 ft. tall, often less than 3 ft. tall, usually with some pubescence throughout; stem unbranched and leafless in lower portion, branching in upper portion; branches slender, upright.

LEAVES: alternate, deciduous, produced on new shoots, short-petioled;
blade usually glabrous or with some pubescence on lower surface, oblong to
narrowly spatulate, to 4¼ in. long, 2 in. wide, rounded to abruptly pointed
at tip, entire.

INFLORESCENCE: flowers few to several, nodding, pedicelled, in axillary
umbels forming an elongated raceme on leafless branches of last season; pedicels glabrous, with 2 small bracts at base. *Flower*: white to pinkish, to ½ in.
long; calyx 5-lobed; corolla slenderly urn-shaped, 5-lobed, ¼–½ in. long.

FRUIT: capsule, glabrous, ovoid, to 2/5 in. long, surrounded by appressed
sepals; seeds pale brown, shiny, minute.

NOTE: foliage reported poisonous to young grazing animals.

LBU   (BGB, LBS)   March–June

Indian-pipe   [p. 81]
Monotropa uniflora L.
(Moh-no-troh'-pah   yoo-nih-floh'-rah)

Erect, saprophytic, glabrous perennial 4–10 in. tall from mass of short
brittle roots; plant contains no chlorophyll, varying from waxy white to dark
rosy pink, becoming black when dry; stems 1–several, succulent, brittle.

LEAVES: alternate, sessile, white, reduced to small scalelike bracts, ¼–½
in. long, clasping at base.

INFLORESCENCE: flower solitary, terminal, nodding, becoming erect at
maturity. *Flower*: white, without fragrance, to 1¼ in. long; sepals 2–4, soon
falling; petals usually 5, oblong, deeply cupped at base, glabrous on outer
surface, pubescent on inner surface, exceeding sepals; filaments pubescent.

FRUIT: capsule, erect, ovoid, about ½ in. long; seeds pale brown, with
taillike appendage at each end.

BMLS   (SOF, LBU)   April–October

PRIMULACEAE
(Primrose Family)

Trailing loosestrife   [p. 50]
Lysimachia radicans Hook.
(Lis-ih-mak'-ee-ah   rad'-ih-kanz)

Sprawling or trailing glabrous perennial; stem branched; branches slender, elongated, to 3 ft. long, soon lying on ground and rooting at nodes.

LEAVES: opposite or whorled, petioled; petiole to 1¼ in. long, slender, narrowly winged, with bristly pubescence; blade thin, soft, lanceolate to broadly lanceolate, to 3½ in. long, 1 in. wide, entire.

INFLORESCENCE: flowers usually facing downward, long-pedicelled, from leaf axils. *Flower*: yellow, to ½ in. across; calyx deeply 5-parted; petals 5, short-clawed, irregularly cut and toothed at tip and with short rigid point.

FRUIT: capsule, exceeding calyx, globelike; seeds few to many.
SOF   May–July

Scarlet pimpernel   [p. 93]
Anagallis arvensis L.
(An-ah-gal'-lis   ar-ven'-sis)

Erect, spreading or sprawling annual usually forming mats; stem 4-angled, to 12 in. long, commonly much-branched, often rooting at lower nodes.

LEAVES: opposite, sessile, or somewhat clasping; blade broadly lanceolate, to 1¼ in. long.

INFLORESCENCE: flowers solitary, long-pedicelled, from upper leaf axils. *Flower*: scarlet to salmon, occasionally blue or white, to about ½ in. across, opening only in fair weather; calyx 5-lobed, divided almost to base; petals 5, united at base then spreading wide.

FRUIT: capsule, glabrous, globelike, to ¼ in. across, opening around the middle; seeds many, dark brown, minute.
R   (MGP, LBU)   March–November

STYRACACEAE
(Storax Family)

Silver-bell (snowdrop-tree)   [p. 81]
Halesia diptera Ellis
(Hay-lee'-zee-ah   dip'-ter-ah)

Large shrub or small tree to 24 ft. tall, often much lower.

LEAVES: alternate, deciduous, petioled; petiole ½–1 in. long, pubescent;

blade dark green and glabrous on upper surface when mature, pale green and pubescent on lower surface, with pale and conspicuous veins, elliptic to spatulate, 2–7 in. long, 3½ in. wide, abruptly pointed at tip; margins remotely toothed, the teeth coarse.

INFLORESCENCE: flowers pedicelled, drooping, in clusters of 2–6 from axils of young leaves on branches of previous season; pedicels slender, pubescent, ½–2 in. long. *Flower*: snowy white, to ¾ in. long; calyx 4-toothed, pubescent; petals 4, united at base, opening wide, pubescent; stamens 8–16, strictly erect; filaments and style pubescent.

FRUIT: dry and hard upon aging, prominently beaked, narrowly ellipsoid, broadly and conspicuously 2-winged; seed cylindrical.

BMLS   March–May

Mock-orange (storax) [p. 57]
Styrax americana Lam.
(Sty′-rax a-mer-ih-kay′-nah)

Shrub or low tree, somewhat pubescent, to 18 ft. tall, usually much lower; bark dark, streaked.

LEAVES: alternate, petioled, deciduous; petiole to ⅜ in. long; blade essentially glabrous, paler on lower surface and sometimes with minute rough pubescence, broadly elliptic to somewhat spatulate, to 5 in. long, 3⅛ in. wide, tapering to base, sharp-pointed at tip; margins irregularly toothed, especially in upper portion of blade.

INFLORESCENCE: flowers showy, solitary or in short raceme, axillary, peduncled, along short lateral leafy branches; peduncles drooping. *Flower*: white, fragrant, about ½ in. long; calyx pubescent, 5-lobed, united only to base of ovary; petals 5, with soft pubescence, spreading or conspicuously recurved; stamens 10, united at base into short tube.

FRUIT: capsule, hard, dry, pubescent, somewhat globelike, to ⅜ in. long, with persistent calyx attached to lower portion; seeds usually only 1 per capsule, erect, hard, globelike.

BGB   April–May

OLEACEAE
(Olive Family)

Fringe-tree [p. 82]
Chionanthus virginica L.
(Kye-oh-nan′-thus vir-jin′-ih-kah)

Large shrub or low tree 25–30 ft. tall, often much lower; young branches stout, pubescent.

LEAVES: opposite to alternate, deciduous, petioled; petiole to 1 in. long;

blade dark green and shiny on upper surface, paler and glabrous to densely pubescent below, oval to oblong or sometimes wider in tip portion, to 8 in. long, 2½ in. wide, usually much smaller, wedge-shaped at base and extending onto petiole, entire.

INFLORESCENCE: flowers numerous, delicate, pedicelled, in graceful showy panicle; panicles open, drooping, 5–10 in. long, from leaf axils of preceding year; flowers opening before or with first leaves. *Flower*: white to greenish white; calyx 4-parted, very small, persistent; petals 5–6, narrowly linear, to 1¼ in. long, about 1/16 in. wide.

FRUIT: drupe, blue or purple, fleshy, ovoid to ellipsoid, to ¾ in. long; seed usually 1.

BMLS   (SOF)   March–April

LOGANIACEAE
(Logania Family)

Carolina-jessamine   [p. 71]
Gelsemium sempervirens (L.) Jaume St.-Hil.
(Jel-see′-mee-um   sem-per-vye′-renz)

High-climbing or trailing, glabrous perennial vine; stem slender, woody, freely branching, wiry, reddish brown, to 20 ft. long; plant sometimes forming large carpets on ground.

LEAVES: opposite, semievergreen or evergreen, petioled; petiole about ¼ in. long; blade glabrous, elliptic to broadly lanceolate, to 3 in. long, 1¼ in. wide.

INFLORESCENCE: flowers in clusters of 1–6 from leaf axils, showy. *Flower*: yellow, strongly and pleasantly fragrant, 1–1½ in. long, 1 in. across; calyx deeply 5-lobed, subtended by several small bracts; corolla funnel-shaped, 5-lobed, the lobes wide-spreading.

FRUIT: capsule, flattened, elliptic, about ¾ in. long; seeds numerous, dull brown, flat, narrowly winged.

NOTE: frequently cultivated. Parts of this plant are poisonous.

LBU   (BMLS)   January–April

Indian-pink   [p. 51]
Spigelia marilandica L.
(Spy-gee′-lee-ah   mair-ih-lan′-dih-kah)

Erect, glabrous perennial to 32 in. tall, frequently much lower; stem 4-angled, sometimes branched at base.

LEAVES: opposite, sessile, 4–7 pairs on stem; blade broadly lanceolate, to 4 in. long. 1½ in. wide.

INFLORESCENCE: flowers few to several, in showy terminal 1-sided spike;

spikes often bending downward at tip, sometimes forked. *Flower*: red on outside, yellow within, 1½ in. long; calyx 5-lobed, less than ½ in. long; corolla
erect, tubular, 5-lobed; corolla lobes short, sharp-pointed, spreading.

FRUIT: capsule, broader than long, separating into 2 parts at maturity;
seeds numerous, blackish brown, angled.

NOTE: uncommon in the Big Thicket; more common eastward.

SOF   (BMLS)   May–October

Hornpod   [p. 51]
Cynoctonum mitreola (L.) Britt.
(Sye-nok′-toh-num   mit-ree′-oh-lah)

Glabrous annual to 20 in. tall; stem frequently reddish, unbranched or
freely branching; branches slender, weak.

LEAVES: opposite, stipuled, petioled; blade thin, elliptic to broadly lanceolate, ¾–3⅛ in. long, rounded to sharp-pointed at tip.

INFLORESCENCE: flowers numerous, sessile, very small, arranged along
one side of branches in long-peduncled terminal or axillary cymes; cyme
branches coiled in bud, uncoiling at maturity. *Flower*: white or pink-tinged;
sepals 5, united at base; corolla funnel-shaped, twice as long as sepals, 5-
lobed, pubescent in throat; stamens not exserted.

FRUIT: capsule, essentially smooth, ⅛–¼ in. long, deeply 2-lobed, each
lobe horned; capsules widely spaced on cyme branches; seeds many, black,
pebbled on surface, minute.

SOF   (POF)   May–December

Wand hornpod   [p. 63]
Cynoctonum sessilifolium (Walt.) J. F. Gmel.
(Sye-nok′-toh-num   ses-sih-lih-foh′-lee-um)

Stiffly erect, glabrous annual to 20 in. tall; stem usually unbranched, or
if branched, the branches strictly erect.

LEAVES: opposite, stipuled, sessile; blade firm, elliptic to oval or almost
round, rarely more than ¾ in. long and wide; margins usually with noticeable minute projections.

INFLORESCENCE: flowers numerous, very small, arranged tightly along
one side of branches of terminal cyme. *Flower*: white to pale pink; calyx 5-
lobed, the lobes prominently keeled; corolla only slightly longer than calyx.

FRUIT: capsule, conspicuously covered with minute projections on outer
surface, ⅛–¼ in. long, deeply 2-lobed; capsules crowded on cyme branches;
seeds many, smooth and shiny on surface, minute.

LBS   June–October

Juniper-leaf [p. 86]

Polypremum procumbens L.

(Pol-ih-pree'-mum proh-kum'-benz)

Erect or spreading glabrous annual or perennial 2–12 in. tall; stem 4-angled, ribbed, much-branched.

LEAVES: opposite, sessile, connected at base by thin membrane, often with smaller leaves clustered in axils; blade narrowly linear, to 1¼ in. long, rarely more than 1/16 in. wide.

INFLORESCENCE: flowers solitary, sessile, small, inconspicuous, terminal and axillary. *Flower*: white, about ¼ in. across; calyx 4-lobed, divided nearly to base; corolla 4-lobed, almost flat, bearded in throat; stamens 4.

FRUIT: capsule, notched at tip, slightly flattened, ovoid, very small; seeds many, minute.

OFS   (SOF)   April–November

GENTIANACEAE
(Gentian Family)

Pine-woods rose-gentian [p. 63]

Sabatia gentianoides Ell.

(Sa-bay'-shee-ah   jen-shee-an-oh'-ih-deez)

Strictly erect, glabrous annuals 12–20 in. tall; stem usually unbranched, occasionally few-branched in upper portion.

LEAVES: opposite, sessile; basal leaves in wide-spreading rosette, oblong to very broadly spatulate, to 1¼ in. long, ½ in. wide; stem leaves erect or appressed, linear, to 4¾ in. long, ⅛ in. wide.

INFLORESCENCE: flowers 1–several, essentially sessile, in showy compact terminal or axillary cluster; clusters subtended by conspicuous, linear, leaflike bracts. *Flower*: pink to dark rose; calyx 10-lobed, the lobes recurved; corolla deeply cleft into 7–12 lobes; corolla lobes to 1¼ in. long, ⅜ in. wide, appearing as petals; style 2-branched, at first twisted and lying flat with stigmas concealed, becoming erect and uncoiling after anthers shed pollen.

FRUIT: capsule, ovoid, to ⅜ in. long; seeds numerous, small, gray green.

LBS   May–August

Rose-pink [p. 63]

Sabatia angularis (L.) Pursh

(Sa-bay'-shee-ah   an-gyoo-lair'-is)

Erect, stout, glabrous annual to 28 in. tall; stem conspicuously 4-angled, winged on the edges, unbranched or much-branched in upper portion.

LEAVES: opposite, sessile; basal leaves absent or present at flowering time; stem leaves thin, 3- to 7-veined, from almost round to broadly lanceolate, to 1½ in. long, 1 in. wide, notched at base and clasping stem.

INFLORESCENCE: flowers usually solitary, at ends of branches, forming showy terminal panicle; branches opposite. *Flower*: pink or rose, rarely white, with greenish central star, delicately fragrant; calyx tube cleft into 5 threadlike lobes; corolla deeply cleft into 5 lobes, the lobes to ¾ in. long; style elongated; stigmas 2, maturing before anthers shed pollen.

FRUIT: capsule, ellipsoid, to ⅜ in. long, angled, not winged; seeds numerous, blackish brown, minute.

LBS (MGP, LBU)   May–July

Meadow-pink   [p. 63]
Sabatia campestris Nutt.
(Sa-bay'-shee-ah kam-pes'-tris)

Erect, slender or wide-spreading glabrous annual to 20 in. tall; stem 4-angled, branched in upper portion.

LEAVES: opposite, sessile, clasping basally; blade thin, oblong to broadly lanceolate, to 1¾ in. long, ¾ in. wide.

INFLORESCENCE: flowers solitary, at ends of branches and on long peduncles from leaf axils, forming showy terminal panicle; branches alternate. *Flower*: pink to rose, with yellow central star; calyx deeply 5-lobed, conspicuously 5-winged; corolla deeply cleft into 5 lobes; corolla lobes to about 1 in. long, ½ in. wide; style 2-branched, elongated, at first lying flat and twisted together concealing stigmas, becoming erect and uncoiling after anthers shed pollen.

FRUIT: capsule, to ⅜ in. long, angled, winged on edges; seeds numerous.

LBS (MGP, LBU)   April–July

Prairie rose-gentian   [p. 64]
Sabatia campanulata (L.) Torrey
(Sa-bay'-shee-ah kam-pan-yoo-lay'-tah)

Erect to sprawling, glabrous perennial 12–28 in. tall from short rhizome; stems 1–few, slender, delicate, usually branched.

LEAVES: opposite, sessile; basal leaves absent; stem leaves 3-veined, narrowly oblong to elliptic, becoming threadlike to linear in upper portion.

INFLORESCENCE: flowers solitary at ends of branches and on peduncles from leaf axils; branches alternate. *Flower*: pink, rarely white, with yellow central star; calyx 5-lobed; calyx lobes linear to bristlelike, ¼–¾ in. long; corolla united at base, deeply cleft into usually 5 lobes; corolla lobes to ¾ in. long, ⅜ in. wide; style elongated, lying flat, twisted, concealing stigmas, becoming erect and uncoiling after anthers shed pollen.

FRUIT: capsule, ellipsoid, to ¼ in. long; seeds numerous.

NOTE: rare in the Big Thicket.

LBS   May–August

Centaury [p. 37]

Centaurium pulchellum (Sw.) Druce

(Sen-taw'-ree-um   pul-kel'-lum)

Erect, slender, delicate, glabrous perennial 3–8 in. tall; stem solitary, much-branched in upper portion.

LEAVES: opposite, sessile; basal leaves absent; lower stem leaves elliptic to broadly lanceolate, to ¾ in. long; upper leaves usually smaller.

INFLORESCENCE: flowers solitary at ends of opposite branches and on short peduncles from leaf axils, forming showy terminal panicle. *Flower*: pink to dark rose; calyx about ¼ in. long, deeply cleft into 5 narrow segments; corolla trumpet-shaped, 5-lobed, the slender tube portion 1½–2 times longer than lobes; corolla lobes short, wide-spreading to almost closed.

FRUIT: capsule, about ¼ in. long.

NOTE: rare in the Big Thicket.

MGP   May–August

Bluebell gentian [p. 37]

Eustoma exaltatum (L.) G. Don

(Yoo-stoh'-mah   ex-al-tay'-tum)

Erect, glabrous, glaucous annual or short-lived perennial to 28 in. tall; stems 1–several, branched in upper portion of plant.

LEAVES: opposite, sessile, clasping basally; basal leaves usually in rosette, broadly spatulate; stem leaves broadly lanceolate or oblong to narrowly elliptic, to 3½ in. long, 1¼ in. wide, rounded to abruptly sharp-pointed at tip.

INFLORESCENCE: flowers usually solitary, long-pedicelled, from upper leaf axils, usually forming showy terminal cluster; pedicels to 4 in. long. *Flower*: blue, dark lavender, or white, prominently blotched with darker purple in throat, deeply cupped; calyx deeply cleft into 5 lobes; calyx lobes long-pointed, to about ¾ in. long; corolla with short basal tube, deeply divided into 5 lobes at rim; corolla lobes twisted in bud, erect when opened, about ¾ in. long, less than ⅝ in. wide.

FRUIT: capsule, ellipsoid, to ¾ in. long, separating into 2 sections; seeds many.

NOTE: uncommon in the Big Thicket.

MGP   June–October

Bluebells   [p. 37]

Eustoma grandiflorum (Raf.) Shinners

(Yoo-stoh'-mah   grand-dih-floh'-rum)

Erect, glabrous, glaucous, usually short-lived perennial to 28 in. tall; stems 1–several, branched in upper portion.

LEAVES: opposite, sessile, clasping basally; blade noticeably 3-veined, broadly lanceolate to broadly oblong, to 3⅛ in. long, 1¼ in. wide.

INFLORESCENCE: flowers solitary, showy, pedicelled, from upper leaf axils; pedicels to 2⅜ in. long. *Flower*: variable in color from white or white tinged with purple or yellow to pinkish or blue purple prominently marked in center with darker purple, deeply cupped; calyx deeply cleft into 5 lobes, the lobes to about 1⅛ in. long; corolla with short basal tube, deeply divided into 5 lobes at rim; corolla lobes erect when opened, 1¼–1½ in. long, at least 3 times as long as tube.

FRUIT: capsule, ellipsoid, to ¾ in. long, separating into 2 sections; seeds many.

NOTE: uncommon, becoming rare in the Big Thicket.

MGP   June–September

Bottle-gentian   [p. 63]

Gentiana saponaria L.

(Jen-shee-ay'-nah   sap-oh-nair'-ee-ah)

Erect, often clumped, usually glabrous, glaucous perennial to 3 ft. tall, often lower; from coarse roots.

LEAVES: opposite, sessile, whorled below inflorescence; blade pale green, thick, narrowly elliptic to lanceolate, to 4 in. long, abruptly narrowed at base.

INFLORESCENCE: flowers few–several in dense terminal cluster and 1–few in upper leaf axils, showy. *Flower*: pale to dark blue or purplish, erect, cylindrical, to 2 in. long, appearing closed or only slightly open near tip; calyx 5-lobed; calyx lobes firm, lanceolate to oblong; corolla tubular, shallowly lobed near tip, the lobes alternating with folded membranous tissue.

FRUIT: capsule, ellipsoid; seeds numerous.

NOTE: possibly near extinction in the Big Thicket due to destruction of habitat.

LBS   September–November

Spring bartonia   [p. 64]

Bartonia verna (Michx.) Muhl.

(Bar-toh'-nee-ah   ver'-nah)

Stiffly erect, delicate, inconspicuous annual or biennial 2–8 in. tall; stem threadlike, wiry, purplish or rarely yellowish; plants usually in colonies.

LEAVES: essentially opposite, minute, scalelike, erect or appressed, to ⅛ in. long.

INFLORESCENCE: flowers very small, inconspicuous, solitary and terminal or also from elongated axillary peduncles and forming terminal panicle. *Flower*: white or yellowish; calyx deeply 4-parted, the segments lanceolate and keeled; corolla bell-shaped, deeply 4-lobed, the lobes to ½ in. long.

FRUIT: capsule, ovoid, to ¼ in. long, abruptly beaked at tip; seeds numerous, brown, minute.

NOTE: Because of its diminutive nature in its natural habitat, this plant is difficult to see.

LBS   February–April

Floating-heart   [p. 57]
Nymphoides aquatica (Gmel.) O. Ktze.
(Nim-foh′-ih-deez   a-kwah′-tih-kah)

Aquatic, glabrous perennial from short, thick tuber.

LEAVES: from tuber, long-petioled, floating; petiole slender, purple, pitted, to 10 in. long; blade glabrous, rather thick, spongy, prominently veined, pale green above, usually purple and pitted on lower surface, almost round to wider than long, to 6 in. wide, deeply cleft at base.

INFLORESCENCE: flowers few to several, pedicelled, in showy umbel along petiole below blade; pedicels to 3⅛ in. long, elongating in fruit; after flowering a cluster of tubers sometimes forming below leaf blade. *Flower*: white, about ⅝ in. across; calyx less than ¼ in. long, 5-parted nearly to base; corolla deeply 5-lobed, the lobes with glandular appendages near base.

FRUIT: capsule, ellipsoid, to ⅝ in. long; seeds few to many, yellowish to tan, shiny, with roughened projections.

BGB   May–August

APOCYNACEAE
(Dogbane Family)

Blue-star   [p. 51]
Amsonia glaberrima Woodson
(Am-soh′-nee-ah   gla-ber′-rih-mah)

Erect, glabrous perennial to 32 in. tall; stems usually several from woody rhizome.

LEAVES: alternate, short-petioled; blade glabrous, dull on both surfaces, firm, narrowly lanceolate to broadly oblong, to 3⅛ in. long, ¾ in. wide, narrowed at base, slowly tapering to tip; upper leaves usually broader than lower leaves.

INFLORESCENCE: flowers several to many, short-pedicelled, in loose open terminal panicle. *Flower*: pale to bright blue; calyx glabrous, small, shallowly 5-lobed; corolla trumpet-shaped, deeply divided into 5 lobes, glabrous on outer surface; tube slender, about 1/4 in. long; corolla lobes about 1/4 in. long, wide-spreading, not constricted at base; stamens 5, alternate with corolla lobes; ovaries 2; styles united into 1; stigma conspicuously large, thick.

FRUIT: follicle, glabrous, narrowly cylindrical, 3–4 in. long, in pairs at tip of pedicel; seeds numerous, rather corky.

SOF   (POF, LBS)   March–May

Climbing dogbane   [p. 51]
Trachelospermum difforme (Walt.) Gray
(Tray-kee-loh-sper'-mum   dif-for'-mee)

Twining or low-climbing, glabrous to variously pubescent perennial vine; stem slender, woody, reddish.

LEAVES: opposite, petioled, deciduous, often of different forms on same plant; petiole to 1/2 in. long; blade thin, lanceolate or elliptic to broadly lanceolate or sometimes broadly spatulate, to 4¾ in. long, 3 in. wide, rounded or wedge-shaped at base, tapering or abruptly pointed at tip.

INFLORESCENCE: flowers numerous, small, pedicelled, in axillary cyme; cymes long-peduncled; only 1 cyme per pair of leaves. *Flower*: pale yellow or greenish; calyx deeply 5-lobed; corolla funnel-shaped, 5-lobed at rim; corolla lobes shorter than tube, spreading; anthers united; ovaries 2, surrounded at base by 5 nectar-bearing structures.

FRUIT: follicle, glabrous, narrowly cylindrical, 6–9 in. long; follicles in pairs; seeds numerous, with tuft of hair at tip.

SOF   (POF, LBU)   April–June

Indian hemp   [p. 72]
Apocynum cannabinum L.
(A-pos'-ih-num   kan-nab'-ih-num)

Erect, glabrous to variously pubescent perennial to about 3 ft. tall from horizontal bud-bearing roots; stem solitary, usually much-branched in upper portion, often reddish; plants usually forming large colonies.

LEAVES: opposite, petioled or occasionally sessile; blade glabrous on upper surface, glabrous to pubescent on lower surface, ovate to lanceolate, to 5½ in. long, 2¾ in. wide, somewhat rounded at base, rounded to sharp-pointed at tip, entire.

INFLORESCENCE: flowers usually several in cyme, pedicelled; cymes terminal or axillary, usually overtopped by leafy branches. *Flower*: white to greenish, to 1/4 in. long; calyx deeply 5-lobed, glabrous; corolla tubular to urn-shaped, shallowly 5-lobed; stamens 5.

FRUIT: follicle, glabrous, slender, 4¾–8 in. long, to ⅛ in. wide, drooping at maturity; follicles usually paired; seeds numerous, longer than wide, smooth, with small tuft of hairs.

LBU (SOF) April–August

ASCLEPIADACEAE
(Milkweed Family)

Antelope-horn [p. 37]
Asclepias viridis Walt.
(As-klee′-pee-us vir′-ih-dis)

Erect to somewhat sprawling, rather stout, essentially glabrous perennial to 2 ft. tall, with milky sap; stems unbranched or occasionally branched from base.

LEAVES: alternate, occasionally almost opposite, short-petioled; blade yellowish green, firm, broadly lanceolate to elliptic, 1½–5⅛ in. long, ⅜–2⅜ in. wide, abruptly to broadly rounded at base, rounded or abruptly pointed at tip.

INFLORESCENCE: flowers several to many, pedicelled, crowded in showy peduncled cymelike terminal or axillary umbels; peduncle to 2⅜ in. long, with scattered pubescence. *Flower*: pale green, purple in center; calyx deeply 5-lobed; corolla deeply 5-lobed, the lobes erect for most of length; anthers 5, united with stigma; hoods 5, to ¼ in. long, abruptly reflexed at tip; each tip with small, blunt structure.

FRUIT: follicle, erect on deflexed pedicel, inflated, broadly ovoid, to 1⅛ in. across; follicles usually 1 per peduncle; seeds many, flattened, oval, with conspicuous tuft of whitish or yellowish hair.

MGP (LBS, LBU) March–September

Blunt-leaf milkweed [p. 86]
Asclepias amplexicaulis Sm.
(As-klee′-pee-us am-plex-ih-kaw′-lis)

Erect or occasionally sprawling, stout, glabrous perennial to 40 in. tall, usually lower, with milky sap.

LEAVES: opposite, sessile, prominently clasping basally; blade thick, firm, glaucous, broadly lanceolate to narrowly oblong, 3–6 in. long, 2–3 in. wide, broadly notched at base, broadly rounded or blunt at tip; margins usually conspicuously crisped or wavy.

INFLORESCENCE: flowers several, pedicelled, in usually solitary showy peduncled terminal umbel; peduncle stout, to 3¼ in. long. *Flower*: greenish, tinged with purple or rose; calyx deeply 5-lobed, glabrous; corolla deeply 5-

lobed; corolla lobes about ⅜ in. long, reflexed; anthers 5, united with stigma; hoods 5, tubular, with small horn attached near middle of tube; horn longer than hood, curved inward.

FRUIT: follicle, erect on deflexed pedicel, smooth, glabrous, rather glaucous, narrowly ellipsoid, tapering at both ends, 4–6½ in. long, to ¾ in. across; usually 1 follicle per peduncle; seeds many, flattened, with conspicuous tuft of brownish yellow hair.

OFS   April–June

Savannah milkweed [p. 72]
Asclepias obovata Ell.
(As-klee′-pee-us   ob-oh-vay′-tah)

Erect, rather stout, herbaceous perennial 6–20 in. tall, with milky sap, softly pubescent mostly throughout; stem usually solitary, occasionally branching.

LEAVES: opposite, short-petioled; blade firm, densely pubescent especially on lower surface, variable in size and shape, broadly lanceolate to oblong or elliptic, to 3⅛ in. long, 1½ in. wide, rounded or blunt at base, broadly rounded or abruptly pointed at tip.

INFLORESCENCE: flowers several, pedicelled, in compact umbel; umbels 1–3, essentially sessile, densely pubescent, from upper nodes. *Flower*: pale greenish yellow; calyx 5-lobed; corolla 5-lobed; corolla lobes to ⅜ in. long, reflexed; anthers 5, united with stigma; hoods 5, broadly oblong, broadly rounded or notched at tip; horn prominently curved inward.

FRUIT: follicle, erect on deflexed pedicel, pubescent, ellipsoid, tapering at both ends, 4¾ in. long or more; usually 1 follicle per peduncle; seeds many, flattened, with conspicuous tuft of hair.

LBU   May–September

Butterfly-weed [p. 86]
Asclepias tuberosa L.
(As-klee′-pee-us   too-beh-roh′-sah)

Erect to sprawling, stout, conspicuously pubescent perennial to 32 in. tall, often lower, without milky sap; stems solitary or several and forming clump, usually branching only in inflorescence.

LEAVES: alternate, numerous, somewhat crowded, short-petioled; blade firm, pubescent especially on lower surface, narrowly lanceolate to broadly spatulate, to 4¼ in. long, 1¼ in. wide, wedge-shaped to rounded and broadly notched at base, rounded to sharp-pointed at tip; margins often crisped or wavy, occasionally rolled toward lower surface.

INFLORESCENCE: flowers numerous, in showy cymelike umbels from nodes of reduced terminal leaves; umbel branches twisted or spiraled. *Flower*:

orange to orange red, occasionally yellowish; calyx 5-lobed; corolla 5-lobed; corolla lobes about ¼ in. long, reflexed; anthers 5, united with stigma; hoods 5, lanceolate, erect; horns slightly longer than hoods, gradually arching over anther structure.

FRUIT: follicle, erect on deflexed pedicel, smooth, pubescent, narrowly ellipsoid, tapering at both ends, 3–6 in. long, about ½ in. across; follicles usually 1 per peduncle, sometimes 2; seeds many, flattened, broadly oval, with conspicuous tuft of white hair.

OFS   (MGP, POF, LBU)   April–September

Green milkweed [p. 72]
Asclepias viridiflora Raf.
(As-klee'-pee-us   vir-ih-dih-floh'-rah)

Stiffly erect or occasionally somewhat sprawling, glabrous or pubescent herbaceous perennial to 3 ft. tall, sometimes lower, with milky sap; stem usually solitary, sometimes branched from base, often zigzag in upper portion.

LEAVES: opposite, essentially sessile to short-petioled; blade firm, thick, glabrous to roughly pubescent, variable in shape and size, linear to lanceolate, elliptic or almost round, 1½–5⅛ in. long, ⅜–2⅜ in. wide; margins often rough, usually wavy.

INFLORESCENCE: flowers many, pedicelled, in compact umbel; umbels somewhat globelike, essentially sessile, pubescent, terminal or from upper leaf axils and appearing to be placed on side of stem. *Flower*: pale green; calyx 5-lobed; corolla deeply 5-lobed; corolla lobes about ¼ in. long, prominently reflexed; hoods 5, erect, appressed to anther structure; horns absent.

FRUIT: follicle, erect on deflexed pedicel, glabrous to roughly pubescent, narrowly ellipsoid, slenderly pointed at tip, 2¾–6 in. long, ½–¾ in. across; follicles usually 1 per peduncle, sometimes 2; seeds many, flattened, with conspicuous tuft of brownish yellow hair.

LBU   (MGP, OFS)   April–August

White-flowered milkweed [p. 72]
Asclepias variegata L.
(As-klee'-pee-us   vair-ee-eh-gay'-tah)

Erect, stout, herbaceous perennial to 3½ ft. tall, often lower, with milky sap; stems solitary or few and forming clump, slender, unbranched, sparsely pubescent to glabrous.

LEAVES: opposite, 2–5 pairs, the lowermost pair much reduced in size, petioled; petiole to ¾ in. long; blade thick, dark green and glabrous on upper surface, glaucous and sparsely pubescent beneath, broadly lanceolate to broadly oblong, 3–6 in. long, 1½–3½ in. wide, broadly rounded at base, usually broadly rounded with sharp point at tip.

INFLORESCENCE: flowers numerous, pedicelled, in showy umbel; umbels compact, globelike, peduncled, terminal or from uppermost nodes. *Flower*: white; calyx 5-lobed; corolla deeply 5-lobed; corolla lobes about ¼ in. long, somewhat spreading; anthers 5, purple, united with stigma; hoods 5; each hood folded together, inflated, angular on each side near base; horn much shorter than hood.

FRUIT: follicle, erect on deflexed pedicel, glaucous, minutely pubescent, narrowly ellipsoid, tapering at both ends, 4–6 in. long, to ¾ in. across; usually 1 follicle per peduncle, sometimes 2; seeds many, flattened, with conspicuous tuft of white hair.

LBU   (BMLS)   April–July

Red milkweed   [p. 58]
Asclepias rubra L.
(As-klee'-pee-us   roo'-brah)

Erect, slender, rather delicate, glabrous or inconspicuously pubescent herbaceous perennial to 40 in. tall, commonly lower, with milky sap.

LEAVES: opposite, essentially sessile; blade firm, dark green on upper surface, glaucous beneath, narrowly to broadly lanceolate, rounded to somewhat notched at base; margins usually sparsely pubescent, crisped or wavy.

INFLORESCENCE: flowers several, pedicelled, in showy peduncled umbel; peduncles to 4 in. long; umbels 1–4, rather open, terminal or from upper nodes, commonly paired when terminal. *Flower*: pale pink to dull red or lavender; calyx 5-lobed, glabrous; corolla 5-lobed; corolla lobes about ¼ in. long, spreading; anthers 5, united with stigma; hoods 5, lanceolate, erect; horns shorter than hoods.

FRUIT: follicle, erect on deflexed pedicel, smooth, glabrous, narrowly ellipsoid, tapering at both ends, 3–4¾ in. long, about ½ in. across; usually 1 follicle per peduncle, sometimes 2; seeds many, flattened, broadly oval, about ¼ in. long, with conspicuous tuft of long white hair.

BGB   May–August

Whorled milkweed   [p. 38]
Asclepias verticillata L.
(As-klee'-pee-us   ver-tih-sil-lay'-tah)

Erect, slender, delicate, sparsely pubescent herbaceous perennial to 28 in. tall, with milky sap; stem solitary, usually unbranched.

LEAVES: usually whorled, with 3 or 4 per node, sometimes opposite in pairs, essentially sessile, usually strictly erect; blade firm, glabrous or sparsely pubescent, threadlike to linear, to 2¾ in. long; margins often rolled toward lower surface.

INFLORESCENCE: flowers few to many, pedicelled, in peduncled umbel;

umbels solitary or paired from upper nodes. *Flower*: greenish white, occasionally tinged with rose purple; calyx 5-lobed; corolla deeply 5-lobed; corolla lobes about 1/16 in. long, reflexed, curved upward at tips; anthers 5, united; hoods 5, oval, much shorter than horns; horns incurved, exserted.

FRUIT: follicle, erect on erect pedicel, smooth, glabrous, narrowly ellipsoid, tapering at both ends, 2½–4 in. long, about ¼ in. across; usually 1 follicle per peduncle, occasionally 2; seeds many, flattened, oval, about ¼ in. long, with conspicuous tuft of white hair.

MGP   (LBS)   April–August

Long-leaf milkweed [p. 64]
Asclepias longifolia Michx.
(As-klee'-pee-us   lon-jih-foh'-lee-ah)

Sprawling to trailing, minutely pubescent, herbaceous perennial with milky sap; stem slender, unbranched, 8–28 in. long.

LEAVES: opposite or almost so, numerous, essentially sessile, erect; blade glabrous to sparsely pubescent along veins on lower surface, linear to narrowly lanceolate, 2⅜–7¼ in. long, to ⅜ in. wide.

INFLORESCENCE: flowers several to many, pedicelled, in peduncled umbel; peduncles slender, to 2½ in. long; umbels somewhat globelike, rather loose, terminal or from upper nodes, often 1 on each side of stem at same node. *Flower*: pale greenish white tinged with purple; calyx 5-lobed; corolla deeply 5-lobed; corolla lobes about ¼ in. long, reflexed; anthers 5, united with stigma; hoods 5, broadly spatulate; horns absent.

FRUIT: follicle, erect on deflexed pedicel, minutely pubescent, narrowly ellipsoid, tapering at both ends, 3–4¾ in. long, ⅜ in. across; usually 1 follicle per peduncle; seeds many, flattened, broadly oval, about ⅜ in. long, with conspicuous tuft of white hair.

LBS   April–July

Shore milkweed [p. 51]
Asclepias perennis Walt.
(As-klee'-pee-us   pe-ren'-nis)

Erect, slender, rather delicate, glabrous or sparsely pubescent herbaceous perennial 12–15 in. tall; stem solitary, slender, usually branching only from base.

LEAVES: opposite, 3–5 pairs on stem, petioled; petiole to ⅝ in. long; blade thin, glabrous, narrowly lanceolate to narrowly elliptic, 2–5½ in. long, ⅝ in. wide, tapering to base.

INFLORESCENCE: flowers several to many, pedicelled, in umbel; umbels peduncled, rather loose, showy, from uppermost nodes; peduncles slender, to 1½ in. long; pedicels usually reddish or purplish. *Flower*: white tinged with pale pink; calyx 5-lobed, pubescent; corolla deeply 5-lobed; corolla lobes about ⅛ in. long, reflexed; hoods 5, rounded at tip, somewhat spreading; horns somewhat longer than hoods, curved inward.

FRUIT: follicle, hanging downward on deflexed pedicel, smooth, glabrous, broadly ellipsoid, short-tapered at base, slenderly beaked at tip, 1½–2¾ in. long, to 1 in. across; usually only 1 follicle per peduncle; seeds many, flattened, broadly oval, about ⅝ in. long, with no tuft of hair present.
SOF (POF, BGB) April–August

Milkvine [p. 51]
Matelea gonocarpa (Walt.) Shinners
(Ma-teh-lee′-ah gon-oh-kar′-pah)

Twining or high-climbing, slender, pubescent herbaceous perennial vine; stem wiry, usually branched.

LEAVES: opposite, petioled; petiole pubescent, longer than inflorescence; blade pale on lower surface, broadly lanceolate, to 6 in. long, 4 in. wide, lobed at base and narrowly notched, abruptly sharp-pointed at tip.

INFLORESCENCE: flowers numerous, inconspicuous, pedicelled, in peduncled umbellike axillary clusters. *Flower*: brownish purple to greenish purple; calyx 5-lobed, the lobes fringed with hairs; corolla deeply 5-lobed; corolla lobes narrowly lanceolate, to ⅝ in. long, glabrous, spreading.

FRUIT: follicle, long-pedicelled, smooth, glabrous, prominently angled, ovoid, to 4¾ in. long; seeds many, flattened, with tuft of hair.
SOF (POF, BMLS) May–July

CONVOLVULACEAE
(Morning Glory Family)

Purple stylisma [p. 38]
Stylisma aquatica (Walt.) Raf.
(Sty-liz′-mah a-kwah′-tik-kah)

Trailing or twining, delicate, pubescent perennial vine; stems several to many, to 5 ft. long; older plants often forming large mats or clumps.

LEAVES: alternate, short-petioled; blade with dense short pubescence on both surfaces, oblong to lanceolate, to 1¼ in. long, ⅜ in. wide, blunt or somewhat notched at base.

INFLORESCENCE: flowers 1–3, short-pedicelled, on peduncle from leaf axil; peduncles longer than leaves. *Flower*: lavender, to ⅝ in. long; sepals 5, separate, stiff, pubescent; corolla funnel-shaped, shallowly lobed; stamens 5; filaments essentially glabrous; style divided more than half its length.

FRUIT: capsule, densely pubescent, ovoid; seeds 1–4, about ¼ in. long, ⅛ in. wide.

NOTE: uncommon in the Big Thicket.
MGP   May–June

White stylisma [p. 72]
Stylisma humistrata (Walt.) Chapm.
(Sty-liz′-mah hyoo-mih-stray′-tah)

Trailing or twining, delicate, pubescent perennial vine; stems slender, unbranched or with few long branches, to 8 ft. long, usually shorter.

LEAVES: alternate, short-petioled; blade sparsely to densely pubescent especially on lower surface, elliptic to somewhat oblong, to 2⅜ in. long, 1⅛ in. wide, usually somewhat notched at base, with short sharp point at rounded tip.

INFLORESCENCE: flowers 1–3, short-pedicelled, on peduncle from leaf axil; peduncles very slender, much longer than subtending leaf. *Flower*: white, to ¾ in. long; sepals 5, glabrous on outer surface; corolla funnel-shaped, shallowly 5-lobed; stamens 5; filaments pubescent; style divided ⅔ or more of length.

FRUIT: capsule, glabrous, ovoid, about as long as sepals; seeds 1–4.
LBU   (SOF)   June–August

Bracted stylisma [p. 87]
Stylisma pickeringii (Torr.) Gray var. *pattersonii* (Fern. & Schub.) Myint
(Sty-liz′-mah pik-eh-ring′-ee-eye pat-ter-soh′-nee-eye)

Trailing or sprawling on other plants, delicate, pubescent herbaceous perennial; stem very slender, commonly much-branched, to 7 ft. long.

LEAVES: alternate, essentially sessile; blade glabrous on upper surface, pubescent below, threadlike to linear, to 2⅛ in. long, ⅛ in. wide, narrowed at base.

INFLORESCENCE: flowers 1–3, short-pedicelled, on axillary peduncle; pedicel subtended by 2 small linear bracts; peduncles slender, equaling or exceeding subtending leaf. *Flower*: white, to ¾ in. long; sepals 5, densely pubescent on outer surface; corolla funnel-shaped, 5-lobed; stamens 5; filaments glabrous; style usually undivided or sometimes slightly so.

FRUIT: capsule, pubescent, ovoid, longer than sepals; seeds 1–4.
OFS   (SOF)   May–September

Hairy cluster-vine [p. 93]
Jacquemontia tamnifolia (L.) Griseb.
(Jak-eh-mon′-chee-ah tam-nih-foh′-lee-ah)

Erect, becoming elongate and trailing or twining, pubescent annual vine to 7 ft. long.

LEAVES: alternate, long-petioled; blade occasionally sparsely pubescent on both surfaces, elliptic to broadly lanceolate, 1¼–4¾ in. long, ¾–3½ in. wide, usually notched at base; margins with soft straight pubescence.

INFLORESCENCE: flowers several to many in dense headlike cyme; cymes terminal or on long peduncles from leaf axils, subtended by leaflike bracts; flowers opening 1–few at a time in cyme. *Flower*: blue, to ¾ in. across; sepals 5, separate, linear, with stiff brownish yellow pubescence; corolla funnel-shaped, 5-angled; stamens 5.

FRUIT: capsule, globelike, to ¼ in. across; seeds 4, brownish black, glabrous.

R   (POF, SOF)   July–October

Cypress vine [p. 94]
Ipomoea quamoclit L.
(Eye-poh-mee′-ah   kwam′-oh-klit)

Twining or low-climbing, slender, delicate, glabrous annual vine 10–20 ft. long.

LEAVES: alternate, short-petioled; blade thin, to 2 in. long, 1¾ in. wide, deeply cleft almost to midrib into numerous threadlike segments.

INFLORESCENCE: flowers 1–few, pedicelled, peduncled, in axillary cyme; pedicels 1 in. long or more, thickening in fruit; peduncles slender, as long as subtending leaf. *Flower*: scarlet, to 1½ in. long, remaining open all day; sepals 5, united at base, with soft spinelike tips; corolla trumpet-shaped; tube long, slender; rim flat, 5-lobed; stamens and stigma exserted.

FRUIT: capsule, on erect pedicel, broadly ovoid, ⅛–¼ in. long, about twice as long as sepals; seeds 4–6.

NOTE: native of tropical America.

R   July–November

Wild potato [p. 94]
Ipomoea pandurata (L.) Mey.
(Eye-poh-mee′-ah   pan-doo-ray′-tah)

Trailing or twining and low-climbing, essentially glabrous herbaceous perennial vine from large tuberous root; stems strong, often several from base, usually purplish, branched in upper portion, to 15 ft. long.

LEAVES: alternate, petioled; petiole to 3⅛ in. long; blade glabrous or with dense soft pubescence on lower surface, broadly lanceolate, often with indented sides and appearing 3-lobed, 1¼–4 in. long, ¾–3½ in. wide, deeply notched at base.

INFLORESCENCE: flowers 1–5, large, pedicelled, in showy peduncled cyme; peduncles from leaf axils, elongating in fruit. *Flower*: white with purple red center, open for only a few hours in early morning, to 3¼ in. long, about as wide; sepals 5, unequal in length, glabrous; corolla funnel-shaped; tube short, rim 5-lobed; stamens 5.

FRUIT: capsule, ovoid, about ⅜ in. long; seeds 2–4, densely woolly on angles.

NOTE: In old plants the root may be several feet long and weigh up to 25 pounds.

R   (SOF, LBU, OFS)   June–September

Salt-marsh morning glory   [p. 38]
Ipomoea sagittata Poir.

(Eye-poh-mee'-ah   saj-it-tay'-tah)

Trailing, tightly twining or low-climbing, glabrous perennial vine from creeping root, usually forming colonies.

LEAVES: alternate, petioled; blade narrowly lanceolate to broadly lanceolate, deeply lobed at base with the lobes extending downward, 1½–4 in. long, to 2 in. wide above lobes.

INFLORESCENCE: flowers solitary, large, showy, on long peduncle from leaf axils. *Flower*: dark pink to red purple, to 3½ in. long, about as wide; sepals 5, conspicuously unequal in length, glabrous; corolla funnel-shaped, essentially unlobed at rim; stamens and stigma not exserted.

FRUIT: capsule, globelike, about ⅜ in. across; seeds 2–6, with stiff pubescence on angles.

MGP   (POF)   April–October

Pitted morning glory   [p. 51]
Ipomoea lacunosa L.

(Eye-poh-mee'-ah   lak-oo-noh'-sah)

Trailing or twining and low-climbing, slender-stemmed pubescent annual 2–10 ft. long, from slender taproot.

LEAVES: alternate, petioled; blade thin, variable, usually broadly lanceolate, entire to toothed or prominently 3-lobed, ¾–4 in. long, ½–3½ in. wide, notched at base; margins usually maroon or purple.

INFLORESCENCE: flowers 1–3, on long, solitary peduncle from leaf axils. *Flower*: white, occasionally pinkish, about ¾ in. long, not as wide as long; sepals 5, leathery, fringed with hairs; corolla funnel-shaped, 5-lobed; stamens and stigma not exserted.

FRUIT: capsule, glabrous in top portion, globelike, to ⅜ in. across; seeds 2–6.

SOF   (POF)   September–October

Dodder   [p. 42]
Cuscuta spp.
(Kus-kyoo'-tah)

Twining, glabrous, herbaceous parasitic vine; stems numerous, often covering vegetation and becoming matlike, leafless and rootless, fleshy, pale yellow to orange, the basal portion at ground level soon withering away and leaving the plant attached to the host plant by structures penetrating host tissue.

LEAVES: none, or reduced to minute scales.

INFLORESCENCE: flowers few to many, small, essentially sessile, in cymelike clusters along stem. *Flower*: white; calyx united basally, usually 5-lobed; corolla funnel-shaped to tubular, usually 5-lobed; stamens 5, exserted, attached between corolla lobes, with scalelike fringed appendage near base of each stamen; stamens usually 5; styles usually 2.

FRUIT: capsule, globelike to ovoid; seeds usually 4.

NOTE: Several species of *Cuscuta* are found in East Texas and western Louisiana and are quite difficult to identify. Most species will grow on several host plants, but some exhibit a definite plant preference.

POF   (MGP, SOF, LBU, BMLS, OFS)   May–November

POLEMONIACEAE
(Phlox Family)

Standing cypress   [p. 87]
Ipomopsis rubra (L.) Wherry
(Eye-poh-mop'-sis roo'-brah)

Strictly erect, rather coarse, sparsely pubescent biennial to 6 ft. tall, commonly about 3 ft. tall.

LEAVES: alternate, in basal rosette and also crowded along stem, essentially sessile; blade deeply cleft into numerous thread-like segments; segments to 2¼ in. long, sharply and firmly pointed at tip.

INFLORESCENCE: flowers numerous, in showy slender elongated terminal panicle; panicle often ¼–⅓ total height of plant. *Flower*: bright red or scarlet, rarely yellow, with darker spots on inner surface, 1–1¼ in. long; calyx tubular, 5-lobed, the lobes sharp-tipped; corolla trumpet-shaped, deeply 5-lobed; corolla lobes wide-spreading, blunt at tip; stamens 5, unequally exserted.

FRUIT: capsule, to ⅜ in. long, separating into 3 sections; seeds numerous, elongated and angular or ovoid, often waxy.

NOTE: plants showy, worthy of cultivation.

OFS   June–August

Trailing phlox [p. 87]

Phlox nivalis Lodd. subsp. *texensis* Lundell

(Flox nih-vay'-lis tex-en'-sis)

Tufted or mat-forming, somewhat woody shrublike perennial; sterile stems evergreen; flowering stems erect, deciduous.

LEAVES: opposite, crowded, with conspicuous clusters of smaller leaves in axils; blade pubescent, often with gland-tipped hairs, narrowly lanceolate, to 1 in. long, usually sharp-pointed at tip.

INFLORESCENCE: flowers mostly 3–6 in cyme; cymes usually numerous, showy; entire top portion of plant often covered with flowers. *Flower*: pink to rose or lavender, usually darker in center; sepals 5, united for about half of length by a flat or wrinkled membrane; corolla trumpet-shaped, 5-lobed; corolla tube slender, to ¾ in. long; corolla lobes narrowed at base, notched at tip; stamens 5, shorter than corolla tube.

FRUIT: capsule, papery, globelike to ellipsoid, to ¼ in. long, separating into 3 sections; seeds usually 1 per section, ellipsoid.

NOTE: uncommon to rare in the Big Thicket; endemic to southeastern Texas.

OFS   March–May

Prairie phlox [p. 38]

Phlox pilosa L.

(Flox pye-loh'-sah)

Erect, herbaceous perennial to 2 ft. tall, with gland-tipped pubescence; stems 1–few, slender, with 7–15 nodes, unbranched or with few branches from upper nodes.

LEAVES: opposite, sessile; blade glabrous or pubescent, linear in lower portion of stem, becoming lanceolate in upper portion, to 5 in. long, ⅜ in. wide, narrowed or rounded at base, fringed with hairs.

INFLORESCENCE: flowers numerous, pedicelled, in several few-flowered cymes forming large showy panicle; longest pedicels to ¾ in. long. *Flower*: pink to dark lavender; calyx deeply 5-lobed to below middle, with gland-tipped pubescence; corolla trumpet-shaped; corolla tube very short, to ⅝ in. long, usually pubescent; corolla lobes 5, to ½ in. long, narrowed at base, broader and abruptly sharp-pointed at tip; stamens 5, not exserted.

FRUIT: capsule, papery, shorter than calyx, globelike to ellipsoid, to ¼ in. long, opening into 3 sections; seeds usually 1 in each section.

MGP   (POF, LBU)   April–May

Drummond phlox   [p. 38]

Phlox drummondii Hook.

(Flox   drum-mun'-dee-eye)

Erect, pubescent annual 4–20 in. tall, varying with environment; stem usually solitary, unbranched or much-branched in upper portion.

LEAVES: opposite and essentially sessile in lower portion of plant, becoming alternate and sessile or clasping basally in upper portion; leaves usually at only 3–5 nodes; blade elliptic, oblong, or spatulate, the largest usually 1½–3⅛ in. long, to ⅝ in. wide.

INFLORESCENCE: flowers numerous, arranged in 2–6 cymes; cymes grouped in showy somewhat spiraled terminal cluster. *Flower*: white to red, lavender, or purple, occasionally variegated or bicolored, usually with different-colored center; sepals 5, united basally; corolla trumpet-shaped, 5-lobed; corolla tube slender, to ⅝ in. long; corolla lobes spreading flat, wider in tip portion, to ⅝ in. long; stamens 5, not exserted.

FRUIT: capsule, papery, globelike to ellipsoid, very pale tan, opening into 3 sections; seeds usually 1 in each section.

NOTE: native; often planted along roadsides by Texas Highway Department.

MGP   (OFS)   May–September

HYDROPHYLLACEAE
(Waterleaf Family)

Prairie phacelia   [p. 38]

Phacelia strictiflora (Engelm. & Gray) Gray

(Fah-see'-lee-ah   strik-tih-floh'-rah)

Erect annual 6–14 in. tall, with coarse shaggy loosely spreading pubescence; stem solitary, unbranched or few-branched from base.

LEAVES: alternate, in conspicuous basal rosette and with few along stem; blade oblong to oval, ⅜–2⅜ in. long, ¼–1¼ in. wide; margins with 1–6 pairs of shallow teeth or lobes; basal rosette usually withering early; leaves along stem sessile.

INFLORESCENCE: flowers several, pedicelled, in coiled cyme; cyme terminal, uncoiling as flowers open. *Flower*: purplish lavender, to ¾ in. across; calyx deeply 5-lobed, increasing in size in fruit; corolla funnel-shaped, exceeding calyx.

FRUIT: capsule, somewhat globelike, to about ¼ in. across; seeds 10–20.

MGP   (OFS)   March–May

Blue waterleaf [p. 42]

Hydrolea ovata Choisy

(Hye-droh'-lee-ah oh-vay'-tah)

Erect to sprawling, stout, spiny, roughly pubescent aquatic perennial to 30 in. tall; stems solitary or several from base and clumplike, usually branching in upper portion; usually forming large colonies of plants around edges of lakes, ponds, or streams.

LEAVES: alternate, short-petioled or sessile, subtended by conspicuous spine; blade broadly lanceolate to oblong or elliptic, 1–2½ in. long, to 1 in. wide.

INFLORESCENCE: flowers numerous, arranged in several few-flowered cymes and forming large showy terminal or axillary panicle; axillary cymes often long-peduncled. *Flower*: bright blue or purplish, occasionally white, to 1 in. across; calyx deeply 5-lobed, pubescent; corolla broadly funnel-shaped, exceeding calyx, deeply 5-lobed to below middle; stamens 5, conspicuous.

FRUIT: capsule, ovoid or globelike; seeds many, wrinkled, minute.

POF (SOF) September–October

One-flowered waterleaf [p. 42]

Hydrolea uniflora Raf.

(Hye-droh'-lee-ah yoo-nih-floh'-rah)

Erect or sprawling, slender, spiny, glabrous aquatic perennial 10–30 in. tall; stems solitary or several from base and clumplike, sometimes branched in upper portion; plants usually forming colonies in or near edge of water.

LEAVES: alternate, short-petioled to essentially sessile, subtended by conspicuous spine; blade dark green, shiny, lanceolate, tapering at both ends, 2–3⅛ in. long, to ¾ in. wide.

INFLORESCENCE: flowers few to several, inconspicuous, in small cyme; cymes dense, sessile, from leaf axils; flowers opening 1 or 2 at a time in cyme. *Flower*: bright blue to purplish, to ½ in. across; sepals 5, united basally, as long as corolla, glabrous; corolla 5-lobed to below middle, the lobes somewhat erect; stamens 5.

FRUIT: capsule, glabrous, ovoid or globelike; seeds many, wrinkled, minute.

POF (SOF) September–October

BORAGINACEAE
(Borage Family)

Seaside heliotrope [p. 39]

Heliotropium curassavicum L.

(Hee-lee-oh-troh'-pee-um koo-ras-sav'-ih-kum)

Usually sprawling or trailing, succulent, rubbery, glabrous, glaucous perennial to 16 in. long; stems 1–several, much-branched.

LEAVES: alternate, sessile or short-petioled; blade thick, juicy, pale green, prominently flattened, linear to narrowly spatulate, to 1½ in. long, to about ¼ in. wide, rounded or blunt at tip.

INFLORESCENCE: flowers numerous, very small, inconspicuous, in solitary or paired peduncled axillary cymes; cymes coiled when young, uncoiling as flowers open, becoming up to 4 in. long in fruit. *Flower*: white; calyx deeply 5-lobed, fleshy, persistent; corolla 5-lobed, glabrous.

FRUIT: schizocarp; nutlets 4, covered with a thick layer of firm bladdery tissue which apparently aids in water dissemination; seeds 1 in each nutlet.

NOTE: native of tropical America.

MGP   February–November

Four-spike heliotrope   [p. 52]
Heliotropium procumbens Mill.
(Hee-lee-oh-troh'-pee-um   proh-kum'-benz)

Erect to loosely sprawling, pale green, pubescent annual; stems 1–several, often branched above base, not succulent or glaucous.

LEAVES: alternate, numerous, petioled; petiole to ⅜ in. long; blade elliptic to narrowly spatulate, alike in coloration and amount of pubescence on both surfaces, to 1½ in. long, ¾ in. wide, usually wedge-shaped at base.

INFLORESCENCE: flowers numerous, very small, inconspicuous, in peduncled terminal or axillary cymes; cymes usually in pairs, coiled when young, uncoiling as flowers open, 1¼–4 in. long. *Flower*: white to creamy yellow; calyx 5-lobed, slightly longer than corolla tube, becoming almost twice as large in maturity; corolla sparsely pubescent in throat.

FRUIT: schizocarp; nutlets 4, dry, bony; seeds 1 in each nutlet.

NOTE: native of American tropics.

SOF   (POF)   April–November

Turnsole   [p. 52]
Heliotropium indicum L.
(Hee-lee-oh-troh'-pee-um   in'-dih-kum)

Erect, coarse, loosely branched annual to 40 in. tall, usually much lower, with long stiff pubescence rough to the touch.

LEAVES: alternate, petioled; petiole 1½–4 in. long; blade conspicuously veined, broadly lanceolate to elliptic, to 6 in. long, 4 in. wide, rounded or somewhat notched at base; margins usually somewhat crisped or wavy.

INFLORESCENCE: flowers numerous, very small, sessile, in 2 rows along upper side of terminal cyme; cymes coiled when young, uncoiling as flowers open, to 12 in. long. *Flower*: blue or violet, rarely white, about ⅛ in. across; calyx 5-lobed; corolla 5-lobed, pubescent on outer surface.

FRUIT: schizocarp; nutlets 2, dry, hard, smooth, prominently ribbed; seeds 1 in each nutlet.

SOF   (POF)   June–October

Puccoon   [p. 72]

Lithospermum caroliniense (Walt.) MacM.

(Lith-oh-sper′-mum   kair-oh-lin-ee-en′-see)

Erect, stout, frequently clumped, pubescent perennial 12–40 in. tall from taproot; root deep, woody, with purple-staining juice; stems 1–several, commonly branched in upper portion, with rough pubescence.

LEAVES: alternate, numerous, sessile; blade with rough pubescence, broadly linear to lanceolate, to 1½ in. long, ⅜ in. wide, narrowed at base.

INFLORESCENCE: flowers several, short-pedicelled, subtended by small leaflike bracts, in somewhat coiled cyme; cymes terminal, loosely flowered, straightening with age. *Flower*: orange yellow, to 1 in. across; calyx deeply 5-lobed; corolla trumpet-shaped, 5-lobed, sparsely pubescent on outer surface; tube pubescent on inner surface near base.

FRUIT: schizocarp, on erect pedicel; nutlets 4, dry, hard, essentially smooth, white, shiny, broadly ovoid; seeds 1 in each nutlet.

LBU   March–May

VERBENACEAE
(Vervain Family)

Tuber vervain   [p. 94]

Verbena rigida Spreng.

(Ver-bee′-nah   rij′-ih-dah)

Erect, pubescent perennial 8–24 in. tall from elongated rhizomes; stems 1–few, 4-angled, branched in upper portion; plants usually forming colonies.

LEAVES: opposite, sessile, clasping basally; blade with rough, stiff pubescence on both surfaces, lanceolate to somewhat spatulate, 1½–4¼ in. long, to 1¼ in. wide, coarsely and sharply toothed.

INFLORESCENCE: flowers several, subtended by bracts, in short dense cylindrical spike; spikes 1–few, stiffly arranged in cymes; lateral cymes long-peduncled; bract usually longer than calyx, with gland-tipped pubescence. *Flower*: purple to magenta; calyx tubular, 5-ribbed, unequally 5-toothed, pubescent; corolla trumpet-shaped; tube 2 or 3 times as long as calyx, pubescent on outer surface; stamens 4, attached to corolla tube, not exserted.

FRUIT: schizocarp; nutlets 4, brown on outer surface, tan on inner surface, warty, oblong, remaining somewhat loosely united; seeds 1 per nutlet.

NOTE: native of South America, now escaped from cultivation and becoming wild.

R　(MGP)　　April–October

Brazilian vervain [p. 39]
Verbena brasiliensis Vell.

(Ver-bee'-nah　bra-sil-ee-en'-sis)

Erect, stout perennial to 8 ft. tall, usually much lower, essentially glabrous in lower portion of plant, somewhat roughly and sharply pubescent in upper portion; stems 1–several, prominently 4-angled, commonly much-branched.

LEAVES: opposite, sessile or short-petioled; blade with short stiff pubescence on upper surface, sparsely pubescent on lower surface, elliptic or lanceolate, $1\frac{1}{2}$–4 in. long, to 1 in. wide, tapering at base, sharply toothed or lobed.

INFLORESCENCE: flowers several, very small, subtended by bracts, in short compact spike; spikes loosely arranged in numerous open cymes; bracts about equaling calyx, fringed with hairs. *Flower*: bluish purple, lilac, or purple; calyx 5-lobed, pubescent; corolla trumpet-shaped, 5-lobed, pubescent on outer surface; tube slightly longer than calyx; stamens 4, attached to corolla tube, not exserted.

FRUIT: schizocarp; nutlets 4, brown on outer side, gray and roughened with spines on inner side; seeds 1 per nutlet.

NOTE: native to most of South America, now widely naturalized.

MGP　(POF, SOF)　　May–October

Texas vervain [p. 39]
Verbena halei Small

(Ver-bee'-nah　hay'-lee-eye)

Erect, pubescent perennial 1–$2\frac{1}{2}$ ft. tall; stems usually several from woody base, 4-angled, branched in upper portion; branches slender, erect.

LEAVES: opposite, petioled; blade with short stiff pubescence on both surfaces, very diverse in shape, varying from deeply to shallowly cleft or lobed in lower portion of plant to toothed or entire in upper portion of plant, $\frac{3}{4}$–$3\frac{1}{8}$ in. long, to $1\frac{1}{2}$ in. wide.

INFLORESCENCE: flowers several, very small, subtended by small leaflike bracts in graceful spike; spikes slender, elongated, loosely flowered, terminal and from upper leaf axils, usually several and forming panicle. *Flower*: bluish to lavender, rarely white, about $\frac{1}{4}$ in. across; calyx pubescent; corolla trumpet-shaped, 5-lobed, twice as long as calyx, pubescent on outer surface; stamens 4, attached to corolla tube, not exserted.

FRUIT: schizocarp; nutlets 4, brown on outer side; seeds 1 per nutlet.
MGP   (POF, LBU, OFS)   February–November

Rose vervain [p. 72]
Verbena canadensis (L.) Britt.
(Ver-bee'-nah   kan-ah-den'-sis)

Erect to sprawling or creeping, pubescent perennial 6–16 in. tall; stem 4-angled, branched, rooting at nodes, forming large dense colonies of plants.

LEAVES: opposite, petioled; petiole to 1 in. long; blade thin, glabrous or pubescent on both surfaces, deeply cleft or lobed to merely toothed or entire, 1–3½ in. long, to 1½ in. wide, wedge-shaped at base.

INFLORESCENCE: flowers many, sessile, subtended by very small leaflike bracts, in showy solitary terminal spike; spikes erect, peduncled, at first short and dense, conspicuously elongating in fruit. *Flower*: pale pink to rose or magenta, occasionally blue or lavender, with darker center, fragrant; calyx 5-lobed, pubescent; corolla trumpet-shaped, 5-lobed, frequently with gland-tipped pubescence on outer surface; stamens 4, attached to corolla tube, not exserted.

FRUIT: schizocarp; nutlets 4, brown on outer side, white and warty on inner side, remaining somewhat loosely attached; seeds 1 per nutlet.
LBU   (MGP, POF)   March–June

Dakota vervain [p. 94]
Verbena bipinnatifida Nutt.
(Ver-bee'-nah   bye-pin-na-tif'-ih-dah)

Mat-forming, pubescent perennial 6–18 in. tall from creeping stems; stem branching from base, 4-angled, rooting at lower nodes.

LEAVES: opposite, petioled; blade with dense appressed pubescence on both surfaces, ¾–2½ in. long, several times cleft or lobed with the segments again cleft or lobed.

INFLORESCENCE: flowers many, small, subtended by very small leaflike bracts, in terminal spike; spikes peduncled, at first short and dense, becoming conspicuously elongated in fruit. *Flower*: pink, lavender, or purple, to ⅜ in. across; calyx 5-lobed, pubescent; corolla trumpet-shaped, 5-lobed, pubescent on outer surface; stamens 4, attached to corolla tube, not exserted.

FRUIT: schizocarp; nutlets 4, brown on outer surface; seeds 1 per nutlet.
R   (MGP, SOF, LBU, OFS)   Throughout year

Carolina vervain [p. 87]
Stylodon carneus (Medic.) Moldenke
(Sty'-loh-don   kar'-nee-us)

Erect, pubescent perennial to about 3 ft. tall, often lower; stem usually solitary, 4-angled, unbranched or sparsely branched in upper portion.

LEAVES: opposite, sessile; blade with rough pubescence on upper surface, less roughly pubescent on lower surface and prominently net-veined, oblong to spatulate, to about 4¾ in. long, 1½ in. wide, shallowly toothed.

INFLORESCENCE: flowers many, subtended by very small leaflike bracts, in terminal and axillary spikes; spikes peduncled, wandlike; bracts with glandular pubescence. *Flower*: pale pink or blue; calyx sharply 5-lobed, with glandular pubescence; corolla trumpet-shaped, slightly longer than calyx, pubescent on outer surface; stamens 4, attached to corolla tube, not exserted.

FRUIT: schizocarp; nutlets 4, tightly united and appearing as one, ridged, with 4 broad surfaces at tip forming caplike beak, tardily separating; seeds 1 per nutlet.

NOTE: uncommon in East Texas and western Louisiana.

OFS   (LBU)   April–September

West Indian lantana [p. 94]
Lantana camara L.

(Lan-tay′-nah   ka-mair′-ah)

Erect or sprawling, clumped, stout, pubescent perennial to 7 ft. tall, usually much lower; stems usually several from base, 4-angled, often with small prickles along edges, branching in upper portion.

LEAVES: opposite, petioled; petiole to ¾ in. long; blade net-veined and with rough stiff pubescence on upper surface, with short pubescence mostly along veins beneath, broadly lanceolate to broadly oblong, 2–4¼ in. long, 1–2¾ in. wide, shortly narrowed or abruptly rounded to the wedge-shaped base; margins toothed, the teeth numerous, sharp, regularly spaced, appressed.

INFLORESCENCE: flowers many, sessile, small, subtended by very small leaflike bracts, in showy headlike spike; spikes dense, short, not elongating as flowers open, on peduncles from upper leaf axils; peduncles ¾–3⅛ in. long, pubescent. *Flower*: yellow to orange, pink, or red; calyx very small; corolla trumpet-shaped, unequally 4-lobed, the larger 2 lobes with small sharp point at tip; stamens 4, attached to corolla tube, not exserted.

FRUIT: drupe, black, fleshy; seeds 2.

NOTE: native of American tropics.

R   May–December

Texas frog-fruit [p. 94]
Phyla incisa Small

(Fye′-lah   in-sye′-zah)

Trailing or creeping, pubescent perennial; stems often purplish, 4-angled, rooting at nodes, commonly erect in tip portion, unbranched or branched, usually forming large matlike colonies.

LEAVES: opposite, essentially sessile; blade often thick, with appressed stiff pubescence on both surfaces, narrowly oblong to broadly spatulate, to 2 in. long, ⅝ in. wide, wedge-shaped near base, sharp-pointed to rounded at tip; margins with only 1–4 pairs of coarse, spreading teeth.

INFLORESCENCE: flowers many, sessile, subtended by very small leaflike bracts, in small headlike spike; spikes axillary, peduncled, pubescent, at first globelike, elongating and becoming somewhat cylindrical in fruit; peduncles long, usually at alternate nodes. *Flower*: white with yellow center; calyx very small; corolla trumpet-shaped, 5-lobed; stamens 4, united to corolla tube, not exserted.

FRUIT: schizocarp; nutlets 2, yellowish tan, rounded on one side, flat on the other, minute; seeds 1 per nutlet.
R   (MGP, POF, SOF, LBS)   March–November

LABIATAE
(Mint Family)

Forked blue curls   [p. 73]
Trichostema dichotomum L.
(Trik-oh-stee′-mah   dye-kot′-oh-mum)

Erect, pubescent annual to 3½ ft. tall, usually much lower; stem solitary, slender, obscurely 4-angled, much-branched in upper portion.

LEAVES: opposite, petioled; petiole to about ½ in. long; blade pubescent, broadly lanceolate to oblong, to 2½ in. long, 1 in. wide, tapering basally to petiole, abruptly sharp-pointed or rounded at tip; margins entire, toothed, or rarely lobed.

INFLORESCENCE: flowers 3–7, pedicelled, subtended by small leaflike bract, in peduncled axillary cyme; cymes usually paired, somewhat coiled, forming large loose terminal panicle; pedicels and peduncles glandular, pubescent. *Flower*: blue to lavender, occasionally white; calyx 2-lipped; lower calyx lip 2-lobed, shorter than upper lip; upper calyx lip 3-lobed; calyx twisting at maturity with larger upper lip appearing as the lower; corolla deeply 5-lobed; upper 4 corolla lobes erect; lowest corolla lobe liplike, longer than upper lobes, prominently extending downward; stamens 4, much exserted, prominently curled forward, conspicuous.

FRUIT: schizocarp; nutlets 4, small, conspicuously net-veined, obovoid, remaining united basally; seeds 1 per nutlet.
LBU   July–October

American germander   [p. 52]
Teucrium canadense L.
(Too′-kree-um   kan-ah-den′-see)

Erect, pubescent perennial to 3 ft. tall, usually lower, from creeping rhizome; stem solitary, 4-angled, branched in upper portion; plants usually forming dense colonies.

LEAVES: opposite, petioled; basal leaves absent; petiole to ¾ in. long; blade glabrous or variably pubescent on upper surface, usually with conspicuous silvery pubescence on lower surface, narrowly elliptic to broadly lanceolate, 2¼–4 in. long, ¾–1½ in. wide, tapering or rounded at base, obscurely to prominently toothed.

INFLORESCENCE: flowers numerous, essentially sessile, subtended by small leaflike bracts, in elongated spike; spikes usually dense, axillary or terminal, 8–12 in. long. *Flower*: pink to lavender, ½–¾ in. long; calyx 5-lobed, pubescent; lower 2 calyx lobes longer than upper 3; corolla 2-lipped; upper corolla lip very short and deeply notched; lower corolla lip spreading, with small lateral lobes, conspicuous; stamens 4, erect, exserted from between cleft of upper corolla lip, prominently curved downward, conspicuous.

FRUIT: schizocarp; nutlets 4, yellowish brown, glabrous, wrinkled, ellipsoid to obovoid; seeds 1 per nutlet.

SOF   (POF, LBS)   May–September

Rough skullcap [p. 64]

Scutellaria integrifolia L.

(Skoo-tel-lair′-ee-ah   in-teg-rih-foh′-lee-ah)

Strictly erect, pubescent perennial to 3 ft. tall, usually lower; stems solitary or few from base and forming clump, slender, 4-angled, unbranched or branched in upper portion.

LEAVES: opposite, petioled, with 3–8 pairs below inflorescence; lower leaves broadly lanceolate, to 1⅜ in. long, ¾ in. wide, sharply toothed; petiole slender, to 1 in. long; middle and upper leaves pubescent, gland-dotted, lanceolate to narrowly elliptic, becoming narrower in tip portion of plant, ¾–2⅜ in. long, to ⅝ in. wide, entire to remotely toothed; petiole to ⅜ in. long, usually obscured by blade tissue.

INFLORESCENCE: flowers several, short-pedicelled, subtended by bracts, in showy raceme; racemes usually solitary and terminal, occasionally many axillary and forming panicle. *Flower*: blue to violet and whitish, to 1 in. long; calyx 2-lipped, pubescent; upper calyx lip crested, enlarging in fruit, conspicuous; corolla 2-lipped; tube exserted from calyx, curved at base, compressed at throat; upper corolla lip small, essentially unlobed; lower corolla lip 3-lobed, the lateral lobes mostly united to upper corolla lip; middle lobe largest, broad, spreading; stamens 4, not exserted.

FRUIT: schizocarp; nutlets 4, black, somewhat globelike, covered with small projections, small; seeds 1 per nutlet.

LBS   April–June

Egg-leaf skullcap   [p. 73]
Scutellaria ovata Hill
(Skoo-tel-lair′-ee-ah   oh-vay′-tah)

Erect to occasionally sprawling, pubescent perennial to 32 in. tall, usually much lower, from stolons; stems slender, 4-angled, unbranched or forking.

LEAVES: opposite, petioled; petiole slender, 1–2¾ in. long; blade glabrous or pubescent, very broadly lanceolate, to 5⅛ in. long, 3½ in. wide, deeply notched at base, shallowly or sharply toothed.

INFLORESCENCE: flowers many, subtended by bracts, in pubescent terminal raceme; raceme sometimes forking, often forming panicle. *Flower*: blue and white, to ¾ in. long; calyx 2-lipped, with glandular pubescence; upper calyx lip crested, becoming enlarged in fruit, conspicuous; corolla 2-lipped, curved at base; upper corolla lip essentially entire; lower corolla lip 3-lobed, the lateral lobes united with upper lip; lowermost lobe broad, spreading; stamens 4, not exserted.

FRUIT: schizocarp; nutlets 4, pale brown to orange, very small, covered with small projections; seeds 1 per nutlet.
LBU   (LBS)   April–June

Desert-lavender   [p. 64]
Hyptis alata (Raf.) Shinners
(Hip′-tis   a-lay′-tah)

Erect, stout, sparsely pubescent perennial to 8 ft. tall, usually much lower, from woody rhizome; stem 4-angled, unbranched or rarely branched.

LEAVES: opposite, short-petioled to almost sessile; blade narrowly to broadly lanceolate or somewhat diamond-shaped, 2–6 in. long, to 2⅜ in. wide, tapering at base, coarsely and irregularly toothed.

INFLORESCENCE: flowers many, in dense globelike peduncled axillary head; heads surrounded by numerous small bracts; peduncles to 2¼ in. long, the lower ones longest; bracts pale green to whitish near base. *Flower*: white, spotted with lavender, about ¼ in. long; calyx prominently cross-ribbed; corolla 2-lipped; upper corolla lip 4-lobed; lower corolla lip saclike, curved downward at base; stamens 4, resting on lower corolla lip.

FRUIT: schizocarp; nutlets 4, black, smooth, oval, very small, seeds 1 per nutlet.
LBS   June–November

Self-heal   [p. 94]
Prunella vulgaris L.
(Proo-nel′-lah   vul-gair′-is)

Erect to occasionally sprawling, often clumplike, glabrous or pubescent perennial to 24 in. tall, usually 4–12 in. tall; stems solitary or few from base, 4-angled, occasionally branched in upper portion.

LEAVES: opposite, petioled to essentially sessile in upper portion of plant; longest petioles to 2 in. long; blade thin, elliptic to broadly lanceolate, 1¼–3½ in. long, ⅜–1½ in. wide, basally tapering to petiole, entire or occasionally sparsely and irregularly toothed.

INFLORESCENCE: flowers sessile, subtended by bracts, in clusters of 3; clusters arranged in showy terminal or occasionally axillary spikes; bracts small, rounded, leaflike, often tinged with purple, fringed with hairs; spikes ¾–2 in. long. *Flower*: purple or violet and lavender, rarely solid white, to ¾ in. long; calyx deeply 2-lipped, closed in fruit; corolla erect, prominently 2-lipped; upper corolla lip unlobed, curved forward; lower corolla lip 3-lobed, spreading, the middle lobe finely fringed along margin.

FRUIT: schizocarp; nutlets 4, dark brown, shiny, ovoid, small; seeds 1 per nutlet.

R   (POF, SOF, LBU)   April–June

Intermediate false dragon-head [p. 95]

Physostegia intermedia (Nutt.) Engelm. & Gray

(Fye-soh-stee′-jee-ah   in-ter-mee′-dee-ah)

Erect, glabrous perennial 12–60 in. tall from rhizome; stem solitary, slender, 4-angled, unbranched or sparsely branched in upper portion; plants usually forming large colonies, mostly in standing water.

LEAVES: opposite, widely spaced, sessile; blade rather thick, dark green, linear to narrowly lanceolate, 2–3 in. long, to ½ in. wide; margins wavy and entire or rarely toothed; leaves much reduced in upper portion of plant.

INFLORESCENCE: flowers numerous, opposite, sessile, in slender usually solitary showy terminal spike. *Flower*: lavender, spotted with purple, to ⅝ in. long; calyx bell-shaped, 5-toothed; corolla 2-lipped, inflated at throat; upper corolla lip erect, essentially unlobed; lower corolla lip 3-lobed, spreading; middle lobe broad, rounded, notched at tip; stamens 4, curved forward below upper corolla lip.

FRUIT: schizocarp; nutlets 4, smooth, ovoid; seeds 1 per nutlet.

NOTE: Flowers may be moved laterally and will remain in the position in which they are placed, thus giving this genus one of its common names, "obedient-plant."

R   (POF, SOF)   April–June

Blunt false dragon-head [p. 73]

Physostegia praemorsa Shinners

(Fye-soh-stee′-jee-ah   pree-mor′-sah)

Erect, glabrous perennial to 4 ft. tall, often lower, from rhizomes; stem usually solitary, slender, unbranched to occasionally branched in upper portion.

LEAVES: opposite, short-petioled in lower portion of plant, sessile in upper portion; blade lanceolate to narrowly oblong, 1⅛–2¾ in. long, ¼–½ in. wide, sharply toothed except near base; leaves becoming reduced to bracts in upper portion of plant.

INFLORESCENCE: flowers many, sessile, in large showy terminal or occasionally axillary spikes; spike pubescent, occasionally branched. *Flower*: lavender to violet, occasionally whitish, spotted with rose purple, to 1¼ in. long; calyx bell-shaped, 5-toothed; corolla 2-lipped, inflated at throat; upper corolla lip erect; lower corolla lip 3-lobed, spreading; middle lobe broad, rounded, notched at tip; stamens 4, curved beneath upper corolla lip.

FRUIT: schizocarp; nutlets 4, dark brown, sharply 3-angled, about ⅛ in. long; seeds 1 per nutlet.

NOTE: the only species of *Physostegia* flowering in autumn in East Texas and western Louisiana.

LBU   (MGP)   August–October

False dragon-head [p. 65]

Physostegia digitalis Small

(Fye-soh-stee'-jee-ah   dij-ih-tay'-lis)

Erect, stout, glabrous perennial to 6 ft. tall, frequently lower; stem solitary, prominently 4-angled, unbranched or sparsely branched in upper portion.

LEAVES: opposite, sessile, partially clasping basally; blade somewhat thick, leathery, oblong to narrowly elliptic, to 8¾ in. long, 3 in. wide; margins wavy or toothed in tip portion of blade.

INFLORESCENCE: flowers many, short-pedicelled, subtended by small bracts, in large showy terminal raceme; raceme pubescent, often branched. *Flower*: pale lavender to whitish, spotted with reddish purple, ¾–1 in. long; calyx bell-shaped, 5-toothed; corolla 2-lipped, inflated at throat; upper corolla lip wavy; lower corolla lip 3-lobed; middle lobe broad, notched at tip, about twice as long as lateral lobes; stamens 4, curved beneath upper corolla lip.

FRUIT: schizocarp; nutlets 4, smooth, ovoid; seeds 1 per nutlet.

LBS   June–August

Slender-leaf betony [p. 52]

Stachys tenuifolia Willd.

(Stak'-is   ten-yoo-ih-foh'-lee-ah)

Erect to somewhat sprawling, rather coarse, essentially glabrous perennial 2–4 ft. tall from creeping rhizomes; stems 4-angled, unbranched or branching in upper portion; plants usually forming large colonies.

LEAVES: opposite, petioled; petiole to ¾ in. long, less than ¼ length of blade; blade glabrous or pubescent on one or both surfaces, linear or narrowly lanceolate, to about 5 in. long, 2⅜ in. wide, tapering, wedge-shaped or rounded at base, sharply toothed.

INFLORESCENCE: flowers few in whorl; whorls subtended by leaflike bracts, forming interrupted terminal or occasionally axillary spikes. *Flower*: pale pink to purplish or reddish, about ⅜ in. long; calyx bell-shaped, glabrous or pubescent, 5-toothed, the teeth soon curving outward; corolla prominently 2-lipped; upper corolla lip erect, cupped, pubescent on outer surface; lower corolla lip 3-lobed, spreading, drooping; stamens 4, curved beneath upper corolla lip.

FRUIT: schizocarp; nutlets 4, shiny, small; seeds 1 per nutlet.

SOF   (POF)   August–November

Hedge-nettle [p. 52]

Stachys floridana Shuttlew.

(Stak′-is   floh-rih-day′-nah)

Erect, slender, rather delicate pubescent perennial 8–16 in. tall from creeping elongated tubers; stem 4-angled, commonly much-branched; plants forming colonies.

LEAVES: opposite, petioled; petiole ⅓–½ length of blade; blade elliptic to broadly lanceolate, to ¾ in. long, toothed.

INFLORESCENCE: flowers sessile with few in whorl; whorls subtended by leaflike bracts, forming showy interrupted terminal or occasionally axillary spikes. *Flower*: pale pink to rose or lavender, spotted or marked with darker color, about ⅜ in. long; calyx bell-shaped, pubescent, 5-toothed, the teeth soon curving outward; corolla 2-lipped; upper corolla lip erect, cupped; lower corolla lip 3-lobed, spreading, somewhat drooping.

FRUIT: schizocarp; nutlets 4, dark brown, smooth, ovoid; seeds 1 per nutlet.

SOF   (LBS)   March–June

Henbit [p. 95]

Lamium amplexicaule L.

(Lay′-mee-um   am-plex-ih-caw′-lee)

Erect to sprawling, sparsely pubescent annual or biennial to 18 in. tall; stem 4-angled, freely branching from base and lower leaf axils, often rooting at lower nodes.

LEAVES: opposite, short-petioled to sessile; blade thick, conspicuously veined, broadly lanceolate to almost round, blunt or rounded and notched at base, coarsely toothed; basal leaves to ⅜ in. wide, petioled; upper leaves to 1 in. wide, sessile or clasping.

INFLORESCENCE: flowers 6–10 per cluster, sessile, whorled; clusters axillary and terminal. *Flower*: purple and pale lavender, spotted with darker coloring, to ¾ in. long; calyx sharply 5-toothed, pubescent; corolla 2-lipped; upper corolla lip erect, cupped, not lobed; lower corolla lip 3-lobed; middle lobe contracted at base, deeply notched at tip; stamens 4, curved beneath upper corolla lip.

FRUIT: schizocarp; nutlets 4, brown mottled with white, smooth, shiny, somewhat 3-angled, ovoid; seeds 1 per nutlet.

R   (MGP, LBU, OFS)   February–April

Lion's-ears   [p. 52]
Leonotis nepetaefolia A. Br.

(Lee-oh-noh'-tis   nep-eh-tee-foh'-lee-ah)

Erect, stout, pubescent annual to 8 ft. tall, often much lower; stem solitary, 4-angled, unbranched or much-branched.

LEAVES: opposite, petioled; petiole to 2¾ in. long; blade broadly lanceolate, 2–4¾ in. long, 1½–4 in. wide, blunt or wedge-shaped or rounded and notched at base, coarsely toothed; leaves below inflorescence conspicuously drooping.

INFLORESCENCE: flowers many in cluster; clusters dense, encircling stem, globelike, few to many and forming interrupted terminal spikes. *Flower*: orange yellow, occasionally red, to 1 in. long; calyx 2-lipped, pubescent, lobed; calyx lobes 8–10, unequal, tipped with bristles; corolla 2-lipped, densely pubescent; upper corolla lip hoodlike; lower corolla lip 3-lobed, much shorter than upper lip; stamens 4.

FRUIT: schizocarp; nutlets 4, brown, smooth, 3-angled; seeds 1 per nutlet.

SOF   April–September

Lyre-leaf sage   [p. 95]
Salvia lyrata L.

(Sal'-vee-ah   lye-ray'-tah)

Strictly erect, pubescent perennial 1–3 ft. tall from somewhat tuberous root; stem solitary, 4-angled, unbranched or with 1 or 2 pairs of branches in upper portion.

LEAVES: mostly basal, in rosette, petioled; stem leaves 1 or 2 pairs, small, sessile; blade of basal leaves entire to deeply cleft or lobed, with terminal lobe largest, to 8 in. long; winter leaves pubescent, often purple-tinged.

INFLORESCENCE: flowers few, sessile, subtended by small bracts, in cluster; clusters 3–10, whorled around stem, forming showy terminal or axillary spikes. *Flower*: pale blue to violet, ¾–1¼ in. long; calyx 2-lipped, bell-shaped, sharply 5-toothed; corolla 2-lipped; upper corolla lip short, not lobed; lower corolla lip 3-lobed, much larger than upper lip; stamens 2, exserted.

FRUIT: schizocarp; nutlets 4, dark brown, dull, obovoid; seeds 1 per nutlet.

R   (MGP, SOF, LBU, OFS)   December–May

Blue sage [p. 73]

Salvia azurea Lam. var. *grandiflora* Benth.

(Sal'-vee-ah a-zoo'-ree-ah gran-dih-floh'-rah)

Erect, pubescent perennial to 5 ft. tall; stems solitary or few from base, 4-angled, branching in upper portion.

LEAVES: opposite, petioled; basal leaves absent; blade narrowly lanceolate or lanceolate to narrowly oblong, to 2 in. long, ½ in. wide, tapering basally to petiole, rounded or sharp-pointed at tip, entire to irregularly toothed.

INFLORESCENCE: flowers few, sessile, subtended by bracts, in clusters; clusters several, forming interrupted pubescent showy axillary and terminal spikes. *Flower*: dark blue to pale blue, occasionally white, to 1 in. long; calyx bell-shaped, obscurely 2-lipped, prominently ribbed, pubescent; corolla 2-lipped; upper corolla lip erect, cupped, not lobed, pubescent on outer surface; lower corolla lip 3-lobed, spreading; middle lobe large, deeply notched at tip; stamens 2, curved beneath upper corolla lip.

FRUIT: schizocarp; nutlets 4, olive brown, sticky, dull, ellipsoid to obovoid; seeds 1 per nutlet.

LBU (MGP, LBS, OFS) May–November

Tropical sage [p. 73]

Salvia coccinea Murr.

(Sal'-vee-ah kok-sin'-ee-ah)

Strictly erect, pubescent perennial 1–3 ft. tall; stem 4-angled, usually much-branched in upper portion.

LEAVES: opposite, petioled; petiole to 1¼ in. long; blade thin, prominently veined, with soft pubescence on lower surface, broadly lanceolate, to 2¾ in. long, 2 in. wide, blunt to rounded at base, rounded or sharp-pointed at tip, sharply toothed.

INFLORESCENCE: flowers few to several, short-pedicelled, in cluster; clusters several, forming interrupted showy slender axillary and terminal racemes. *Flower*: scarlet or dark red, usually about 1 in. long; calyx 2-lipped, usually tinged with red, pubescent; corolla 2-lipped, pubescent; upper corolla lip short, not lobed, slightly cupped; lower corolla lip 3-lobed; middle lobe large, deeply notched, wide-spreading; stamens 2, exserted beyond upper corolla lip.

FRUIT: schizocarp; nutlets 4, dark brown, smooth, dull, ellipsoid; seeds 1 per nutlet.

NOTE: only native red-flowered species of *Salvia* in East Texas and western Louisiana.

LBU February–November

Wild bergamot   [p. 87]
Monarda fistulosa L.
(Moh-nar'-dah fis-tyoo-loh'-sah)

Erect, clumped, aromatic, mostly pubescent perennial to 5 ft. tall, often lower; stems usually several from base, 4-angled, unbranched or commonly branched in upper portion.

LEAVES: opposite, petioled; petiole to 5/8 in. long; blade firm, pale green, pubescent on lower surface, lanceolate, 1½–4¼ in. long, to 1½ in. wide, wedge-shaped to rounded and notched at base, sharply toothed; uppermost leaves and leaflike bracts often pink-tinged.

INFLORESCENCE: flowers many, sessile, in showy solitary globelike terminal head. *Flower*: lavender, pubescent, 3/4–1¼ in. long; calyx tubular, 5-toothed, to ½ in. long, densely pubescent on inner surface; corolla prominently 2-lipped, pubescent; upper corolla lip erect, short, slender, with tuft of hair at tip; lower corolla lip spreading, 3-lobed; stamens 2, elongated, exserted.

FRUIT: schizocarp; nutlets 4, smooth, shiny, ovoid; seeds 1 per nutlet.
OFS (LBU)   May–July

Spotted beebalm   [p. 87]
Monarda punctata L.
(Moh-nar'-dah punk-tay'-tah)

Erect, often clumplike, aromatic, pubescent perennial to 3½ ft. tall, usually lower; stems 1–several from base, 4-angled, unbranched or branched in upper portion.

LEAVES: opposite, petioled; petiole to 1 in. long; blade pale green, pubescent, lanceolate to oblong, much varied in size, 5/8–3¾ in. long, usually toothed.

INFLORESCENCE: flowers many, sessile, in dense cluster subtended by leaflike bracts; clusters 2–6, forming slender interrupted terminal or axillary spikes; bracts yellowish or purple-tinged, lanceolate, spreading or reflexed, toothed on margins. *Flower*: yellowish or rarely pinkish, conspicuously spotted with dark maroon, to 3/4 in. long; calyx tubular, ribbed, 5-toothed, pubescent; corolla prominently 2-lipped; upper corolla lip narrow, unlobed, curved forward; lower corolla lip 3-lobed; stamens 2, curved beneath upper corolla lip, not exserted.

FRUIT: schizocarp; nutlets 4, brown to blackish, smooth, ellipsoid; seeds 1 per nutlet.
OFS (MGP, POF, LBU)   May–August

Water-horehound   [p. 58]

Lycopus rubellus Moench

(Lye′-koh-pus   roo-bel′-lus)

Erect to somewhat sprawling, nonaromatic, essentially glabrous perennial
to 4 ft. tall from slender creeping stolons and rhizomes; stem 4-angled, usually branched in upper portion.

LEAVES: opposite, petioled; blade thin, prominently veined, elliptic to
lanceolate, to 6 in. long, 2 in. wide, prominently and sharply toothed.

INFLORESCENCE: flowers many, very small, sessile, subtended by minute
bracts, in cluster; clusters at leaf axils, appearing whorled around stem. *Flower*: white, sometimes spotted with purple; calyx bell-shaped, 5-toothed, pubescent; corolla bell-shaped, 4-lobed, the upper lobe slightly larger than the
others; stamens 2.

FRUIT: schizocarp; nutlets 4, smooth, somewhat 3-angled, obovoid, flattened on top and several-pointed, much shorter than calyx; seeds 1 per nutlet.

BGB   (POF, SOF)   August–December

Mountain-mint   [p. 73]

Pycnanthemum albescens T. & G.

(Pik-nan′-the-mum   al-bes′-senz)

Erect, stout, aromatic perennial to 5 ft. tall, commonly lower, from elongated rhizome; stem usually solitary, slender, 4-angled, much-branched in
upper portion.

LEAVES: opposite, petioled; petiole to ½ in. long; blade thin, conspicuously whitened, minutely pubescent on lower surface, 1–2¾ in. long, ⅜–1
in. wide, sharply toothed.

INFLORESCENCE: flowers many, sessile, in dense terminal head; flowers
intermixed with small bracts; heads subtended by several conspicuously whitened leaflike bracts. *Flower*: white or lavender, usually spotted; calyx tubular, 5-toothed, pubescent; corolla 2-lipped; upper corolla lip erect, short, unlobed; lower corolla lip spreading, 3-lobed; stamens 4, exserted.

FRUIT: schizocarp; nutlets 4, brown, pubescent, cylindrical to ellipsoid;
seeds 1 per nutlet.

NOTE: plants with mint fragrance.

LBU   (SOF)   July–November

SOLANACEAE
(Nightshade Family)

Cut-leaf ground-cherry   [p. 52]

Physalis angulata L.

(Fis′-ah-lis   ang-yoo-lay′-tah)

Erect to somewhat lax, essentially glabrous annual to about 3 ft. tall, commonly lower; stem usually solitary, angled, much-branched in upper portion.

LEAVES: alternate, petioled; petiole slender, 1½–3⅛ in. long; blade thin, broadly lanceolate, 2–4¼ in. long, 1⅜–3⅛ in. wide; margins entire to deeply and irregularly sharply toothed to wavy-toothed.

INFLORESCENCE: flowers solitary, pedicelled, from upper leaf axils. *Flower*: yellow, without dark spot in center, to ½ in. long, ½ in. wide; calyx bell-shaped, 5-toothed, glabrous, becoming much inflated at maturity and surrounding fruit; corolla somewhat bell-shaped, shallowly 5-lobed; stamens 5; anthers bluish or violet.

FRUIT: berry, mealy, globelike, to about ⅜ in. across, surrounded by calyx; calyx conspicuously inflated, 10-ribbed, ¾–1⅜ in. long, to 1 in. wide; seeds many, flattened, finely pitted.
SOF (LBU) May–October

Silver-leaf nightshade
[p. 95]

Solanum elaeagnifolium Cav.

(Soh-lay′-num el-ee-ag-nih-foh′-lee-um)

Erect, somewhat prickly, pubescent perennial to 3½ ft. tall, usually much lower; stem solitary, often woody at base, usually much-branched in upper portion, armed with slender brownish prickles; plant with conspicuous, silvery pubescence mostly throughout.

LEAVES: alternate, petioled; petiole to 2 in. long; blade thin, velvety with dense pubescence, linear to oblong or narrowly lanceolate, to about 6 in. long, 1¼ in. wide, usually tapering basally to petiole; margins entire, often conspicuously wavy.

INFLORESCENCE: flowers few, pedicelled, in axillary panicles near ends of branches; pedicels long, curved downward in bud and fruit. *Flower*: violet to pale lavender or rarely white, to 1 in. across; calyx shallowly bell-shaped, deeply 5-lobed, pubescent; corolla shallowly to deeply 5-lobed; stamens 5, exserted; anthers large, yellow, erect, remaining close together.

FRUIT: berry, yellowish or eventually black, fleshy, globelike, to about ⅝ in. across; seeds numerous, flattened.
R (MGP, LBU, OFS) March–October

Carolina horse-nettle
[p. 87]

Solanum carolinense L.

(Soh-lay′-num kair-oh-lih-nen′-see)

Erect, coarse, prickly, branched, pubescent perennial to 3½ ft. tall, usually much lower, from creeping horizontal rhizome.

LEAVES: alternate, petioled; petiole to 1¼ in. long; blade pubescent on both surfaces and with conspicuous spines along veins on lower surface, broadly lanceolate to elliptic, to 4¾ in. long; margins with several teeth or shallow lobes.

INFLORESCENCE: flowers several, pedicelled, in terminal racemelike cluster; clusters elongating at maturity. *Flower*: white to pale violet, ¾–1¼ in. across; calyx deeply 5-lobed, persistent; corolla wide-spreading, 5-lobed; stamens 5; anthers yellow, erect, remaining close together.

FRUIT: berry, yellow when mature, fleshy, globelike, to ¾ in. across; seeds numerous, flattened.

OFS   (SOF, LBU)   April–October

SCROPHULARIACEAE
(Figwort Family)

Carolina water-hyssop   [p. 58]
Bacopa caroliniana (Walt.) Robins
(Ba-koh'-pah   kair-oh-lin-ee-ay'-nah)

Erect or floating, succulent, aromatic, pubescent perennial to 16 in. tall from creeping rhizome; stems often forming extensive mats at water's edge.

LEAVES: essentially opposite, sessile, clasping basally, somewhat erect in tip portion of stem; blade with transparent glands, broadly lanceolate, to 1 in. long, rounded at tip.

INFLORESCENCE: flowers solitary, pedicelled, usually subtended by 2 minute bracts, from upper leaf axils. *Flower*: blue, about ⅜ in. long; calyx 5-lobed, with 1 lobe larger than others; corolla bell-shaped, 4-lobed; 1 corolla lobe larger than others, pubescent on inner surface; ovary surrounded by a disk with 10–12 slender teeth; stamens 4, not exserted.

FRUIT: capsule, ovoid; seeds numerous.

NOTE: plants with fragrance of lemon when crushed.

BGB   May–October

Disc water-hyssop   [p. 42]
Bacopa rotundifolia (Michx.) Wettst.
(Ba-koh'-pah   roh-tun-dih-foh'-lee-ah)

Creeping or floating, succulent, pubescent perennial to 24 in. long; plants usually forming large mats at water's edge or floating in water.

LEAVES: opposite, sessile, clasping basally, erect in tip portion of stem; blade thin, not conspicuously gland-dotted, prominently veined from base, broadly lanceolate to almost round, to 1⅜ in. long, 1 in. wide, rounded at tip.

INFLORESCENCE: flowers 2–4 at each upper node, pedicelled; not subtended by minute bracts; pedicels slender, pubescent, to ¾ in. long. *Flower*:

white, yellow in center, to ⅜ in. long; calyx 5-lobed; corolla somewhat bell-shaped, 4-lobed, the upper lobe slightly notched; no disk surrounding ovary, or if present, then without teeth.

FRUIT: capsule, globelike, about as long as sepals; seeds numerous.

NOTE: plants not aromatic when crushed.

POF   May–November

Yellow-flowered mecardonia   [p. 95]
Mecardonia vandellioides (H.B.K.) Penn.
(Meh-kar-doh′-nee-ah   van-del-lee-oh′-ih-deez)

Erect or widely spreading, glabrous herbaceous perennial to 16 in. tall; stem 4-angled, often much-branched from base, blackening on drying.

LEAVES: opposite, sessile; blade gland-dotted, broadly lanceolate to spatulate, ⅜–1 in. long, tapering basally to petiole, rounded to abruptly sharp-pointed at tip, somewhat sharply toothed in tip portion.

INFLORESCENCE: flowers solitary, long-pedicelled, from upper leaf axils; pedicels usually much exceeding subtending leaf, subtended by 2 small leaf-like bracts. *Flower*: pale yellow with dark veins on upper lobes, to ½ in. long; calyx 5-parted; corolla prominently 2-lipped, always longer than calyx; upper corolla lip 2-lobed; lobes essentially united, somewhat erect, bearded at base; lower corolla lip 3-lobed, the lobes commonly spreading.

FRUIT: capsule, ellipsoid, equal to or shorter than calyx; seeds numerous, net-veined, cylindrical.

R   (MGP, SOF, LBU)   March–November

Monkey-flower   [p. 52]
Mimulus alatus Ait.
(Mim′-yoo-lus   a-lay′-tus)

Erect, glabrous, herbaceous perennial to 4 ft. tall, commonly lower, from stolons; stem 4-angled, winged on angles, usually branching in upper portion.

LEAVES: opposite, petioled; petiole to 1 in. long; blade broadly lanceolate, to 6 in. long, 2⅜ in. wide, tapering basally to petiole, sharply toothed.

INFLORESCENCE: flowers solitary, pedicelled, from upper leaf axils; pedicels stout, usually shorter than the calyx. *Flower*: blue or violet to whitish, to 1 in. long; calyx tubular, 5-toothed, prominently 5-angled, ½–¾ in. long; corolla 2-lipped; upper corolla lip 2-lobed, the lobes prominently curved backward; lower corolla lip 3-lobed, wide-spreading; throat nearly closed; stamens 4; stamens and style included.

FRUIT: capsule, obovoid, enclosed by persistent calyx; seeds numerous, yellow.

SOF   June–November

Cup-leaf penstemon   [p. 88]

Penstemon murrayanus Hook.

(Pen'-steh-mon   mur-ray-ay'-nus)

Erect, glabrous, glaucous, herbaceous perennial to 6 ft. tall, commonly about 3 ft. tall.

LEAVES: opposite, thick, glaucous; basal leaves sessile, lanceolate or oblong, to 3 in. long; stem leaves united at base and completely encircling stem, somewhat cupped, to 3 in. long, 2 in. wide, becoming reduced in upper portion of stem, entire.

INFLORESCENCE: flowers in pairs, pedicelled, from upper leaf axils, forming an elongated showy terminal panicle. *Flower*: bright red, about 1¼ in. long; sepals 5; corolla somewhat trumpet-shaped, 2-lipped; upper corolla lip 2-lobed; lower corolla lip 3-lobed; fertile stamens 4, exserted; sterile stamen glabrous.

FRUIT: capsule, ovoid, long-beaked at tip; seeds numerous, many-angled, rough.

NOTE: uncommon in East Texas and western Louisiana.

OFS   April–May

Sharp-sepal penstemon   [p. 42]

Penstemon tenuis Small

(Pen'-steh-mon   ten'-yoo-is)

Erect, minutely pubescent perennial 16–36 in. tall; stem usually solitary, unbranched or branched in upper portion.

LEAVES: opposite, sessile, clasping basally; blade thin, pale green, 2¾–4 in. long, ⅝–1¼ in. wide, sharply but shallowly toothed.

INFLORESCENCE: flowers many, in loose showy glabrous terminal panicle. *Flower*: pale pink to dark rose, about ¾ in. long; sepals 5, less than ¼ in. long; corolla 2-lipped; upper corolla lip 2-lobed, short; lower corolla lip 3-lobed, spreading; fertile stamens 4, not exserted; sterile stamen bearded with yellow hairs in tip portion.

FRUIT: capsule, ovoid, beaked at tip; seeds numerous, many-angled, rough.

NOTE: uncommon in East Texas and western Louisiana.

POF   April–May

Loose-flowered penstemon   [p. 73]

Penstemon laxiflorus Penn.

(Pen'-steh-mon   lax-ih-floh'-rus)

Erect to sprawling, glabrous or sparsely pubescent perennial 1–2 ft. tall; stem slender, branched in upper portion.

LEAVES: opposite, sessile, clasping basally; blade thin, narrowly lanceolate, to about 4 in. long, ¾ in. wide, conspicuously toothed.

INFLORESCENCE: flowers many, in showy somewhat glandular pubescent terminal panicle. *Flower*: white to pink, ¾–1¼ in. long; sepals 5, very small; corolla 2-lipped, narrow; upper corolla lip deeply 2-lobed, short; lower corolla lip 3-lobed, spreading; fertile stamens 4; sterile stamen densely bearded with golden hair for most of length, exserted.

FRUIT: capsule, ovoid, beaked at tip; seeds numerous, many-angled, rough.

LBU   March–June

Texas toad-flax [p. 88]

Linaria texana Scheele

(Lin-air′-ee-ah   tex-ay′-nah)

Erect, glabrous annual or winter biennial to 28 in. tall; stem solitary, with short spreading branches forming small rosette at base.

LEAVES: opposite on basal branches, alternate on stem, sessile; basal leaves thick, flat, pale green, shorter and wider than stem leaves; stem leaves rather sparse in upper portion of stem, thinner than basal leaves, pale green, narrowly linear, ¾–1½ in. long.

INFLORESCENCE: flowers few to many, pedicelled, in spikelike solitary terminal raceme; raceme often becoming to 12 in. long. *Flower*: pale blue to violet, ½–⅝ in. long exclusive of spur; calyx deeply 5-parted; corolla 2-lipped; upper corolla lip 2-lobed, short, erect; lower corolla lip 3-lobed, spreading, spurred at base; spur very slender, curved, to about ¼ in. long; stamens 4, included.

FRUIT: capsule, somewhat globelike, about ⅛ in. across; seeds many, gray, rough, very small.

OFS (LBU)   February–May

Old-field toad-flax [p. 73]

Linaria canadensis (L.) Dum.

(Lin-air′-ee-ah   kan-ah-den′-sis)

Erect, delicate, glabrous annual or winter biennial to 28 in. tall, usually lower; stem solitary, with a small rosette of short spreading sterile branches often produced at base.

LEAVES: opposite on basal branches, alternate on stem, sessile; basal leaves thick, flat, pale green, shorter and wider than stem leaves; stem leaves sparse, usually below middle of stem, pale green, linear to narrowly lanceolate, ⅜–1⅛ in. long.

INFLORESCENCE: flowers usually few, pedicelled, in spikelike solitary terminal raceme; raceme congested at flowering, later becoming to 6 in. long. *Flower*: pale blue to pale lavender, to ⅜ in. long excluding spur; calyx deeply 5-parted; corolla 2-lipped; upper corolla lip 2-lobed, erect; lower corolla lip 3-lobed, wide-spreading, spurred at base; spur slender, curved, to about ⅛ in. long; stamens 4, included.

FRUIT: capsule, somewhat globelike, to ⅛ in. across; seeds many, black, usually smooth, very small.

LBU   March–May

False foxglove   [p. 74]
Aureolaria grandiflora (Benth.) Penn.
(Aw-ree-oh-lair′-ee-ah   gran-dih-floh′-rah)

Usually somewhat sprawling pubescent perennial to 5 ft. tall, often much lower; stems solitary or several from base, slender, much-branched.

LEAVES: opposite, may be nearly alternate in upper portion of stem, sessile; lower leaves deeply cleft or lobed; upper leaves entire, much reduced; leaves subtending flowers bractlike, pubescent.

INFLORESCENCE: flowers solitary, pedicelled, showy, from upper leaf axils; pedicels stout, minutely pubescent, abruptly curved upward. *Flower*: yellow, about 1½ in. long; calyx bell-shaped, somewhat 5-lobed, pubescent; corolla 2-lipped; upper corolla lip 2-lobed, with sometimes 1 or both lobes cupped forward; lower corolla lip spreading, deeply 3-lobed; stamens 4, not exserted.

FRUIT: capsule, glabrous, ovoid, to ¾ in. long; seeds few to several.

NOTE: reported to be parasitic on the roots of *Quercus*.

LBU (BMLS)   June–October

Green gerardia   [p. 64]
Agalinis viridis (Small) Penn.
(Ag-ah-lye′-nis   vih′-rih-dis)

Erect, essentially glabrous annual to 2 ft. tall, frequently lower; stem solitary, much-branched; branches long, slender, wiry, angled, commonly reddish in tip portion.

LEAVES: opposite, sessile, strictly erect along stem; blade minutely roughly pubescent on upper surface, threadlike to linear, to ⅔ in. long, less than 1/16 in. wide; leaves becoming smaller in upper portion of plant.

INFLORESCENCE: flowers 1–9, pedicelled, from upper leaf axils, forming raceme; pedicels slender, wide-spreading. *Flower*: pale pink, to ½ in. long; calyx bell-shaped, 5-lobed; corolla 2-lipped; upper corolla lip 2-lobed; lower corolla lip 3-lobed, spreading; stamens 4, slightly exserted; filaments pubescent.

FRUIT: capsule, pale brown, globelike, about ¼ in. long; seeds numerous.

NOTE: the smallest-flowered species of *Agalinis* in East Texas and western Louisiana; plants partially parasitic on roots of grasses and other herbs.
LBS   September–October

Scale-leaved gerardia [p. 74]
Agalinis oligophylla Penn.
(Ag-ah-lye′-nis   ol-ih-goh-fil′-lah)

Erect to somewhat sprawling, pubescent annual 12–32 in. tall; stem usually solitary, ridged, obscurely 4-angled in upper portion, usually much-branched; branches very slender, somewhat erect to wide-spreading.

LEAVES: opposite, sessile, usually closely appressed to stem; blade with rough pubescence on upper surface, threadlike to linear, to ⅜ in. long; leaves on flowering branches reduced to minute bracts.

INFLORESCENCE: flowers 1–8, short-pedicelled, showy, from axils of upper leaves and forming raceme; pedicels rather thick, pubescent to glabrous. *Flower*: pink, ¾–1 in. long; calyx bell-shaped, 5-toothed, very small; corolla 2-lipped; upper corolla lip 2-lobed, erect; lower corolla lip 3-lobed, spreading, somewhat curved upward; stamens 4; filaments pubescent.

FRUIT: capsule, globelike, less than ¼ in. long; seeds numerous.

NOTE: plants partially parasitic on roots of grasses or other herbs.
LBU   (MGP, LBS)   September–November

Purple gerardia [p. 74]
Agalinis purpurea (L.) Penn.
(Ag-ah-lye′-nis   pur-poo′-ree-ah)

Erect to somewhat sprawling, glabrous or pubescent annual to 4 ft. tall, usually much lower; stem solitary, commonly angled, much-branched in upper portion; branches slender, wide-spreading.

LEAVES: opposite, frequently alternate in tip of flowering branches, sessile, widely spreading or somewhat erect, sometimes with clusters of smaller leaves in axils; blade with rough pubescence or glabrous with rough margins, linear, to about 1½ in. long, ⅛ in. wide.

INFLORESCENCE: flowers few to several, short-pedicelled, from upper leaf axils, not forming distinct raceme. *Flower*: pale to dark pink lined with yellow and spotted with purple in throat, pubescent, 1–1¼ in. long; calyx bell-shaped, 5-toothed, very small; corolla 2-lipped; upper corolla lip 2-lobed, erect, conspicuously bearded at base in throat; lower corolla lip 3-lobed, spreading; stamens 4, slightly exserted.

FRUIT: capsule, globelike, to ¼ in. across; seeds numerous.

NOTE: plants partially parasitic on roots of grasses or other herbs.
LBU   (MGP, BGB, LBS)   August–November

American bluehearts [p. 65]
Buchnera americana L.
(Buk′-ner-ah a-mer-ih-kay′-nah)

Strictly erect, slender, delicate perennial to 2 ft. tall, with rough stiff pubescence; stem solitary, ribbed, unbranched, turning black when dried.

LEAVES: opposite, sessile; blade prominently 3-veined, with rough pubescence, broadly lanceolate to broadly spatulate, to 4 in. long; upper leaves reduced in size, coarsely toothed.

INFLORESCENCE: flowers few to several, opposite, subtended by minute bracts, in open terminal spike. *Flower*: dark purple, to $\frac{3}{4}$ in. long; calyx tubular, obscurely veined, 5-lobed, to about $\frac{1}{4}$ in. long; corolla somewhat trumpet-shaped, deeply 5-lobed; fertile stamens 4, not exserted.

FRUIT: capsule, narrowly ovoid, about $\frac{1}{4}$ in. long; seeds many.

NOTE: plants apparently parasitic on roots of other plants.
LBS   (MGP)   June–December

Florida bluehearts [p. 39]
Buchnera floridana Gand.
(Buk′-ner-ah floh-rih-day′-nah)

Strictly erect, slender, delicate pubescent perennial to 2 ft. tall, commonly from thickened root; plant turning black on drying.

LEAVES: opposite, occasionally alternate in upper portion of stem, sessile; blade obscurely 3-veined or not veined, with rough stiff pubescence, broadly lanceolate, to 4 in. long, $\frac{3}{4}$ in. wide, tapering basally to petiole, entire to wavy-toothed.

INFLORESCENCE: flowers few, opposite, sessile, subtended by very small bracts, in loose terminal spike. *Flower*: violet to purplish, rarely whitish, about $\frac{1}{2}$ in. long; calyx tubular, obscurely veined, 5-lobed, to about $\frac{1}{4}$ in. long; corolla somewhat trumpet-shaped, deeply 5-lobed; fertile stamens 4, not exserted.

FRUIT: capsule, narrowly ovoid, less than $\frac{1}{4}$ in. long; seeds many.

NOTE: plants apparently parasitic on roots of other plants.
MGP   (LBU)   April–November

Sticky parentucellia [p. 95]
Parentucellia viscosa (L.) Caruel.
(Pa-ren-too-sil′-lee-ah vis-koh′-sah)

Erect, stout, pubescent annual to about 20 in. tall, often much lower; pubescence glandular, sticky to touch; stem solitary, unbranched or branched in upper portion.

LEAVES: opposite, alternate, or spiraled around stem, sessile, clasping basally; blade thick, pubescent on upper surface, pubescent except between ribs on lower surface, broadly lanceolate, 1¼–2 in. long, rounded or broadly wedge-shaped at base, prominently and deeply toothed.

INFLORESCENCE: flowers few to many, essentially sessile, arranged in loose, spikelike racemes; racemes terminal on main stem or branches. *Flower*: golden yellow, about ⅝ in. long; calyx somewhat tubular, 4-lobed; corolla 2-lipped; upper corolla lip small, unlobed, cupped forward and forming hood; lower corolla lip deeply 3-lobed, spreading.

FRUIT: capsule, less than ⅜ in. long, with stiff brown pubescence in tip portion; seeds minute.

R   April–June

Wood-betony   [p. 82]
Pedicularis canadensis L.

(Pee-dik-yoo-lair'-is kan-ah-den'-sis)

Erect, stout, clustered, unbranched, pubescent perennial 4–16 in. tall from thickened, fibrous roots; plants usually forming dense, matlike colonies.

LEAVES: opposite or alternate, mostly toward base and long-petioled or essentially sessile in upper portion of plant and much reduced in size; blade thick, deeply cleft or lobed into segments, the segments shallowly lobed or toothed.

INFLORESCENCE: flowers few to many, sessile, in dense terminal spike; spike 1¼–2 in. long in flower, elongating to 8 in. in fruit. *Flower*: pale to dark yellow, to almost 1 in. long; calyx somewhat flattened, split in front; corolla 2-lipped; upper corolla lip flattened, curved forward and forming hood, 2-toothed at tip; lower corolla lip 3-lobed, spreading; stamens 4, not exserted.

FRUIT: capsule, flattened, somewhat oblong, twice as long as calyx; seeds many, flat, wingless.

BMLS (SOF, LBU)   March–May

Texas paintbrush (Indian paintbrush)   [p. 95]
Castilleja indivisa Engelm.

(Kas-til-lee'-ah in-dih-vye'-sah)

Strictly erect, clumped, pubescent annual 8–16 in. tall from slender taproot.

LEAVES: alternate, sessile; blade pubescent on both surfaces with longer softer hairs on veins and margins, linear to narrowly lanceolate, 1–4 in. long, entire or often with 1 or 2 pairs of small lobes.

INFLORESCENCE: flowers sessile, inconspicuous, usually not noticed, in axils of red-tipped conspicuous leaflike bracts; flowers and bracts numerous, forming large showy terminal spike; bracts broadly lanceolate, about ¼ in. long. *Flower*: whitish or greenish, ¾–1 in. long, usually enclosed by calyx; calyx tubular, entire to somewhat 4-lobed, whitish or pinkish rimmed with red, to 1 in. long, conspicuous; corolla very slender, 2-lipped; stamens 4.

FRUIT: capsule, ovoid; seeds numerous.

NOTE: plants apparently parasitic on roots of grasses and other herbs.

R   (MGP)   May–June

BIGNONIACEAE
(Catalpa Family)

Cross-vine   [p. 53]
Bignonia capreolata L.
(Big-noh'-nee-ah   kap-ree-oh-lay'-tah)

Usually high-climbing, woody, glabrous perennial vine, climbing by tendrils at ends of leaves; tendrils several-branched, the branches ending in small flat disks.

LEAVES: opposite, evergreen, petioled, compound; petiole to ¾ in. long; blade of 2 lateral leaflets, with third leaflet modified into tendril; leaflet short-petioled, glabrous, firm, narrowly lanceolate to oblong or elliptic, to 6 in. long, 2 in. wide, rounded or abruptly pointed at tip, rounded and notched at base, entire.

INFLORESCENCE: flowers 2–5, pedicelled, in showy cyme; pedicels ¾–1½ in. long; cymes short-stalked, axillary. *Flower*: reddish orange and yellow, 1½–2 in. long, fragrant; calyx bell-shaped, shallowly 5-lobed; corolla somewhat trumpet-shaped, 5-lobed; corolla lobes rounded, curved backward; stamens 4, included.

FRUIT: capsule, flattened, linear, to 6 in. long, 1 in. wide; seeds thin, papery, winged, elliptic, to 1¼ in. long, ⅜ in. wide.

NOTE: The leaflets may appear as 4 downward-pointing leaves when seen growing on the trunks of trees.

SOF   (LBU, BMLS)   March–May

Trumpet-creeper   [p. 53]
Campsis radicans (L.) Seem.
(Kamp'-sis   rad'-ih-kanz)

Sprawling to high-climbing, woody, shrubby, somewhat pubescent vine to 40 ft. long, climbing by small roots along stem.

LEAVES: opposite, deciduous, petioled, compound; blade usually pale green, divided into 9–11 leaflets; leaflets short-petioled, usually somewhat pubescent on lower surface, broadly lanceolate to broadly elliptic, to 3½ in.

long, 1½ in. wide, broadly rounded to wedge-shaped at base, prominently toothed.

INFLORESCENCE: flowers few to several, pedicelled, in showy terminal panicles. *Flower*: orange or red, to 3½ in. long; calyx somewhat tubular, 5-lobed, to 1 in. long, pale orange, leathery; corolla somewhat trumpet-shaped, 5-lobed, soft leathery; fertile stamens 4, glabrous, included.

FRUIT: capsule, hard, woody, beaked at tip, cylindrical, 3–4¾ in. long, persistent; seeds numerous, flattened, with 2 large wings.

SOF   (MGP, POF, LBU, BMLS)   May–October

MARTYNIACEAE
(Unicorn-plant Family)

Common devil's claw   [p. 88]
Proboscidea louisianica (Mill.) Thell.
(Proh-bos-sid'-ee-ah   loo-iz-ee-an'-ih-kah)

Erect to sprawling, coarse, unpleasantly scented annual 1–3 ft. tall, commonly lower, with glandular pubescence mostly throughout; stem solitary, opposite-branched.

LEAVES: opposite, frequently alternate in upper portion of plant, petioled; petiole to 8 in. long, densely pubescent; blade pubescent, broadly lanceolate to almost round, to 12 in. wide, slightly wider than long, entire to shallowly lobed and usually wavy.

INFLORESCENCE: flowers 1–20, pedicelled, showy, in raceme; racemes open, terminal, axillary, or at ends of branches. *Flower*: dull white, purplish, or pinkish, mottled or spotted with reddish purple and yellow, to 2¼ in. long; calyx 5-lobed, to ¾ in. long; corolla somewhat trumpet-shaped, 5-lobed; upper 2 corolla lobes recurved, glandular pubescent at base; lower 3 corolla lobes wide-spreading; fertile stamens 4.

FRUIT: capsule, broadly ellipsoid; tip portion of capsule extending as long beak; beak 1½–3 times longer than body and splitting at maturity into 2 curved hornlike structures; body portion of capsule to 4 in. long; seeds blackish, angled, to ⅜ in. long.

OFS   (SOF, LBU)   June–September

OROBANCHACEAE
(Broomrape Family)

Beech-drops   [p. 82]
Epifagus virginiana (L.) Bart.
(Ep-ih-fay'-gus   vir-jin-ee-ay'-nah)

Erect, clump-forming, fleshy, glabrous, parasitic perennial to 18 in. tall;

stems slender, brittle, delicate, reddish purple, apparently with no chlorophyll, unbranched or much-branched in upper portion.

LEAVES: alternate, reduced to minute scales, sessile; blade broadly lanceolate, about 1/16 in. long.

INFLORESCENCE: flowers few to several, sessile, scattered along branches; chasmogamous flowers along upper portion of branches, sterile; cleistogamous flowers in lower portion, fertile. *Flower*: tan to purplish, mottled or banded with darker coloring, about ⅜ in. long; calyx of sterile flowers cup-shaped, 5-lobed; corolla of sterile flowers tubular, 4-lobed, to ½ in. long; calyx of fertile flowers cup-shaped, essentially unlobed; corolla of fertile flowers caplike, pushed off by developing capsule.

FRUIT: capsule, brown, papery, globelike; seeds numerous, yellowish white, ellipsoid, minute.

BMLS   February–November

LENTIBULARIACEAE
(Bladderwort Family)

Zigzag bladderwort   [p. 58]
Utricularia subulata L.
(Oo-trik-yoo-lair′-ee-ah   sub-yoo-lay′-tah)

Glabrous, terrestrial, carnivorous perennial; stems below ground, creeping, threadlike, branched; branches small, below ground, with minute bladderlike traps which capture and digest minute organisms; flower scape above ground.

LEAVES: alternate, sessile, below ground; blade threadlike to linear, to ⅜ in. long.

INFLORESCENCE: flowers 1–12, pedicelled, on leafless scape; scape erect, threadlike, to 8 in. tall; pedicels subtended by very small bract. *Flower*: yellow, to ½ in. long; calyx 2-lobed, very small; corolla 2-lipped; upper corolla lip erect, unlobed; lower corolla lip 3-lobed, spurred, with large conspicuous projection at base closing throat; spur curved, appressed to lower lip.

FRUIT: capsule, brown, glabrous, globelike, about 1/16 in. across; seeds numerous, minute.

BGB   March–June

Rush bladderwort   [p. 65]
Utricularia juncea Vahl.
(Oo-trik-yoo-lair′-ee-ah   jun′-see-ah)

Glabrous, terrestrial or aquatic, carnivorous perennial; stems below ground or floating on water, threadlike, delicate, branched, creeping, mat-forming; branches with small bladderlike traps which capture and digest minute organisms; flower scape above ground or above water.

INFLORESCENCE: flowers 1–12, very short-pedicelled, on leafless scape; scape erect, threadlike, to 16 in. tall; flowers distant, not crowded; pedicels subtended by very small bract. *Flower*: yellow, to ⅝ in. long, ⅜ in. across; calyx 2-lobed, very small; corolla 2-lipped; upper corolla lip somewhat erect, unlobed; lower corolla lip 3-lobed, spurred, with large, conspicuous projection at base closing throat; spur straight or only slightly curved, about ¼ in. long.

FRUIT: capsule, brown, glabrous, globelike, about 1/16 in. across; seeds numerous, net-veined, minute.

LBS   (BGB)   May–September

Purple bladderwort [p. 58]
Utricularia purpurea Walt.

(Oo-trik-yoo-lair′-ee-ah   pur-poo′-ree-ah)

Floating, glabrous, carnivorous, aquatic perennial; stems submersed, slender, delicate, branched, to 40 in. long; branches with small bladderlike traps which capture and digest minute organisms; flower scape above water.

LEAVES: whorled, 5–7 at node, numerous, submersed; blade divided into whorled, threadlike segments, the segments often with terminal bladder.

INFLORESCENCE: flowers 1–4, very short-pedicelled, on leafless scape; scape erect, to 6 in. tall. *Flower*: rose purple to violet, about ⅜ in. long; calyx 2-lobed, very small; corolla 2-lipped; upper corolla lip erect, flat or cupped, unlobed; lower corolla lip 3-lobed, spurred; lateral corolla lobes forming prominent structure at base, closing throat; spur curved, appressed to lower lip.

FRUIT: capsule, globelike, about 1/16 in. across; seeds numerous, rough, minute.

NOTE: uncommon to rare in the Big Thicket.

BGB   May–September

Floating bladderwort [p. 58]
Utricularia radiata Small

(Oo-trik-yoo-lair′-ee-ah   ray-dee-ay′-tah)

Floating, glabrous, carnivorous aquatic perennial; stems delicate, submersed, few-branched; branches with small bladderlike traps which capture and digest minute organisms; flower scape above water.

LEAVES: stem leaves submersed, alternate, 4–6 times divided into segments; segments delicate, threadlike, bearing small ovoid bladders; leaves along flower scape floating, in whorls of 4–10, petioled; petiole inflated; blade divided into numerous short, threadlike segments; bladders absent.

INFLORESCENCE: flowers 3 or 4, very short-pedicelled, on leafless scape;

scape erect, very slender, ¾–2 in. tall; pedicel elongating to 1⅜ in. long in
fruit, usually stiffly erect, subtended by very small bract. *Flower*: yellow,
about ⅝ in. across; calyx 2-lobed; corolla 2-lipped; upper corolla lip erect,
unlobed; lower corolla lip 3-lobed, spurred, with large conspicuous projection
at base closing throat; spur curved, appressed to lower lip.

FRUIT: capsule, glabrous, globelike; seeds numerous, minute.

BGB   (POF, SOF)   March–July

Cone-spur bladderwort   [p. 58]
Utricularia gibba L.

(Oo-trik-yoo-lair'-ee-ah   gib'-bah)

Floating or creeping, glabrous, terrestrial or aquatic, carnivorous perennial; stems and branches delicate, threadlike, numerous, often forming thick
entangled mats, submersed or below ground; branches with small, bladderlike
traps which capture and digest minute organisms; flower scape above ground
or above water.

LEAVES: alternate, sessile, below ground or submersed; blade divided
into usually 2 threadlike segments; segments with few scattered bladders.

INFLORESCENCE: flowers 1–3, short-pedicelled, on leafless scape; scape
erect, threadlike, to 4 in. tall; pedicels somewhat lax, subtended by very
small bract. *Flower*: yellow, to ½ in. long, ⅜ in. across; calyx 2-lobed, very
small; corolla 2-lipped; upper corolla lip erect, not lobed; lower corolla lip
3-lobed, spurred, with prominent projection at base closing throat; spur thick,
blunt, much shorter than lower lip.

FRUIT: capsule, glabrous, globelike; seeds numerous, flat, winged, angled,
minute.

BGB   (POF, SOF, LBS)   June–August

Small butterwort   [p. 65]
Pinguicula pumila Michx.

(Pin-gwik'-yoo-lah   pyoo'-mih-lah)

Low, succulent, carnivorous perennial from fibrous roots.

LEAVES: basal, forming rosette, sessile; blade soft, fleshy, pale green,
greasy to the touch, elliptic to broadly spatulate, to 1⅛ in. long, narrowed at
base, blunt or rounded at tip; blades capturing insects on the sticky surface;
margins rolling inward over the trapped prey until it is digested.

INFLORESCENCE: flower solitary, terminal on erect scape; scapes threadlike, to 8 in. tall, usually much lower, glandular, pubescent. *Flower*: whitish
or pale violet, to ¾ in. across; calyx 5-lobed, very small, pubescent; corolla
somewhat 2-lipped, 5-lobed, spurred at base; corolla lobes similar, spreading,
somewhat notched at tip; stamens 2; anthers coming together, appearing as
one.

FRUIT: capsule, globelike; seeds several, yellow, rough, minute.
LBS   (BGB)   March–June

ACANTHACEAE
(Acanthus Family)

Violet ruellia [p. 39]

Ruellia nudiflora (Gray) Urban
(Roo-el'-lee-ah   noo-di-floh'-rah)

Erect or sprawling perennial to 28 in. tall; stem solitary, usually branched in upper portion, densely pubescent when young, becoming essentially glabrous with age.

LEAVES: opposite, petioled; blade gray-green, with dense showy pubescence, prominently net-veined on lower surface, oblong to somewhat lanceolate, to 2⅜ in. long, 1⅛ in. wide, basally extending onto petiole; margins conspicuously crisped or wavy-toothed, narrowly fringed; summer leaves to about 4¾ in. long or much reduced in upper portion of plant.

INFLORESCENCE: flowers few to many, pedicelled, in loose showy terminal panicle; small, lateral panicles of cleistogamous flowers produced earlier in season. *Flower*: purplish blue, to 2¼ in. long, 1½ in. across, opening about sunrise, falling in early afternoon; calyx deeply 5-lobed, with dense gland-tipped pubescence but not sticky to touch; corolla trumpet-shaped, 5-lobed, conspicuously curved; stamens 4.

FRUIT: capsule, pubescent, somewhat flattened, shortly cylindrical; seeds several, brown, from persistent hook-shaped stalks.
MGP   (POF)   February–November

Low ruellia [p. 74]

Ruellia humilis Nutt. var. *longiflora* (Gray) Fern.
(Roo-el'-lee-ah   hyoo'-mih-lis   lon-jih-floh'-rah)

Erect to somewhat sprawling, clumped, rather stout, conspicuously pubescent perennial to 32 in. tall, commonly much lower, from shortened knotty rhizomes; stems usually several in cluster, often prominently 4-angled, branched; branches slender, often arching or lying on ground.

LEAVES: opposite, essentially sessile, somewhat crowded on stem; blade leathery, pubescent, densely so on veins and margins, lanceolate to narrowly lanceolate or narrowly elliptic, to 3⅛ in. long, 1¾ in. wide, blunt to broadly wedge-shaped at base and extending onto petiole, blunt or short-pointed at tip.

INFLORESCENCE: flowers few, in essentially sessile cluster; clusters from middle and upper leaf axils; cleistogamous flowers rarely present. *Flower*: lavender to light blue with darker markings in throat, 2–3⅛ in. long, usually about ¾ in. across; calyx deeply 5-lobed, pubescent; corolla trumpet-shaped, 5-lobed; stamens 4.

FRUIT: capsule, brownish, glabrous, somewhat flattened, to ⅝ in. long, less than ¼ in. wide; seeds few, pale, from persistent hook-shaped stalks.
LBU   April–October

Dicliptera   [p. 53]
Dicliptera brachiata (Pursh) Spreng.
(Dye-klip'-ter-ah   bray-kee-ay'-tah)

Erect or sprawling, rather coarse, glabrous or pubescent perennial to 28 in. tall; stem solitary, slender, somewhat angled, branched; branches many, opposite, spreading.

LEAVES: opposite, petioled; petiole to 2½ in. long; blade thin, broadly lanceolate to broadly elliptic, to 4 in. long, 2 in. wide, tapering basally onto petiole, usually sharp-pointed at tip.

INFLORESCENCE: flowers 1–several, essentially sessile, in paniclelike axillary cluster; clusters subtended by several small leaflike bracts. *Flower*: purple to pale lavender or pink, to ¾ in. long, pubescent; calyx bell-shaped, 5-parted, transparent; corolla deeply 2-lipped, pubescent; upper corolla lip narrow, unlobed; lower corolla lip narrow, unlobed to shallowly 3-lobed; stamens 2.

FRUIT: capsule, pubescent, ovoid, about ¼ in. long; seeds usually 2, brown, flattened, oval, from persistent hook-shaped stalks.
SOF (POF)   July–October

Green-flowered yeatesia   [p. 43]
Yeatesia viridiflora (Nees) Small
(Yayt'-see-ah   vih-rih-dih-floh'-rah)

Erect, glabrous or pubescent perennial to 2 ft. tall, commonly lower; stem somewhat glaucous, unbranched or branched; under very dry conditions with indented ring above leaf node and appearing as if jointed.

LEAVES: opposite, short-petioled; blade bright green, thin, sparsely pubescent on upper surface, glabrous on lower surface, broadly lanceolate to lanceolate, to 5 in. long, 2 in. wide, tapering basally to petiole.

INFLORESCENCE: flowers numerous, sessile, subtended by leaflike bracts, in cylindrical spike; spike compact, peduncled, terminal and from upper leaf axils. *Flower*: white, about ⅝ in. long; calyx deeply 5-parted; corolla trumpet-shaped, 4-lobed; stamens 2; filaments slender, included.

FRUIT: capsule, firm; seeds 4, glabrous, from persistent hook-shaped stalks.
POF (SOF)   July–October

Lance-leaved water-willow [p. 43]

Justicia lanceolata (Chapm.) Small

(Jus-tis′-ee-ah lan-see-oh-lay′-tah)

Erect or sprawling, essentially glabrous perennial to 12 in. tall from rhizomes; stems usually branched; plants forming colonies.

LEAVES: opposite, essentially sessile; blade minutely pubescent, linear to narrowly lanceolate or narrowly elliptic, to 4 in. long, 1¼ in. wide, entire.

INFLORESCENCE: flowers numerous, in peduncled axillary spike; spikes slender, 1¼–4 in. long, the flowers scattered evenly along 1 side; peduncles longer than leaves, often branching. *Flower*: pale lavender to purple with darker markings, about ⅜ in. long; calyx deeply 5-lobed; corolla 2-lipped; upper corolla lip 2-lobed, narrow, short; lower corolla lip 3-lobed, broad, spreading; stamens 2, slightly exserted.

FRUIT: capsule, somewhat flattened, larger near tip, about ½ in. long; seeds 4, smooth, flattened, somewhat rounded, from persistent hook-shaped stalks.

POF   (SOF)   March–June

RUBIACEAE
(Madder Family)

Fine-leaf bluets [p. 74]

Hedyotis nigricans (Lamb.) Fosb. var. *filifolia* (Chap.) Shinners

(Hed-ee-oh′-tis nig′-rih-kanz fih-lih-foh′-lee-ah)

Strictly erect to sprawling, glabrous perennial 2–20 in. tall from tough taproot; stems solitary or few from base forming clump, branched in upper portion.

LEAVES: opposite, essentially sessile, often with clusters of smaller leaves in axils; blade usually roughly pubescent along margins and veins of lower surface, threadlike to linear or narrowly lanceolate, ⅜–1½ in. long; margins often rolled toward lower surface.

INFLORESCENCE: flowers few to several, in sessile or short-peduncled cyme; cymes axillary and terminal, forming large panicle. *Flower*: white, pink or purplish, less than ⅜ in. long; calyx 4-lobed, persistent; corolla trumpet-shaped, 4-lobed.

FRUIT: capsule, obovoid, about 1/16 in. long, mostly inferior; seeds few to several.

LBU   (OFS)   April–November

Southern bluets   [p. 74]
Hedyotis australis Lewis & Moore
(Hed-ee-oh'-tis   aw-stray'-lis)

Erect to sprawling, tufted, delicate, glabrous winter annual 1¼–4 in. tall from branched fibrous roots; stems 1–few in clump; plants often forming large, dense colonies.

LEAVES: opposite, essentially sessile; blade broadly lanceolate to spatulate, about ⅜ in. long, ⅛ in. wide; margins entire, glabrous.

INFLORESCENCE: flowers solitary, terminal. *Flower*: white, less than ¼ in. long; calyx 4-lobed; corolla trumpet-shaped, 4-lobed; tube 2–3 times as long as calyx lobes; stamens 4, included.

FRUIT: capsule, erect, glabrous, obovoid, small, mostly inferior; seeds few to several, minute.
LBU   February–April

Small bluets   [p. 75]
Hedyotis crassifolia Raf.
(Hed-ee-oh'-tis   kras-sih-foh'-lee-ah)

Erect to somewhat sprawling, delicate, tufted, essentially glabrous winter annual 1¼–4¾ in. tall from branched fibrous roots; stems usually branched; plants often forming large, showy colonies.

LEAVES: opposite, petioled; blade broadly lanceolate to broadly spatulate, to ⅜ in. long, less than ¼ in. wide, abruptly tapering basally to petiole; margins often pubescent; upper blades many times longer than petiole; lower blades equal to petiole to several times longer.

INFLORESCENCE: flowers solitary, pedicelled, terminal. *Flower*: blue violet to lilac, with darker throat, rarely white, to about ⅜ in. long; calyx 4-lobed; corolla trumpet-shaped, 4-lobed, less than twice the length of calyx lobes; stamens 4, included.

FRUIT: capsule, erect, glabrous, obovoid, small, mostly inferior; seeds few to several, minute.
LBU   (MGP)   January–April

Common buttonbush   [p. 43]
Cephalanthus occidentalis L.
(Sef-ah-lan'-thus   ok-sih-den-tay'-lis)

Shrub or small tree, usually about 5–10 ft. tall; stems solitary or several from base, usually much-branched; branches slender, brown or grayish, glabrous or with short pubescence.

LEAVES: opposite, occasionally in threes or fours, deciduous, petioled; petiole to 1¼ in. long; blade bright green on upper surface, prominently veined, glabrous or pubescent on lower surface, narrowly lanceolate to broadly lanceolate, to 7½ in. long, 3⅜ in. wide, wedge-shaped or rounded and notched at base, entire.

INFLORESCENCE: flowers numerous, small, densely clustered into peduncled almost perfectly spherical heads; peduncles to 4 in. long, terminal and from upper leaf axils. *Flower*: white to yellowish, ¼–⅜ in. long; calyx minute, 4- or 5-toothed; corolla somewhat trumpet-shaped, 4- or 5-lobed; stamens 4; style threadlike, much exserted beyond corolla; stigma often covered with masses of pollen.

FRUIT: capsule, small, at maturity splitting upward from base into 2–4 sections; seeds 1 per section.

POF (SOF) June–September

Partridge-berry [p. 82]

Mitchella repens L.

(Mih-chel′-lah ree′-penz)

Creeping, delicate, glabrous perennial forming low appressed mats of various size.

LEAVES: opposite, evergreen, stipuled, petioled; stipules minute; blade dark green, leathery, shiny, often conspicuously veined, broadly lanceolate to almost round, to 1 in. long or wide, rounded and notched at base.

INFLORESCENCE: flowers in pairs on short peduncle. *Flower*: white, often tinged with pink or purple in bud, fragrant; calyx very small, 4-toothed; corolla trumpet-shaped, 4-lobed; tube long, slender; corolla lobes widespreading, pubescent on inner surface; stamens 4; ovaries of paired flowers united.

FRUIT: drupe, glabrous, bright red, shiny, aromatic, globelike, about ¼ in. across, formed from the united ovaries; edible when ripe; seeds 8 per drupe, small, bony, nutlike.

BMLS (SOF) May–July

Tropical Mexican-clover [p. 88]

Richardia brasiliensis Gomes

(Rih-char′-dee-ah bra-zil-ee-en′-sis)

Erect to sprawling and matted, densely pubescent annual or sometimes perennial to 12 in. tall from deep thickened root; stems 1–several, much-branched.

LEAVES: opposite, stipuled, essentially sessile to short-petioled; stipules fringed with bristles, connecting petioles; blade thick, densely covered with appressed rough pubescence, broadly lanceolate to elliptic, ¾–1½ in. long, to ¾ in. wide, tapering basally to petiole.

INFLORESCENCE: flowers few to several, in dense terminal cluster; cluster surrounded by the 1 or 2 uppermost pairs of leaves. *Flower*: white, about

1/4 in. long; calyx united at base, 6-toothed, pubescent; corolla funnel-shaped, 6-lobed; stamens 6.

FRUIT: schizocarp; nutlets 4, dull red, pubescent, keeled; seeds 1 per nutlet, brown, smooth.

OFS (LBU)   May–October

Virginia buttonweed   [p. 43]
Diodia virginiana L.
(Dye-oh'-dee-ah vir-jin-ee-ay'-nah)

Erect, spreading, or trailing and matlike, glabrous or pubescent herbaceous perennial 4–24 in. long from woody base; stem much-branched, forking.

LEAVES: opposite, stipuled, sessile; stiples sheathing stem, fringed with long bristles on margins; blade bright green, narrowly lanceolate or narrowly elliptic to somewhat spatulate, to 3½ in. long, 1¼ in. wide, usually much smaller, tapering basally to petiole, finely toothed.

INFLORESCENCE: flowers usually solitary, sessile, from upper leaf axils. *Flower*: white, about ½ in. long; calyx pubescent, 2-toothed; corolla trumpet-shaped, 4-lobed; tube very slender; corolla lobes narrow, spreading flat, pubescent on inner surface; stamens 4; style cleft.

FRUIT: schizocarp; carpels 2, rarely separating, ellipsoid, the 2 calyx teeth persistent at tip; seeds 1 per carpel.

POF (MGP, SOF)   May–October

CAPRIFOLIACEAE
(Honeysuckle Family)

Southern arrow-wood   [p. 43]
Viburnum dentatum L.
(Vye-bur'-num den-tay'-tum)

Shrub or small tree, much-branched, mostly pubescent, commonly 5–15 ft. tall, occasionally taller; stem bark gray or reddish brown; young branches and twigs usually densely pubescent.

LEAVES: opposite, deciduous, petioles to ⅝ in. long, pubescent; blade thin, essentially glabrous or with some pubescence on lower surface, broadly lanceolate to almost round, to 6 in. long, 4 in. wide, usually much smaller, broadly wedge-shaped to rounded or rounded and notched at base, broadly rounded to shortly pointed at tip, coarsely toothed.

INFLORESCENCE: flowers numerous, in showy peduncled compound terminal cyme; cymes somewhat flat, formed from 5–7 small clusters. *Flower*: white or creamy, about ¼ in. across; sepals 5, minute; corolla trumpet-shaped, deeply 5-lobed; stamens 5, exserted.

FRUIT: drupe, blue-black when ripe, globelike to ovoid or obovoid, to ⅝ in. long; stone ellipsoid, deeply grooved on one side.

POF (SOF, BMLS)   April–June

Common elder-berry [p. 53]
Sambucus canadensis L.
(Sam-byoo'-kus kan-ah-den'-sis)

Erect, somewhat woody, partially herbaceous perennial to 12 ft. tall, usually lower, from stolons; stems 1–several, with conspicuous corky spots; plants usually forming large colonies; foliage unpleasantly scented when crushed.

LEAVES: opposite, petioled, compound; blade usually once divided into 5–11 leaflets; leaflets glabrous or pubescent, lanceolate to broadly elliptic, to 7¼ in. long, 2¾ in. wide, sharply toothed.

INFLORESCENCE: flowers numerous, small, in large showy terminal compound cyme; cymes flat to convex, to 14 in. across. *Flower*: white, less than ¼ in. across, fragrant; sepals 5, minute; corolla trumpet-shaped, 5-lobed; stamens 5, exserted.

FRUIT: drupe, juicy, purplish to blackish, globelike, to ¼ in. across, edible when ripe; seeds 3 or 4.

NOTE: fruit commonly used for pies, jellies, and wine.

SOF (POF)   May–July

Japanese honeysuckle [p. 53]
Lonicera japonica Thunb.
(Loh-nis'-eh-rah ja-pon'-ih-kah)

Trailing, creeping, twining or high-climbing woody perennial vine; stems tough, branched, often rooting at nodes and forming large mats on ground.

LEAVES: opposite, short-petioled, evergreen; blade thick, firm, leathery, dark green and glabrous on upper surface, paler and usually sparsely pubescent beneath, broadly lanceolate to narrowly elliptic, to 3⅛ in. long, 1½ in. wide, rounded to broadly rounded and notched at base, rounded to pointed at tip; early leaves sometimes toothed or lobed.

INFLORESCENCE: flowers in pairs, subtended by 2 leaflike bracts, on peduncle from leaf axils. *Flower*: white or pink fading yellow, fragrant, to 1½ in. long; calyx 5-parted, minute; corolla 2-lipped, pubescent on outer surface; upper corolla lip 4-lobed; lower corolla lip unlobed, narrow; stamens 5, conspicuous.

FRUIT: berry, black, shiny, glabrous, globelike, about ¼ in. across; seeds several, black, shiny, to about ⅛ in. long.

NOTE: native of Asia; an escaped, persistent, rampant growing plant endangering native vegetation and usually most undesirable.

SOF   (POF, LBS, LBU, BMLS)   March–November

Trumpet honeysuckle (wood-bine) [p. 95]
Lonicera sempervirens L.

(Loh-nis'-eh-rah   sem-per-vye'-renz)

Twining or low-climbing, essentially glabrous, woody perennial vine to 15 ft. or more long.

LEAVES: opposite, partially evergreen, essentially sessile in lower portion of stem, upper 1 or 2 pairs united at base and completely encircling stem; blade thick, firm, glaucous, pale green and glabrous on upper surface, white and occasionally minutely pubescent beneath; lower leaves narrowly oblong to elliptic or spatulate, to 2¾ in. long, 1½ in. wide, rounded to wedge-shaped at base, blunt or rounded at tip.

INFLORESCENCE: flowers 4–6 in cluster; clusters 2–4, sessile, forming interrupted spike; spikes terminal on new growth. *Flower*: red, often yellowish in throat, to 2¼ in. long; calyx bell-shaped, very small; corolla tubular, shallowly 5-lobed; stamens 5, slightly exserted; style much exserted.

FRUIT: berry, red, glabrous, shiny; seeds several.

R   (POF, SOF, LBU)   March–April

VALERIANACEAE
(Valerian Family)

Corn salad [p. 96]
Valerianella stenocarpa (Engelm.) Krok

(Va-ler'-ee-ah-nel'-lah   sten-oh-kar'-pah)

Erect or somewhat sprawling annual or sometimes biennial 4–20 in. tall; stem angled, forked in upper portion, pubescent on angles.

LEAVES: opposite, sessile, succulent; basal leaves spatulate, about 1½–2¼ in. long, united around stem at base, rounded at tip, entire and fringed with hairs; stem leaves broadly lanceolate, sparsely toothed near base and fringed with hairs.

INFLORESCENCE: flowers several, very small, in compact cymes at ends of forking branches; cymes subtended by small, leaflike bracts; bracts lanceolate, usually glabrous. *Flower*: white; calyx minute or none; corolla funnel-shaped, 5-lobed at rim, conspicuous above bracts; stamens and style exserted.

FRUIT: capsulelike, 3-celled, yellowish, narrowly ellipsoid, more than twice as long as wide; only 1 cell fertile; seed 1 per fertile cell.

R   (SOF, LBU)   March–May

CAMPANULACEAE
(Bluebell Family)

Chicken spike   [p. 53]
Sphenoclea zeylanica Gaertn.
(Sfee-nok-lee'-ah   zee-lan'-ih-kah)

Erect, coarse, glabrous annual to 40 in. tall, commonly lower; stem hollow, branched in upper portion.

LEAVES: alternate, petioled; petiole to ¾ in. long; blade pale on lower surface, elliptic, to 4¾ in. long, 2 in. wide, entire.

INFLORESCENCE: flowers numerous, minute, sessile, in dense terminal peduncled spike; peduncles to 4 in. long; spikes erect, cylindrical, leafless, tapering at tip, to 3¼ in. long, ⅜ in. thick; each flower subtended by minute bract. *Flower*: white; calyx minute, 5-parted; corolla 5-parted; stamens 5.

FRUIT: capsule, very small, opening around middle, the top falling off as lid; seeds numerous, yellowish, minute.

NOTE: an introduced Old World species.
SOF   August–November

Venus' looking-glass   [p. 88]
Triodanis perfoliata (L.) Nieuw.
(Try-oh-day'-nis   per-foh-lee-ay'-tah)

Erect to sprawling, pubescent annual to 3½ ft. tall, usually 4–20 in. tall; stem solitary, unbranched to sparsely branched.

LEAVES: alternate, sessile, clasping basally; blade with rough pubescence, broadly lanceolate to almost round, to 1 in. across, rounded and deeply notched at base, usually toothed.

INFLORESCENCE: flowers 1–several at a node, sessile; lower flowers cleistogamous; upper flowers chasmogamous, showy, subtended by leaflike bracts. *Flower*: purple to bluish violet, about ¾ in. across; calyx 5-lobed, the lobes narrowed to slender rigid tip; corolla deeply 5-lobed; stamens 5; stigma 3-lobed.

FRUIT: capsule, ellipsoid to obovoid, to ⅜ in. long; seeds numerous, somewhat flattened, shiny, escaping through lateral pores formed by wall tissue rolled upward like a window shade.
OFS   (MGP, LBU)   April–July

Wahlenbergia   [p. 75]
Wahlenbergia marginata (Thunberg) DC.
(Wah-len-berg'-ee-ah   mar-jih-nay'-tah)

Erect to sprawling, usually somewhat clumped, delicate, glabrous or pubescent perennial 4–22 in. tall; stems usually several, branched, leafy usually on lower half.

LEAVES: alternate, essentially sessile, mostly basal or on lower portion of stem; blade linear or lowermost lanceolate or somewhat spatulate, $\frac{3}{8}$–$1\frac{1}{2}$ in. long, sharp-pointed at tip; margins entire to sharply toothed, often wavy.

INFLORESCENCE: flowers few to many in open panicle, pedicelled; pedicels $\frac{3}{8}$–2 in. long. *Flower*: blue to violet, about $\frac{1}{4}$ in. long; calyx deeply divided into 5 lobes; calyx lobes narrow, erect; corolla bell-shaped, divided into 5 lobes at rim; corolla lobes shorter than tube, pointed at tip; stamens 5; stigma 3-lobed.

FRUIT: capsule, somewhat globelike, to $\frac{1}{4}$ in. long, opening by terminal pores; seeds brown, oblong, minute.
LBU   (BMLS)   March–November

Eared lobelia [p. 96]
Lobelia appendiculata A. DC.
(Loh-bee'-lee-ah   ap-pen-dik-yoo-lay'-tah)

Erect to sprawling, essentially glabrous annual or biennial to 3 ft. tall, usually about 14–24 in. tall; stem unbranched or with few branches.

LEAVES: alternate, sessile, sometimes clasping basally; blade thin, broadly lanceolate to oblong, 1–$3\frac{1}{8}$ in. long, $1\frac{1}{4}$ in. wide, rounded or sharp-pointed at tip.

INFLORESCENCE: flowers many, subtended by bracts, pedicelled, in terminal raceme; pedicels less than $\frac{1}{4}$ in. long, pubescent, with pair of bracts at base; bracts linear, exceeding pedicel; raceme usually solitary, often 1-sided, to 15 in. long. *Flower*: pale lilac to violet or bluish white, to $\frac{5}{8}$ in. long; calyx somewhat inflated, pubescent, 5-lobed, with small appendages at base of lobes; calyx lobes linear, fringed with bristly hairs; calyx basal appendages drying blue or purplish; corolla 2-lipped; upper corolla lip deeply 2-lobed, the cleft extending almost to base of tube; lower corolla lip 3-lobed, wide, spreading flat; stamens 5, united into tube.

FRUIT: capsule, partially exserted from calyx, sometimes nodding; seeds many, rough.
R   (MGP, LBU, OFS)   April–June

Soft-leaved lobelia [p. 65]
Lobelia flaccidifolia Small
(Loh-bee'-lee-ah   flak-sid-ih-foh'-lee-ah)

Erect, delicate, glabrous annual to about 40 in. tall, usually much lower; stem unbranched or with few branches.

LEAVES: alternate, essentially sessile, mostly along stem; blade thin, lanceolate to oblong or spatulate, to $4\frac{1}{4}$ in. long, $\frac{5}{8}$ in. wide, often abruptly tapered at base, rounded or sharp-pointed at tip, entire or inconspicuously toothed.

INFLORESCENCE: flowers several to many, short-pedicelled, subtended by bracts, in terminal raceme; pedicels slender, rough, curved, becoming $\frac{1}{4}$–$\frac{1}{2}$ in. long in fruit, with pair of very small bracts near or below middle of pedicel; raceme usually solitary, slender, somewhat spiraled, to 12 in. long. *Flower*: lavender or bluish lavender to nearly white, white near throat, about $\frac{3}{4}$–1 in. long; calyx 5-lobed; calyx lobes with small basal appendages, with gland-tipped teeth along margins; corolla 2-lipped; upper corolla lip deeply 2-lobed, small; lower corolla lip 3-lobed, broad; stamens 5, united into tube.

FRUIT: capsule, surrounded by calyx; seeds many, rough.
LBS   April–August

Downy lobelia   [p. 39]
Lobelia puberula Michx.
(Loh-bee'-lee-ah pyoo-ber'-yoo-lah)

Erect perennial $3\frac{1}{2}$–4 ft. tall, commonly much lower; pubescence dense, short, rough throughout; stem usually unbranched.

LEAVES: alternate, sessile, becoming bracts in upper portion of stem; blade rather thick, lanceolate to oblong or narrowly spatulate, to $4\frac{3}{4}$ in. long, $1\frac{1}{2}$ in. wide, occasionally tapering basally, rounded or sharp-pointed at tip, entire or toothed.

INFLORESCENCE: flowers few to numerous, subtended by bracts, pedicelled, in dense terminal raceme; pedicels stout, to $\frac{1}{4}$ in. long in fruit; raceme usually solitary, commonly 1-sided or with flowers swirled, to 20 in. long. *Flower*: blue to purple, rarely whitish, to 1 in. long; calyx 5-lobed, with very small appendages at base of lobes; corolla 2-lipped, pubescent; upper corolla lip deeply 2-lobed, narrow; lower corolla lip 3-lobed, broad; stamens 5, united into tube.

FRUIT: capsule, about $\frac{1}{4}$ in. long; seeds many, rough.
MGP (LBS)   August–December

Cardinal flower   [p. 54]
Lobelia cardinalis L.
(Loh-bee'-lee-ah kar-dih-nay'-lis)

Erect, coarse, glabrous or pubescent perennial to 6 ft. tall, often $1\frac{1}{2}$–3 ft. tall, from basal offshoots; stem usually unbranched, occasionally with few branches just below inflorescence.

LEAVES: alternate, numerous, petioled, in lower portion of plant, becoming sessile and smaller in upper portion of plant; blade thin, glabrous or pubescent, lanceolate to broadly lanceolate, 2–8 in. long, 1–2 in. wide, sharply and irregularly toothed.

INFLORESCENCE: flowers numerous, pedicelled, subtended by bracts, in dense showy terminal raceme; raceme somewhat 1-sided, to 20 in. long. *Flower*: scarlet or deep red, 1¼–2 in. long; calyx 5-lobed; calyx lobes leaflike, to ⅝ in. long; calyx margins crisped, toothed, fringed with hairs; corolla 2-lipped; upper corolla lip long, slender, deeply 2-lobed, the lobes erect or falling to side; lower corolla lip 3-lobed, broad; stamens 5, united into slender prominently exserted tube; anthers united, bluish gray, conspicuous.

FRUIT: capsule, ovoid to globelike, to ⅜ in. long; seeds many, yellowish brown, rough.

NOTE: uncommon in East Texas and western Louisiana.

SOF   (POF)   May–December

COMPOSITAE
(Sunflower Family)

Western ironweed   [p. 39]

Vernonia baldwinii Torr.

(Ver-noh'-nee-ah   bald-win'-ee-eye)

Erect, strong, coarse, clump-forming, pubescent perennial 2–5 ft. tall; stem unbranched or few-branched in inflorescence.

LEAVES: alternate, essentially sessile; blade firm, pubescent on upper surface, glabrous or pubescent on lower surface and gland-dotted, elliptic or narrowly lanceolate to broadly lanceolate, 3¼–6 in. long, ¾–2⅜ in. wide, tapering basally, sharply toothed.

INFLORESCENCE: flowers 18–34, of disk type, in small compact terminal head; heads numerous, in compact showy terminal cyme; receptacle flat or slightly convex; phyllaries closely appressed, often purplish green, darker along margins and midrib. *Flower*: dark rose to purple; ray flowers absent; disk flowers perfect, fertile, 5-lobed; stamens 5; style branches 2, slender; pappus of numerous barbed rusty white bristles.

FRUIT: achene, 6- to 10-ribbed, resin-dotted between ribs.

NOTE: uncommon in the Big Thicket.

MGP   (POF, SOF)   July–October

Missouri ironweed   [p. 43]

Vernonia missurica Raf.

(Ver-noh'-nee-ah   mis-soo'-rih-kah)

Erect, stout, rather coarse, clump-forming pubescent perennial 3–5 ft. tall; stem solitary, branching in inflorescence.

LEAVES: alternate, numerous, sessile or short-petioled; blade firm, dark green and with rough pubescence on upper surface, pubescent beneath at least along veins, lanceolate to broadly lanceolate, 2¼–6 in. long, ⅝–2 in.

wide, rounded or tapering at base, essentially entire to coarsely and sharply toothed.

INFLORESCENCE: flowers commonly 34–55, of disk type, in small compact terminal head; heads numerous, in showy terminal cyme; receptacle flat or slightly convex; phyllaries closely appressed, purplish or greenish, with midrib not prominent. *Flower*: dark rose to purple; ray flowers absent; disk flowers perfect, fertile, 5-lobed; stamens 5; style branches 2, slender; pappus of numerous barbed rusty white bristles.

FRUIT: achene, 6- to 10-ribbed, resin-dotted between ribs.

POF (MGP) July–October

Texas ironweed [p. 54]
Vernonia texana (Gray) Small
(Ver-noh'-nee-ah tex-ay'-nah)

Erect, slender, clump-forming glabrous or pubescent perennial 16–32 in. tall; stem unbranched or few-branched in inflorescence.

LEAVES: alternate, sessile, somewhat erect; blade firm, roughly pubescent on upper surface, pubescent and gland-dotted on lower surface, linear to narrowly lanceolate, 2¼–4¾ in. long, ⅜–¾ in. wide, tapering basally, entire to sharply toothed; upper leaves much reduced and narrowed.

INFLORESCENCE: flowers 18–21, of disk type, in small compact terminal head; heads few to several, in loose terminal cyme; receptacle flat or slightly convex; phyllaries closely appressed or spreading, tinged with purple. *Flower*: dark rose to purple; ray flowers absent; disk flowers perfect, fertile, 5-lobed; stamens 5; style branches 2, slender; pappus of numerous barbed rusty white bristles.

FRUIT: achene, 6- to 10-ribbed, pubescent on ribs, resin-dotted between ribs.

SOF July–October

Elephant's-foot [p. 82]
Elephantopus nudatus Gray
(El-eh-fan'-toh-pus noo-day'-tus)

Erect, coarsely pubescent perennial 8–16 in. tall; stems 1–few from base, branching in upper portion.

LEAVES: alternate, basally forming conspicuous rosette; few small leaves scattered along stem, sessile; basal leaves lanceolate to broadly spatulate or elliptic, 1¼–6 in. long, ¾–2¾ in. wide, finely and sharply toothed; stem leaves much reduced, only ¾–1¼ in. long.

INFLORESCENCE: flowers 2–4, of disk type, in head; heads few, sessile, forming small terminal cluster surrounded by 3 small leaflike bracts; clusters several, forming larger somewhat showy cluster; receptacle flat or nearly so;

phyllaries appressed, straw-colored. *Flower*: pinkish white to lavender; ray flowers absent; disk flowers perfect, fertile, 5-lobed; stamens 5; style branches 2, slender; pappus of 5–10 stiff bristles.

FRUIT: achene, pubescent, ribbed, cylindrical, tapered at base.

BMLS (LBU)   August–October

Sharp gay-feather   [p. 65]
Liatris acidota Engelm. & Gray
(Lye-ay'-tris a-sih-doh'-tah)

Stiffly erect, slender, glabrous or pubescent perennial 20–32 in. tall from corm; corm globelike, slightly elongated, to about 1⅛ in. across; stems solitary or in threes or fours, with remnants of old basal leaves.

LEAVES: alternate, sessile, numerous, crowded on stem, becoming smaller in upper portion of stem; basal leaves glabrous, linear to narrowly lanceolate, 8–16 in. long, to ¼ in. wide; leaves becoming narrower, abruptly shortened, erect and bractlike in inflorescence.

INFLORESCENCE: flowers 3–5, of disk type, in small compact head; heads numerous, forming an elongated terminal raceme; raceme 4–8 in. long, the flowers opening from tip downward; receptacle essentially flat; phyllaries few, appressed, glabrous, sometimes becoming purplish. *Flower*: dark lavender to purple; ray flowers absent; disk flowers perfect, fertile, 5-lobed; stamens 5; style branches 2, club-shaped; pappus of numerous finely barbed hairlike bristles.

FRUT: achene, about 10-ribbed, pubescent, somewhat cylindrical, tapered at base.

LBS (MGP, LBU)   July–December

Slender gay-feather   [p. 75]
Liatris tenuis Shinners
(Lye-ay'-tris ten'-yoo-is)

Stiffly erect pubescent perennial 12–22 in. tall from corm; stems 1–few, unbranched.

LEAVES: alternate, sessile, crowded on stem; stem leaves linear, pubescent, gland-dotted, to 6 in. long, less than ¼ in. wide; leaves along midstem becoming abruptly smaller; uppermost leaves reduced to bracts.

INFLORESCENCE: flowers 10 or 11, of disk type, in small axillary compact head; heads numerous, in slender raceme; raceme solitary, terminal, 6–10 in. long, opening from tip downward; receptacle essentially flat; phyllaries recurved at tips, fringed with hairs. *Flower*: lavender to purple, about ¼ in. long; ray flowers absent; disk flowers perfect, fertile, 5-lobed; stamens 5; style branches 2, club-shaped; pappus of numerous finely barbed hairlike bristles.

FRUIT: achene, ribbed, prominently pubescent along ribs, somewhat cylindrical, tapered at base.

NOTE: infrequent in the Big Thicket; endemic to southeastern Texas.

LBU   June–August

Kansas gay-feather [p. 65]
Liatris pycnostachya Michx.
(Lye-ay'-tris pik-noh-stak'-ee-ah)

Stiffly erect perennial 2–5 ft. tall from globelike or elongated corm; glabrous or with short stiff pubescence rough to the touch; stems 1–many, finely ribbed, unbranched.

LEAVES: alternate, sessile, numerous; lower leaves glabrous or roughly pubescent, gland-dotted, linear, to 4 in. long, less than 1/4 in. wide; leaves gradually decreasing in size upward, becoming bracts in inflorescence.

INFLORESCENCE: flowers 5–12, of disk type, in small compact head; heads sessile, numerous, crowded in dense solitary terminal spike; spike pubescent, 6–20 in. long, 3/4–1 1/4 in. across, opening from tip downward; receptacle essentially flat; phyllaries often purplish, recurved at tips, crisped or fringed with hairs. *Flower*: lavender to dark purple, about 3/8 in. long; ray flowers absent; disk flowers perfect, fertile, 5-lobed; stamens 5; style branches 2, club-shaped; pappus of numerous finely barbed bristles.

FRUIT: achene, ribbed, somewhat cylindrical, tapered at base.

LBS   (MGP)   June–October

Pink-scale gay-feather [p. 88]
Liatris elegans (Walt.) Michx.
(Lye-ay'-tris el'-eh-ganz)

Strictly erect perennial 1–4 ft. tall from globelike or elongated corm; stems 1 or 2, pubescent.

LEAVES: alternate, sessile, numerous, crowded on stem; lower leaves glabrous, gland-dotted, linear to narrowly lanceolate, to 4 in. long, less than 1/4 in. wide; leaves gradually decreasing in size upward, becoming bracts in inflorescence.

INFLORESCENCE: flowers usually 5, of disk type, in small compact head; heads essentially sessile, numerous, crowded in solitary terminal spike; spike cylindrical, 6–20 in. long, opening from tip downward to base; receptacle essentially flat; phyllaries colored and petallike at tip, elongated, longer than corolla and pappus. *Flower*: purple to pale lavender or white, about 1/2 in. long; ray flowers absent; disk flowers perfect, fertile, 5-lobed; stamens 5; style branches 2, club-shaped; pappus of numerous long feathery bristlelike hairs.

FRUIT: achene, ribbed, somewhat cylindrical, tapered at base.

NOTE: the most common but least showy species of *Liatris* in the Big Thicket.

OFS (LBU)   August–October

Climbing hemp-weed   [p. 54]
Mikania scandens (L.) Willd.

(Mih-kay′-nee-ah   skan′-denz)

Sprawling, twining or low-climbing, glabrous or pubescent herbaceous perennial vine; stems slender, slightly 4-angled, to 12 ft. long or more.

LEAVES: opposite, petioled; petiole slender, to 2 in. long; blade thin, very broadly lanceolate, to 4 in. long, 3 in. wide, broadly rounded and widely notched at base, wavy or shallowly lobed.

INFLORESCENCE: flowers 4, of disk type, in small head; heads numerous, forming terminal compound cluster; receptacle essentially flat, minute; phyllaries 4. *Flower*: whitish; ray flowers absent; disk flowers perfect, fertile, 5-toothed; stamens 5; style branches 2, club-shaped; pappus of about 30 rather stiff bristles.

FRUIT: achene, 5-ribbed, black, with resinous glands, cylindrical, tapered at base.

NOTE: infrequent in East Texas and western Louisiana.

SOF (POF)   June–November

Hyssop-leaf eupatorium   [p. 65]
Eupatorium hyssopifolium L.

(Yoo-pah-toh′-ree-um   his-sop-ih-foh′-lee-um)

Erect, glabrous to pubescent perennial commonly 12–20 in. tall from short rhizome; stems solitary or few from base forming clump.

LEAVES: opposite or in whorls of 3 or 4, essentially sessile, often with clusters of smaller leaves in axils; blade glabrous or pubescent, gland-dotted, linear to elliptic, 1–3⅛ in. long, to ⅝ in. wide, tapering basally, entire or obscurely toothed in tip portion.

INFLORESCENCE: flowers 3–7, of disk type, in small cylindrical head; heads numerous, terminal on short pubescent branches, forming somewhat flat-topped terminal cluster; receptacle flat to cone-shaped; inner phyllaries narrowly oblong, rounded or blunt at tip; phyllary margins thin, narrow, whitish. *Flower*: white; ray flowers absent; disk flowers perfect, fertile, 5-toothed; stamens 5; style branches 2, club-shaped; pappus of slender bristles.

FRUIT: achene, 5-ribbed, blackish, dotted with resinous glands, somewhat cylindrical.

NOTE: uncommon in the Big Thicket.

LBS   August–October

Justice-weed   [p. 65]
Eupatorium leucolepis (DC.) T. & G.
(Yoo-pah-toh'-ree-um   loo-ko-leep'-is)

Stiffly erect, slender, minutely pubescent perennial 2½–4 ft. tall from knotty rhizome and fibrous roots; stems solitary or several from base and forming clump, branched in upper portion.

LEAVES: opposite, essentially sessile; blade firm, thick, dull grayish green, gland-dotted, broadly linear to narrowly oblong, 1¼–3¼ in. long, to ⅜ in. wide, toothed in tip half of leaf; leaves generally smaller in upper portion of plant.

INFLORESCENCE: flowers 5, of disk type, in small cylindrical head; heads numerous, terminal on short branches, forming loose terminal panicle; receptacle flat to cone-shaped; longer phyllaries white in tip portion and along margins. *Flower*: whitish; ray flowers absent; disk flowers perfect, fertile, 5-toothed; stamens 5; style branches 2, club-shaped; pappus of slender bristles.

FRUIT: achene, 5-ribbed, blackish, somewhat cylindrical.

NOTE: uncommon in the Big Thicket.

LBS   September–November

Joe-Pye-weed   [p. 58]
Eupatorium fistulosum Barr.
(Yoo-pah-toh'-ree-um   fis-tyoo-loh'-sum)

Stiffly erect, stout, coarse, glabrous, glaucous perennial 3–10 ft. tall from rhizomelike root; stem solitary or several and somewhat clump-forming, purplish green, sometimes hollow between nodes, usually unbranched.

LEAVES: whorled, with 4–7 at each node, petioled; petiole blackish, ¾–2¾ in. long; blade prominently veined, occasionally minutely gland-dotted, broadly lanceolate to broadly elliptic, 4–8 in. long, to 3 in. wide, coarsely toothed.

INFLORESCENCE: flowers 5–8, of disk type, in small cylindrical head; heads numerous, terminal on short branches, the whole forming large showy round-topped or domed mass at top of stem; receptacle flat; phyllaries pale or whitish, striped with purple. *Flower*: lilac pink to purple or brownish lavender, less than ¼ in. long; ray flowers absent; disk flowers perfect, fertile, 5-toothed, scarcely exserted from phyllaries; stamens 5; style branches 2, club-shaped; pappus of numerous slender bristles.

FRUIT: achene, 5-ribbed, blackish, somewhat cylindrical.

NOTE: infrequent in the Big Thicket.

BGB   July–August

Mist-flower [p. 54]

Eupatorium coelestinum L.

(Yoo-pa-toh′-ree-um　see-les-tye′-num)

Erect to sprawling or somewhat climbing, pubescent perennial 1–3 ft. tall from long slender rhizomes; stem solitary, weak, branched in upper portion; plants usually forming extensive colonies.

LEAVES: opposite, petioled; petiole to 1 in. long; blade pubescent, minutely resin-dotted, broadly lanceolate or somewhat triangle-shaped, 3/4–2 3/4 in. long, 3/4–2 in. wide, rounded or shallowly notched at base, sharply toothed.

INFLORESCENCE: flowers 40–50, of disk type, in small head; heads numerous, forming dense showy cluster; clusters terminal on stem and slender branches; receptacle cone-shaped; longer phyllaries pubescent, obscurely 3-veined. *Flower*: blue or purplish blue; ray flowers absent; disk flowers perfect, fertile, 5-toothed; stamens 5; style branches 2, club-shaped; pappus of slender bristles.

FRUIT: achene, 5-ribbed, blackish, somewhat cylindrical.

SOF　　July–December

Scratch-daisy [p. 88]

Croptilon divaricatum (Nutt.) Raf.

(Krop′-tih-lon　dih-vair-ih-kay′-tum)

Erect, slender annual, sometimes overwintering, to 3 ft. tall; pubescence long, sometimes glandular; stem solitary, usually much-branched.

LEAVES: alternate, sessile; blade roughly pubescent, narrowly elliptic to lanceolate, 1–4 in. long, to 1/2 in. wide, tapering basally, bristle-pointed at tip; margins fringed with stiff spreading bristles.

INFLORESCENCE: flowers numerous, of ray and disk types, in small head; heads numerous, peduncled, scattered in widely branched panicle; receptacle flat or convex, often very rough; phyllaries with pale midrib and thin papery margins. *Flower*: ray flowers 5–29, pistillate, fertile, yellow; disk flowers 10–40, perfect, fertile, 5-toothed, yellow; stamens 5; style branches 2, flattened and pubescent at tips; pappus of brownish barbed bristles.

FRUIT: achene, dark, not ribbed, ellipsoid.

OFS　　June–December

Golden-aster [p. 89]

Heterotheca latifolia Buckl.

(Het-er-oh-thee′-kah　lat-ih-foh′-lee-ah)

Erect to sprawling, aromatic annual to 6 ft. tall, usually 1–3 ft. tall; pubescence long, dense, intermixed with gland-tipped hairs, making plant sticky to touch; stem solitary, usually much-branched; branches slender, usually few-leaved.

LEAVES: alternate; lower leaves petioled, soon deciduous; upper leaves sessile, clasping basally, densely pubescent, lanceolate to broadly lanceolate, to 1 in. long, ¾ in. wide, entire or toothed.

INFLORESCENCE: flowers numerous, of ray and disk types, in small head; heads numerous, peduncled, in widely branched terminal panicle; receptacle flat or slightly convex; phyllaries pubescent and with gland-tipped hairs. *Flower*: ray flowers 15–35, pistillate, usually fertile, yellow; disk flowers 35–40, perfect, fertile, 5-toothed, yellow; stamens 5; style branches 2, flattened and pubescent at tips; ray-flower pappus absent; disk-flower pappus of numerous stiff bristles and very small conspicuous scales.

FRUIT: achene, obovoid; those of ray flowers glabrous and without pappus; those of disk flowers densely pubescent and with pappus.
OFS   May–December

Silk-grass [p. 75]
Heterotheca graminifolia (Michx.) Shinners
(Het-er-oh-thee′-kah   gra-min-ih-foh′-lee-ah)

Erect perennial 8–24 in. tall from stolons, with soft, silvery white pubescence throughout; stems solitary or several and somewhat clumplike, branched in upper portion; plants usually scattered in thin colonies.

LEAVES: alternate, grasslike, appressed to stem, becoming smaller in upper portion of stem, finally grading into the phyllaries; blade narrow, flexible, 3- to 5-veined, with dense silvery white silky pubescence.

INFLORESCENCE: flowers numerous, of ray and disk types, in small head; heads several, peduncled, forming showy open panicle; receptacle flat; phyllaries linear, appressed, with gland-tipped pubescence. *Flower*: ray flowers 4–15, pistillate, usually fertile, yellow; disk flowers 5–15, perfect, fertile, 5-toothed, yellow; style branches 2, flattened and pubescent at tips; pappus of numerous stiff cinnamon-colored bristles and minute scales.

FRUIT: achene, reddish brown to black, prominently ribbed, pubescent, ellipsoid.
LBU   April–December

Maryland golden aster [p. 75]
Heterotheca mariana (L.) Shinners
(Het-er-oh-thee′-kah   mair-ee-ay′-nah)

Erect, stout perennial commonly 1–2 ft. tall from thick rhizome, with loose silky pubescence when young, becoming more or less glabrous with age; upper portion of plant minutely but densely glandular; stems 1–several, branched in upper portion.

LEAVES: alternate, short-petioled or sessile; blade thin, green, softly pubescent, spatulate, commonly 2–4 in. long, to 1¼ in. wide, tapering basally, generally rounded at tip; upper leaves smaller, elliptic to lanceolate, essentially sessile.

INFLORESCENCE: flowers numerous, of ray and disk types, in small flat showy head; heads several, peduncled, forming rather dense terminal paniclelike cluster; receptacle flat; phyllaries linear, with gland-tipped hairs; margins fringed with hairs. *Flower*: ray flowers 12–25, pistillate, usually fertile, to ¾ in. long, golden yellow; disk flowers several, perfect, fertile, 5-toothed, yellow; style branches 2, flattened and pubescent at tips; pappus of numerous stiff bristles and small scales.

FRUIT: achene, reddish to brown, pubescent, slightly flattened, obovoid.

NOTE: infrequent in East Texas and western Louisiana.

LBU   (OFS)   July–November

Slender-headed euthamia   [p. 39]
Euthamia leptocephala (T. & G.) Greene
(Yoo-thay'-mee-ah   lep-toh-sef'-ah-lah)

Strictly erect, essentially glabrous perennial 16–32 in. tall from rhizome; stems usually several from base and clumplike, much-branched in upper portion; branches slender, leafy, stiffly erect, reaching to top of stem.

LEAVES: alternate, sessile; blade thin, dark green, gland-dotted and somewhat sticky, linear, 1½–3½ in. long, to about ¼ in. wide; margins minutely roughened.

INFLORESCENCE: flowers several, of ray and disk types, in small head; heads several, essentially sessile, solitary or in clusters of 2–4, forming large showy terminal panicle; receptacle very small, convex; phyllaries firm, erect, appressed, oblong, usually blunt at tip, dark in tip portion. *Flower*: ray flowers few, pistillate, fertile, minute, yellow; disk flowers 10–15, perfect, fertile, 5-toothed, only slightly exceeding phyllaries, yellow; style branches 2, flattened and pubescent at tips; pappus of hairlike bristles.

FRUIT: achene, pubescent, obovoid.

MGP   (LBU, OFS)   September–November

Slender bigelowia   [p. 66]
Bigelowia virgata (Nutt.) DC.
(Big-eh-loh'-ee-ah   vir-gay'-tah)

Rigidly erect, slender perennial 20–40 in. tall from rhizomes or woody base; stems usually several, forming clump, wiry, branched in inflorescence.

LEAVES: alternate, mostly crowded in lower portion of plant, sessile; blade firm, often resinous, linear; leaves remotely scattered or absent in upper portion of plant.

INFLORESCENCE: flowers few, of disk type, in small head; heads numerous, densely crowded in terminal paniclelike cluster; receptacle flat or nearly so; phyllaries firm, erect, appressed, resinous, sticky, dark in tip portion: *Flower*: yellow; ray flowers absent; disk flowers 4–6, perfect, fertile, deeply 5-lobed; style branches 2, flattened and pubescent at tips; pappus of numerous bristles somewhat flattened basally.

FRUIT: achene, densely covered with stiff white pubescence, narrowly obovoid, somewhat 3-angled.

LBS   July–September

Thin-leaf goldenrod [p. 96]
Solidago delicatula Small
(Sol-ih-day′-goh   del-ih-kat′-choo-lah)

Strictly erect, slender, essentially glabrous perennial to 5 ft. tall from rhizome; stem solitary, branching in inflorescence.

LEAVES: alternate, sessile; lower leaves always withered and absent at flowering time; middle stem leaves thin, smooth, narrowly elliptic, 2½–4 times as long as broad, to 2¾ in. long including the petiolelike base, which is up to 1¼ in. long; margins sharply toothed in tip portion; uppermost leaves elliptic, 2–3 times as long as broad.

INFLORESCENCE: flowers 8–12, of ray and disk types, in small head; heads numerous, on very short branches along longer branches, the whole forming large showy terminal cluster; receptacle small, flat or nearly so, not chaffy; phyllaries appressed, narrowly lanceolate, straw-colored with darker middle stripe. *Flower*: ray flowers 3–5, pistillate, fertile, minute, yellow; disk flowers perfect, fertile, 5-toothed, yellow; style branches 2, flattened and pubescent at tips; pappus of numerous hairlike bristles.

FRUIT: achene, pubescent, very small.

R (LBU)   July–January

Boott goldenrod [p. 75]
Solidago boottii Hook.
(Sol-ih-day′-goh   boot′-tee-eye)

Strictly erect, slender, essentially glabrous perennial to 4 ft. tall; stem solitary, branching in inflorescence.

LEAVES: alternate, firm, persistent; lower leaves usually withered at flowering time but still attached; blade 2¾–8 in. long, slenderly tapering to petiolelike base, coarsely toothed; blade of midstem leaves not 3-veined, smooth on both surfaces, about 3–4 times as long as broad, toothed in upper two-thirds of length; upper leaves 2–3 times as long as broad.

INFLORESCENCE: flowers several, of ray and disk types, in small head; heads numerous, crowded, on very short branches along one side of longer whiplike branches, the whole forming large showy terminal cluster; receptacle small, flat or nearly so, not chaffy; phyllaries appressed. *Flower*: ray flowers pistillate, fertile, yellow; disk flowers perfect, fertile, 5-toothed, yellow; style branches 2, flattened and pubescent at tips; pappus of numerous hairlike bristles.

FRUIT: achene, pubescent, very small.

LBU   (OFS)   August–October

Wrinkle-leaved goldenrod   [p. 54]
Solidago rugosa Ait. var. *celtidifolia* (Small) Fern.
(Sol-ih-day'-go   roo-goh'-sah   sel-ti-di-foh'-lee-ah)

Erect, stout, coarse, pubescent perennial 2½–7 ft. tall from creeping rhizomes; stems usually many, forming small clumps or colonies of plants.

LEAVES: alternate, numerous, crowded, sessile, gradually becoming somewhat smaller in upper portion of plant; blade dark green, somewhat wrinkled, sparsely roughly pubescent on upper surface, usually pubescent on lower surface and prominently veined, lanceolate to broadly lanceolate, commonly 1½–4 in. long, to 1¾ in. wide, tapering at base and petiolelike, conspicuously toothed.

INFLORESCENCE: flowers several, of ray and disk types, in small head; heads numerous, on very short branches along one side of longer branches, the whole forming large loose terminal cluster; receptacle flat or nearly so, not chaffy; phyllaries appressed, narrow, straw-colored with darker middle stripe. *Flower*: ray flowers 6–11, pistillate, fertile, very small, yellow; disk flowers 4–7, perfect, fertile, 5-toothed, yellow; style branches 2, flattened and pubescent at tips; pappus of numerous hairlike bristles.

FRUIT: achene, pubescent.

SOF   (POF, LBS)   September–October

Tall goldenrod   [p. 40]
Solidago altissima L.
(Sol-ih-day'-goh   al-tis'-sih-mah)

Erect, stout, coarse pubescent perennial 3–7 ft. tall from rhizome; stems usually numerous and forming large clumps, branched in inflorescence.

LEAVES: alternate, numerous, crowded, sessile; blade dull green, prominently 3-veined, with minute rough pubescence, lanceolate to elliptic, commonly 2¼–6 in. long, ⅜–1¼ in. wide, toothed in upper portion.

INFLORESCENCE: flowers 10–20, of ray and disk types, in small head; heads numerous, on short branches along one side of longer branches, the whole forming a terminal paniclelike cluster; cluster large, loose, showy; receptacle flat or nearly so, not chaffy; phyllaries appressed, narrowly lanceolate, straw-colored with darker middle stripe. *Flower*: ray flowers 9–15, pistillate, fertile, yellow; disk flowers perfect, fertile, 5-toothed, yellow; style branches 2, flattened and pubescent at tips; pappus of numerous hair-like bristles.

FRUIT: achene, pubescent.

MGP (POF, SOF)   August–November

Downy goldenrod
[p. 75]

Solidago petiolaris Ait.

(Sol-ih-day'-goh   pet-ee-oh-lair'-is)

Rigidly erect, slender, pubescent perennial 1½–4 ft. tall from rhizome; stems few, forming small clumps, branched in inflorescence.

LEAVES: alternate, numerous, crowded, sessile; blade pubescent, lanceolate, varying to elliptic or somewhat spatulate, commonly 1½–2¾ in. long, ⅜–⅝ in. wide; margins rough, entire or with few small teeth.

INFLORESCENCE: flowers several, of ray and disk types, in small head; heads numerous, on short branches along longer branches, the whole forming a terminal paniclelike cluster; cluster showy, rather slender; receptacle flat or nearly so, not chaffy; phyllaries appressed, narrowly lanceolate, straw-colored with darker middle stripe. *Flower*: ray flowers rather large, conspicuosu, pistillate, fertile, yellow; disk flowers perfect, fertile, 5-toothed, yellow; style branches 2, flattened and pubescent at tips; pappus of numerous hairlike bristles.

FRUIT: achene, pubescent.

NOTE: species name very misleading, since leaves are sessile; a more western species, not common in East Texas and western Louisiana.

LBU   September–November

Texas aster
[p. 40]

Aster texanus Burgess

(As'-ter   tex-ay'-nus)

Erect, slender, glabrous to sparsely pubescent perennial 12–32 in. tall from rhizomelike base; stems much branched in upper portion; branches slender, wide-spreading.

LEAVES: alternate, sessile to short-petioled; blade becoming thick, brittle and crumbly with age; lower and middle stem leaves with broadly lanceolate bladelike portion and a linear, broadly winged petiolelike basal portion; leaves in inflorescence much reduced.

INFLORESCENCE: flowers several, of ray and disk types, in small head; heads terminal on short leafy branches; branches numerous along longer branches, the whole forming showy terminal paniclelike cluster; receptacle flat or nearly so, not chaffy; phyllaries erect, appressed. *Flower*: ray flowers pistillate, fertile, bluish white; disk flowers perfect, fertile, 5-toothed, yellow; style branches 2, flattened and pubescent at tips; pappus of numerous hairlike bristles.

FRUIT: achene, ribbed, somewhat flattened.

MGP (POF, SOF)   October–November

Calico aster   [p. 54]
Aster lateriflorus (L.) Britt.
(As'-ter   lat-er-ih-floh'-rus)
Erect or sprawling, slender, glabrous to sparsely pubescent perennial to
4½ ft. tall from rhizome; stems 1–several, slender, erect to arching, sometimes
clump-forming, much-branched in upper portion; branches wide-spreading.
LEAVES: alternate, sessile; blade thin, pubescent on lower surface, narrowly lanceolate to elliptic, 2–6 in. long, to 1½ in. wide, sharply toothed;
leaves gradually reduced upward, becoming minute in inflorescence.
INFLORESCENCE: flowers numerous, of ray and disk types, in small head;
heads short-peduncled, terminal; peduncles numerous, arranged along long
leafy branches, the whole forming showy terminal paniclelike cluster; receptacle flat or nearly so; phyllaries erect, appressed, whitish with green midrib.
Flower: ray flowers 10–20, pistillate, fertile, white; disk flowers perfect, fertile, 5-lobed, yellow or reddish; style branches 2, flattened and pubescent at
tips; pappus of numerous whitish hairlike bristles.
FRUIT: achene, minutely pubescent.
SOF   (POF, LBS)   September–November

Meadow aster   [p. 75]
Aster pratensis Raf.
(As'-ter   pra-ten'-sis)
Stiffly erect, slender, pubescent perennial commonly 20–32 in. tall from
woody base and fibrous roots; stem solitary, unbranched or with few stiffly
erect branches in upper portion.
LEAVES: alternate, sessile; blade firm, elliptic; uppermost leaves not reduced in size, extending onto flower head as supplementary phyllaries; most
lower leaves falling before time of flowering.
INFLORESCENCE: flowers numerous, of ray and disk types, in head; heads
showy, terminating branches, only few on plant; receptacle flat or nearly so;
true phyllaries firm, appressed in upper portion, fringed with hairs. *Flower*:
ray flowers pistillate, fertile, purple; disk flowers perfect, fertile, 5-lobed,
yellow; style branches 2, flattened and pubescent at tips; pappus of numerous
coarse brownish white bristles.
FRUIT: achene, glabrous, with several ribs on each side, flattened.
LBU   (MGP)   September–November

Annual aster   [p. 40]
Aster subulatus Michx. var. *ligulatus* Shinners
(As'-ter   sub-yoo-lay'-tus   lig-yoo-lay'-tus)
Erect, robust, slender, glabrous annual 1½–6 ft. tall, commonly only to

2½ ft. tall, from short taproot; stem solitary, few to much-branched and somewhat bushy in upper portion.

LEAVES: alternate, sessile; blade fleshy, linear to narrowly elliptic, ⅜–4 in. long, less than ¼ in. wide, sharp-pointed at tip; leaves much reduced in upper portion of plant.

INFLORESCENCE: flowers several, of ray and disk types, in small head; heads terminating short branches, forming open panicle; receptacle flat or nearly so; phyllaries erect, appressed, pale, with darker linear midrib. *Flower*: ray flowers pistillate, fertile, longer than pappus and disk corollas, white; disk flowers perfect, fertile, 5-lobed, yellow; style branches 2, flattened and pubescent at tips; pappus of numerous very soft fine white hairs.

FRUIT: achene, pubescent, ellipsoid.

NOTE: probably the most common species of *Aster* in East Texas and western Louisiana; usually growing in standing water of ditches, swales, margins of ponds, and poorly drained areas.
MGP   (LBS)   July–January

Low aster   [p. 66]
Heleastrum hemisphaericum (Alex.) Shinners
(Hee-lee-as'-trum   hem-ih-sfeer'-ih-kum)

Strictly erect, essentially glabrous perennial 12–28 in. tall from swollen corms along slender rhizome; stem solitary, usually few-branched in inflorescence.

LEAVES: alternate, somewhat erect, sessile, often with clusters of smaller leaves in the axils; blade firm, leathery, linear, to 4¾ in. long, less than ¼ in. wide; leaves becoming smaller in upper portion of stem.

INFLORESCENCE: flowers numerous, of ray and disk types, in head; heads showy, terminal on short branches, with only few on plant; receptacle flat or nearly so; phyllaries broad, in several rows, wide-spreading, green and broad at tips. *Flower*: ray flowers pistillate, fertile, usually dark lavender; disk flowers perfect, fertile, 5-lobed, yellow; style branches 2, flattened and pubescent at tips; pappus of numerous rather coarse bristles, with at least some bristles expanded in tip portion.

FRUIT: achene.

NOTE: infrequent in East Texas and western Louisiana.
LBS   July–April

Flat-top aster   [p. 66]
Doellingeria umbellata (Mill.) Nees var. *latifolia* (Gray) House
(Del-lin-jer'-ee-ah   um-bel-lay'-tah   lat-ih-foh'-lee-ah)

Erect, glabrous or pubescent perennial to 4 ft. tall, usually lower, from rhizome; stem solitary, branching in inflorescence; branches erect, usually reaching to top of stem.

LEAVES: alternate, sessile; blade usually somewhat pubescent, prominently veined, elliptic to broadly lanceolate, 1½–6½ in. long, to 1½ in. wide; leaves in lower portion of plant smaller, becoming larger in upper portion.

INFLORESCENCE: flowers many, of ray and disk types, in small head; heads numerous, peduncled, the whole forming large showy somewhat flat-topped cluster; receptacle flat or nearly so; phyllaries appressed, straw-colored with green midrib. *Flower*: ray flowers pistillate, fertile, whitish; disk flowers perfect, fertile, 5-lobed, yellow; pappus of numerous unequal hairlike bristles.

FRUIT: achene, ribbed, sparsely to densely pubescent.

NOTE: uncommon in the Big Thicket.

LBS   (BGB)   September–October

Savory-leaf aster   [p. 76]
Ionactis linariifolia (L.) Greene
(Eye-oh-nak'-tis   lin-air-eye-ih-foh'-lee-ah)

Stiffly erect, slender, pubescent perennial 4–20 in. tall; stems usually several and clumplike, wiry, unbranched or few-branched in upper portion.

LEAVES: alternate, sessile, numerous, crowded; blade minutely roughly pubescent, linear, to 1¼ in. long, about ⅛ in. wide, fringed with rough hairs; lower leaves reduced to very small scales; upper leaves much reduced, threadlike, to about ⅜ in. long.

INFLORESCENCE: flowers numerous, of ray and disk types, in head; heads showy, terminal, 1–few per stem; receptacle flat or nearly so; phyllaries firm, mostly appressed, straw-colored with green midrib slightly expanding near tip. *Flower*: ray flowers pistillate, fertile, violet blue; disk flowers perfect, fertile, 5-lobed, yellow; pappus of numerous tan hairlike bristles and short minute bristles.

FRUIT: achene, black, with long silky silvery pubescence, tapered basally.

NOTE: uncommon in the Big Thicket.

LBU   September–November

Philadelphia fleabane   [p. 96]
Erigeron philadelphicus L.
(Eh-rij'-eh-ron   fil-ah-del'-fih-kus)

Erect, slender, conspicuously pubescent short-lived perennial 8–28 in. tall from fibrous roots; stem solitary, soft, branched in upper portion.

LEAVES: alternate, essentially sessile; lower leaves narrowly to broadly spatulate, 1½–6 in. long, ⅜–1½ in. wide, tapered basally to petiolelike base, toothed or somewhat lobed; stem leaves clasping basally, entire or toothed.

INFLORESCENCE: flowers numerous, of ray and disk types, in small head;

heads peduncled, nodding in bud, terminal on the few branches, the whole forming showy terminal cluster; receptacle flat or nearly so, not chaffy; phyllaries somewhat lanceolate, sharp-pointed at tip, with thin narrow margins. *Flower*: ray flowers 150 or more, pistillate, fertile, threadlike, white; disk flowers perfect, fertile, 5-toothed, yellow; pappus of numerous hairlike bristles.

FRUIT: achene, essentially glabrous, flattened, prominently 2-ribbed.

NOTE: White-top, *Erigeron strigosus*, is the common fleabane blooming in summer and fall, often forming long, showy borders along roadsides or in large patches in open areas, frequently blooming with brown-eyed Susans (*Rudbeckia hirta*). The less common *E. annuus* is found in some areas, also blooming summer and fall.

R   (LBU)   February–May

Small-head boltonia   [p. 76]
Boltonia diffusa Ell.
(Bohl-toh'-nee-ah   dif-fyoo'-sah)

Erect, slender, essentially glabrous perennial to 4 ft. tall from slender creeping rhizome and fibrous roots; stem solitary, wiry, much-branched in upper portion.

LEAVES: alternate, essentially sessile; blade linear, commonly 3/8–1¼ in. long, less than ¼ in. wide; leaves gradually becoming smaller upward, finally becoming very small and bractlike.

INFLORESCENCE: flowers many, of ray and disk types, in small head; heads terminal on short branches, the whole forming long slender showy paniclelike cluster; receptacle cone-shaped, not chaffy; phyllaries with pale papery margins and darker midrib. *Flower*: ray flowers pistillate, fertile, white; disk flowers perfect, fertile, shallowly 5-lobed; pappus of several small pointed scales or broad bristles and 2 or 3 longer awns.

FRUIT: achene, brown, flattened, 2- or 3-winged.

NOTE: infrequent in East Texas and western Louisiana.

LBU   September–November

Arkansas lazy daisy   [p. 89]
Aphanostephus skirrhobasis (DC.) Trel.
(A-fah-nos'-teh-fus   skir-roh'-bah-sis)

Erect to sprawling perennial to 20 in. tall, with dense fine soft gray pubescence mostly throughout; stem solitary, branching in upper portion.

LEAVES: alternate, essentially sessile; blade pubescent, somewhat spatulate, 1–4 in. long, tapering basally, entire to toothed or lobed.

INFLORESCENCE: flowers numerous, of ray and disk types, in head; heads showy, at ends of branches; receptacle somewhat cone-shaped, rough, not chaffy; phyllaries narrowly lanceolate, in 4 or 5 rows, with coarse rough pubescence. *Flower*: ray flowers pistillate, fertile, white; disk flowers more than 250 per head, perfect, fertile, 5-lobed, yellow, becoming whitened and enlarged in age; style branches 2, flattened and pubescent at tips; pappus of an uneven scaly crown around tip of achene.

FRUIT: achene, glabrous or sparsely pubescent, obscurely ribbed, somewhat cylindrical to angled, expanded in tip portion.

OFS   March–June

Fragrant cudweed [p. 89]
Gnaphalium obtusifolium L.
(Na-fal′-ee-um   ob-too-sih-foh′-lee-um)

Strictly erect, aromatic annual 10–20 in. tall, with long dense woolly and glandular pubescence; stems 1–several, often forming clumps, branched in upper portion.

LEAVES: alternate, sessile; blade thin, woolly when young, soon becoming bright green, glandular, and sticky to the touch on upper surface, linear to lanceolate, 1–3¼ in. long, to ⅜ in. wide, tapering basally, often wavy.

INFLORESCENCE: flowers numerous, of disk type, in small head; heads in clusters of 3–5; clusters on short branches, the whole forming terminal paniclelike cluster; receptacle essentially flat, not chaffy; phyllaries oblong, dull white, becoming rusty-tinged, papery, pubescent at base. *Flower*: whitish; ray flowers absent; disk flowers pistillate and perfect, both fertile; outer pistillate corollas threadlike, numerous; inner perfect corollas tubular, 5-toothed, few; anthers 5; style branches 2, slender; pappus of minute hairlike bristles, not united basally as in some species.

FRUIT: achene, brown, glabrous, sometimes slightly 3- or 4-veined, somewhat flattened.

OFS   (LBU)   September–November

Everlasting [p. 76]
Antennaria fallax Greene
(An-ten-nair′-ee-ah   fal′-lax)

Erect, pubescent perennial, commonly 2¼–8 in. tall from rhizome or stolons; stolons dark, slender, leafy, producing new plants at tips.

LEAVES: alternate, mostly crowded near ground, sessile or very short-petioled; blades olive green and glabrous on upper surface, with grayish woolly pubescence on lower surface, somewhat spatulate, to about 2¼ in. long; ½–1½ in. wide, tapering to petiolelike base; leaves along stem few, much smaller.

INFLORESCENCE: flowers numerous, of disk type, in small head; heads in terminal clusters; receptacle convex, occasionally with minute projections;

phyllaries linear, shiny white or silvery at tip; pistillate and staminate flowers occurring on different plants. *Flower*: whitish; ray flowers absent; pistillate plants with threadlike corolla and pappus of numerous hairlike bristles; staminate plants with flaring 5-toothed corolla, 5 anthers, and pappus of club-shaped bristles.

FRUIT: achene, brownish, rough, somewhat ovoid; pappus somewhat united basally.

NOTE: staminate plant shown.

LBU   (OFS)   March–May

Camphor-weed [p. 54]
Pluchea camphorata (L.) DC.
(Ploo'-kee-ah   kam-foh-ray'-tah)

Erect, pubescent, aromatic annual or perennial to about 4 ft. tall, usually lower, stem solitary, branching in upper portion.

LEAVES: alternate, petioled; petiole to 1 in. long; blade gland-dotted, pubescent on lower surface, elliptic to lanceolate, 2¼–6 in. long, 1¼–2¾ in. wide, entire to sharply toothed.

INFLORESCENCE: flowers numerous, of disk type, in small head; heads numerous, crowded in large showy terminal paniclelike cluster; receptacle flat, not chaffy; phyllaries prominently overlapping, resin-dotted; outer phyllaries sparsely pubescent. *Flower*: rose to rose purple; ray flowers absent; disk flowers pistillate and fertile in outer portion of head, perfect but sterile in center of head; perfect corolla tubular, 5 lobed; perfect-flower anthers 5, tailed; pistillate corolla threadlike, 3-lobed, with anthers absent; pappus of fine barbed bristles.

FRUIT: achene, 4- to 6-angled or -ridged, cylindrical, minute.

SOF   (POF, LBS)   July–November

Stinking-fleabane [p. 43]
Pluchea foetida (L.) DC.
(Ploo'-kee-ah   feh'-tih-dah)

Erect, stout, aromatic, pubescent perennial 20–32 in. tall; stem solitary, usually branched in upper portion.

LEAVES: alternate, sessile; blade pale green, glandular on upper surface, pubescent on lower surface, lanceolate, spatulate or elliptic, commonly 1¼–4 in. long, ⅜–1¼ in. wide, wedge-shaped or clasping at base, rounded or sharp-pointed at tip, shallowly to sharply toothed.

INFLORESCENCE: flowers numerous, of disk type, in small head; heads numerous, arranged in rather showy somewhat flat-topped terminal paniclelike cluster; receptacle flat, not chaffy; phyllaries prominently overlapping, resin-dotted; outer phyllaries sparsely pubescent, blunt at tip. *Flower*: creamy white; ray flowers absent; disk flowers pistillate and fertile in outer portion of head, perfect but sterile in center of head; perfect corolla tubular, 5-lobed; perfect-flower anthers 5, tailed; pistillate corolla threadlike, 3-lobed, with anthers absent; pappus of numerous fine barbed bristles.

FRUIT: achene, pinkish, cylindrical, 4- to 6-angled or -ridged, pubescent on angles, minute.

NOTE: uncommon in the Big Thicket.

POF   (SOF, LBS)   July–November

Slender silphium [p. 40]
Silphium gracile Gray
(Sil'-fee-um   gras'-ih-lee)

Stiffly erect, stout, coarse pubescent perennial to 6 ft. tall, often lower, from stout rhizomelike base; stem solitary, unbranched or with few branches in upper portion.

LEAVES: opposite, sessile or short-petioled, few, mostly crowded near base of stem; blade coarse, pubescent, rough to the touch, toothed; stem leaves only few or none, very reduced, bractlike, usually alternate if present.

INFLORESCENCE: flowers numerous, of ray and disk types, in head; heads large, showy, terminal on short branches; only 1 or 2 flowers opening at same time on plant; receptacle flat or slightly convex, chaffy throughout; phyllaries in several rows, coarse, rough, somewhat leaflike. *Flower*: ray flowers several, pistillate, fertile, to 1½ in. long, yellow; disk flowers apparently perfect but sterile, 5-toothed, usually obscured by long scalelike chaff, yellow; pappus may be present or absent, of 2 minute awns if present.

FRUIT: achene, flattened, broadly firm-winged on edges.

NOTE: infrequent in East Texas and western Louisiana.

MGP   June–August

Green-eyes [p. 89]
Berlandiera × *betonicifolia* (Hook.) Small
(Ber-lan-dee-er'-ah   bet-oh-nis-ih-foh'-lee-ah)

Erect to somewhat sprawling, coarsely pubescent perennial 1–3 ft. tall from fleshy taproot; stem solitary, usually much-branched.

LEAVES: alternate, petioled; blade with coarse pubescence, rough to the touch, broadly lanceolate to somewhat triangular, ½–1¼ times as broad as long, sharply toothed to coarsely double-toothed.

INFLORESCENCE: flowers numerous, of ray and disk types, in head; heads on long peduncles from leaf axils; receptacle somewhat top-shaped, with flattened or slightly depressed center, chaffy; phyllaries large, rounded at tip, exceeding disk, remaining after flowers fall and conspicuous. *Flower*: ray flowers usually 8, fertile, to ¾ in. long, orange yellow with green veins beneath; disk flowers mostly staminate, maroon; pappus essentially absent.

FRUIT: achene, flattened parallel to phyllary, not winged, about ¼ in. long, not quite as wide.

OFS May–August

False ragweed [p. 96]
Parthenium hysterophorus L.
(Par-thee'-nee-um his-ter-of'-oh-rus)

Erect, stout, coarse, pubescent annual 12–40 in. tall from taproot; stem solitary, marked with inconspicuous lines or ridges, usually much-branched.

LEAVES: alternate, sessile or short-petioled; lower leaves forming basal rosette; blade thin, soft, with stiff pubescence, often glandular on upper surface, deeply cleft or lobed into numerous segments.

INFLORESCENCE: flowers numerous, of ray and disk types, in very small head; heads numerous, densely pubescent, the whole forming large showy terminal paniclelike cluster; receptacle essentially flat, chaffy throughout, the scales small; phyllaries broad, green. *Flower*: ray flowers 5, pistillate, fertile, minute, white; disk flowers apparently perfect but sterile, white; pappus of 2 petallike scales closely adjoining corolla.

FRUIT: achene, flattened, with corolla and styles persistent at tip; at maturity 1 achene, 2 attached disk flowers, and 1 phyllary falling together as unit.

R August–October

Ox-eye [p. 96]
Heliopsis gracilis Nutt.
(Hee-lee-op'-sis gras'-ih-lis)

Erect, slender, glabrous to sparsely pubescent perennial 12–16 in. tall; stem unbranched or few-branched in upper portion.

LEAVES: opposite, petioled; petiole to ⅜ in. long; blade dark green and pubescent on upper surface, bright green and glabrous on lower surface, lanceolate to broadly lanceolate, to 2¼ in. long, ¾ in. wide, sharply toothed.

INFLORESCENCE: flowers numerous, of ray and disk types, in head; heads large, showy, peduncled, terminal; peduncles to 9 in. long; receptacle rather broad, slightly convex, often hollow, chaffy; phyllaries in 2 rows, pubescent, spreading. *Flower*: ray flowers 6–8, pistillate, fertile, glabrous, linear, to ⅞ in. long, golden yellow; disk flowers perfect, 5-toothed, glabrous, less than ¼ in. long, dull yellow; pappus of 1–3 pointed teeth.

FRUIT: achene, dull brown, glabrous to minutely pubescent; ray achenes 3-angled; disk achenes 4-angled.

NOTE: infrequent in the Big Thicket.

R   (LBU)   May–November

Creeping spot-flower [p. 43]

Spilanthes americana (Mutis) Hieron. var. *repens* (Walt.) A. H. Moore
(Spy-lan'-theez a-mer-ih-kay'-nah ree'-penz)

Erect to trailing and creeping, sparsely pubescent perennial from rhizomes; stems many, rooting at the nodes, much branched, 20–40 in. long; flowering branches erect.

LEAVES: opposite, petioled; petiole to ¾ in. long; blade glabrous or sparsely pubescent, broadly lanceolate, sharply toothed.

INFLORESCENCE: flowers numerous, of ray and disk types, in small head; heads solitary, peduncled, terminal; peduncles to 6 in. long, from leaf axils; receptacle cone-shaped, chaffy throughout with small scales, the scales enfolding flowers; phyllaries in 2 rows, linear. *Flower*: ray flowers few, pistillate but sterile, 3-toothed at tip, yellow; disk flowers numerous, perfect, fertile, 5-toothed, yellow; pappus usually absent.

FRUIT: achene, blackish, somewhat flattened.

POF   (SOF)   July–December

Purple cone-flower [p. 76]

Echinacea sanguinea Nutt.
(Ek-ih-nay'-see-ah san-gwin'-ee-ah)

Stiffly erect, slender, glabrous to sparsely pubescent perennial 1½–3 ft. tall; stems solitary or several and clumplike, usually unbranched.

LEAVES: alternate, mostly toward base; basal leaves petioled, lanceolate to elliptic, 4–9½ in. long; upper leaves becoming sessile, with rough stiff pubescence.

INFLORESCENCE: flowers numerous, of ray and disk types, in head; heads solitary, terminating long pedunclelike stem; receptacle convex, becoming cone-shaped in fruit and to ¾ in. long, chaffy; scales small, spine-tipped, folded together lengthwise; phyllaries lanceolate, to ⅜ in. long, pubescent. *Flower*: ray flowers sterile, rather persistent, often conspicuously drooping, 1½–3¾ in. long, rose pink; disk flowers perfect, fertile, shorter than scales, 5-lobed, expanded basally, purplish; pappus of low crown at tip of achene.

FRUIT: achene, 4-angled, terminated by pappus crown.

LBU   (MGP)   May–June

Late brown-eyed Susan [p. 96]

Rudbeckia hirta L. var. *pulcherrima* Farw.
(Rood-bek'-ee-ah hir'-tah pul-ker'-rim-ah)

Rigidly erect to somewhat sprawling, slender, coarse annual 16–40 in.

tall, with stiff pubescence rough to the touch; stems usually several and clump-like, commonly with few branches above the middle.

LEAVES: alternate, sessile or very short-petioled, mostly toward base; blade roughly pubescent, lanceolate to broadly lanceolate or elliptic, 2–7¼ in. long, ⅜–3¼ in. wide, entire or somewhat toothed.

INFLORESCENCE: flowers numerous, of ray and disk types, in head; heads large, showy, long-peduncled, terminal; receptacle cone-shaped, chaffy throughout; scales small, sharp-pointed; phyllaries linear, overlapping, spreading, in 2 or more rows, to 1 in. long, pubescent. *Flower*: ray flowers sterile, to 2 in. long, yellow; disk flowers perfect, fertile, 5-toothed, brown; style branches 2, slender, sharp-pointed; pappus absent or a crown of 2–4 minute teeth.

FRUIT: achene, glabrous, 4-angled, blunt at tip.

NOTE: very similar to *R. hirta* var. *angustifolia*.

R   (MGP, LBU, OFS)   May–October

Brown-eyed Susan [p. 76]

Rudbeckia hirta L. var. *angustifolia* (T. V. Moore) Perdue

(Rood-bek′-ee-ah hir′-tah an-gus-tih-foh′-lee-ah)

Rigidly erect, slender, coarse, short-lived perennial 16–40 in. tall, with stiff pubescence and rough to touch; stems usually several and clumplike, usually with few branches at or near the middle.

LEAVES: alternate, sessile or very short-petioled, mostly toward base; blade roughly pubescent, lanceolate to broadly lanceolate or elliptic, 2–7¼ in. long, ⅜–3¼ in. wide, sometimes tapered to petiolelike base, entire or obscurely toothed.

INFLORESCENCE: flowers numerous, of ray and disk types, in head; heads large, showy, long-peduncled, terminal; receptacle cone-shaped, chaffy throughout; scales small, sharp-pointed; phyllaries linear, overlapping, spreading, in 2 or more rows, linear to lanceolate, to 1 in. long, pubescent. *Flower*: ray flowers sterile, ¾–2 in. long, yellow often basally spotted with red brown; disk flowers perfect, fertile, 5-toothed, brown; style branches 2, slender, sharp-pointed; pappus absent or a crown of 2–4 minute teeth.

FRUIT: achene, glabrous, 4-angled, blunt at tip; pappus often absent.

LBU   (OFS)   May–September

Rough cone-flower [p. 76]

Rudbeckia grandiflora (Sweet) DC.

(Rood-bek′-ee-ah gran-dih-floh′-rah)

Strictly erect, coarse perennial 1½–3½ ft. tall, with stiff rough pubescence mostly throughout; plants usually forming colonies.

LEAVES: alternate, mostly in basal portion of plant; basal leaves long-petioled, rigid, prominently 3- to 5-ribbed, with stiff rough pubescence on both surfaces, lanceolate to broadly elliptic, 2½–6 in. long, shallowly toothed; stem leaves similar but smaller, essentially sessile.

INFLORESCENCE: flowers numerous, of ray and disk types, in head; heads large, showy, long-peduncled, terminal; receptacle cone-shaped, chaffy throughout; scales pubescent at tip, with short somewhat sticky hairs; phyllaries overlapping, in 2 or more rows. *Flower*: ray flowers sterile, drooping, yellow; disk flowers perfect, fertile, 5-toothed, brown; style branches 2, short, blunt; pappus of a conspicuous low crown.

FRUIT: achene, 4-angled, with sides unequal.

NOTE: uncommon and local in East Texas and western Louisiana.

LBU   (MGP)   June–August

Marsh cone-flower   [p. 40]
Rudbeckia missouriensis Boynt. & Beadle
(Rood-bek′-ee-ah   mih-zoo-ree-en′-sis)

Rigidly erect, slender perennial 16–32 in. tall, with dense long rough pubescence mostly throughout; stems few to several, forming clump, leafy, occasionally branched; branches slender, erect, close to stem.

LEAVES: alternate, sessile; blade densely pubescent, linear to narrowly lanceolate, to ¾ in. wide.

INFLORESCENCE: flowers numerous, of ray and disk types, in head; heads solitary, showy, long-peduncled, terminal; receptacle cone-shaped, chaffy with small scales throughout; phyllaries linear, to ⅜ in. long, somewhat pubescent. *Flower*: ray flowers usually 12–14, sterile, to 1 in. long, yellow; disk flowers perfect, fertile, 5-toothed, brown; style branches 2, short, blunt; pappus of a very short crown.

FRUIT: achene, 4-angled, the sides almost equal.

NOTE: uncommon in the Big Thicket.

MGP   July–September

Cut-leaf cone-flower   [p. 54]
Rudbeckia laciniata L.
(Rood-bek′-ee-ah   la-sin-ee-ay′-tah)

Erect, coarse, glaucous, glabrous or pubescent perennial 3–8 ft. tall from rhizomes; stem solitary, ribbed or angled, usually branched; plants forming colonies.

LEAVES: alternate, sessile or short-petioled; blade glabrous, smooth or rough on upper surface, deeply divided into several segments or upper ones entire, rounded or blunt at base, usually toothed.

INFLORESCENCE: flowers numerous, of ray and disk types, in head; heads showy, long-peduncled, terminal, receptacle cone-shaped, chaffy throughout;

scales pubescent at tip; phyllaries linear, essentially glabrous, to ¾ in. long, reflexed. *Flower*: ray flowers sterile, ¾–1¼ in. long, yellow; disk flowers perfect, fertile, 5-lobed, greenish yellow; style branches 2, pubescent at tips; pappus of a short crown of 2–4 teeth.

FRUIT: achene, brown, 4-angled, somewhat flattened.

NOTE: infrequent in the Big Thicket.

SOF   June–September

Shiny cone-flower [p. 40]

Rudbeckia nitida Nutt. var. *texana* Perdue

(Rood-bek´-ee-ah   nit´-ih-dah   tex-ay´-nah)

Strictly erect, slender, glabrous perennial 1–4 ft. tall, usually less than 3½ ft. tall; stem solitary, unbranched or few-branched in upper portion; branches slender, erect, close to stem.

LEAVES: alternate, sessile, mostly toward base; blade thick, shiny, narrowly to broadly elliptic or spatulate, 4–6 in. long, 1⅛–2⅜ in. wide, tapering to long slender petiolelike base, entire or toothed.

INFLORESCENCE: flowers numerous, of ray and disk types, in head; heads showy, long-peduncled, terminal; receptacle cone-shaped to somewhat cylindrical, to 1¾ in. long, chaffy throughout; scales small, sharp-pointed; phyllaries linear, in 2 or more rows. *Flower*: ray flowers sterile, yellow; disk flowers perfect, fertile, 5-toothed, brown; style branches 2, pubescent at tips; pappus of a short crown.

FRUIT: achene, 4-angled, to ⅜ in. long.

NOTE: uncommon in East Texas and western Louisiana.

MGP   April–October

Clasping cone-flower [p. 66]

Dracopis amplexicaulis (Vahl) Cass

(Dra-ko´-pis   am-plex-ih-kaw´-lis)

Erect, glaucous, glabrous annual 12–28 in. tall; stem solitary, branching in upper portion.

LEAVES: alternate, sessile, clasping basally; blade thick, 1-ribbed, net-veined, lanceolate to broadly lanceolate, entire or sparsely toothed.

INFLORESCENCE: flowers numerous, of ray and disk types, in head; heads showy, long-peduncled, terminal; receptacle slender, elongated, cylindrical; phyllaries few, lanceolate, to ⅜ in. long. *Flower*: ray flowers 5–9, sterile, to 1 in. long, yellow or often red brown at base; disk flowers perfect, fertile, 5-toothed, brown; style branches 2, with pubescent appendages; pappus absent.

FRUIT: achene, somewhat cylindrical, minutely wrinkled, to about 1/16 in. long.

LBS   (SOF, POF)   June–August

Mexican-hat　　　　　　　　　　　　　　　　　　　　　　　　[p. 40]

Ratibida columnaris (Sims) D. Don

(Ra-tib′-ih-dah　kol-um-nair′-is)

Erect or somewhat sprawling perennial 8–48 in. tall, with stiff appressed pubescence throughout, occasionally resin-dotted; stem solitary, slender, branching from base.

LEAVES: alternate, sessile or petioled; blade thick, deeply divided into 5–13 narrow segments; segments entire or again lobed or cleft; basal leaves sometimes undivided, slender-petioled.

INFLORESCENCE: flowers numerous, of ray and disk types, in head; heads showy, long-peduncled, terminal; receptacle slender, elongated, cylindrical, to $2\frac{1}{4}$ in. long, to $\frac{3}{8}$ in. wide; phyllaries in 2 rows, linear, to $\frac{1}{2}$ in. long, the inner row much smaller than the outer row. *Flower*: ray flowers 4–10, sterile, drooping, inconspicuously 3-lobed, yellow often spotted basally with red brown; disk flowers numerous, perfect, fertile, 5-lobed, brown; style branches 2, short, blunt; pappus of 2 toothlike projections, 1 on each edge of crown.

FRUIT: achene, essentially glabrous, short, flattened, winged on edges, terminated by pappus.

MGP　(POF)　　May–November

Stiff-haired sunflower　　　　　　　　　　　　　　　　　　　[p. 76]

Helianthus hirsutus Raf.

(Hee-lee-an′-thus　hir-soo′-tus)

Erect, slender, coarse perennial $1\frac{1}{2}$–$5\frac{1}{2}$ ft. tall from coarse roots and stout much-branched rhizomes, with dense stiff pubescence, very rough to touch; stem solitary, branching in upper portion.

LEAVES: opposite, petioled; petiole to $\frac{3}{4}$ in. long, sometimes winged; blade thick, roughly pubescent on upper surface, somewhat pubescent below, lanceolate to broadly lanceolate, $2\frac{3}{8}$–6 in. long, to $2\frac{3}{4}$ in. wide, rounded or somewhat tapering at base, toothed.

INFLORESCENCE: flowers numerous, of ray and disk types, in head; heads showy, long-peduncled, terminal; receptacle essentially flat, chaffy throughout; scales keeled, with 3 sharp rigid points at tip, folded around disk achene; phyllaries lanceolate, pubescent, loose, recurved. *Flower*: ray flowers usually pistillate, sterile, 3-toothed, to 1 in. long, yellow; disk flowers numerous, perfect, fertile, 5-lobed, yellow to brownish or purplish; style branches 2, short, blunt; pappus of 2 short pubescent awns, promptly falling.

FRUIT: achene, glabrous, dark brown, inflated, about $\frac{1}{4}$ in. long; pappus usually absent.

LBU　　July–November

Ashy helianthus [p. 66]

Helianthus mollis Lam.

(Hee-lee-an'-thus mol'-lis)

Rigidly erect, coarse perennial 2–6 ft. tall from creeping rhizomes and fine fibrous roots, with conspicuous dense rough pubescence mostly throughout; stems 1–several, tufted, usually branched in upper portion.

LEAVES: opposite, sessile, clasping basally; blade densely pubescent on both surfaces, broadly lanceolate, 2–5 in. long, 1–2½ in. wide, rounded and notched at base, sharply toothed.

INFLORESCENCE: flowers numerous, of ray and disk types, in head; heads large, showy, long-peduncled, terminal; receptacle essentially flat, chaffy throughout; scales small, folded around disk achenes; phyllaries erect, lanceolate, densely pubescent. *Flower*: ray flowers 15–25, usually pistillate, sterile, 3-toothed, to 2 in. long, yellow; disk flowers numerous, perfect, fertile, 5-lobed, yellow; pappus of 2 broadly lanceolate awns, promptly falling.

FRUIT: achene, black, pubescent at tip, to about ¼ in. long.

LBS   July–October

Swamp sunflower [p. 76]

Helianthus angustifolius L.

(Hee-lee-an'-thus an-gus-tih-foh'-lee-us)

Erect, slender, pubescent perennial 3–6 ft. tall from slender rhizomes and fibrous roots; stem solitary, much-branched in upper portion.

LEAVES: alternate, sessile; blade very firm, with rough pubescence on upper surface, pubescent and often with resin dots beneath, linear, 4–8 in. long, to ⅝ in. wide; margins often rolled toward lower surface.

INFLORESCENCE: flowers numerous, of ray and disk types, in head; heads large, showy, long-peduncled, terminal; receptacle essentially flat, chaffy throughout; scales with 3 sharp rigid points at tip; phyllaries narrowly lanceolate, very loose, roughly pubescent. *Flower*: ray flowers usually pistillate, sterile, 3-toothed, yellow; disk flowers numerous, perfect, fertile, 5-toothed, somewhat pubescent, purplish red; pappus of 2 lanceolate awns, promptly falling.

FRUIT: achene, dark brown, slender, glabrous, somewhat rounded at tip.

LBU   (MGP, LBS)   August–November

Weak-stem sunflower [p. 89]

Helianthus debilis Nutt.

(Hee-lee-an'-thus deb'-ih-lis)

Erect, coarse annual 1½–6 ft. tall, glabrous or pubescent, usually rough to touch; stem solitary, often reddish, usually much-branched; branches slender, wide-spreading.

LEAVES: alternate, long-petioled; petiole to 4¾ in. long; blade green, occasionally pubescent, broadly lanceolate, 1¼–3¼ in. long, ¾–2 in. wide, very broad at the rounded and notched base, irregularly and sharply toothed.

INFLORESCENCE: flowers numerous, of ray and disk types, in head; heads terminal on long slender peduncles; receptacle essentially flat, chaffy throughout; scales with 3 sharp rigid points at tip; phyllaries narrowly lanceolate, loose. *Flower*: ray flowers commonly 11–16, usually pistillate, sterile, 3-toothed, to 1 in. long, yellow; disk flowers numerous, perfect, fertile, 5-toothed, reddish purple; pappus of 2 short slender awns, promptly falling.

FRUIT: achene, slender, flattened, pubescent at tip.

OFS   (LBU)   June–October

Frostweed [p. 55]
Verbesina virginica L.
(Ver-bee-sye′-nah   vir-jin′-ih-kah)

Erect, coarse, pubescent perennial 3–7 ft. tall; stem solitary, branching only in inflorescence, conspicuously 4- or 5-winged in lower portion.

LEAVES: alternate, petioled; petiole extending down stem as narrow wings; blade thin, pubescent and rough on upper surface, with soft pubescence below, 4–8 in. long, 1–3 in. wide, tapering basally, coarsely toothed; upper leaves usually smaller, sessile.

INFLORESCENCE: flowers numerous, of ray and disk types, in small head; heads short-pedicelled, numerous, the whole forming large showy terminal paniclelike cluster; receptacle essentially flat or slightly cone-shaped, chaffy; scales small, partly enfolding achenes; phyllaries appressed, lanceolate, pubescent. *Flower*: ray flowers 1–few, pistillate, sterile, 3-lobed, white; disk flowers numerous, perfect, fertile, 5-toothed, white; style branches 2, sharp-pointed at tips; pappus of 2 awns.

FRUIT: achene, dark brown, pubescent, flattened, winged on edges, larger in tip portion, awned.

SOF   (POF, LBU)   August–November

Lance-leaved coreopsis [p. 96]
Coreopsis lanceolata L.
(Koh-ree-op′-sis   lan-see-oh-lay′-tah)

Erect, clumped, glabrous perennial 8–48 in. tall from short rhizomes.

LEAVES: opposite, occasionally alternate in upper portion of stem; lower leaves long-petioled, glabrous or pubescent, to 6 in. long, usually entire, sometimes with few lobes or segments; upper leaves sessile.

INFLORESCENCE: flowers numerous, of ray and disk types, in head; heads long-peduncled, terminal; receptacle flat or nearly so, chaffy throughout;

phyllaries often in 2 rows; outer phyllaries 8–10, somewhat lanceolate. *Flower*: ray flowers pistillate, sterile, to 1¼ in. long, yellow; disk flowers numerous, perfect, fertile, 5-toothed, yellow; style branches 2, with taillike appendages, sharp-pointed at tips; pappus of 2 short chaffy teeth.

FRUIT: achene, black, flattened, winged.

NOTE: infrequent in the Big Thicket.

R   March–May

Plains coreopsis   [p. 89]
Coreopsis tinctoria Nutt.
(Koh-ree-op'-sis   tink-toh'-ree-ah)

Erect to sprawling, rather delicate, glabrous annual 1–4 ft. tall, usually 1–2 ft. tall; stem solitary, leafy, much-branched.

LEAVES: opposite, essentially sessile, mostly in lower portion of plant; blade once or twice divided into numerous linear segments; upper leaves often undivided.

INFLORESCENCE: flowers numerous, of ray and disk types, in head; heads long-peduncled, in loose terminal clusters; receptacle essentially flat, chaffy throughout; phyllaries in 2 rows; outer phyllaries about 8, often triangular, much shorter than inner row. *Flower*: ray flowers about 7 or 8, pistillate, sterile, usually prominently 3-lobed, to ⅝ in. long, yellow often with reddish or brownish basal spot or occasionally entirely reddish; disk flowers numerous, perfect, fertile, 5-toothed, reddish or brownish; style branches 2, blunt at tips; pappus of 2 minute awns or essentially absent.

FRUIT: achene, black, flattened, without wings.

OFS (MGP)   May–August

Flax-leaved coreopsis   [p. 66]
Coreopsis linifolia Nutt.
(Koh-ree-op'-sis   lin-ih-foh'-lee-ah)

Erect, slender, rather delicate, glabrous perennial 20–28 in. tall; stem solitary, branched in upper portion.

LEAVES: opposite, occasionally alternate in lower portion of stem, petioled; petiole to 1½ in. long; lower leaves somewhat spatulate, shorter than internodes, commonly to ⅜ in. wide, rounded at tip; upper leaves sometimes sessile, linear, blunt at tip, much smaller.

INFLORESCENCE: flowers numerous, of ray and disk types, in head; heads long-peduncled, terminal; receptacle essentially flat, chaffy throughout; phyllaries in 2 rows; outer phyllaries 6–11, essentially glabrous, broadly lanceolate, finely lined lengthwise, papery on margins, shorter than inner phyllaries. *Flower*: ray flowers 7 or 8, in 2 rows, pistillate, sterile, 3-lobed, about ½ in.

long, yellow; disk flowers numerous, perfect, fertile, 5-toothed, reddish brown; style branches 2, somewhat cone-shaped; pappus of 2 small awns or essentially absent.

FRUIT: achene, black, flattened, winged.

NOTE: uncommon in the Big Thicket.

LBS   April–August

Tickseed [p. 76]

Bidens aristosa (Michx.) Britt.

(Bye′-denz   a-ris-toh′-sah)

Erect, glabrous or sparsely pubescent annual or biennial 1–5 ft. tall; stem solitary, often reddish, branched in upper portion.

LEAVES: opposite, petioled; petiole to ⅝ in. long; blade once or twice divided into segments; segments thin, sparsely pubescent on lower surface, narrowly lanceolate to lanceolate; margins sharply toothed or somewhat lobed, fringed with hairs.

INFLORESCENCE: flowers numerous, of ray and disk types, in head; heads long-peduncled, terminal; receptacle flat or nearly so, chaffy throughout; scales small, narrow, flat; phyllaries in 2 rows; outer phyllaries 8–10, linear, to ½ in. long, fringed with hairs. *Flower*: ray flowers 6–10, sterile, to 1 in. long, golden yellow with darker basal spot; disk flowers numerous, perfect, fertile, 5-toothed, yellow; style branches 2, bearded, tipped with short appendages; pappus of 2 smooth or barbed awns.

FRUIT: achene, blackish or yellowish black, somewhat flattened, to ¼ in. long; pappus commonly persistent.

NOTE: barbed fruits frequently and freely catch in clothing and the fur of animals.

LBU   (MGP)   July–November

Green-thread [p. 90]

Thelesperma flavodiscum (Shinners) B. L. Turner

(Thee-leh-sper′-mah   flay-voh-dis′-kum)

Erect, slender, delicate, essentially glabrous annual 28–36 in. tall from taproot; stems 1–3 from base, usually branching in upper portion.

LEAVES: opposite, mostly crowded toward base of stem; blade once or twice divided into segments; ultimate segments threadlike, to 3¼ in. long, usually in a loose arrangement.

INFLORESCENCE: flowers numerous, of ray and disk types, in head; heads long-peduncled, terminal, often drooping in bud; receptacle flat, chaffy; phyllaries in 2-rows; inner phyllaries 8, lanceolate, red brown, partially united, often reflexed at tip; outer phyllaries 7–9, usually threadlike, shorter than inner ones. *Flower*: ray flowers usually 8, sterile, 3-notched at tip, to ⅝ in. long, yellow; disk flowers numerous, perfect, fertile, unequally 5-lobed, yellow; pappus of 2 barbed awns.

FRUIT: achene, of various forms, rounded to flattened, smooth or warty, usually with barbed hairs near tip; inner achenes erect; outer achenes curved inward.

NOTE: endemic to the Big Thicket.

OFS   June–August

White marshallia   [p. 40]
Marshallia caespitosa DC.

(Mar-shal'-lee-ah   ses-pih-toh'-sah)

Erect, clumped, glabrous perennial, commonly 8–16 in. tall from short rhizome.

LEAVES: alternate, essentially sessile, crowded near base of plant; blade thick, obscurely 3-veined, linear to narrowly lanceolate, commonly to 3¼ in. long, ⅜ in. wide, rounded or sharp-pointed at tip.

INFLORESCENCE: flowers numerous, of disk type, in head; head solitary on stem, showy, terminal; receptacle somewhat cone-shaped, chaffy throughout; scales narrow, linear, rather rigid; phyllaries in 2 rows, green with white margins, glabrous. *Flower*: white; ray flowers absent; disk flowers numerous, perfect, fertile, funnel-shaped, deeply 5-lobed; style branches 2, long, blunt at tips; pappus of 5 scales.

FRUIT: achene, 5-angled, ribbed, resin-dotted between ribs; pappus scales erect, forming crown at tip of achene.

MGP   April–June

Barbara's-buttons   [p. 66]
Marshallia tenuifolia Raf.

(Mar-shal'-lee-ah   ten-yoo-ih-foh'-lee-ah)

Erect, clumped, essentially glabrous perennial 16–40 in. tall from woody base; stem sometimes branched near middle; branches slender, strictly erect.

LEAVES: alternate, sessile, somewhat clasping basally, gradually becoming smaller in upper portion of plant; lower leaves thin, glabrous, prominently 1- to 3-veined, linear to narrowly lanceolate, broadest near middle, 1½–8 in. long, to about ½ in. wide, tapering to base; upper stem leaves narrowly linear, gradually reduced in size upwards to the very small bracts of the peduncles.

INFLORESCENCE: flowers numerous, of disk type, in head; head solitary on stem, showy; receptacle somewhat cone-shaped, chaffy throughout; scales narrow, rigid; phyllaries in 2 rows, glabrous. *Flower*: dark rose to purple or lavender; ray flowers absent; disk flowers numerous, perfect, fertile, funnel-shaped, deeply 5-lobed, to ⅝ in. long; style branches 2, long, blunt at tips; pappus of 5 scales.

FRUIT: achene, 5-angled, ribbed; pappus scales erect, forming crown at tip of achene.

NOTE: uncommon in the Big Thicket.

LBS   July–October

Indian blanket [p. 97]

Gaillardia pulchella Foug.

(Gay-lar′-dee-ah   pul-kel′-lah)

Erect to sprawling, taprooted, pubescent annual 12–16 in. tall; stems branched, becoming woody at base late in season, furrowed and with lines of short fine hairs.

LEAVES: alternate, sessile and clasping basally or tapering into short petiole; blade with some pubescence on both surfaces, oblong to somewhat spatulate, ¾–3¼ in. long, ¼–¾ in. wide; margins coarsely toothed to lobed or entire, somewhat fringed with hairs.

INFLORESCENCE: flowers numerous, of ray and disk types, in head; heads showy, terminal on long peduncles; receptacle convex, pitted, with sharp-pointed bristles; phyllaries in 2 or 3 rows, lanceolate, stiff and papery basally, prominently reflexed in fruit. *Flower*: ray flowers 6–10, sometimes pistillate, sterile, 3-toothed or -lobed at tip, red tipped with yellow; disk flowers numerous, perfect, fertile, 5-toothed; disk-flower teeth yellowish or brownish, terminally covered with fine hairs; style branches 2; pappus of 5–7 awned scales.

FRUIT: achene, brown, pubescent in basal portion only, obovoid.

R   (OFS)   June–August

Winkler gaillardia [p. 89]

Gaillardia aestivalis (Walt.) Rock var. *winkleri*

(Gay-lar′-dee-ah   es-tih-vay′-lis   wink′-ler-eye)

Erect to sprawling, pubescent perennial 12–28 in. tall; stem solitary, sometimes reddish, with lengthwise furrows, branched in upper portion.

LEAVES: alternate, sessile or petioled; blade thick, with short fine pubescence on both surfaces, gland-dotted, linear to somewhat spatulate, 2–4 in. long, fringed with hairs; lower leaves generally larger than upper leaves, petioled.

INFLORESCENCE: flowers numerous, of ray and disk types, in head; heads solitary, showy, long-peduncled, terminal; receptacle convex, pitted, with short weak bristles; phyllaries in 2 or 3 rows, lanceolate, covered with short fine pubescence, prominently reflexed in fruit. *Flower*: ray flowers 12–18, usually pistillate, sterile, conspicuously tubular at base, deeply 3-lobed, white; disk flowers numerous, perfect, fertile, 5-toothed, creamy white to yellow; style branches 2; pappus of several awned scales.

FRUIT: achene, brown, densely pubescent, obovoid.

OFS   May–September

Bitterweed [p. 97]
Helenium amarum (Raf.) Rock
(Heh-lee′-nee-um   a-mair′-um)

Erect, moundlike, bitterly aromatic, essentially glabrous annual 4–20 in. tall; stem solitary, slender, with few to numerous branches.

LEAVES: alternate, sessile; blade with microscopic resin glands, threadlike to linear or somewhat lobed, spatulate, ½–2¾ in long, tapering basally; lower leaves early deciduous and usually absent at flowering time.

INFLORESCENCE: flowers numerous, of ray and disk types, in head; heads small, terminal, numerous, the whole forming a usually showy terminal paniclelike cluster; receptacle globelike; phyllaries about 16, in 2 rows; outer row longer than inner row, usually reflexed at maturity. *Flower*: ray flowers about 8, usually pistillate, sometimes fertile, 3-lobed, somewhat drooping, yellow; disk flowers numerous, perfect, fertile, 5-lobed, yellow; style branches 2, without appendages; pappus of 5 spine-tipped translucent scales.

FRUIT: achene, dark brown, pubescent, ribbed, obovoid.

NOTE: Milk from cows eating this plant is extremely distasteful.

R   (POF, SOF, LBU, OFS)   May–December

Purple-head sneezeweed [p. 66]
Helenium flexuosum Raf.
(Heh-lee′-nee-um   flex-yoo-oh′-sum)

Erect, glabrous or pubescent perennial, 16–40 in. tall; stems 1–several, branching in upper portion, conspicuously winged in lower portion.

LEAVES: alternate, sessile; stem leaves linear to narrowly lanceolate, 1½–3 in. long, to ½ in. wide, basally extending down stem as wings, entire or sparsely toothed; lower leaves much larger, tapering basally, usually withered at flowering time.

INFLORESCENCE: flowers numerous, of ray and disk types, in head; heads long-peduncled, forming loose, open terminal cluster; receptacle globelike; phyllaries about 16, in 2 rows; outer row longer than inner row, usually reflexed. *Flower*: ray flowers usually pistillate, sterile, 3-lobed, to about ¾ in. long, often drooping, yellow or reddish brown; disk flowers perfect, fertile, with corolla tubular, usually 4-lobed, red brown to red purple; style branches 2, without appendages; pappus of 5 spine-tipped translucent scales.

FRUIT: achene, brown, pubescent, short, cylindrical, minute.

NOTE: uncommon in the Big Thicket.

LBS　(MGP)　　May–June

Fringed sneezeweed [p. 66]

Helenium drummondii Rock

(Heh-lee′-nee-um　drum-mun′-dee-eye)

Erect, clumped, glabrous perennial commonly 18–22 in. tall; stems solitary or few in clump, unbranched, winged in lower portion.

LEAVES: alternate, sessile; blade thin, linear, becoming reduced to mere bracts near middle of stem; lower leaves usually present at flowering time, somewhat spatulate, entire to cleft or lobed.

INFLORESCENCE: flowers numerous, of ray and disk types, in head; head solitary on stem, showy, terminal; receptacle somewhat globelike; phyllaries in 2 rows; outer row longer than inner row, usually reflexed. *Flower*: ray flowers sterile, 3-lobed, to about ¾ in. long, yellow; disk flowers perfect, fertile, 5-lobed, yellow; style branches 2, without appendages; pappus of 5–10 translucent scales deeply divided into threadlike segments.

FRUIT: achene, short, somewhat cylindrical, pubescent on ribs, minute.

NOTE: uncommon in the Big Thicket.

LBS　March–May

Bristle-leaf dyssodia [p. 90]

Dyssodia tenuiloba (DC.) Robins

(Dis-soh′-dee-ah　ten-yoo-ih-loh′-bah)

Erect to sprawling, sometimes forming dense clumps, strongly scented, annual or short-lived perennial 4–12 in. tall, glabrous or sparsely roughly pubescent.

LEAVES: alternate, sessile, blade dotted with translucent orange or dark brown oil glands, to 1¼ in. long, entire or deeply cleft into 7–15 threadlike or linear segments or lobes.

INFLORESCENCE: flowers numerous, of ray and disk types, in head; heads numerous, usually peduncled, sometimes sessile or nearly so, forming terminal cymelike clusters; receptacle essentially flat; phyllaries 12–22, glandular, united almost to tip, subtended by 3–8 phyllarylike glandular bracts. *Flower*: ray flowers mostly about 13, pistillate, golden yellow; disk flowers numerous, perfect, 5-lobed, yellow; style branches 2, long, slender, tipped with short appendages; pappus of 10–12 awned scales.

FRUIT: achene, glabrous, slender, cylindrical.

OFS　September–November

Reverchon palafoxia [p. 89]
Palafoxia reverchonii (Bush) Cory
(Pal-ah-fox'-ee-ah rev-er-choh'-nee-eye)

Erect to somewhat sprawling, glandular annual 12–20 in. tall, sometimes taller; stem solitary, widely branching in upper portion, with gland-tipped pubescence only in inflorescence.

LEAVES: alternate, petioled; blade firm, very linear to very narrowly lanceolate, 1½–2⅜ in. long, less than ¼ in. wide.

INFLORESCENCE: flowers numerous, of ray and disk types, in head; heads showy, terminal on slender branches, the whole forming loose wide-spreading terminal cluster; receptacle essentially flat; phyllaries 7–9, rather thick, green. *Flower*: ray flowers 4–6, pistillate, fertile, often with 1 or more missing, conspicuously and deeply 3-lobed at tip, pink to rose; disk flowers perfect, fertile, 5-lobed; anthers dark brown; style branches 2, purple, linear, spreading or curled, pubescent; pappus of 7–10 scales.

FRUIT: achene, 4-angled, somewhat obovoid, about ¼ in. long.

NOTE: uncommon in the Big Thicket; endemic to East Texas.

OFS July–October

Hooker palafoxia [p. 89]
Palafoxia hookeriana T. & G.
(Pal-ah-fox'-ee-ah hook-er-ee-ay'-nah)

Stiffly erect, rather stout, glandular annual 2–4 ft. tall; stem solitary, branching from near middle, with gland-tipped pubescence in inflorescence and extending well below, often sticky to the touch.

LEAVES: alternate, petioled; blade firm, very linear to narrowly lanceolate, to about 3⅛ in. long, to ¾ in. wide.

INFLORESCENCE: flowers numerous, of ray and disk types, in head; heads terminal on branches, the whole forming somewhat dense, showy terminal cluster; receptacle essentially flat; phyllaries 7–9, thick, green, pubescent, with some pubescence glandular. *Flower*: ray flowers pistillate, fertile, often with 1 or more missing, ⅜–½ in. long, deeply 3-lobed, dark rose; disk flowers perfect, fertile, 5-lobed, rose; style branches 2, linear, spreading or curled, pubescent; pappus of 7–10 scales.

FRUIT: achene, 4-angled, somewhat obovoid, to about ⅜ in. long.

NOTE: endemic to southern portions of Texas; plant showy and worthy of cultivation.

OFS September–October

Woolly-white   [p. 77]

Hymenopappus artemisiaefolius DC.

(Hye-men-oh-pap'-pus   ar-tih-miz-ee-eh-foh'-lee-us)

Erect, rather stout, glabrous or pubescent biennial 1½–3 ft. tall from unbranched taproot; stem solitary, branched in upper portion.

LEAVES: alternate, in basal rosette and along stem; basal leaves long-petioled, mostly densely pubescent on lower surface, 3¼–7¼ in. long, usually deeply cleft into broad segments; stem leaves much smaller, essentially sessile.

INFLORESCENCE: flowers numerous, of disk type, in head; heads small, peduncled, terminal with 30–60 per stem, the whole forming large showy terminal cluster; receptacle essentially flat to convex; phyllaries 6–14, in 2 rows; principal phyllaries snowy white for about ½ length, erect, appearing somewhat petallike. *Flower*: rose to dark wine; ray flowers absent; disk flowers perfect, funnel-shaped, 5-lobed; style much exserted, 2-branched, the branches with small cone-shaped appendages at tips; pappus of 16–18 oblong scales.

FRUIT: achene, 4-sided, somewhat obovoid, pubescent on angles.

LBU   (OFS)   March–May

Common yarrow   [p. 97]

Achillea millefolium L.

(A-kil-lee'-ah   mil-lee-foh'-lee-um)

Strictly erect, pubescent perennial 8–40 in. tall from rhizome; stems 1–several, from base, unbranched or forking in upper portion; plants usually forming small colonies.

LEAVES: alternate, sessile or short-petioled; blade pubescent, 2 or 3 times divided into threadlike or linear segments, fernlike, ¾–6 in. long, to 1½ in. wide; basal leaves often longer, petioled.

INFLORESCENCE: flowers few to many, of ray and disk types, in head; heads small, peduncled, terminal, about 10–20 in dense cluster; clusters few, forming larger showy terminal cluster; receptacle somewhat cone-shaped, chaffy; scales small, stiff, oblong; phyllaries in about 4 rows, pubescent. *Flower*: ray flowers 5–12, pistillate, fertile, usually white, sometimes pink; disk flowers perfect, fertile, 5-toothed, whitish or yellowish white; style branches 2, flat at tips; pappus absent.

FRUIT: achene, glabrous, shiny, somewhat flattened.

R   (SOF, LBU, OFS)   April–June

Woolly groundsel [p. 77]
Senecio tomentosus Michx.
(Seh-nee'-she-oh   toh-men-toh'-sus)

Erect perennial 10–20 in. tall, usually with soft woolly pubescence throughout; stems 1–several, often tufted, occasionally branched in upper portion.

LEAVES: alternate, mostly crowded toward base; basal leaves usually with conspicuous woolly pubescence, broadly lanceolate to oblong, 2–4 in. long, sharply toothed, petioled; petiole linear, to 6½ in. long; upper leaves much reduced, often sessile, sometimes shallowly lobed, becoming bracts near inflorescence.

INFLORESCENCE: flowers few to many, of ray and disk types, in head; heads small, terminal on short branches, forming showy terminal cluster; receptacle flat or nearly so; phyllaries about 21, in 2 rows; inner row much longer than outer one, usually persistently pubescent. *Flower*: ray flowers pistillate, fertile, linear, 3-toothed, yellow; disk flowers numerous, perfect, fertile, equally 5-toothed, yellow; style branches 2, spreading or curled; pappus of numerous hair-like bristles.

FRUIT: achene, somewhat cylindrical, several-ribbed.

NOTE: uncommon in the Big Thicket.

LBU   March–April

Butterweed [p. 55]
Senecio glabellus Poir.
(Seh-nee'-she-oh   gla-bel'-lus)

Erect, rather stout, succulent, glabrous annual 1–3 ft. tall; stem solitary, hollow, unbranched or branched in upper portion.

LEAVES: alternate; lower leaves petioled; blade 2–8 in. long, ¾–2¾ in. wide, divided to midrib into many segments or lobes; segments rounded and lobed or toothed; upper segments not constricted at base; leaves gradually becoming smaller in upper portion of plant, but not much reduced, sessile.

INFLORESCENCE: flowers many, of ray and disk types, in head; heads small, terminal on short branches, forming showy terminal cluster; receptacle flat or nearly so; phyllaries usually in 1 row. *Flower*: ray flowers pistillate, fertile, linear, 3-toothed, to ½ in. long, yellow; disk flowers perfect, fertile, equally 5-toothed, yellow; style branches 2, spreading or curled; pappus of numerous white hairlike bristles.

FRUIT: achene, brown, glabrous or pubescent, narrowly ellipsoid, minute.

NOTE: uncommon in the Big Thicket.

SOF (POF)   March–April

Lance-leaf Indian plantain   [p. 40]
Cacalia lanceolata Nutt.
(Ka-kay'-lee-ah lan-see-oh-lay'-tah)

Strictly erect, stout, essentially glabrous perennial 2–5 ft. tall; stem solitary, branching only in extreme tip portion.

LEAVES: alternate; lower leaves glaucous, prominently 5-veined, lanceolate to broadly lanceolate, 4–7 in. long, 1¼–2 in. wide, long-petioled, entire or toothed, upper leaves smaller, sessile.

INFLORESCENCE: flowers 5, of disk type, in head; heads peduncled, terminal, arranged in large loose somewhat flat-topped terminal cluster; receptacle convex; phyllaries about 5, erect, broad, yellow green. *Flower*: white; ray flowers absent; disk flowers few, perfect, fertile, equally 5-toothed; pappus of numerous slender white bristles.

FRUIT: achene, dark brown to blackish, ribbed, essentially smooth, somewhat obovoid.

NOTE: infrequent in the Big Thicket.
MGP   (POF, LBS)   July–October

Bull thistle   [p. 97]
Cirsium horridulum Michx.
(Sir'-see-um hor-rid'-yoo-lum)

Erect, stout, coarse, glabrous or pubescent winter annual or biennial 1–5 ft. tall; stem solitary, thick, usually not branched, covered with thick soft pubescence.

LEAVES: alternate, mostly in basal rosette, sessile; blade commonly pubescent on lower surface, once divided into several shallow lobes; margins toothed and with spines; each lobe and each tooth usually ending in longer sharper spine.

INFLORESCENCE: flowers numerous, of disk type, in head; heads peduncled, large, showy, terminal, often few to several in terminal cluster; receptacle covered with soft hairlike bristles; phyllaries numerous, in many rows, prominently overlapping, lanceolate, with weak flat tips; head subtended by several appressed, very spiny leaflike bracts. *Flower*: pink, rose, purple, or yellow; ray flowers absent; disk flowers numerous, perfect, fertile, deeply 5-lobed; style branches 2; pappus of numerous bristles united in ring at base.

FRUIT: achene, glabrous, smooth, flattened, somewhat oblong; entire pappus deciduous as a unit.
R   (POF, SOF, LBS, LBU, OFS)   March–May

Soft thistle   [p. 97]
Cirsium carolinianum (Walt.) Fern. & Schub.
(Sir'-see-um kair-oh-lin-ee-ay'-num)

Erect, slender, glabrous or pubescent biennial or perennial to 3½ ft. tall from short taproot and fibrous roots; stem solitary, usually branched in upper portion.

LEAVES: alternate; blade thin, pliable, green and essentially glabrous on upper surface, with dense white pubescence on lower surface, to 12 in. long, 2 in. wide; margins spine-toothed or with spine-tipped lobes; lower leaves petioled; stem leaves few, much smaller, essentially sessile.

INFLORESCENCE: flowers numerous, of disk type, in head; heads showy, peduncled, terminating branches; receptacle covered with soft hairlike bristles; phyllaries numerous, spine-tipped; spine tips purplish, spreading. *Flower*: lavender, rose, or purple; ray flowers absent; disk flowers numerous, perfect, fertile, deeply 5-lobed; style branches 2; pappus of numerous bristles united in ring at base.

FRUIT: achene, glabrous, smooth, flattened, somewhat oblong; entire pappus deciduous as a unit.

R (LBU) June–August

Sunbonnets [p. 67]

Chaptalia tomentosa Vent.

(Chap-tay'-lee-ah toh-men-toh'-sah)

Tufted pubescent perennial to 14 in. tall from short rhizome and abundant fibrous roots; flower scape erect, slender, leafless, unbranched.

LEAVES: in basal rosette, essentially sessile; blade pubescent on upper surface, becoming glabrous, with dense white pubescence on lower surface, 3¼–4 in. long, ½–1¼ in. wide, tapering to somewhat petiolelike base, entire or shallowly lobed.

INFLORESCENCE: flowers many, of ray and disk types, in head; head solitary on scape, terminal, erect when fully open, nodding in bud and after flowering; receptacle flat; phyllaries in 4 or 5 rows, often pubescent. *Flower*: ray flowers about 20, pistillate, white; outermost disk flowers 5–11, pistillate, 2-lipped; innermost disk flowers about 25, staminate, 2-lipped, yellow; pappus of numerous rigid buffy white bristles.

FRUIT: achene, glabrous, 5- to 7-ribbed, beaked at tip.

NOTE: uncommon in the Big Thicket.

LBS (LBU) February–April

Potato-dandelion [p. 97]

Krigia dandelion (L.) Nutt.

(Krig'-ee-ah dan-dee-lye'-on)

Erect, tuftlike, glaucous, essentially glabrous perennial 4–18 in. tall from fibrous roots and slender rhizome bearing tuberlike enlargements; plant with milky sap.

LEAVES: alternate, numerous, crowded at base, very short-petioled; blade linear, elliptic, or narrowly spatulate, 2–8 in. long, to ¾ in. wide, tapering to petiolelike base; margins entire, toothed, or lobed.

INFLORESCENCE: flowers numerous, of ray type, in head; heads solitary, showy, terminal on slender scape; receptacle flat or somewhat cupped, becoming convex in fruit; phyllaries 15, erect, in 2 rows, green, with thin margins, becoming shriveled and reflexed in age. *Flower*: yellow; disk flowers absent; ray flowers numerous, perfect, fertile, to ¾ in. long; pappus in 2 rows, the outer row of 10 minute scales, the inner row of 25–45 rough bristles to almost ⅜ in. long.

FRUIT: achene, reddish brown, pubescent, 10- to 15-ribbed, somewhat cylindrical, very small.

R   (LBU)   March–May

Dwarf dandelion [p. 97]
Krigia occidentalis Nutt.
(Krig′-ee-ah   ok-sih-den-tay′-lis)

Low, tufted annual 1½–7 in. tall from inconspicuous taproot and fibrous roots; stems several, slender, scapelike, glabrous or with pubescence of short stiff hairs, commonly glandular.

LEAVES: alternate, crowded and rosettelike, sessile; blade narrowly lanceolate to spatulate, narrowing to petiolelike base; margins entire, lobed, or deeply cleft.

INFLORESCENCE: flowers numerous, of ray type, in head; heads solitary, terminal on scapes; receptacle flat or somewhat cupped, becoming convex in fruit; phyllaries usually 5, lanceolate, with thin margins, united in basal portion, remaining erect in fruit, becoming closed by shriveling after fruit has fallen. *Flower*: yellow or yellow orange; disk flowers absent; ray flowers numerous, perfect, fertile, 5-toothed, less than ¼ in. long; pappus an outer row of 5 very small transparent broadly wedge-shaped scales and an inner row of rough bristles.

FRUIT: achene, cinnamon or red brown, 10- to 15-ribbed, somewhat cylindrical, more or less angular, very small.

R   (LBU, OFS)   March–May

Carolina false dandelion [p. 97]
Pyrrhopappus carolinianus (Walt.) DC.
(Pir-oh-pap′-pus   kair-oh-lin-ee-ay′-nus)

Erect or occasionally somewhat sprawling, essentially glabrous annual commonly 12–28 in. tall from slender taproot; stems 1–few, slender, commonly branched in upper portion.

LEAVES: alternate, mostly crowded near base, sessile, becoming smaller in upper portion of plant; blade narrowly elliptic to somewhat spatulate, 3¼–

10 in. long, to 2¼ in. wide, tapering basally; margins toothed, lobed, or cleft; upper leaves usually unlobed.

INFLORESCENCE: flowers numerous, of ray type, in head; heads showy, terminating stem or branches; receptacle essentially flat; phyllaries in 2 rows, reflexed at maturity; outer row much shorter than inner row. *Flower*: yellow; disk flowers absent; ray flowers numerous, perfect, fertile, 5-toothed, to 1 in. long; pappus of numerous soft tawny white hairlike bristles.

FRUIT: achene, pubescent, brownish, 5-ribbed, cylindrical, tapered at both ends, less than ¼ in. long, tapering into long beak with tuft of pappus attached at tip.

R   February–July

Cat's-ear [p. 77]
Hypochoeris microcephala (Sch. Bip.) Cabrera var. *albiflora* (O. Ktze.) Cabrera
(Hye-pok'-eh-ris mye-kroh-sef'-ah-lah al-bih-floh'-rah)

Erect, slender, rather delicate glabrous perennial 12–28 in. tall from stout roots; stems 1–3, branched in upper portion.

LEAVES: alternate, sessile; basal leaves once deeply divided into linear segments; stem leaves few, usually lobed; upper leaves reduced to sharp-pointed bracts.

INFLORESCENCE: flowers many, of ray type, in head; heads small, terminating ultimate branches; receptacle convex, chaffy; scales thin, lanceolate, subtending flowers; phyllaries several, erect, green with white midrib. *Flower*: white; disk flowers absent; ray flowers numerous, perfect, fertile, 5-toothed; pappus of about 20 feathery bristles.

FRUIT: achene, in 2 distinct portions; lower portion brown, 10-ribbed, ellipsoid; upper portion a slender beak; pappus tuft attached at tip of beak.

NOTE: native of southern South America; uncommon and local in the Big Thicket.

LBU   May–September

Sow thistle [p. 98]
Sonchus asper (L.) Hill
(Son'-chus as'-per)

Erect, rather coarse, glabrous, or essentially so, winter annual to 6 ft. tall, commonly only to 3 ft. tall or lower; stem glabrous or glandular in upper portion, usually several-branched in tip portion of plant; plant with milky juice.

LEAVES: alternate, clasping basally; blade of lower leaves glabrous, often lobed, sharply toothed and with spines; upper leaves smaller and less lobed.

INFLORESCENCE: flowers numerous, of ray type, in head; heads small, terminating branches; receptacle flat or slightly convex, without chaff; phyllaries in several rows, often with glandular crest near midnerve; inner phyllaries longer, thin, green, the margins dry and not green; outer phyllaries short, the bases and broad midnerve becoming thick and whitish after flowering. *Flower*: yellow; disk flowers absent; ray flowers numerous, perfect, fertile; pappus of 50–60 extremely fine white persistent hairs surrounding 6–10 white flattened bristles.

FRUIT: achene, reddish brown, flattened, rough or central ones nearly smooth, about 2–2½ times as long as broad, broadest near middle.

NOTE: A native of Europe, this species is very similar to *S. oleraceus*, and identification is often difficult.

R   (LBU)   February–November

Rattlesnake root [p. 55]
Prenanthes barbata (T. & G.) Milstead
(Pree-nan'-theez   bar-bay'-tah)

Erect, slender or stout, glabrous perennial 1½–5 ft. tall from thick taproot or corm; stem solitary, often purplish, repeatedly branched in upper portion.

LEAVES: alternate, sessile; blade shallowly or deeply lobed; lower leaves usually withered before flowering.

INFLORESCENCE: flowers many, of ray type, in head; heads small, terminal on short drooping branches; branches numerous, the whole forming large showy terminal paniclelike cluster; receptacle essentially flat; phyllaries in 2 rows, green or purplish, glabrous or pubescent; outer row lanceolate, shorter than inner row; inner row 6–8, linear, overlapping at margins. *Flower*: white, usually tinged with cream or rose; disk flowers absent; ray flowers 10–12, perfect, 5-toothed; pappus of several buffy white bristles.

FRUIT: achene, smooth, 5-ribbed, narrowly cylindrical, to ⅜ in. long.

NOTE: uncommon in the Big Thicket.

SOF   September–October

Red-seeded dandelion [p. 98]
Taraxacum erythrospermum Besser
(Ta-rax'-ah-kum   eh-rith-roh-sper'-mum)

Tufted or erect, pubescent perennial 1¼–8 in. tall from deep taproots; stems 1–few, hollow, leafless.

LEAVES: alternate, numerous, crowded in basal rosette; blade oblong to spatulate in outline, shallowly to deeply lobed, 2–6 in. long, ½–2½ in. wide, tapering to petiolelike base, toothed.

INFLORESCENCE: flowers numerous, of ray type, in head; heads solitary, large, showy, terminal, on slender scape; receptacle essentially flat; phyllaries in 2 rows, gland-tipped, reflexed at maturity; outer row shorter than inner row. *Flower*: yellow; disk flowers absent; ray flowers numerous, perfect, fertile, 5-toothed; styles exserted, 2-branched, curled; pappus of numerous white hairlike bristles.

FRUIT: achene, in 2 distinct portions; lower portion reddish brown, somewhat flattened, with about 5 major ribs; upper portion a long, slender beak; pappus tuft attached at tip of beak; at maturity the whole forming spherical, fluffy ball.

NOTE: native of Europe, now widespread.

R   November–May

Glossary

ACHENE. A small, dry, usually hard, one-seeded, nonopening fruit with the outer tissue wall firmly adnate to the seed.

ALTERNATE. Arranged other than opposite or whorled; borne at different levels; situated between other organs or plant parts.

ANNUAL. Growing from seed to maturity and dying in one year or season.

ANTHER. The part of the stamen that bears the pollen.

APPRESSED. Pressed closely against another plant part.

AQUATIC. Living in water.

AROMATIC. Having a noticeable, not unpleasant scent; pungent. Often refers to crushed plant parts; not usually used of flowers.

AWN. The continuous terminal bristle of a plant part.

AXIL. The vertex of the upper angle between any two structures or organs, as where a leaf or branch joins the stem.

AXILLARY. Situated in or arising from an axil.

BANNER. The unpaired petal of the five petals in a flower of the Legume Family, usually the largest and uppermost.

BARBED. Bearing sharp, rigid, reflexed points, the points similar to the tip of a fishhook.

BASAL. Located at or relating to the base.

BEAK. A firm, prolonged, slender tip, usually of a seed or fruit.

BEARD. A zone of long, stiff hairs.

BERRY. A fleshy or pulpy, nonopening fruit containing 1–many seeds, the seeds without a stony covering.

BIENNIAL. Requiring two years to complete the life cycle.

BLADDER. A thin, usually transparent organ capable of being inflated or expanded.

BLADDERY. Having some characteristics of a bladder.

BLADE. The expanded portion of a leaf, petal, or other organ.

BLUNT. Appearing as if cut straight across; not rounded or lobed.

BRACT. A reduced or modified leaf, most often occurring below or subtending a flower or inflorescence, sometimes brightly colored or petallike. May appear as a scalelike or threadlike structure.

BRISTLE. A very stiff hair or similar structure.

BUD. The relatively small structure which is the undeveloped stem or leaf, usually enclosed by scales. An unexpanded flower, sometimes enclosed by the bracts or the calyx.

BULB. A short underground bud surrounded by layers of thick, fleshy, modified leaves, as an onion.

BULBLET. A small bulb, sometimes borne aerially, as in the inflorescence.

BURLIKE. With a rough, prickly covering, like a bur.

BURLLIKE. With hard, woody knots or lumps, like the knotty burls on trees.

CALYX. The outer whorl of a flower; the sepals collectively, which may be separate or united and may be green or colorful and petallike.

CANE. A stem, commonly used for the genus *Rubus* and sometimes for the genus *Rosa*.

CAPSULE. A dry or sometimes leathery fruit developed from more than one carpel; each carpel may be 1-seeded or many-seeded.

CARNIVOROUS. Flesh-eating; applied to those plants which trap and digest insects or other small organisms.

CARPEL. Synonymous with a pistil if single or with a division of the pistil if the pistil is compound.

CHAFF. Small, dry, thin scales or bracts.

CHASMOGAMOUS. Applied to flowers which open for pollination.

CHLOROPHYLL. The green substance within plant cells which converts light into chemical energy.

CLASPING. Basal edges of a leaf or other organ partly or wholly surrounding the stem or other structure but not united.

CLAW. The narrow, petiolelike basal portion of some sepals and petals.

CLEFT. Deeply cut.

CLEISTOGAMOUS. Applied to flowers which are self-fertilizing and never open, usually small and inconspicuous.

CLIMBING. Reaching upward using the support of other plants or objects.

CLUSTER. A general term for a group of flowers or other plant parts.

COLONY. A relatively dense stand or population of plants of one species more or less isolated from other stands.

COLUMN. The structure formed by the union of the stamens and the style and stigma in the Orchid Family and by the union of the filaments in the Mallow Family.

COMPOUND. Composed of two to many separate similar parts which collectively make a whole, such as a leaf divided into leaflets.

CONCAVE. With a curved depression; bowl- or saucer-shaped.

CONIFER. A tree or shrub with usually evergreen needles or scales, normally bearing woody or berrylike cones.

CONVEX. With a curved or rounded surface, as an overturned bowl or saucer.

CORM. A very short, thick, firm, fleshy underground stem, usually broader than tall; bulblike, but solid instead of in layers.

COROLLA. The inner whorl of a flower; the petals collectively, which may be separate or united; often colorful.

CORONA. A crownlike outgrowth of petals or stamens.

CREEPING. Growing beneath or on the surface of the ground and rooting at nodes.

CREST. An elevated ridge, projection, or appendage on the surface of a structure or organ.

CRISPED. Margins irregularly folded, twisted, or curled.

CROWN. A projection or outgrowth at the top of a structure; a corona.

CULM. The stem of grass or sedge, often pithy or hollow.

CUT. General term used for any dissection.

CYLINDRICAL. Somewhat circular in cross-section, usually longer than wide; herein used of solids.

CYME. A usually flattish inflorescence with the central or terminal flower maturing first.

DECIDUOUS. Not persistent; disattaching after completing rhythmic seasonal function.

DEFLEXED. Bent or turned downward.

DISK. A more or less fleshy portion of the receptacle at the base of the pistil. Applied to the tubular, central flowers of the head in the Sunflower Family.

DRUPE. A fleshy, nonopening fruit containing a hard stone surrounding and enclosing the solitary seed.

DRUPELET. A small drupe.

ELLIPSOID. A three-dimensional shape elliptic in longitudinal section.

ELLIPTIC. A two-dimensional shape like a flattened circle, longer than wide and widest near the middle.

EMERGENT. Rising out of and standing above water.

ENDEMIC. Restricted to a limited geographic area.

ENTIRE. Margins without teeth, lobes, or incisions.

EPIPHYTE. A plant growing on another plant or object but not parasitic, obtaining food from minute airborne particles.

ERECT. Pointing upward; upright. Somewhat perpendicular to the surface.

ESCAPE. A cultivated plant growing and reproducing in the wild.

EVERGREEN. Retaining green leaves throughout the year.

EXSERTED. Projecting out or extending beyond; not included.

FERTILE. Highly productive. Capable of sexual reproductive function. Usually refers to stamens bearing viable pollen or to pistils which can receive pollen spores and produce fruit with seed.

FIBROUS. With or containing fibers.

FILAMENT. Basal portion of stamen supporting anther, usually slender. Any threadlike structure.

FLOWER. A structure consisting of associated plant parts which functions as a reproductive unit.

FOLLICLE. A dry fruit developed from a simple carpel and opening by only one suture; it may be 1-seeded or many-seeded.

FRINGE. Finely cut margins of sepal, petal, tepal, or lip.

FRUIT. The mature ovary and any associated parts which may be fused with it, normally containing seed.

FUNNEL-SHAPED. Tubular at the base, gradually flaring upward.

FURROWED. With lengthwise channels or grooves.

GLABROUS. Without pubescence. Not to be used for SMOOTH, the opposite of ROUGH.

GLAND. Small structures on or near a surface which secretes sticky or volatile oils or fluids.

GLANDULAR. Bearing glands.

GLAUCOUS. With a whitish cast, often due to a somewhat waxy or powdery substance, called "bloom," which can be rubbed off.

GLOBELIKE. Loosely applied herein to objects with the approximate shape of a globe or part of a globe.

GRANULAR. Covered with minute grains; mealy to the touch.

HAIR. Any of the structures occurring on a plant which resemble in appearance the true hairs of animals; they may be microscopic or readily visible.

HEAD. Compact cluster of sessile or nearly sessile flowers or fruits.

HERB. A plant without a persistent, above-ground woody stem, either annual or dying back to the ground each year.

HERBACEOUS. With the characteristics of a herb.

HIP. Common name for the fruit in the genus *Rosa*.

HOOD. A structure usually rising above and arching or extending over some other part. A segment of the corona, formed from modified filaments, in some flowers of the Milkweed Family.

HORN. A specialized structure or appendage associated with the hood in some flowers of the Milkweed Family. Any small, stiff, tapering hornlike structure.

INCLUDED. Not protruding beyond the surrounding organ; not exserted.

INFERIOR. Lower or below. Frequently applied to an ovary visible as an enlargement beneath the other flower parts, which are attached above it.

INFLATED. Bladderlike; appearing blown up; enlarged.

INFLORESCENCE. All of the flowers and the associated parts in a flower cluster; it may be one flower or many. The arrangement of flowers on a stem.

INTRODUCED. A wild or cultivated plant brought in from another region, intentionally or unintentionally, which has become established in the wild.

JOINT. The place of connection of distinct structures; a node. One section of an elongated structure composed of similar parts.

KEEL. A prominent lengthwise ridge. The two lower and united petals in the flowers of the Legume Family.

LANCEOLATE. A two-dimensional shape longer than wide, widest below the middle, tapering to the tip; spearhead-shaped.

LATERAL. On or at the sides.

LAX. Loose, open. Not rigid.

LEAF. The unit of foliage.

LEAFLET. One segment of a compound leaf, itself appearing as a small leaf.

LEGUME. A dry fruit from a solitary ovary, usually opening along two sutures; it may be one- to several-seeded. A fruit of the Legume Family.

LENS-SHAPED. Shaped like the biconvex lens of a reading glass.

LINEAR. A two-dimensional shape much longer than wide, with nearly parallel sides, as a grass leaf.

LIP. The upper or lower portion of a calyx or corolla which has been partially divided into two parts. The odd and uppermost petal in the flowers of the Orchid Family, but often twisted and occurring in the lowermost position.

LOBE. Any projection of a margin, often rounded, normally larger than a tooth.

LOBED. With lobes.

MARGIN. The outer edge of a flattened or somewhat flattened structure.

MEMBRANE. A thin, pliable tissue.

MERICARP. An individual, separated carpel of a schizocarpic fruit type from a compound ovary, each mericarp attached by a stalk upon separation.

MESOPHYTIC. Adapted to conditions of moderate moisture.

MIDRIB. The central or main rib or vein of a leaf or other structure.

NET-VEINED. With veins joined together and resembling a net.

NODDING. Hanging or drooping downward.

NODE. A place on a stem where branches, leaves, or flower stalk are attached; a joint.

NUTLET. An individual, separated, 1-seeded carpel of a schizocarpic fruit type. Any small, dry, hard, nutlike fruit or seed.

OBLONG. With a shape substantially longer than wide, generally rounded at both ends and with nearly parallel sides; herein used of flattened or somewhat flattened structures.

OBOVOID. A somewhat globelike elongated solid structure, larger in the tip portion than at the base.

OPPOSITE. Two like parts connected at the same place but across from each other. Two structures, one occurring directly in front of the other, as a stamen opposite a petal.

OVAL. With a shape noticeably longer than wide, rounded at each end and wider in the middle; herein used for flattened or somewhat flattened structures.

OVARY. Basal portion of the pistil bearing the ovules, which later develop into seeds.

OVOID. A somewhat globelike elongated solid structure, larger at the base than in the tip portion.

PANICLE. A branched inflorescence with the flowers in racemes.

PAPPUS. Modified calyx lobes in the Sunflower Family consisting of bristles, awns, teeth, or scales at the summit of the achene.

PARASITIC. A species which attaches to another species and obtains food from it without returning appreciable benefits.

PEDICEL. The flower stalk of an individual flower in an inflorescence of several flowers.

PEDUNCLE. The stalk of an inflorescence or of a solitary flower.

PERENNIAL. Living for more than two years.

PERFECT. Applied to a flower having both pistils and stamens.

PERSISTENT. Remaining attached for some time after completing living functions.

PETAL. One segment of a corolla.

PETIOLE. The stalk of a leaf.

PHYLLARY. One of a whorl of bracts subtending a flower cluster, as in the heads of the Sunflower Family.

PISTIL. The female reproductive part of the flower containing the ovary, the style (if present), and the stigma.

PISTILLATE. Having a pistil and without fertile stamens; female.

PITH. Spongy center of a woody stem or branch.

PITTED. With small or minute depressions or pits on the surface.

POLLEN. The male spores borne by the anther.

POME. A fruit formed from an inferior ovary surrounded by fleshy tissue which is derived from the receptacle.

PRICKLE. A sharp projection of the outer plant covering which can be separated intact from the plant, as a rose prickle.

PUBESCENCE. A covering of hair, herein used for most types of hair which occur on plants; it may be very sparse to very dense, and microscopic to easily visible.

PUBESCENT. With pubescence.

RACEME. An elongating unbranched inflorescence with flowers pedicelled and opening progressively from the base of the inflorescence upward.

RAY. The outer, flattened, petallike flowers in the flower head of the Sunflower Family. The first stalks off the stem of a compound umbel or umbellike inflorescence.

RECEPTACLE. The terminal portion of a pedicel or peduncle, often enlarged, to which the other flower parts are attached.

RECURVED. Curving or bending backward or downward.

REFLEXED. Abruptly curving or bending backward or downward.

REMOTE. Comparable parts distant; widely spaced; far apart.

RESIN. A sticky, usually aromatic liquid produced by the glands of some plants.

RESINOUS. Producing resin; dotted with resin-producing glands.

RHIZOME. An underground, horizontal, usually elongated stem producing roots and leafy stems at the nodes.

RIB. A primary lengthwise vein of a leaf. A ridge on a fruit.

RIM. The terminal border of a united calyx or corolla.

ROOT. A usually underground part of a plant which normally anchors the plant to the substrate and functions chiefly in obtaining water and minerals.

ROSETTE. A circular cluster of leaves radiating from the center at or near the ground.

ROUGH. With a coarse texture; not smooth to the touch; may be due to hairs or any other unevenness.

ROUND. Herein used for flattened circular structures.

ROUNDED. Somewhat or partly circular; not pointed; somewhat round.

SAPROPHYTIC. Obtaining energy from organic material and containing no chlorophyll.

SCALE. Any small, thin, nongreen, dry structure.

SCAPE. A leafless flower stem rising from the ground.

SCAR. Visible mark left after detachment of some plant part.

SCHIZOCARP. A fruit from a compound ovary that splits between carpels at maturity into 1-seeded portions.

SEED. A fertilized ovule; an embryo and immediate covering, normally capable of germination to produce a new plant.

SEPAL. One segment of a calyx.

SEPARATE. Distinct; like parts not united.

SESSILE. Attached directly at the base; without petiole or pedicel.

SHEATH. A somewhat tubular structure of a plant part which is attached and clasping at its base and wholly or partly surrounding another structure for some distance; a covering.

SHEATHING. Forming a sheath.

SHRUB. Woody plant smaller than a tree, usually with several branches from base.

SILIQUE. A narrow, elongated, dry, many-seeded capsule splitting from the base into two sections, leaving a middle partition between them; the fruit of some species in the Mustard Family.

SIMPLE. Undivided into separate similar parts; not compound.

SINGLE, SINGLY. One; may or may not be part of a cluster. One at a time. Not paired.

SMOOTH. Not rough to the touch. Not to be used for GLABROUS, which means without pubescence.

SOLITARY. Not forming part of a group or cluster.

SPADIX. A fleshy spike partially enclosed by a spathe and with embedded, inconspicuous flowers.

SPATHE. A bract, often conspicuous, sheathing or partially enclosing a spadix.

SPATULATE. A two-dimensional shape rounded at tip, broadest in the tip portion, slowly tapering to the base.

SPIKE. An elongating, unbranched inflorescence with flowers sessile and opening progressively from the base of the inflorescence upward.

SPIKELET. A flower cluster of grasses and sedges. A small spike; a small spikelike structure.

SPINE. A sharp, rigid, woody outgrowth of the stem, not separating from the plant; the equivalent of a leaf or petiole. Any sharp-pointed outgrowth of a leaf or fruit.

SPRAWLING. Leaning over; lax.

SPREADING. Flaring toward a flat or somewhat flat position. Not appressed or pressed together. Parting.

SPUR. A tubular or saclike extension of a sepal or petal, usually containing nectar.

STALK. A general term for the usually elongated structure connecting or supporting an organ or group of organs.

STAMEN. Pollen-bearing male reproductive structure of a flower consisting of filament and anther.

STAMINATE. Having stamens but no functional pistils; male.

STEM. The main stalk of a plant arising from the roots.

STERILE. Not fertile; incapable of sexual reproductive function.

STIGMA. The portion of the pistil adapted for the reception of pollen and consequent fertilization.

STIPULES. The pair of appendages at the base of a petiole, usually small, sometimes united; they may be either persistent or falling early.

STOLON. A somewhat horizontal, above-ground, sometimes below-ground, stem or branch rooting at the tip or nodes and forming new plants.

STONE. The hard, bony structure formed from part of the ovary wall which surrounds the seed in some fruits.

STYLE. The portion of the pistil between the ovary and the stigma, often elongate, sometimes apparently absent.

SUBMERSED. Growing under water.

SUBTEND. To be below and close to.

SUCCULENT. Juicy and fleshy.

SWIRLED. Overlapping and appearing spiraled but not necessarily ascending.

TAPROOT. The primary, mostly vertical, central root of a plant.

TAXA. Plural of TAXON.

TAXON. A taxonomic group, such as a genus or family.

TEETH. Any small marginal protuberances, usually regularly repeated.

TENDRIL. A modified portion of a stem or leaf, usually slender and coiling or twining and functioning as a support.

TEPAL. Used for sepals and petals which are much alike and not easily differentiated.

TERMINAL. At the end or tip.

TERRESTRIAL. Growing on land; not aquatic or epiphytic.

THORN. A sharp, woody projection derived from a modified branch; not separating from the plant.

THROAT. The area at the junction of the tube with the rim in a united calyx or corolla.

TOOTHED. With teeth.

TRAILING. Lying on the ground and elongating but not rooting.

TRUMPET-SHAPED. Tubular at the base, abruptly flaring in the upper portion.

TUBE. The tubular, basal portion of a calyx or corolla. Any tubular structure.

TUBER. A short, thickened portion of a rhizome used for storage of food and for propagation; commonly underground.

TUBEROUS. Bearing a tuber; resembling a tuber.

TUBULAR. Circular in cross-section, hollow, nearly uniform in width, and usually longer than wide.

TUFT. A clump or cluster of stems, leaves, hairs, or other elongated structures, commonly densest at the base and spreading upward.

TWINING. Supporting by wrapping around or encircling other plants or structures.

UMBEL. A flat or convex inflorescence with the rays or pedicels arising from a common point, as the ribs of an umbrella.

UNITED. Fused together; not separate.

URN-SHAPED. Enlarged at the base, contracted at the throat, and without a prominent rim.

VEIN. An externally visible fibrous strand; a rib.

VEINED. With conspicuous or numerous veins; with veins.

WANDLIKE. Slender and more or less flexible.

WAVY. Applied to margins with waves perpendicular to the plane of the blade.

WEDGE-SHAPED. With sides straight for some distance and forming an angle at the point of attachment.

WHORL. A circular arrangement of structures arising from the same location.

WING. A flattened membranous structure extending from an organ. One of a pair of lateral petals in some flowers of the Legume Family. One of a pair of inner sepals, usually enlarged and petallike, in some flowers of the Milkwort Family.

WINGED. With a wing.

WOOLLY. With long, soft, more or less matted pubescence.

XEROPHYTIC. Adapted to conditions of very low moisture.

ILLUSTRATED GLOSSARY

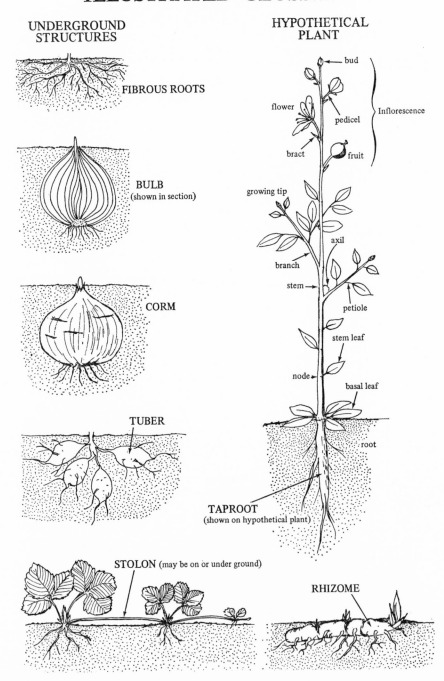

UNDERGROUND
STRUCTURES

HYPOTHETICAL
PLANT

FIBROUS ROOTS

BULB
(shown in section)

CORM

TUBER

TAPROOT
(shown on hypothetical plant)

STOLON (may be on or under ground)

RHIZOME

bud

flower

pedicel

Inflorescence

bract

fruit

growing tip

axil

branch

stem

petiole

stem leaf

node

basal leaf

root

VEGETATIVE STRUCTURES

ARRANGEMENT

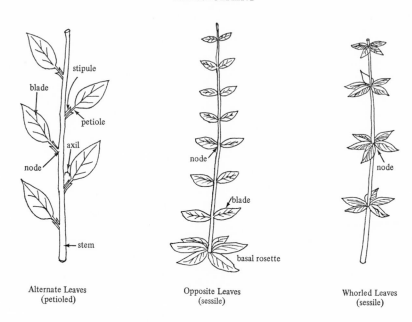

Alternate Leaves
(petioled)

Opposite Leaves
(sessile)

Whorled Leaves
(sessile)

TYPES

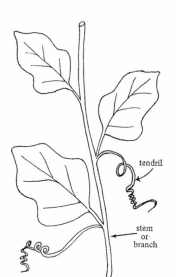

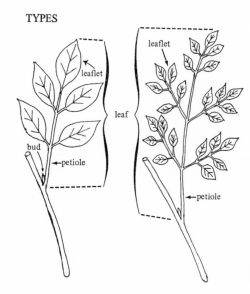

Simple Leaf
(undivided)

Compound Leaf
(once divided)

Compound Leaf
(twice divided)

VEGETATIVE STRUCTURES (cont.)

BLADE SHAPES (Generalized)

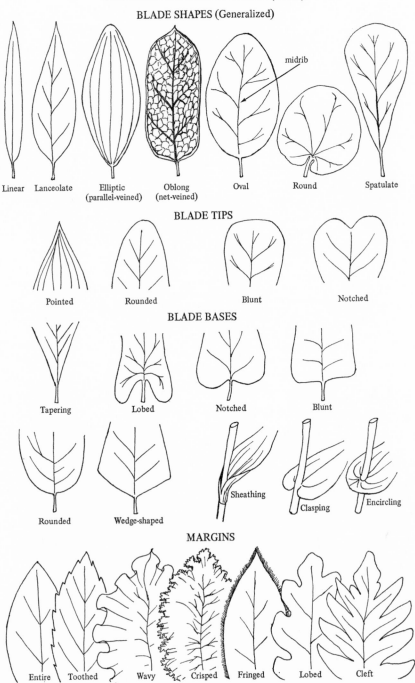

Linear Lanceolate Elliptic (parallel-veined) Oblong (net-veined) Oval midrib Round Spatulate

BLADE TIPS

Pointed Rounded Blunt Notched

BLADE BASES

Tapering Lobed Notched Blunt

Rounded Wedge-shaped Sheathing Clasping Encircling

MARGINS

Entire Toothed Wavy Crisped Fringed Lobed Cleft

FLORAL STRUCTURES

INFLORESCENCE TYPES

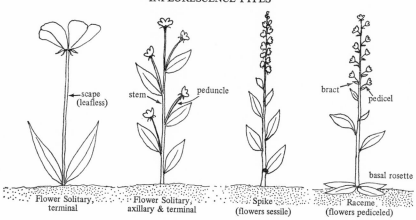

Flower Solitary, terminal

Flower Solitary, axillary & terminal

Spike (flowers sessile)

Raceme (flowers pediceled)

scape (leafless) · stem · peduncle · bract · pedicel · basal rosette

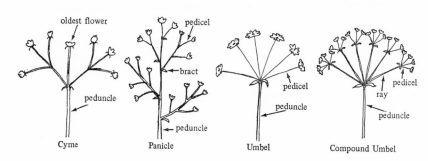

Cyme

Panicle

Umbel

Compound Umbel

oldest flower · pedicel · bract · peduncle · ray

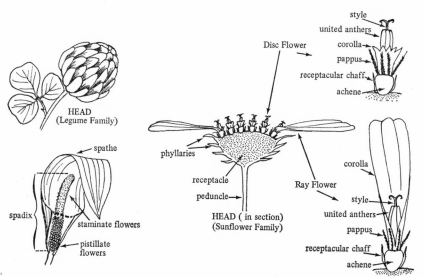

HEAD (Legume Family)

spathe · spadix · staminate flowers · pistillate flowers

Disc Flower · style · united anthers · corolla · pappus · receptacular chaff · achene

phyllaries · receptacle · peduncle

HEAD (in section) (Sunflower Family)

Ray Flower · corolla · style · united anthers · pappus · receptacular chaff · achene

FLORAL STRUCTURES (cont.)

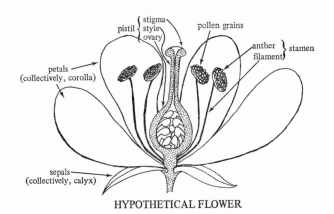

HYPOTHETICAL FLOWER

SOME COMMON CALYX OR COROLLA SHAPES

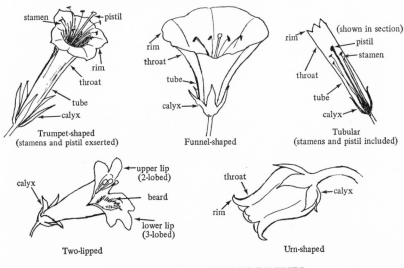

Trumpet-shaped
(stamens and pistil exserted)

Funnel-shaped

Tubular
(stamens and pistil included)

Two-lipped

Urn-shaped

GENERAL COROLLAS OF SOME FAMILIES

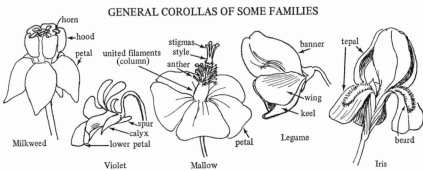

Milkweed

Violet

Mallow

Legume

Iris

FRUITING STRUCTURES

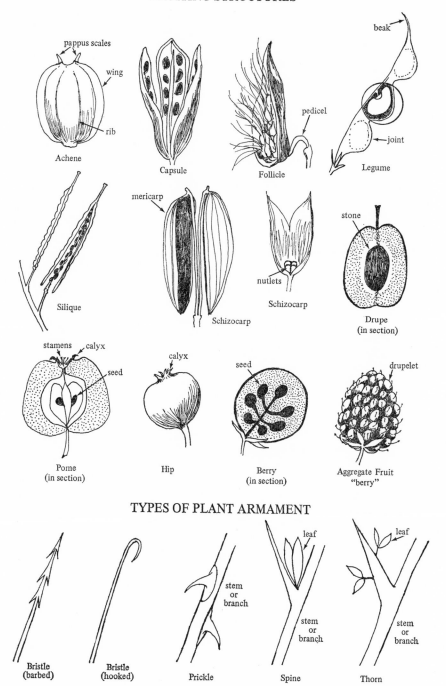

Achene
pappus scales
wing
rib

Capsule

Follicle
pedicel

Legume
beak
joint

Silique

Schizocarp
mericarp

Schizocarp
nutlets

Drupe
(in section)
stone

Pome
(in section)
stamens
calyx
seed

Hip
calyx

Berry
(in section)
seed

Aggregate Fruit
"berry"
drupelet

TYPES OF PLANT ARMAMENT

Bristle
(barbed)

Bristle
(hooked)

Prickle
stem
or
branch

Spine
leaf
stem
or
branch

Thorn
leaf
stem
or
branch

Photographic Notes

THE six years spent in photographing the wild flowers for this book were both educational and rewarding. Because the work was done in one of the most beautiful and biologically interesting parts of the state, there were many opportunities to learn more of photography and botany as well as to add new species of plants to the county and state lists.

Photography in the Big Thicket was exceptionally challenging because of the diverse habitats. The range of light conditions, from glaring sandy-lands to almost lightless bogs and bottomlands, required versatility of both equipment and photographic techniques. The lenses and methods used for one photograph frequently would not work for the next one, requiring the constant changing of lenses, arranging of backgrounds, or, in some instances, erecting of complicated wind or shadow screens.

It was frequently necessary to stand for hours in water or lie prostrate in mud or hot, dry sand in order to get the exact effect of sunlight, shadow, or lighting needed to bring out the best features of the plant. It was also necessary to ignore the heat, humidity, mosquitoes, and poisonous snakes—photographing the flower was concern enough.

Fortunately, the days of sunlight are many and long in the Big Thicket, and the work could be continued for twelve to fourteen hours a day, photographing six to eight species each day. Some days were spent in exploring new territory, and even if no photographs were obtained, discovering new or rare species of flora made the trips exciting and worthwhile.

Due to the necessity of frequently hiking long distances through deep sand or swamps, cameras and equipment were kept to a minimum. During the first four years a 35-mm Pentax H1a with a regular 50-mm lens, a 135-mm telephoto lens, and various close-up rings were used. Later, a Hasselblad was added, but it was used only for the habitat shots. Humidity and constant use almost destroyed the faithful Pentax, and the last two years' work was completed with a Nikon F, using the regular 55-mm lens, a Micro-Nikkor, and a 135-mm telephoto lens with a combination of close-up lenses. A tripod was used at all times. Film was Ektachrome X with an ASA rating of 64. Often a solid black or shaded background was employed to portray the flowers or leaves to better advantage, making identification easier. Exposures were determined with the Pentax clip-on meter and the through-the-lens metering system of the Nikon. Artificial lighting was not used, but sometimes reflecting devices such as aluminum foil or white paper were arranged to reflect light to the smaller flowers or parts of the plant.

In photographing the wild flowers for this book, care was given to illustrate the entire plant when the growth pattern or leaf placement was significant in identification. When the leaf or other features could be adequately described in the text, often a close-up was chosen to show some outstanding feature or simply bring out the beauty of the blossom.

Bibliography

Braun, E. L. 1950. *Deciduous forests of eastern North America.* Philadelphia: Blakiston Co.

Bray, W. L. 1906. Distribution and adaptation of the vegetation of Texas. *Bull. of Univ. of Texas No. 82, Scientific Series No. 10.* Austin: University of Texas.

Britton, N. L., and C. F. Millspaugh. 1920. *The Bahama flora.* New York: published by the authors.

Brown, C. A. 1972. *Wildflowers of Louisiana and adjoining states.* Baton Rouge: Louisiana State University Press.

Burlage, H. M. 1968. *Index of plants of Texas with reputed medicinal and poisonous properties.* Austin: published by the author.

Correll, D. S., and H. B. Correll. 1972. *Aquatic and wetland plants of the southwestern United States.* Washington, D.C.: Environmental Protection Agency.

————, and M. C. Johnston. 1970. *Manual of the vascular plants of Texas.* Renner: Texas Research Foundation.

Dormon, C. 1958. *Flowers native to the Deep South.* Harrisburg, Pa.: Mt. Pleasant Press.

Duncan, W. H., and L. E. Foote. 1975. *Wildflowers of the southeastern United States.* Athens: The University of Georgia Press.

Fernald, M. L. 1950. *Gray's manual of botany.* 8th ed. New York: American Book Co.

Gleason, H. A., and A. Cronquist. 1963. *Manual of vascular plants of northeastern United States and adjacent Canada.* New York: D. Van Nostrand Company.

Gould, F. W. 1969. *Texas plants—a checklist and ecological summary.* MP-585. College Station: Texas Agricultural Experiment Station.

————. 1975. *The grasses of Texas.* College Station: Texas A&M University Press.

Gow, J. E. 1905. An ecological study of the Sabine and Neches Valleys, Texas. *Proc. Iowa Acad. Sci.* 12: 39–47.

Gunter, A. Y. 1972. *The Big Thicket.* Austin: Jenkins Publishing Co.

Jepson, W. L. 1925. *A Manual of the Flowering Plants of California.* Berkeley: Assoc. Students Store, University of California.

Justice, W. S., and R. C. Bell. 1968. *Wild flowers of North Carolina*. Chapel Hill: University of North Carolina Press.

Marks, P. L., and P. A. Harcombe. 1975. Community diversity of Coastal Plain forest in southern East Texas. *Ecology* 56: 1004–1008.

McLeod, C. A. 1972. *The Big Thicket forest of eastern Texas*. Huntsville, Texas: Sam Houston State University.

Moldenke, H. N. 1949. *American wild flowers*. New York: Van Nostrand Co.

Parks, H. B. 1938. The Big Thicket. *Texas Geographic Magazine* 2 (Summer): 16–28.

Parks, H. B., V. L. Cory, et al. 1936. *Biological survey of the East Texas Big Thicket area: The fauna and flora of the Big Thicket area*. Sponsored by Texas Academy of Science.

Penfound, W. T., and E. S. Hathaway. 1938. Plant communities in the marshlands of southwestern Louisiana. *Ecol. Monogr.* 8: 1–56.

Pessin, L. J. 1933. Forest associations in the uplands of the lower Gulf Coastal Plain. *Ecology* 14: 1–14.

Phillips Petroleum Co. 1960. *Native and imported grasses*. 6 vols. Bartlesville, Okla.

Radford, A., H. E. Ahles, and R. C. Bell. 1964. *Manual of the vascular flora of the Carolinas*. Chapel Hill: University of North Carolina Press.

Rechenthin, C. A. 1972. *Native flowers of Texas*. Temple, Texas: U.S. Department of Agriculture, Soil Conservation Service.

Reeves, R. G. 1972. *Flora of Central Texas*. Fort Worth: Prestige Press.

Rickett, H. W. 1967. *Wild flowers of the United States: The southeastern states*. New York: McGraw-Hill.

———. 1969. *Wild flowers of the United States: Texas*. New York: McGraw-Hill.

Shinners, L. H. 1972. *Spring flora of the Dallas and Ft. Worth area*. 2nd ed. Fort Worth: Prestige Press.

Small, J. K. 1933. *Manual of the southeastern flora*. New York: Science Press.

Smith, R. 1966. *Ecology and field biology*. New York: Harper and Row.

Stearn, W. T. 1966. *Botanical Latin*. New York: Hafner.

Stupka, A. 1965. *Wildflowers in color*. New York: Harper and Row.

Tharp, B. C. 1926. Structure of Texas vegetation east of the 98th Meridian. *Univ. of Texas Bull. No. 2606*. Austin: University of Texas.

Turner, B. L. 1959. *The legumes of Texas*. Austin: University of Texas Press.

U.S. Department of Agriculture, Soil Conservation Service. 1965. *Soil survey of Jefferson County and others*. Washington, D.C.: Government Printing Office.

U.S. Department of Commerce. 1968. *Climatological summary*. Austin: University of Texas.

Vines, R. A. 1960. *Trees, shrubs, and woody vines of the Southwest*. Austin: University of Texas Press.

Watson, G. 1975. *Big Thicket plant ecology: An introduction*. Saratoga, Texas: Big Thicket Museum.

Whitehouse, E. 1967. *Texas flowers in natural colors*. 3rd ed. Dallas: Dallas County Audubon Society.

Wills, M. M., and H. S. Irwin. 1961. *Roadside flowers of Texas*. Austin: University of Texas Press.

Index

(Numbers in italics refer to pages of color plates.)

The question now comes, is the Big Thicket to pass into legend as have the other areas, or is this area to be protected and made available to those who enjoy the study of animate nature; who enjoy the beauty of the primeval forest with its age old trees, its undergrowth of flowering shrubs, the delicately colored flowers and moss ground cover that bespeaks an age in making. . . .

H. B. Parks, V. L. Cory, et al.
BIOLOGICAL SURVEY OF THE EAST TEXAS
BIG THICKET AREA (1936)